Introduction to
Catering:

Ingredients for Success

D0144484

Introduction to
Catering:

Ingredients for Success

Stephen B. Shiring, Sr.

R. William "Bill" Jardine

Richard J. Mills, Jr.

DELMAR
CENGAGE Learning™

Australia • Brazil • Japan • Korea • Mexico • Singapore • Spain • United Kingdom • United States

DELMAR
CENGAGE Learning

Introduction to Catering: Ingredients for Success
Stephen B. Shiring, R. William "Bill" Jardine, and Richard J. Mills

Business Unit Director: Susan L. Simpfenderfer

Executive Editor: Marlene McHugh Pratt

Acquisitions Editor: Erin O'Connor Traylor

Editorial Assistant: Alexis Ferraro

Executive Production Manager: Wendy A. Troeger

Project Editor: Amy E. Tucker

Production Editor: Elaine Scull

Executive Marketing Manager: Donna J. Lewis

Channel Manager: Wendy E. Mapstone

Cover Design: Joseph Villanova

© 2001 Delmar, Cengage Learning

ALL RIGHTS RESERVED. No part of this work covered by the copyright herein may be reproduced, transmitted, stored or used in any form or by any means graphic, electronic, or mechanical, including but not limited to photocopying, recording, scanning, digitizing, taping, Web distribution, information networks, or information storage and retrieval systems, except as permitted under Section 107 or 108 of the 1976 United States Copyright Act, without the prior written permission of the publisher.

For product information and technology assistance, contact us at
Cengage Learning Customer & Sales Support, 1-800-354-9706

For permission to use material from this text or product,
submit all requests online at **www.cengage.com/permissions**
Further permissions questions can be emailed to
permissionrequest@cengage.com

Library of Congress Control Number: 00-064505

ISBN-13: 978-0-7668-1660-2

ISBN-10: 0-7668-1660-5

Delmar
Executive Woods
5 Maxwell Drive
Clifton Park, NY 12065
USA

Cengage Learning is a leading provider of customized learning solutions with office locations around the globe, including Singapore, the United Kingdom, Australia, Mexico, Brazil, and Japan. Locate your local office at **international.cengage.com/region**

Cengage Learning products are represented in Canada by Nelson Education, Ltd.

For your lifelong learning solutions, visit **www.cengage.com/delmar**

Visit our corporate website at **www.cengage.com**

Notice to the Reader

Publisher does not warrant or guarantee any of the products described herein or perform any independent analysis in connection with any of the product information contained herein. Publisher does not assume, and expressly disclaims, any obligation to obtain and include information other than that provided to it by the manufacturer. The reader is expressly warned to consider and adopt all safety precautions that might be indicated by the activities described herein and to avoid all potential hazards. By following the instructions contained herein, the reader willingly assumes all risks in connection with such instructions. The publisher makes no representations or warranties of any kind, including but not limited to, the warranties of fitness for particular purpose or merchantability, nor are any such representations implied with respect to the material set forth herein, and the publisher takes no responsibility with respect to such material. The publisher shall not be liable for any special, consequential, or exemplary damages resulting, in whole or part, from the readers' use of, or reliance upon, this material.

Printed in the United States of America
8 9 10 11 12   14 13 12 11 10

ED200

Contents

v

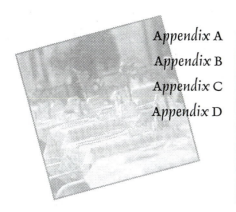

Foreword

Bill Jardine has been a successful restaurateur and caterer in western Pennsylvania for nearly four decades. His operation, Jardine's Farm Restaurant & Catering, was a staple for exceptional country cooking and innovative, down-home, on- and off-premise catering. Jardine's attracted thousands of guests every summer who would walk around the farm, take hayrides, visit the unique gift and antique shops, and dine in casual eloquence in the bright, cheery rooms surrounded by 26 acres of pastoral splendor. He was the primary caterer for his geographic region and his catering operations are legendary. Bill has brought his expertise—honed over forty-years of on-the-job training—to this easy-to-understand-and-apply text that offers *real-life* experiences so others may gain success in the catering profession.

Bill has been a valued friend for 25 years to myself and thousands of young folks he employed and encouraged to pursue a career in the industry with both kind, "fatherly" advice, and financially, through scholarships and other financial incentives. He taught his craft at Butler County Community College and served in high positions in the Western Pennsylvania Restaurant Association and the Pennsylvania Restaurant Association. As Research and Development Chef for a commercial food broker, Bill continues to teach the *how-tos* of professional food preparation, service, and *tricks-of-the-trade* to a new generation of hospitality professionals. There are few people in the food service industry today that are more respected and who bring the technical knowledge and professional expertise that Bill does to the catering experience.

The student of hospitality will find, in this text, all the essential *ingredients for success* needed in this ever-expanding and increasingly sophisticated hospitality niche. The skills acquired through hands-on experiences are evident throughout the text, combining Bill's business acumen with the operating and control details that are necessary for successful catering. Certified Sous Chef Richard Mills supplies recipes, photographs, and menu plans designed around a 15-week online lab course to accompany the text. Dr. Stephen Shiring adds his own management experiences in large chain restaurants and catering operations to ensure a complete catering package.

Wisely, the authors consulted numerous experts in the field, too often missing in texts that relate to task-specific areas. An important ingredient is the *Tips from the Trade* that are based on the contributions of colleagues and current operators who have made their mark in the industry, and continue to create unique, profitable components for the on- and off-premise caterer. The experience and creativity found within these pages will serve the student and present catering operator for decades to come. Your *ingredients for your success* are definitely all here.

Dr. Joseph B. Gregg
Managing Director
DCT International Hotel & Culinary School
Luzern, Switzerland

Preface

◈ OVERVIEW

Catering education has undergone a drastic series of changes over the past one hundred years. It continues to change as industry and business also experience change. Catering education today demands new approaches to teaching and new directions for learning. *Introduction to Catering: Ingredients for Success* is a practical hands-on text written to help you become more efficient and effective as a professional caterer. The student will embark on a journey to learn more innovative catering methods and their application. With the demand of America's eating habits, the need for qualified caterers will always be on the rise. The job market will enable any individual with an interest in catering to start their own business or work in hotels, restaurants, and institutions around the globe. Each catering opportunity will lead to outstanding experiences with both food, beverages, and individual development.

Introduction to Catering: Ingredients for Success is targeted at individuals in both graduate and undergraduate schools, pursuing degrees, or an interest, in the food industry. The combined professional and academic experience of all three authors is a significant asset to this book. Students will gain insight into the necessary steps to either begin building their own catering business or obtain a position in a commercial food service environment.

Introduction to Catering was written to provide a hands-on experience through the eyes of three professionals with twenty-five years in the catering industry. It encompasses three areas of expertise with a seasoned approach: strategic management, culinary arts, and real-life catering. An emphasis is placed on differences between on-premise and off-premise catered events. The text shares the knowledge that any caterer can use, whether organizing an event for one or 14,000 guests. However, the need for further research in the catering industry remains a driving motive for the continued development of catering professionals.

The three parts of this text are divided into fourteen easy-to-read chapters. Each chapter explains how to plan, organize, implement, and execute a catering function. The format of the text complements the authors' direct approach to the subject matter. General *Objectives* and a list of *Key Terms* at the beginning of each chapter explain what should be accomplished before proceeding to the next chapter. *Ingredients for Success*, listed in most chapters, emphasize fundamental catering rules and reinforce general procedures necessary to build a successful catering career. *Tips from the Trade*, found throughout the text, apply real-life situations to the topic being discussed. These tips present critical problem-solving skills demonstrated by leading professionals in the market today. *Handy forms and checklists* being used in the industry are interspersed throughout the text to aid comprehension of processes. *Review Questions* are presented at the end of each chapter, along with *Putting It All Together* exercises for students to apply what they have learned. The text also includes a glossary, containing all the highlighted key terms, and comprehensive appendices with useful industry-related information for the student to use throughout his or her catering career. Web site URLs are found in Appendix D and throughout the book. The authors and Delmar have made every effort to ensure their accuracy at the time of printing. Due to the fluid nature of the *Internet*, we cannot guarantee they will remain so for the life of this edition.

The *Instructor's Manual* to accompany *Introduction to Catering: Ingredients for Success*, is a useful organizational and assessment tool offering several features that allow the instructor to specifically tailor the course to curriculum requirements.

Beginning with an Introduction, the manual moves into a Catering Concepts grid that breaks down key instructional concepts into their respective chapters. A matrix details Gardner's eight Multiple Intelligences and their application to the various chapters. Both the concepts grid and Multiple Intelligence matrix are outlined for the book's *Online Resources* as well.

A section on *Talking the Talk* explains the value of the key terms and includes a complete alphabetic listing of the book's terms. The manual wraps up with complete answers to the Chapter Review questions and Scoring Rubrics for the *Putting It All Together* activities at the culmination of each chapter.

 The accompanying *Online Resources* features a databank of recipes broken down by ingredient list and procedures—with many photos illustrating the completed dishes. Activities, tied to the book's chapter content, utilize the recipe databank and additional Web links to reinforce ideas and concepts. The *Online Resources* is structured around a 15-week lab course with additional activities for longer term schedules and in-depth study. Activities are designed for group and individual participation, both during or outside a classroom environment, and complement both college course-work in catering and culinary school curriculums.

◆ ACKNOWLEDGMENTS

We, the authors, would like to give thanks and acknowledgment to the many professionals, family, and friends who have played a role in the development of this book. It takes a family to write a textbook.

- Executive Chef Doug Noxon, Wilson Lodge, at Ogleby Resort, Wheeling, West Virginia, and Mr. Dan Miller, Manager, Springfield Restaurant Group, Mercer, PA, for sharing their expertise and experiences.

- Mr. Chris Gowdy, Director of Marketing, Mount Vernon Mills, Inc., Riegel Consumer Products Division, for permission to use his reference material.

- Mr. Rafael A. Rivera-Vigo, Benefits Manager, at Hyatt Orlando, Kissimmee, Florida, for his professional assistance in this project.

Steve Bernard, Bernard Food Industries, Inc., for his permission to use their company as an educational reference.

Mr. Tom Rentz, Distributor Sales Representative, U. S. FoodService™, for reference material.

Mr. Bruce Frankel at *http://www.virtualrestaurant.com* for permission to use the information on his Web site concerning the business plan in Chapter 6 and Appendix C.

Mr. Mark Poss, Director of Marketing, The Homer Laughlin China Company for his assistance on this project.

Mr. Jeremy Engle, Banquet Manager, Beaver Run Resort and Conference Center, Breckenridge, Colorado and Ms. Katie Peabody, from the Boca Raton Resort and Club, for their contributions to this text.

Kenneth P. Darling, Executive Pastry Chef, Heidi's Gourmet Desserts, Tucker (Atlanta), GA

Marty Horn, President & CEO, FOODgalaxy.com

Dianne Herzog, Catering Manager, Hyatt Orlando, Kissimmee, FL

Eric J. Fairman, Executive Sous Chef, The Bradley House of Catering, Inc.

Michelle Albright Lennox, Catering/Conventions Service Manager, Hyatt Orlando, Kissimmee, FL

Dirk N. Soma, Director, Kapi' Olani Community College, Culinary Institute of the Pacific, Honolulu, HI

Henry Holthaus, Certified Executive Chef/Instructor, Kapi' Olani Community College, Culinary Institute of the Pacific, Honolulu, HI

Bruce Schmidt, President/Owner, Holstein Manufacturing, Inc., Holstein, Iowa

Mark Sparacino, Chef/Catering Manager, Traveling Fare, River Forest, IL

Michael P. Simon, Jr., Great Lakes Region Manager, MasterFoodServices, A Division of Uncle Ben's, Inc., Houston, TX

Dr. Stephen B. Shiring thanks his wife, Tamara, and children, Stephen Jr. ("Slugger," age 12), Samantha ("Bitsy," age 11), and Elizabeth ("Louie," age 8) for their love and many hours of tremendous support and cooperation. He recognizes and thanks his father, James and his mother, Laura; brothers James, Jr., Erick, and Scott; sisters Laurie Shiring and Letitia Shiring-O'Donnell; Uncle Tony and Aunt Barbara Valasek; and his mother-in-law, Isabel Galzerano. Dr. Shiring sends a special thanks to his mentors and friends: Dr. Richard Seckinger and Dr. Glenn Nelson, Administration and Policy Studies, School of Education, at the University of Pittsburgh, for their encouragement and guidance throughout his career; Bobby and Jill Milliner-Simpson, and the staff at the Ice Connection of Pittsburgh—Victor McCarron, Don Good, Todd Ament, and Robert F. Budash—for providing an office to write this manuscript while Samantha skated and Jill coached; and for his expertise and professional support in writing Chapter 12, Understanding Insurance and Legal Issues, thanks goes to Mr. John Daloisio, CPPC, CLU, of the ESS Insurance Group, Kittanning, PA. Dr. Shiring is in deepest appreciation to Amy E. Tucker,

Project Editor, for her inspired leadership, energizing vision, meticulous guidance, and her valued friendship in the successful completion of this text.

Mr. R. William "Bill" Jardine would like to thank his wife, Joyce, for her love, devotion, and encouragement while catering thousands of functions over the years, and her dedication and support for this project. A special thanks goes to Bart Duva of Bart's Catering & Fine Foods in Apollo, PA, for his enthusiastic support. And, to the Bradley House of Catering, Inc.—thank you for your support.

Chef Richard J. Mills, Jr. would like to extend a special thanks to Chef Tom Degori, Shawn Williams, John Muller, Ajax Williams, Shay Gilliam, and the many faithful employees at the Embassy Suites Hotel, Pittsburgh, PA, for their thoughtful ideas and concerns related to the production of this book. A sincere thank you to General Manager Tom Spoto for granting us permission to research and acquire some of the necessary materials to write this book.

And finally, to the *Fun Bunch*, ALOHA!

The authors and Delmar would like to thank the following individuals for their time and feedback in helping to shape this book to the needs of the industry.

Warren Sackler
Associate Professor
Rochester Institute of Technology
Rochester, NY

Michael Piccinino
Culinary Arts Instructor
Shasta College
Redding, CA

Elaine Madden
Department Chair
Anne Arundel Community College
Arnold, MD

David Hanson
Program Coordinator
Idaho State University
Pocatello, ID

The authors and Delmar would also like to personally thank these individuals and organizations, for supplying photographs and content for the following figures, and granting permission to reprint them for this book.

The following figures are courtesy of Bart's Catering & Fine Foods: 10–4, 12–9a, 12–9b

The following figure is courtesy of Blaze Products Corp.: 9–11

The following figure is courtesy of Bernard Food Industries, Inc.: 8–3

The following figures are courtesy of Carlisle FoodService Products, Oklahoma City, OK: 8–8, 8–16

The following figures are courtesy of Embassy Suites Hotel, Coraopolis, PA: 2–4, 4–6, 6–3, 7–1a, 7–1b, 7–6, 9–1, 9–8, 9–14, 10–2, 10–3, 10–7, 10–14, 10–15, 10–16

The following figures are courtesy of Holstein Manufacturing, Inc.: 1–8, 9–12a-c

The following figure is courtesy of The Homer Laughlin China Co.: 10–12

The following figure is courtesy of Hotshot Delivery Systems, Inc.: 9–10

The following figure is courtesy of Indiana Holiday Inn/Crown American Hotels: 12–11

The following figures are courtesy of Bill Jardine: 4–3, 7–8, 10–13, 11–1, 12–7

The following figure is courtesy of Keating of Chicago, Inc.: 9–13

The following figures are courtesy of Mon General Hospital, Morgantown, WV: 1–5, 1–6

The following figure is adapted from the *Riegel Sales Reference Guide*, reprinted with permission of Mount Vernon Mills, Inc., Riegel Consumer Products Division, Johnston, SC: 10–8

The following figure is adapted from the National Advisory Committee on Microbiological Criteria for Foods (NACMCF), Courtesy of the U.S. Food and Drug Administration: 6–8

The following figures are courtesy of Port-A-Cool, a division of General Shelters of Texas, S.B., Ltd., Center, TX: 6–6a, 6–6b

The following figures are courtesy of Rafael A. Rivera-Vigo, Benefits Manager, Hyatt Orlando, 6375 W. Irlo Bronson Memorial Hwy., Kissimmee, FL: Chapter Openers 1 and 14; Figures 1–7, 10–17, 12–8

The following figures are courtesy of Dr. Stephen Shiring: 4–5, 9–9, 10–5

The following figures are adapted from the 1999 FDA Model Food Code <http://www.fda.gov>, courtesy of the U.S. Food and Drug Administration: 6–5, 6–7, 6–9, 6–10, 6–11, 6–12, 6–13, 8–17, 8–18, 8–19, 8–20, 9–3, 9–5, 9–7, 9–15

The following figures are courtesy of U. S. FoodService™: 8–14, 8–15

◈ ABOUT THE AUTHORS

Introduction to Catering: Ingredients for Success was written by three professional food service experts. Dr. Stephen B. Shiring, Sr., received his doctorate degree from the School of Education, Department of Administrative and Policy Studies at the University of Pittsburgh in Pittsburgh, PA. His Master of Business Administration (M.B.A) and Bachelor of Science in Food Service Management are from Indiana University of Pennsylvania (IUP), where he is currently an Assistant Professor in the Department of Hotel, Restaurant, and Institutional Management. At IUP, Dr. Shiring is actively engaged in on-campus catering activities and has taught, researched, published, and implemented various courses targeted specifically toward the food service industry. He is a member of the International Council on Hotel, Restaurant, and Institutional Education (CHRIE), and co-founder, with Dirk Soma, of the *Fun Bunch*, an association affiliated with CHRIE. Dr. Shiring is a member of advisory committees representing both community colleges and vocational-technical high schools. In addition, he is employed by Foodservice Innovators, Inc., as a consulting food broker.

Dr. Shiring was the Director of the Hospitality Management Program at Butler County Community College (BCCC) previous to IUP. While at BCCC, he received numerous recognitions and awards and was recognized by the Council on Hotel, Restaurant and Institutional Education's Two Year Colleges Catalogue of Exemplary Activities and Educational Training Initiatives Between Colleges and Universities and the Hospitality/Tourism Industry in both 1990 and 1991 for his working relationship with *Jardine's Restaurant, Country Stores and Catering Services.*

Mr. Jardine has twenty-five years of experience as a professional caterer and more than forty years of industry experience. He has also designed, written, and implemented a catering course in both the public and private sectors; served as an officer for both the Western Chapter of the Pennsylvania Restaurant Association and the Pennsylvania Restaurant Association; and was instrumental in organizing and promoting several catering associations. Bill is a member of the American Culinary Federation and serves on various advisory committees representing culinary programs, community colleges, and vocational-technical high schools. He is also a member of the *Fun Bunch.*

Mr. Jardine invited Dr. Shiring and his students to work, as-needed, at many of his catered functions so the students could gain practical work experience. In return, he was recruited to teach in the Hospitality Management Program. Mr. Jardine designed and taught a professional cooking and catering management course at BCCC, and, together with Dr. Shiring, they were the exclusive caterers for all BCCC campus functions, including the president's private functions, state senate events, board of trustees' events, and all college-sponsored activities.

This new experience, combined with his tremendous love for people, led him to a career change in 1992. Mr. Jardine was given the opportunity to join a food brokerage firm and use his knowledge, wisdom, culinary skills, and teaching ability as a Research and Development Chef. In this new position, his motivation and desire was fueled by the idea of teaching the art and science of hospitality and service management to food service professionals such as owners, chefs, and caterers. Bill sold his catering and restaurant business to start this new career based on the opportunity to share what he had learned through practical experience. He is currently employed as a Research and Development Chef for Foodservice Innovators, Inc., one of the largest food service brokers in Pennsylvania.

Chef Richard J. Mills, Jr., has many years of both professional and academic experience. He is currently a certified Sous Chef through the American Culinary Federation and has worked in the industry as a professional cook and chef for twelve years. He is presently teaching in the Communications and Hospitality & Tourism departments at Robert Morris College, Coraopolis, PA. Chef Mills holds two masters degrees, an MLS and MA, and has taught, researched, and published. He implemented various courses at the Undergraduate level, in food production management and quantity food production, at several colleges and universities.

Many of the recipes featured on the book's *Online Resources* were developed and prepared by Chef Mills during his career. He is currently pursuing his Doctorate Degree in the Communications Department at Duquense University in Pittsburgh, PA, and Chef Mills is a member of the *Fun Bunch.*

PART ONE

What Is Catering?

Chapter One

The Catering World: Types of Catering

Key Terms

catering management
commercial segment
noncommercial segment
military segment
on-premise catering
hospital catering
high school catering
private or nonprofit caterers
customer appeal
university/college caterers
off-premise catering
supermarket catering
dual-restaurant catering
exclusive caterer
distinct competence
private-party catering
convention catering
one-stop shop
mobile catering
seasonal niche
home-based caterers

Objectives

After studying this chapter, you should be able to:

◆ Discuss the catering industry.

◆ Identify catering segments.

◆ Define on-premise and off-premise catering.

◆ Explain the different types of catering events held on-premise and off-premise.

◆ Provide examples of the different kinds of on-premise and off-premise operations.

◈ CATERING INDUSTRY

Catering is a multifaceted segment of the food service industry. There is a niche for all types of catering businesses within the segment of catering. The food service industry is divided into three general classifications: commercial segment, noncommercial segment, and military segment. **Catering management** may be defined as the task of planning, organizing, and controlling. Each activity influences the preparation and delivery of food, beverage, and related services at a competitive, profitable price. These activities work together to meet and exceed the customer's perception of value.

◈ CATERING SEGMENTS

Catering management is executed in many diverse ways within each of the three segments. The first, **commercial segment**, traditionally considered the *for profit* operations, includes the independent caterer, the restaurant caterer, and the home-based caterer. In addition, hotel/motel and private club catering operations are also found in this category.

The **noncommercial segment**, or the *not-for-profit* operations, consists of the following types of catering activities: business/industry accounts, college and university catering, health care facilities, recreational food service catering, school catering, social organizations, and transportation food service catering. The **military segment** encompasses all catering activities involved in association with the armed forces and/or diplomatic events. Figure 1–1 illustrates how the food service catering industry is segmented.

FOOD SERVICE CATERING INDUSTRY		
Military Segment	**Commercial Segment**	**Noncommercial Segment**
Military Functions	Independent Caterers	Business/Industry Accounts
Diplomatic Functions	Hotel/Motel Caterers	College and University Catering
	Home-Based Caterers	Health Care Facilities
	Restaurant/Catering Firms	Recreational Food Service
	Private Clubs	(amusement and theme
		parks, conference and
		convention facilities,
		museums, libraries, stadiums,
		and sport arenas)
		School Catering
		Social Organizations (fraternal
		and social clubs,
		associations, and fire halls)
		Transportation Food Service
		Catering (in-flight catering)

Figure 1-1 *Modern American catering categories.*

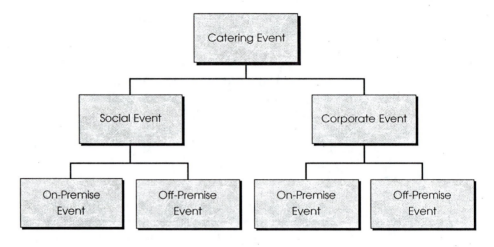

Catering Event

Social Event

Corporate Event

On-Premise Event

Off-Premise Event

On-Premise Event

Off-Premise Event

Figure 1-2 *The catering event.*

◆ ON-PREMISE CATERING

There are two main types of catering (on-premise and off-premise) that may be a concern to a large and small caterer. Figure 1–2 illustrates the different types of catering events. First, **on-premise catering** indicates that the function is held exclusively within the caterer's own facility. All of the required functions and services that the caterer executes are done exclusively at their own facility. For instance, a caterer within a hotel or banquet hall will prepare and cater all of the events without taking any service or food outside the facility. Many restaurants have specialized rooms on-premise to cater to the *private-party* niche.

A restaurant may have a layout strategically designed with three separate dining rooms (Figure 1–3) attached to a centralized commercial food production

Figure 1-3 *Dual restaurant and catering dining rooms.*

Figure 1-4
Production kitchen.

kitchen (Figure 1–4). These separate dining rooms are available at the same time to support the restaurant's operation and for reservation and overflow seating. In addition, any of the three dining rooms may be contracted out for private-event celebrations and may require their own specialized service and menu options.

Hospital Catering

An example of **hospital catering** is an on-premise catering operation for events that occur within a hospital's environment. It is very rare for a hospital to sponsor an off-premise event. One exception could occur if the hospital is sponsoring a fund raiser.

There are great demands placed on the food service department within a hospital environment when an active catering service is used. Special functions are held by the internal hospital associations. There are many *visible* and *invisible* associations conducting business within a hospital's environment. Associations having special requests for internal catered functions (Figures 1–5 and 1–6) may be the medical technologists in the laboratories, ladies' auxiliary, physicians' meetings, nurses' organizations, employees in all departments, or x-ray departments.

Many hospitals have beautiful dining rooms that are primarily used for catering internal events. In addition, they may have other dining areas to have breakfast meetings, luncheon events, and special dinner events in a private setting.

High School/Elementary School Catering

It is very unlikely that a high school would cater an on-premise event for a customer who is not associated with the school. **High school catering** operations service events exclusively for the high school population; high schools

---

SPECIAL CATERING FUNCTION REQUEST

Name of Group/Department/Association _____

Contact Person _____ E-mail _____ Extension _____

Group/Department/Association Location _____

Function Day and Date _____ Function Location _____

Number of Guests _____ Beginning Time _____ Ending Time _____

Menu

Appetizer

Entree

Sandwich

Starch

Vegetable

Salad

Dressing

Bread

Butter/spread

Dessert

Beverage

Other

Special Services

Flowers _____

Decorations _____

Entertainment _____

Napkins _____

Table Seating and Arrangements

☐ Classroom   ☐ Conference   ☐ Theater   ☐ Banquet   ☐ Sit-down   ☐ Buffet

Invoice To _____

Deposit Required $ _____

Cost Per Person $ _____

I agree to the arrangements as outlined on this special function request form.

_____ Date _____

Figure 1-5 A *hospital special catering function request form.*

CATERING SCHEDULE

Time	Location of Function	Group or Association	Number of Guests	Contact Person E-mail/Extension	Menu
7:00 A.M.					
8:00 A.M.					
9:00 A.M.					
10:00 A.M.					
11:00 A.M.					
12:00 P.M.					
1:00 P.M.					
2:00 P.M.					
3:00 P.M.					
4:00 P.M.					
5:00 P.M.					
6:00 P.M.					
7:00 P.M.					

NOTES

Figure 1-6 *Hospital catering schedule form.*

frequently cater athletic banquets, teachers' meetings, events on the football field for fall and spring celebrations, and other sporting events. They may hold a catered event anywhere on the school property, but the preparation of the food is done in the high school cafeteria. One logical reason for this policy is that insurance and liability costs would escalate, and therefore be prohibitive.

Private or Nonprofit Caterers

Why does a school cater internal events by using its on-premise food service facilities? There are certain advantages for maintaining an on-premise food service: catering their own activities provides an exceptional opportunity to increase profits and raise profit margins for the purpose of strengthening their internal fiscal health. The school directors can lower operational food costs in the cafeteria or use the additional revenue to expedite the purchase of new pieces of production equipment.

Usually those facilities can provide food and service for less cost than an independent caterer because they have the facility, their labor costs are built in, and they are not paying certain kinds of taxes. Churches, fraternal organizations, and fire halls are other examples of where an entirely on-premise catering operation may take place. Not many **private or nonprofit caterers** will cater off-premise events because they lack the expertise and equipment to do so; these organizations usually provide the hall, food, beverage, and servers for an occasion. They employ catering as a supplement to their internal financial budgets to help raise money to fund special projects.

There are three strategic advantages these organizations have over the independent caterer.

1. They have no labor costs because the labor is "donated" by the members themselves.

2. They do not pay taxes.

3. Many of them do not incur the expense of carrying any kind of liability insurance.

These organizations can charge $10.00 per plate for a meal and generate a profit. In contrast, the independent caterer would have to charge at least $15.00 per plate for the same job because of the above costs and responsibilities. Since it is difficult for the independent caterer to compete against these organizations on price, they must find another means of competition. They may become a specialist or create a proficiency, strengthen a concept, or create a distinction that leads to satisfying and exceeding customer expectations in ways other organizations cannot do.

Customer Appeal

Fire halls are not decorated and do not offer many fine accompaniments. This is one area where the independent caterer may show individuality and thus compete with a nonprofit group. They can expend resources on a continual training program resulting in superior customer service. Whereas fire halls have volunteers serving the client, they may not be well trained in proper food preparation techniques or proper sanitation practices. The independent caterer can provide **customer appeal** by offering more variety, attractive presentations with china and glassware, and a higher quality of food and expertise. This may assure the caterer that the customer will come to the independent caterer rather than a nonprofit group.

For example, at Christmas time, the decorations supplied by the independent caterer would be more elaborate and could be tailored to decorations that fit the clients' tastes and needs. The caterer strives to be a specialist and to satisfy the customer's needs. If you are able to satisfy more needs, you will benefit with a broader customer base. Ultimately, you will achieve success because more customers will recommend you to do work for their friends and other associates.

University/College Caterers

The management of college and university food service is either contracted to a company which specializes in food management services or handled internally by the institution itself. Regardless of the type of management selected, **university/ college caterers** are responsible for providing food and related services to the students, faculty, administrators, and guests.

College or university campus facilities are often utilized for on-premise catering. Universities and colleges have a myriad of activities happening simultaneously by many diverse organizations. Campus organizations, individual departments, educational conferences, or any other independent groups on campus make it necessary for the college or university to maintain an active on-premise caterer. The caterer can supply food and beverages ranging from cheese and crackers to buffets and elaborate dinners. On-campus requests for catered events can be held seven days a week, 24-hours a day, and range from such locations as individual classrooms to faculty clubs, renovated historical locations, and open-air functions.

The campus caterer will offer the client a choice from a standardized menu book or will customize a menu to fulfill special requests and needs. Functions held on a campus will include dessert receptions for visiting dignitaries, premeeting dinners for the members of the board of trustees, and special requests for the university president. The on-campus caterer is the exclusive caterer for the president and his activities. The president may request weekly or monthly meal plans that will provide breakfast, lunch, or dinner. The catering services are available for the president and visiting dignitaries.

The caterer will also be involved in special university events. Graduation ceremonies, homecoming activities, and sporting events such as football games are important to the university. For homecoming activities, the caterer may set up tents to support both food and beverages for the president and the school's alumni. For football games, the caterer will prepare elaborate pre-game buffets, and during the game may provide food, beverages, and service for the president and his invited guests in his personal box.

The university caterer only services functions on campus for university personnel. Not many events are catered outside the university property for the local community since they do not want to compete against community caterers.

◆ OFF-PREMISE CATERING

The second type of catering, **off-premise catering**, is accomplished exclusively by the caterer. The off-premise caterer transports all of the food, serving products, and personnel to a location other than the building or facility where the food is prepared. An important consideration for off-premise catering is that there must be access to equipment needed to prepare the food. Caterers must also furnish their own refrigerated trucks or other equipment to keep food hot or cold. Food must be the right serving temperature to be satisfactorily served. Salads must be ice cold and soups should be served at a minimum 140°F and not lukewarm. In addition, transportation must be provided for the staff to get to the site. Some off-premise events are so large that a caterer will have to rent buses to get the wait-staff to the location so they all arrive dressed properly at the same time.

TIPS FROM THE TRADE

Jardine's Farm Restaurant & Catering provided a huge chicken barbeque for a corporation's 50th Anniversary. This special event celebration included all of the corporation's employees and their families totalling 13,500 guests. The caterer had approximately 100 employees working that day to support the effort to provide exceptional customer service. The event was held on a very hot August day. Two buses were chartered to transport the employees to the location. An agreement with the bus company was made to keep the buses running all day with the air conditioners on so that if the employees became physically exhausted from working in the August heat, combined with the heat from the charcoal grills, they could go into the motor coaches and get refreshed and cooled down. With this size event, located 30 miles from a centralized location, the caterer had to be organized. Attention to details and planning were the keys of the game. The contract with the corporation was made nine months in advance and the caterer worked on organizing this event continually up to the last minute through planning and focusing on all the details. The caterer had to answer questions such as: "How much coleslaw is needed for 13,500 guests?" "How much charcoal would be needed to prepare the food?" "How was the caterer going to set up stations to expedite the service of the food?" With the details and planning process, the caterer eventually determined how many people they could serve per minute.

Bill Jardine
Jardine's Farm Restaurant & Catering
Sarver, PA

Supermarket Evolution into Catering

Supermarkets are also attracted to the opportunities associated with the catering business. Supermarkets have staff and facilities to get into the business with very little additional costs however, **supermarket catering** is usually limited to what can be served, not what can be prepared.

The evolution of the supermarket and its ability to provide catering service began when they first started offering cheese trays, vegetable trays, and items that people could pick up and take home while shopping in the store. Some of the more upscale supermarkets deducted that since they already had kitchen production facilities for the preparation of hot foods and gourmet foods, they could easily diversify into other related food items.

Supermarkets also use many of the value-added or convenience foods available in the market today. With the use of prepared foods, a menu can be built entirely around these prepared food items. A shopper can conveniently purchase prepared salads and heat-and-serve entrees. Since many of these supermarkets are already serving these items in their deli departments, they can increase their sales by offering similar foods to people who come in and pick up their food and take it home with them. Another development in the prepared food departments in supermarkets is the hiring of highly trained, certified chefs. Certified chefs now manage supermarket gourmet departments, providing an upscale and professional touch to the preparation and presentation of the food.

Dual Restaurant-Catering Operations

Many restauranteurs will cater on-premise special events and pursue off-premise opportunities. One strategic reason for **dual restaurant-catering** is that restauranteurs have invested in professional production equipment and can thus increase efficiencies. This effort will lower the overall fixed costs of the operation. Another reason to pursue off-premise catering functions is to increase incremental gross sales without having to incur a capital expenditure of expanding either the dining room area, the kitchen area, or building another restaurant.

Restaurant facilities have a fixed capacity-sized dining room and are only limited by increasing incremental sales while serving more customers within a given time period. Therefore, a strategy is to serve more people off-premise because they lack the space to hold two functions simultaneously. By complementing an on-site location with off-premise catering, a restauranteur can gain greater efficiencies in the use of production equipment and professional staff, lower overall fixed costs of business, incrementally increase gross sales, increase cash flow and profits, achieve better efficiencies in purchasing, and gain a much broader customer base.

◆ EXCLUSIVE CATERING RIGHTS

One of the most important strategic decisions for a successful off-premise function is the design of the menu. It is necessary to create a menu that will complement the equipment in the kitchen facility. Many caterers serve both on- and off-premise catering quite successfully. The Bradley House of Catering is an example of a caterer who has designed their facilities to handle both on-premise and off-premise functions simultaneously, catering off-premise events from fifty to five thousand people.

TIPS FROM THE TRADE

The Bradley House of Catering maintains exclusive dining rights in its catering facility. Off-premise catering includes events at local museums, cultural centers, grand halls, centers for the arts, historical mansions, conservatories, and library social halls. Their market niche for both on-premise and off-premise functions is quite specialized: banquets and weddings, business meetings, exhibits/trade shows, private/corporate picnics, senior citizen functions, and personal celebrations have all experienced their expertise.

The Bradley House of Catering is the **exclusive caterer** to a major cultural center. This means their facility has the exclusive rights to all catering functions held in the cultural center. The cultural center features a three-tiered, 11,500 square foot ballroom/auditorium that can accommodate up to 1,000 people. In addition to the cultural center's activities, special events such as banquets, weddings, concerts, dinner theaters, group meetings, and other business and social affairs are frequently held at the cultural center. On-site parking for approximately 500 vehicles is one advantage at this facility.

Distinct competence in on-premise and off-premise catering has given them a strategic advantage over many other caterers in the market. When a caterer is able to define a target market, a competitive advantage is developed that is difficult for others to copy. Because of their expertise, The Bradley House of Catering is often called upon to service significant events at national art galleries and other special community activities. Their ability to define their market and work toward exceeding their customer's needs has brought them several awards of honor including The Best Caterer Award at The Caterer Showcase and The Five Star Award by The National Caterers Association.

Eric J. Fairman
Executive Sous Chef
The Bradley House of Catering, Inc.
Pittsburgh, PA

◈ ON-PREMISE AND OFF-PREMISE COMBINATIONS

Although the distinct description between on-premise and off-premise catering does exist, actual operations blend both types of catering so there is some fluctuation between on-premise and off-premise catering services. Many caterers may prepare their foods within their own facility and possibly use labor from another. Hotels and small restaurants may prepare food in their production kitchens and transport food off-premise to another location to serve their guests.

There are many instances when a caterer may be selected to provide either off-premise or on-premise work. For on-premise catering to be successful, the caterer must know how many people can be comfortably seated in their facility. Can *entertainment* be provided? Can a wide variety of *menu items* be prepared efficiently at the last minute? The capabilities of getting food off the grill or out of the oven is a serious consideration. However, going off-premise to a facility may find the caterer feeding many people inside a building, twenty-five or thirty people in a *private home*, at a *church* facility feeding two or three hundred people, or even outside for a picnic or fund-raising event. These are issues a caterer must consider.

A caterer must decide and determine, in advance, the specific *clientele* for their business. It is imperative that a caterer understands the relationship between the potential clients' needs, the caterer's knowledge base and skill levels, the event's labor requirements, and the facility's capabilities and availability.

Advantages and Disadvantages

While there is an advantage for both on-premise and off-premise catering, some inherent problems may occur. The distinct advantage of catering a banquet on-premise for one hundred-fifty people is that everything is within reach. If an unforeseen problem strikes, a better opportunity to create a successful alternative may be implemented. If a customer receives a steak they do not like, a caterer can immediately prepare another one. If serving at an off-premise location, this may not be an alternative. Because every job is different, experience teaches what has worked in similar circumstances in the past and will most likely work again in the present.

Private Parties

Many restaurants will do on-premise work, but the size event they can accommodate depends on how many seats they have available. Some restaurants have separate rooms where customers can have private parties catered. If it is a small restaurant, they may offer **private-party catering** for twenty-five or thirty people. They could cater bridal showers, a small retirement dinner, or a small awards dinner for a special occasion. If the caterer did off-premise work, he could provide the same services by catering the event at an individual's home. The caterer might provide a mini menu such as hors d'oeuvres and sandwiches. If the caterer has access to a hotel where there is seating for hundreds of people, the options are completely different. This opens a window of opportunity for the caterer to offer multiple services for large weddings, business meetings, conventions, or trade organizations. Meetings can be held in one section of the hotel, while dinner and dancing can take place in another. These types of events are quite profitable for hotels and very important to the overall function of the facility.

Conventions and Weddings

Wedding and **convention catering** are two of the most profitable events for caterers because of all the extra purchases that can be incorporated into a single event. A wedding (Figure 1–7) will usually require wine and champagne which is provided by the caterer; in addition, the caterer may also provide the wedding cake, the floral service, and the limousine service. The challenge for a caterer is to understand both the Jewish and Christian wedding ceremonies. Many caterers have a bridal consultant on staff to assist the prospective bride in her decisions. Often, caterers can receive a percentage of the money from those outside suppliers working with them, providing the caterer with additional profit. These multifaceted events are quite important for the caterer.

One-Stop Shop Catering

When building an off-premise or on-premise business, many caterers evolve into a full service or **one-stop shop** for the client. The caterer will work with rental companies to provide tables, chairs, and tents. The client appreciates this worry-free service provided by the caterer.

Today, caterers can provide many additional services based upon the needs of the client. Many caterers will provide entertainment, photography, videography service, invitations, ice sculptures, and any other services needed for a

Figure 1-7 A *wedding banquet setup.*

memorable occasion. In addition, some caterers provide a champagne toast for the bridal party, disposable cameras placed on each table or at key locations around the reception area with same day development, wedding favors, personalized take-home money boxes, and flower preservation. A caterer may have worked out a program for a large corporation picnic to provide services such as entertainment for the children, registration of guests, and valet parking. The keys to success are understanding the customer's needs and determining how the caterer can better satisfy those needs.

Mobile Catering

Another interesting facet of the catering segment is mobile catering. **Mobile catering** employs trucks that are equipped with a body that has built-in facilities, such as gas-fired coffee urns (Figure 1–8). Many mobile caterers have developed a seasonal menu and a picnic table concept on the back of their truck. It is necessary for their units to be approved by the local health department because of the many sites and types of foods they serve. Mobile caterers keep hot soups in the winter, and their fleet of 25–30 trucks are dispatched to a variety of sites and locations from construction sites to automobile dealerships. They furnish a wide assortment of hot or cold sandwiches, beverages, soup, coffee, doughnuts, bagels, burritos, and other menu items for the construction workers or mechanics to eat.

Seasonal Niche

Off-premise catering opportunities will also enable many restaurants and hotels to develop a **seasonal niche**. Based upon the time and season of the year there are special events, some that occur on an annual basis, of which the caterer should be aware. These events may involve food such as barbequed chicken and ribs that are prepared at a restaurant or hotel and served off-premise. An advantage of this

Figure 1-8 *Mobile catering units supply a variety of hot and cold items to their patrons.*

type of special event is that the restaurant gains publicity that will help build their client base.

Another advantage that a restaurant can experience by doing off-premise catering is the opportunity to serve more people than they can at their facility. A county fair might attract thousands of people requiring a great deal of planning, organizing, and menu writing. It is not impossible for a small restaurant that seats forty people during the week to do an off-premise event serving five thousand meals every Saturday at a fair or public event. The most important aspect to consider when planning and organizing this kind of service is the design of the menu.

The caterer arrives at the menu based on the needs of the client and what the kitchen equipment is designed to do in food preparation. A caterer cannot expect to do much sautéing without adequate burner space, or roasting without the necessary oven capacity. A caterer must understand that the design of the facility determines the ability to cater at an off-premise location and must be sure the food items on the menu match the production capability of the kitchen. Before selecting the type and categories of food for the menu, the caterer must have a clear understanding of the relationship between the equipment, production capability, and production scheduling.

Summer Outdoor Events

When catering summer off-premise jobs a caterer must be prepared in advance for the unexpected. Is the caterer prepared with the necessary resources if inclement weather threatens the event? The caterer needs to consider having tent rentals available for the day of the event, especially if the client does not have a rain date. Tents will be needed to protect the guests and the food. Additional production details must be coordinated to the type of menu and style of preparation.

◆ QUESTIONS CATERERS NEED TO ASK

A caterer must make a decision to work with a client. Every caterer must develop a standard set of questions that will assist them in making this determination. See the Client Checklist for a list of questions that may help a caterer decide whether or not to accept a function.

Location Considerations

To illustrate the importance of location in off-premise catering, a caterer agreed to cater an off-premise event at a familiar banquet hall. Unfortunately, days before the event, a fire erupted at this facility, rendering it unusable. The event was shifted to another location. At this new location, the function was held on its third floor. Therefore, the job became more difficult and demanding. Food, china, equipment, and supplies had to be transported up and down two flights of

---

Client Checklist

1. Is the location of the event conducive to the caterer's capabilities to produce the food and service necessary to satisfy the guests' needs?

2. Is the caterer comfortable with the management at the hall or facility? Is the caterer comfortable with the client? Is the caterer comfortable with the personalities?

3. Can the caterer work within the quoted budget specified by the guest?

4. Is the caterer's staff compatible with the hall's staff?

5. Was a background check completed on the financials of the hall and client?

---

stairs. After this experience, the caterer never catered another event in this facility. This is a good legal example for a caterer to cite when including a clause in the contract that allows them to assess an extra fee.

When catering social events, especially in the client's home, the caterer must determine if there is enough area to effectively handle the invited guests. If forty or fifty people will attend the event, is it possible to work in the home with that many guests? What is the size of the kitchen? Is room available to prepare the food and to get the food served properly and expeditiously?

◆ HOME-BASED CATERERS

One of the most challenging aspects of the catering business is the presence of **home-based caterers**—caterers who operate from their own homes. In many instances, these caterers may have limited experience, smaller insurance policies, and less knowledge in proper sanitation techniques. Operating out of the home may limit storage facilities, adequate refrigeration, proper food production, and equipment for holding hot food. Many of these home-based caterers are forced to learn techniques on the job. They have a small margin for error.

Equipment

Many home-based caterers are required by local health departments to have separate kitchens in their homes. This may be a disadvantage to the amount of money necessary to start, but on the other hand, may be an advantage because of the amount of equipment a home-based caterer can purchase. Their equipment may consist of a four-burner stove and a small domestic refrigerator. They may lack a commercial dish machine to sanitize the equipment. The local health departments have a concern over these sanitation issues. If the home-based caterer is preparing mayonnaise-based salads in the summer time, how will they hold it at the proper storage temperature (below 41°F)? What kind of transportation equipment will they use, a car or pick-up truck? A professional, licensed, insured caterer will most often own a refrigerated truck and will rent more as demand necessitates.

Professional Training

Another potential weakness of a home-based caterer is a lack of professional training for their staff. Many do not have the time or resources to adequately train their staff in professional service techniques. In addition, they may not have workman's compensation coverage for their staff.

Home-based caterers can do a good job catering out of their home and charge less money than a licensed, professional caterer. They can handle small jobs between 50–100 people at less cost per plate than the licensed caterer. Many however, are not equipped to handle large events.

Unfair Competitive Advantage

Home-based caterers are sometimes viewed as unfair competition to a licensed caterer because the professional caterer is required to have a license, must be inspected by the proper authorities, must conform to the rules and regulations of the health department, and many must have on-staff personnel certified in sanitation. The home-based caterer does not have this expense or the overhead of having commercial equipment, professionally-trained staff, and the required insurance coverage to compete in today's market.

Finally, it is important to understand that food prepared in a private home may not be used or offered for human consumption in a food establishment.

Summary

Restaurants and hotels are holding banquets on-premise, which permits these events to flow smoothly. The functions may be completed with fewer problems at an on-premise facility than an off-premise location because an on-premise event allows a caterer to have all the equipment at their complete disposal. At an off-premise event, a caterer has to know who is responsible for any cooking, if there is equipment available to heat the food, if the kitchen is large enough to get the food out to serve the guests, and if it is a dinner or stand-up cocktail party. The off-premise catering challenge does give a caterer more hassle, but many times the intrinsic reward and personal satisfaction of completing the event and satisfying the customer is well worth the effort.

Review Questions

Brief Answers

1. Identify and discuss features that distinguish on-premise catering from off-premise catering.

2. Define *catering management*. Discuss and provide examples of how catering fits into three general classifications of the food service industry.

3. Identify and discuss different types of catering events which may occur on-premise and/or off-premise.

4. Identify eight ways restauranteurs benefit from catering off-premise events.

5. Discuss how private or nonprofit caterers have a competitive *advantage* over the independent caterer.

6. Explain competitive *disadvantages* a private nonprofit caterer has compared to an independent caterer.

7. Identify the types of catering events a university-based caterer would execute on campus.

8. Discuss the role a *one-stop shop caterer* provides for a prospective bride and groom when planning their wedding.

9. Identify eight ways off-premise catering events can contribute to increased profitability for the restauranteur.

10. What are the key questions caterers must ask themselves before accepting off-premise functions?

11. Explain why the home-based caterer may be viewed as a competitive threat to the professional caterer.

Multiple Choice

Select the single best answer for each question.

1. Which of the following catering businesses would be found in the commercial segment of the food service industry?
   a. business/industry accounts
   b. college and university
   c. healthcare
   d. independent caterer
   e. diplomatic functions

2. When all required tasks, functions, and related services the caterer executes in preparation and implementation of the food and service for a client are done exclusively at the caterer's own facility, that is called __ .
   a. off-premise catering
   b. on-premise catering
   c. corporate catering
   d. social catering
   e. recreational catering

3. Restauranteurs will pursue off-premise catering opportunities for which one of the following reasons?
   a. It raises the overall fixed costs of business.
   b. It incrementally increases gross sales.
   c. It will decrease cash flow.
   d. It will decrease the customer base.
   e. It will decrease purchasing efficiencies.

True or False

Read each of the following statements and determine if it is true or false.

1. The commercial segment of catering management represents the not-for-profit operations which include business and industry, health care, and private clubs.

2. The evolution of supermarkets and their ability to provide catering service began when they first hired highly trained, certified chefs to upscale the food.

3. Off-premise catering is accomplished when the caterer transports all the food, serving products, and personnel to a location other than the building or facility where the food was prepared.

Putting It All Together

Visit an independent caterer, the catering department of a hotel or restaurant, a health care facility, college/university, or a home-based caterer. Identify and discuss the different types of catering events they have executed in the past year. Identify how their facilities benefit from catering off-premise events. Discuss how private or nonprofit caterers may have a competitive advantage over the independent caterer. Write a short report summarizing your visit.

Chapter Two

The Caterer and the Client

Key Terms

reputation

referrals

word-of-mouth advertising

personality conflicts

hidden costs

corporate catering

primary caterer

secondary caterer

fund-raising events

creativity

amusement park catering

social catering

Objectives

After studying this chapter, you should be able to:

◆ Explain why a caterer's reputation may influence a potential client's decision.

◆ Explain how clients select caterers.

◆ Describe why referrals are important to a caterer.

◆ Explain how developing a market, targeting it, and working toward it creates success.

◆ Explain why a caterer may refuse catering jobs and clients.

◆ Provide examples of unanticipated inconveniences a caterer may confront.

◆ Provide examples of how a caterer can be safeguarded against unanticipated problems.

◆ Explain corporate and social catering.

21

INGREDIENTS FOR SUCCESS

1 "Every customer served at the event is a possible referral."

2 "We cannot be all things to all people."

3 "Research every job."

4 "Build a relationship of trust."

5 "Everything must be 100%, 100% of the time."

6 "Never confuse being a nice person with being an astute business person."

◆ WHY CLIENTS DECIDE ON A CATERER

It is important for a caterer to understand how the potential customer's decision-making process works. A potential client looking for a caterer who has the capabilities to do both on-premise and off-premise catering is certainly beneficial. There are many advantages that ultimately attract a potential customer. The caterer must understand how the needs of the customer will influence their decision to select the *right* caterer.

Reputation

One of the most important considerations a client uses in the decision-making process is a caterer's **reputation**. It is imperative that the caterer is reliable. There are four requirements when choosing a caterer.

1. Is the caterer well respected and well known?

2. Does the caterer do most of the catering in the client's area?

3. Are the customers satisfied?

4. Are clients recommending the caterer to others?

If all these issues are answered satisfactorily, the client can be confident in this decision-making choice (Figure 2–1).

POTENTIAL CLIENTS WILL SUBCONSCIOUSLY REVIEW THE FOLLOWING QUESTIONS FOR INFORMATION

1. How many people will attend the event? What is the maximum and minimum number of guests ever to attend their catered function?
2. Is the location convenient?
3. Will the caterer be able to serve the party in a timely manner?
4. Can the caterer take care of any unexpected needs?
5. Can the caterer exceed expectations? (A portfolio of pictures, testimonial letters, and thank you cards can be requested.)
6. Can the caterer solve problems? What procedures exist for emergencies?
7. Is the caterer reliable? Will the caterer supply references?
8. Does the caterer serve quality food and provide exceptional service? What are the prices?
9. Does the caterer use a contract? What are the policies?
10. How many years has the caterer been in business? How many years has the caterer been at this current location?
11. If the function must be canceled, what will happen to the deposit?
12. Can the food be sampled at a private taste-testing session?

Figure 2-1 *Criteria for selecting a caterer.*

The client must also meet and interview the caterer. This interview will help answer such questions as:

1. Is the client comfortable with the caterer?

2. Is the client comfortable with the caterer's personality?

3. Is the client comfortable with the caterer's suggestions and promises for the event?

4. Where does the client need the caterer to execute the function (location)?

When selecting a caterer who has been in business for a long time, the caterer need not make false promises. Their reputation, based on their track record, should be proven by a satisfied clientele.

Referrals

Referrals may be a caterer's best vehicle for advertising his skills and expertise. A referral in the catering trade occurs when a customer is satisfied with the quality and workmanship of the caterer. If the caterer satisfies their needs, clients will share their experiences with friends and associates.

TIPS FROM THE TRADE

Jardine's Catering turned down numerous requests by prospective clients who were located too far from the location. We believed that the distance would hinder a successful job. One of the customers I worked for was an international cosmetic company. I did an upscale job for them in Pittsburgh, Pennsylvania. The company was so pleased with the work that they asked me to consider traveling to Washington, D.C., to cater a breakfast or a brunch. It was to be a much larger job. This was just totally out of the question for Jardine's. It was their opinion that I could successfully execute this function four to five hours away in a different state, at a different facility. I recommended they select a caterer from that area. I believe they were trying to save money by having us do the job in addition to being pleased with our work.

Bill Jardine
Jardine's Farm Restaurant & Catering
Sarver, PA

Referral Concerns

Referrals also bring other issues to the caterer. One concern is when a referral is searching for something inexpensive. A good operator must rely on personal attributes and strengths in the preparation of food and delivery. They must avoid competing with other organizations solely on price, but in contrast compete through their own expertise. There is always one client who is looking for a service that you cannot provide for the price they have in mind. For example, they may prefer less service to satisfy preconceived cost estimates.

Satisfied clients who recommend a caterer to others become a caterer's best advertising agent (Figure 2–2). Remember, we cannot be all things to all people,

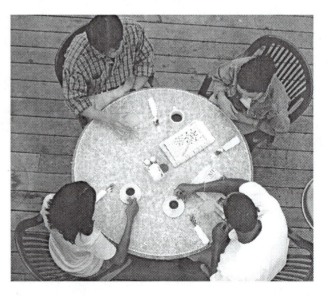

Figure 2-2 *Satisfied customers will share their experiences with others.*

and therefore it would be extremely difficult to attract a client who is shopping for a caterer with only one dimension: price. Those customers may be attracted to your competitor, the nonprofit organization.

Word-Of-Mouth

Word-of-mouth advertising is the best type of advertising for a caterer. If the client is bragging about the job executed by a caterer, the person in need of a catering service will get excited. A potential client may believe that the caterer is as good as a friend says. Satisfied customers are always willing to recommend a caterer they are excited about. Current functions, as well as future jobs, offer the opportunity to attract new customers from the guests in attendance. This introduces *Ingredient for Success 1: "Every customer served at the event is a possible referral."* Guests can be impressed with the food, service, or the caterer's attitude displayed during the function. For this purpose, it is important for the caterer to project a positive attitude regarding the presentation of food and related services. A satisfied client will potentially tell at least three friends, family members, or business associates.

TIPS FROM THE TRADE

We hosted a three-day meeting for a group. The preplanning process went well. The client's needs and special requests were reviewed and the details were finalized with the client. The meeting came and happened. Due to the detailed preplanning the program went off without any problems the client could see. He was very happy because the process was very smooth for him. We checked with the client throughout the day to see if his needs were being met and if any new items were needed. New requests were handled in a very quick and quiet manner. It was made easy for the client. He was made to feel that he was the most important client in house. At the end of the program the client referred three new meetings to us.

Michelle Albright Lennox
Catering/Conventions Services Manager
Hyatt Orlando
Kissimmee, FL

Many caterers are successful at creating new business through referrals from their current clients. Several jobs were acquired because a pleased CEO, who was golfing with his peers, bragged about the exceptional job that a caterer had done for him. This kind of recommendation is a compliment to the caterer and ensures their continued business growth. It is estimated that one satisfied customer will relate this experience to three others; however, an unsatisfied customer will tell eleven other people.

◆ DECIDING WHETHER TO TAKE THE EVENT

An important rule to guide your decision to pursue taking on a catering function is *Ingredient for Success 2: "We cannot be all things to all people."* This ingredient cannot be stressed enough.

TIPS FROM THE TRADE

One of my clients was Lee Trevino, who participated each year in the Senior Skins Tournament on the Big Island of Hawaii. Mr Trevino, Arnold Palmer, Chi Chi Rodriguez, and Jack Nicklaus were all departing the same day and same time from the airport when they saw the food I was delivering for Lee. He made a remark to them that "This is what you get when you win the tournament!" They were impressed by the variety and presentation and from that year on, whoever played in the tournament (win or lose) would contract my company for catering.

Dirk N. Soma
Director
Culinary Institute of the Pacific
Honolulu, HI

A caterer must determine, in advance, the specific market niche to establish for the business, then develop the market, target it, and work toward it. Since caterers cannot be all things to all people, it is imperative to understand the relationship between potential clients and their needs, the caterer's knowledge-base and skill-levels, labor requirements, and facility resources and availability. Developing a market, targeting it, and working toward it will help the caterer create the best plan and contribute to his or her success as a caterer.

We must recognize that a caterer can perform different on-premise tasks easier than can be performed at an off-premise location. One must attempt to understand the natural characteristics of food. Foods differ in how they are handled, stored, prepared, and served. A caterer must know the effect heat will have on the quality of food while being held on a hot serving line or in refrigeration. A sauce should never be made that cannot withstand the required holding period for an off-premise function (See Chapter 6). Because of the nature of some foods, they are better if they are prepared at the last minute. If catering a breakfast event, it is best to do "eggs to order" rather than preparing them ahead of time and transporting them to an off-premise location.

Personality Conflicts

There are times when a caterer must refuse jobs based on lack of comfort with the client. **Personality conflicts** *will* exist. The caterer must also follow intuitive feelings when it is obvious how impossible it would be to meet a client's expectations because of extreme demands. Therefore, when a caterer develops a potential customer list and client base, mutual respect should be perceived on all levels.

Unanticipated Inconveniences

A caterer must always be vigilant and mentally prepared when confronted with unanticipated inconveniences while executing an off-premise assignment.

Bad Politics

One unanticipated inconvenience a caterer may experience is the unpleasant sting of *bad politics*. The following illustration best describes this situation. A caterer is contacted to provide the food for a client who has rented a hall for their special event. The caterer is a third party to the event. The caterer prepares for the event and arrives at the facility with the understanding they are to have full use of the kitchen and production area. Upon the caterer's arrival, they discover that the kitchen and production areas are locked. Apparently a dispute between the client and the facility's management caught the caterer in a bad position. The caterer must develop creative alternatives to serve the food and provide the best service possible.

Hidden Costs

Another potential problem occurs when the off-premise caterer encounters additional *hidden-to-the-client* expenses from the rented facility's management. These **hidden costs** are not usually discussed with the client who rents the catering hall or banquet facility.

The client has made a contract with the management of the banquet hall and has paid the rental fee for its use. The management of this facility contacts the caterer and demands an additional *catering fee* per plate while they are in the banquet facility. The caterer may have already agreed to the price per plate with the client. The client has already paid the rental for the facility but the management levies an additional charge on the caterer for doing business in the hall. If the caterer is overwhelmed with these hidden charges, they have one of two choices: The caterer can absorb the additional cost per plate or can modify the client's original contracted agreement. At this point, the contract must be voided and renegotiated to accommodate the additional charge. This could anger the client, who has already paid for the hall and was not informed of any additional costs.

Gratuities

Another dilemma may occur when people are looking for financial compensation that was not included in the contract. When the caterer is contracted by a third party to enter a banquet hall and serve the food, often the catering hall uses their own service staff and/or bartenders to serve the food or beverages. The caterer is notified by the hall's management to contribute a gratuity for the bartenders and servers. This additional fee, however, could be kept by the management team and never find its way to the servers.

What Experience Teaches

How can a caterer safeguard against these poor business practices?

Explore Options

Caterers have to explore all options. Someone will say that they have cooking facilities, but their idea of cooking facilities may be a two-burner hot plate. Touring the facility before the event is scheduled is important to help determine what options are available at an off-premise facility. Make sure all things are in place *before* the event to avoid getting caught in an unsatisfactory situation.

Research the Job

Caterers have to research every job. **Ingredient for Success 3: "Research every job."** The caterer must be aware of and understand all situations that can potentially occur at the event. Food service, personnel, the type of service be it buffet or sit-down, and the china must be decided in advance. A well-planned catered function should include a schedule that specifies when the event will happen, where the event will happen, and how jobs will be completed.

TIPS FROM THE TRADE

Experience is the best teacher. Experience of handling food teaches one, over time, how much effort is required for each recipe being prepared. This is how to determine the prep work. The caterer may have to schedule prep work the day before or even on the same day of the function. Other factors that affect prep work include the quantity of food being prepared; type of production equipment available; amount of storage space, including cold storage; and complexity of the recipes.

Avoid problems by being completely organized, especially if it is an off-premise catering function. If something is forgotten, it may be difficult to return to the premises. To eliminate that potential problem, make checklists of what you have to do.

Everything is generated from the menu, based on what you are going to cook. You start with a list of all ingredients for every item to be cooked. The first list is a shopping list. The next list is the prep list. The prep list is very important, especially when you are working with inexperienced help. I have prepared these recipes so many times that I have everything stored in my head. Although I know what needs to be done, my staff needs direction. I have to make a prep list and itemize what needs to be done for each recipe. The list will be based on the pre-prep required for both the day before and the day of the event.

For example, we catered a fund-raising event for a political candidate at an off-premise location. We set up twelve action stations for 600 people. It was a lot of volume for each one of these stations. Depending on the recipe and the menu, the amount of prep work varied. One item served was a goat-cheese wonton. We made this item the day before the event. The goat cheese mix was very easy to make and we assembled the wonton's. We had a lili koi (also known as passionfruit) wasabi dipping sauce that was prepared the day before and stored. Everything was ready the day before, completing the prep work. So, you have your checklist done. Everything on that checklist is out of the way. Now, on the day of the event, all you have to do is get to the event, set up, and cook. This becomes another checklist.

Based on the recipe, what equipment will you need to take to the event? To make the equipment list, I recommend building your equipment from the floor up! To begin, I need three banquet tables. I need table cloths and skirting. I need a big, thick cutting board because the burner holding the wok that is cooking the wontons will burn through the table cloths into the table without it. What is next? What type of safety equipment is needed? You should have a first-aid kit in case someone gets burned, and a fire extinguisher in case of fire. Either bring a fire extinguisher with you or make sure one is close by at the cooking site. Always make sure you are permitted to have an open flame at the site. Next, the caterer transports the cooking oil to the event in a clean plastic container, but how will the caterer bring it back? This cooking oil is now at 300°F. When you are finished with the event, you will want to leave right away. You do not want to wait three hours for the oil to cool down. A very large pot should be added to the equipment list. This pot must be larger than the amount of oil needed to transport back. Pour it into the pot and cover it. Make sure the pot is not filled more than one-third.

An important catering task is to make these checklists. First, the food, then the prep work, next the actual cooking, and finally, the equipment list. On the day of the event, make sure you have the checklist. As everything is being packed into the truck or van, it should be checked off. This job should be assigned to one person. Each time I have an event, this job is mine because I want to make sure that I am not going to be missing anything. I do not take anything for granted. Many times I have heard employees say "Yes, we got it, let's go, let's go." Then you get to the site, and the employee says "Oh, I must have forgotten it, Chef." Then you go back to the home base and find it sitting on the loading dock. I prefer a *double checklist*. One checklist that verifies that I have procured the item from the storeroom or kitchen, and the second checklist is used to verify that I actually saw it get on the truck. This system helps to ensure that everything you need gets on the truck including hand towels, fuel, lighter, and matches. I have forgotten matches to light the fuel for the chafing dishes many times. You get to the site and guess what? No one has any matches if no one smokes. Making sure everything is on the list is the best way to prevent a last minute crisis. Then, if you have last minute problems, they are usually surmountable and you can deal with them.

Henry Holthaus
Certified Executive Chef/Instructor
Culinary Institute of the Pacific
Honolulu, HI

Know The Customer

Caterers need to get to know their customers. It is possible to cater a dinner with fine china, glassware, silver, and no facilities out in the middle of a meadow as long as the caterer is prepared and willing to do so. The key to doing these events is to design some kind of checklist to organize and plan all activities and equipment needs before arriving at the event. Figure 2–3 illustrates examples of checklists that a caterer may use.

Before Leaving the Facility

Insulated Transport Boxes

_____ clean and sanitize all insulated hot-food and cold-food transport boxes before and after use to prevent cross-contamination

_____ preheat hot-food transport boxes

_____ chill cold-food transport boxes

Food Production Area

_____ turn off food warming units

_____ unplug steam table unit

_____ remove water from steam table unit, dry with a towel

_____ clean and sanitize food warming units

_____ clean and sanitize food preparation work stations

_____ turn off equipment (fryers, ovens, steam table, steam kettle, tilting skillet, grill, broiler)

Menu Review

_____ review food production sheets

_____ place food and servings into each appropriate steam table pan

_____ cover steam table pan and place in transport (hot-food and cold-food holding) boxes

_____ using masking tape and permanent marker, label food transport boxes with type of food and approximate portions/size.

Small Wares and Equipment

Scoops

_____ scoop number 6—2/3 cup volume or 5 – 5 1/3 oz weight

_____ scoop number 8—1/2 cup volume or 4 oz weight

_____ scoop number 10—3 fl. oz or 3 1/4 oz weight

_____ scoop number 12—1/3 cup volume or 2 1/2 – 3 oz weight

_____ scoop number 16—1/4 cup volume or 2 – 2 1/2 oz weight

_____ scoop number 20—1 1/2 fl. oz volume or 1 3/4 oz weight

_____ scoop number 24—1 1/3 oz weight

_____ scoop number 30—1 oz weight

Ladles

_____ ladle 1 oz (29.6 ml)	_____ ladle 4 oz (118.3 ml)
_____ ladle 2 oz (59.1 ml)	_____ ladle 6 oz (177.4 ml)
_____ ladle 3 oz (88.7 ml)	_____ ladle 8 oz (236.6 ml)

(continued)

Figure 2–3a *Sample catering checklists help the caterer organize the event.*

Spoons
_____ solid
_____ perforated
_____ slotted

French Whip	*Piano Whip*
_____ 10 in. (25.4 cm)	_____ 10 in. (25.4 cm)
_____ 12 in. (30.5 cm)	_____ 12 in. (30.5 cm)
_____ 14 in. (35.6 cm)	_____ 14 in. (35.6 cm)
_____ 16 in. (40.6 cm)	_____ 16 in. (40.6 cm)

Tongs	*Spatulas/Scraper*
_____ 6 in. (15.2 cm)	_____ 9 5/8 in. (24.4 cm)
_____ 9 in. (22.9 cm)	_____ 13 5/8 in. (34.6 cm)
_____ 12 in. (30.5 cm)	_____ 16 5/8 in. (42.2 cm)

Stainless Steel Mixing Bowls	*Cutting Boards*
_____ 1/2 qt (0.5 L)	_____ 12 x 18 x 1/2 in. (30.5 x 45.7 x 1.3 cm)
_____ 3/4 qt (0.7 L)	_____ 15 x 20 x 1/2 in. (38.1 x 50.8 x 1.3 cm)
_____ 1 1/2 qt (1.4 L)	_____ 18 x 24 x 1/2 in. (45.7 x 61.0 x 1.3 cm)
_____ 3 qt (2.8 L)	
_____ 4 qt (3.8 L)	

Table Service

Forks	*Spoons*	*Knives*
_____ dinner	_____ teaspoon	_____ dinner
_____ 4-tine dinner fork	_____ dessert spoon	_____ butter
_____ 3-tine salad	_____ bouillon teaspoon	_____ steak
_____ 4-tine salad	_____ iced tea spoon	
_____ oyster/shrimp		

China		
_____ entree plate	_____ service plate	_____ dessert plate
_____ bread & butter plate	_____ platter	_____ salad plate
_____ plate covers	_____ bowls	_____ coffee mugs
_____ salt & pepper	_____ bouillon cup	_____ underliner
_____ oatmeal bowl	_____ saucer	_____ sauceboats
_____ bud vase	_____ ashtray	_____ celery tray
_____ side plate	_____ sugar packet	_____ carafe
_____ pitcher/creamer	_____ fruit or monkey dish	_____ grapefruit

Linen
_____ table cloths
_____ napkins

Trays	
_____ round	_____ gallery
_____ oval	_____ bread tray
_____ rectangular	_____ server or hostess
_____ oblong	_____ tray stands
_____ square	

(continued)

Figure 2–3a *Sample catering checklists help the caterer organize the event (continued).*

Pitchers
_____ straight-sided
_____ bell-shaped
_____ water

Chafers
_____ chafer frame   _____ cover   _____ fuel holder   _____ fuel   _____ water pan

Insert chafer food pan
Full size = 20 3/4 x 12 3/4 in. (530 x 325 mm)
_____ depth 1 1/4 in. (35 mm)
_____ depth 2 1/2 in. (65 mm)
_____ depth 4.0 in. (100 mm)
_____ depth 6.0 in. (150 mm)

Two-thirds size = 13 7/8 x 12 3/4 in. (354 x 325 mm)
_____ depth 1 1/4 in. (35 mm)
_____ depth 2 1/2 in. (65 mm)
_____ depth 4.0 in. (100 mm)
_____ depth 6.0 in. (150 mm)

One-half size long = 10 3/8 x 12 3/4 in. (325 x 265 mm)
_____ depth 1 1/4 in. (35 mm)
_____ depth 2 1/2 in. (65 mm)
_____ depth 4.0 in. (100 mm)
_____ depth 6.0 in. (150 mm)

One-third size long = 6 7/8 x 12 3/4 in. (325 x 176 mm)
_____ depth 1 1/4 in. (35 mm)
_____ depth 2 1/2 in. (65 mm)
_____ depth 4.0 in. (100 mm)
_____ depth 6.0 in. (150 mm)

One-fourth size long = 6 3/8 x 10 3/8 in. (265 x 162 mm)
_____ depth 2 1/2 in. (65 mm)
_____ depth 4.0 in. (100 mm)
_____ depth 6.0 in. (150 mm)

One-sixth size long = 6 7/8 x 6 1/4 in. (176 x 162)
_____ depth 2 1/2 in. (65 mm)
_____ depth 4.0 in. (100 mm)
_____ depth 6.0 in. (150 mm)

One-ninth size long = 6 7/8 x 4 1/4 in. (176 x 108 mm)
_____ depth 2.0 in. (50 mm)
_____ depth 4.0 in. (100 mm)

Buffetware
_____ 9 in. (22.9 cm) length, 2 oz ladle (59.1 ml)
_____ 12 in. (30.5 cm) length, 4 oz ladle (30.5 cm)
_____ 13 in. (33.0 cm) length fork

(continued)

Figure 2–3a *Sample catering checklists help the caterer organize the event (continued).*

Buffetware (continued)
_____ 11 1/2 in. (29.2 cm) spoon
_____ 13 in. (33.0 cm) spoon
_____ coffee decanter
_____ cake stand

Disposables
_____ plates   _____ bowls   _____ platters   _____ paper napkins
_____ plastic forks   _____ plastic knives _____ plastic spoons   _____ paper towels

Other
_____ plastic wrap   _____ aluminum wrap   _____ hot pads
_____ frill picks   _____ plain picks   _____ doilies
_____ disposable chef's caps _____ duck tape   _____ stapler gun
_____ staplers   _____ masking tape   _____ thumbtacks
_____ screwdrivers, assorted _____ extension cords   _____ power strips
_____ can opener   _____ bottle opener   _____ corkscrew
_____ hammer   _____ scissors   _____ crowbar

Baskets
_____ oblong   _____ round   _____ oval

Cleaning and Sanitation (HACCP Plan, See Chapter 6)
_____ sanitizer   _____ dish soap   _____ scrubbing pads
_____ broom   _____ garbage cans   _____ disposable
_____ buckets   _____ vacuum cleaner   sanitary gloves

Cooking Equipment
_____ portable stove   _____ portable fryer
_____ butane cooking elements _____ propane gas tanks

Stock Pot   **Saucepans**   **Frypans**
_____ 7 1/2 qt (7.1 L)   _____ 1 qt (0.9 L)   _____ 8 1/2 in. (21.6 cm)
_____ 11 1/2 qt (10.9 L)   _____ 2 qt (1.9 L)   _____ 9 3/8 in. (23.8 cm)
_____ 16 qt (15.1 L)   _____ 3 qt (2.8 L)   _____ 11 in. (27.0 cm)

Aluminum Bun Pans
_____ 25 3/4 x 17 3/4 x 1 in. (65.0 x 45.0 x 2.5 cm)—full size pan
_____ 12 7/8 x 17 3/4 x 1 in. (33.0 x 45.0 2.5 cm)—one-half size pan
_____ double boiler

Presentation
_____ heating lamps   _____ extra bulbs   _____ punch bowls
_____ punch fountain   _____ tables

Skirting
Pleat Style
_____ shirred pleat   _____ accordion pleat   _____ box pleat
_____ Skirting clips

Figure 2–3a *Sample catering checklists help the caterer organize the event.*

Front-of-the-House
Bulletin Board Worksheet

Event _____

Event Date _____ Guest Count_____

Buffet _____ Served _____ Combination _____ Other _____

Menu Item: Utensils/Equipment Needed:

Room Setup

Table Setup   Check for a Room Setup Diagram:

Linen:

Special Concerns and Instructions:

Figure 2–3b *Front-of-the-house bulletin board worksheet.*

**Kitchen
Bulletin Board Worksheet**

Event _____

Event Date _____

Confirmed Guest Count _____

Menu Item: Preparation Instructions/Recipe Number:

Special Instructions:

Figure 2–3c *Kitchen bulletin board worksheet.*

◆ TYPES OF CATERING

Professional caterers have distinct types of catering functions in which they can become involved. We can identify all catering functions and place them into two categories, known as *off-premise* and *on-premise*. All catering functions can be identified further as either corporate catering or social catering. One advantage of a catering business is the caterer can decide in advance on the kind of catering function and the clientele to be serviced. A caterer can have the opportunity to aggressively pursue either category. The caterer is in control to select the preferable kind of catering function.

Corporate Catering

Corporate catering is a wonderful form of catering where the professional caterer will build a clientele comprised of large or small corporate and business accounts. These corporate catering events can vary depending on the situation. Many caterers decide to specialize in corporate catering.

One corporate caterer named his business *Strictly Business Catering*. His business strictly caters breakfasts and lunches to small business organizations. This type of caterer does not do any socially catered events. Examples of corporate catering events encompass employee training sessions, board of directors' luncheons, and company-specific picnics for employees and their families.

Organizations will select a caterer based on specific needs and the function they must perform. One advantage of corporate catering is a continual need for food at corporate sponsored events.

One cannot stress enough the importance of **Ingredient for Success 4: "Build a relationship of trust."** Corporate accounts will usually notify the caterer to prepare for an event in 30 or 60 days for 100 people and instruct them to "just invoice us with the costs." This is one advantage of building a relationship based on *mutual trust*.

Relationships Built on Mutual Trust

A second advantage for the caterer is avoiding a bidding war against other caterers. Once the business relationship has been established, and the customer knows what can be done, the client will usually call and give a date. This is done to avoid the hassle of putting the event out for a bid. The building of trust is a mutual process based on what the caterer can do for the client and what the client can do for the caterer.

A disadvantage of having to bid on events against other caterers happens because one caterer will provide "extra" things, such as service, that another caterer is not equipped to do.

Jardine's Catering began its service to the corporate segment with a picnic for 1800 guests attending a banking organization's function. Eventually they merged with another bank and Jardine's began to supply food for employee training programs. Jardine's Catering usually catered lunch for between fifty and one hundred employees involved in each training class. In addition, at the end of each one-day training program, Jardine's would serve them a steak dinner. Often, they would be contracted to provide two and sometimes three meals a day for the bank's employees. On many occasions, Jardine's also provided either a continental breakfast or a full breakfast buffet featuring eggs to order. As a result of this one function, Jardine's became the primary caterer for this bank.

They had clients they serviced for 15–20 years. This relationship was built on mutual respect. Both parties knew what the other expected. Jardine's Catering would be hired for two or three events each year. The client usually liked one specific menu item and requested this item for each event. Even if Jardine's suggested another item, they would refuse and order the same thing. In a way, the client's dedication to the one menu item gives the caterer satisfaction as well. It communicates a strong message. This tells the caterer the client wants them to do the job and at the same time make a profit. A profit is guaranteed in a situation like this because it is known as a repeat business built upon mutual trust.

A **primary caterer** is different from an exclusive caterer. A primary caterer will handle approximately seventy-five percent of a client's needs. The other twenty-five percent of the work will be awarded to a **secondary caterer**. A secondary caterer is usually maintained as a back up. A secondary caterer may lack certain skills or may not be large enough to handle certain jobs.

Bill Jardine
Jardine's Farm Restaurant & Catering
Sarver, PA

Financial Security

Money is another advantage of catering to the corporate segment. The profit is better and is more guaranteed than in social catering. It is very seldom that a caterer ever loses money when catering for a corporation. Caterers pursue corporate accounts because of the willingness of the corporation to issue money up front to the caterer in the form of a deposit. Once a relationship built on trust is created, deposits will become a part of the standard operating procedures that a caterer will establish with the client as part of the business agreement.

Corporate Fund-Raising Sponsorship

Another important catering segment is the power of corporate support. It might be an advantage for a caterer to participate in certain types of corporate **fund-raising events** where food and related services can complement their efforts. Usually, corporate accounts support their fund-raising activities at different times during the year. Once they establish an event, it will be supported annually and often continues to grow in size each year. The following illustration describes how many caterers are able to grow their businesses by catering fund raising events.

One caterer may be the primary caterer for a charitable organization. A cultural event, such as a concert, may be held in the summer in any city. The production area would be set beneath a huge tent and the caterer would provide the food, related services, and equipment. The caterer may even be required to supply drinking water. Everything can be supplied in relationship to tents, tables, linens, and silverware. A caterer must understand costs because tent rentals and related services will drive up the price per person for this type of event. It is not unusual for a specialized corporate event to cost as much as one hundred dollars per person.

The cost of such an event varies based on many factors. The client can spend a lot of money for a very elegant event. A caterer may charge up to forty dollars per person depending upon the charitable organization's budget. The fund raiser probably generates about a fifty percent profit based on the ticket prices. Many charitable organizations raise ticket prices depending on response.

A corporate caterer may also cater events such as corporate-sponsored family picnics, employee meetings, and corporate appreciation dinners. Sometimes these more elaborate events incur a huge cost for the caterer so the corporate clientele should be made aware of all costs. They will pay the agreed upon price for a caterer to come into their facilities and satisfy their needs. For the corporate account, money is often no object as long as they are getting value for their dollar with no surprise costs.

Creativity and the Caterer

The corporate caterer can also enjoy success by weaving **creativity** into each event. Creativity is used to exceed the customers' needs and satisfaction. The art of being creative is important in catering. It is especially important when the caterer builds a relationship with a corporate account. A primary caterer is challenged to create enthusiasm for the guests attending a corporate function. They must often fascinate the same group of people.

The primary caterer for a corporate account must anticipate and plan for the evolution of the relationship. The expectations will change as the client's needs change. A subtle pressure to reinvent each function will challenge the caterer as their relationship with the client evolves.

The first event will probably be a typical dinner. The menu may offer a choice of chicken or roast beef. After a few similar events, a comfortable relationship is built on trust. The primary caterer's challenge is to keep the client's event successful. To remain the primary caterer, the excitement and the participants' anticipation for the event must be maintained. The next step in the evolutionary process is for the primary caterer to plan the function around a theme-based dinner.

The next corporate event may be a fund-raising dinner on Saint Valentine's Day. The primary caterer may use the Saint Valentine's theme and have the wait staff dress in tuxedos with red cummerbunds and bow ties. Approximately 250 people will attend the fund-raising event. Instead of having a formal dinner, as was common practice in past years, the primary caterer can design food stations, designed to provide food and desserts, at various locations in the banquet facility. One station may offer only assorted appetizers; another station, a variety of entrees including carving stations. A variety of delicious desserts may be offered at another station. These stations will be staffed and restocked with food and beverages all night. An orchestra, dancing, and entertainment will complement the food stations. The guests can dance, select food, and mingle for an active, successful event.

One can imagine the excitement for the very next fund-raising event. The client so enjoyed the theme-based dinner that he wanted it to continue. The primary caterer was now further challenged. The customer's needs and expectations had been changed by the innovative caterer. A good caterer will strive to exceed customer expectations and will educate the client. A caterer must continue professional growth.

The primary caterer's employees can play an important role in the development of these theme-based dinners (Figure 2–4). Innovation and creativity

Figure 2-4 *Creative catering ideas evolve from a common theme.*

will excite the staff as well as the client. Research the topic. Ask for employees' ideas—have a general brainstorming session. It is important for a caterer to have someone on the staff with decorating talents to create those memorable, unusual events.

During the brainstorming stage, employees may suggest the following themes: a county fair, a circus, a hobo camp, dinner on a dining car, the Roaring '20s, or opening day at the baseball stadium. The next fund-raising theme selected by the client is the circus theme. The circus theme can be featured throughout the entire event. Clown outfits may replace the official uniform. Each table may have a carousel horse as its centerpiece. The *medicine wagon* will serve as the beverage display. The guests may pass through the midway on their way to tables under the big top. They can stop and play games. The music of the calliope steam organ, and the aroma of popcorn, cotton candy, and fresh food will certainly elevate the guests' desire to participate in the event. The fun house will surprise and amuse.

The following year, the client may select an old-fashioned farm hoedown theme. The caterer may emphasize the fact that the event is being held in the middle of a farm. Set the theme in the catering hall as if the event was being held "in the middle of a meadow." The old buckboard may be used as the beverage station. Decorate the buffet table with wild flowers and miniature bales of hay. Decorate the service area with antique farm equipment and tools, such as an old-fashioned plow. Every detail is planned to simulate a farm environment with straw hats and overalls replacing the official uniform.

Chamber of Commerce

A caterer can begin building a client base by contacting the local Chamber of Commerce. The Chamber of Commerce usually sponsors events such as membership drives, golf outings, and fund raisers. These events help the caterer get established. A caterer can establish relationships and develop a reputation from these events. It takes a professional, organized caterer with accurate knowledge and understanding of the business to produce and execute to the *nth* degree.

Amusement Park Catering

Another option for the caterer pursuing a corporate account is an **amusement park catering**. An amusement park may offer more than 100 different eating establishments for the guests who are enjoying the park. Amusement parks cater to corporations and similar businesses that have their annual *day at the park* each summer. These organizations will bring employees and their family members totalling between 50 and 1,500 people. On any given day, multiple corporations will converge on the amusement park's picnic shelters. These organizations need a lunch or dinner for their group. Because of the volume, amusement parks cannot usually handle all of those requests so they will hire an outside caterer.

A caterer must understand the following mechanics before getting involved with an amusement park. First, always begin with the menu. What kind of food does the guest want? Do they want typical picnic foods such as charcoal-grilled hot dogs and hamburgers, or chicken with watermelon and lemonade? Will the caterer supply the decorations, such as red-checkered paper table covers? Will the caterer be responsible for organizing games for the children and adults?

Cost and Profit Relationship

An important consideration for the caterer is the price. The caterer must understand how the amusement park will charge the guest. Usually, the guest will pay a flat price to enter the park. This one price must include the entry fee, use of the park's facilities, and the lunch. Always do the calculations and understand all expenses. If the park charges only a flat price, make sure the caterer's profit is built into this single price. If the caterer's profit is not included, a separate price should be charged by the caterer for each guest served.

A common problem occurs when a caterer agrees to become the primary caterer for an amusement park without fully understanding the true relationship between revenue and expenses. The caterer should never neglect the research needed to ascertain this important relationship. There are two important considerations to evaluating the cost and profit relationship.

1. Make sure the job can be done at the right price. If quoting a price in January for the exclusive right for the summer contract, accurately forecast and predict expenses based on real costs. Some caterers can lose money on these types of arrangements.

2. Make sure the organization is established before pursuing this type of business. Research the event. Explore every detail. This type of an arrangement will require considerable planning.

While working inside the amusement park, park policy may not permit the caterer to engage in any form of advertising. However, they may permit napkins or matches that have the caterer's name or logo on them. It all may depend on what organization is using the facilities. The main reason for not permitting any form of advertising by the primary caterer is the park wants the guest to believe they are providing the food and service themselves.

Social Catering

Social catering is a distinctive field with its own characteristics. Having the event held in a guest's house is one distinguishing facet of social catering. As a social caterer, never promise anything that cannot be done. Clients may ask the caterer for special requests, and at times, clients will be persistent. They may even just tell the caterer, "Research it and do it!" In every situation, a caterer must remain in control and must be comfortable with saying to the client, "We are unable to do that."

A caterer may have friends or clients from a country other than the United States. These visitors may have different food and cultural habits than what a caterer can produce. Weddings are a good example. A caterer may be approached by someone with Asian food and cultural habits. If this happens, the caterer can work with an authentic Asian chef. The Asian chef prepares the Asian cuisine for the bride's family and Asian friends, while the caterer can prepare and serve American-style food. This joint venture between the caterer and Asian chef will provide the specialized knowledge to exceed this customer's needs.

If the caterer is lacking the knowledge, expertise, skill, facilities, equipment, or information to execute a specific function, they should avoid it. If attempting to prepare a specific cuisine without the adequate skills or knowledge base, the caterer, even in his goodwill attempt, can create a disaster. This will guarantee the loss of the client as well as any potential future business. ***Ingredient for Success 5*** sums up this concept: ***"Everything must be 100%, 100% of the time."***

Client's Home

Planning a social function in a client's home can be a challenge. A caterer's role is more than just providing the food, beverages, and related services. A caterer must educate a client. The client must be taught the proper etiquette of being *mine-host* when ceremoniously entertaining friends or strangers in one's home. From the time a guest enters the home until he departs, the host is responsible for satisfying their social and physiological needs. In other words, the host is responsible for the guests' complete comfort and happiness. Some truly great caterers orchestrate the entire function. They will educate the client in the etiquette of being a proper host and guide the host step-by-step without the knowledge of the invited guests.

Selecting the Guests. The first and perhaps most important responsibility is to select the appropriate guests. Proper care in consideration of this list begins with the approximate number of guests who can comfortably be serviced in the home. The actual selection of the guests must be based on the mutual compatibility of each guest. Even when the occasion requires a group of strangers to socialize in one's home, it is still important for the group to be harmonious. They must have the ability to be cordial to each other. Next, the budget for the event must be finalized. The budget should reflect the host's style of living. At this step, the caterer can guide the host in making realistic decisions. Making the right decision is based on the constraints dictated by the budget, layout of the home, available kitchen appliances, the number and social status of the invited guests, and finally, the ability of the caterer to provide the right food and service. These factors will influence the final cost.

Individualized Plan. A caterer must strive to individualize each plan to meet the needs of the host. Never blindly apply the same social plan to each client. Promise what can be done well while considering the environment, budget, and available resources at the function. Remember, executing a simple plan of delivering a simple menu that provides the highest quality food and service has the basic ingredients for success. A simple plan can always satisfy the needs of a host. Avoid complex plans that simply sound good and create unrealistic customer expectations. Customer expectations based on unrealistic plans lead to poor food quality, bad service, and dissatisfied clients. Worse, it can lead to an embarrassed host whose reputation becomes damaged.

In the long-lived spirit of hospitality, a caterer's duty is to always follow a simple, well-designed plan based on a host's style of living, guided by a well-defined budget, and tailored to exceed their guests' needs.

Special Care. If catering an event in a client's home, always treat the home with special care. Use the *white glove* approach. Be alert and cognizant of the production and service staff activities, the host, and their guests at all times. Be aware of the flow of service and observe each guest's behavior. If a guest has a glass, make sure it is not set down on a piece of furniture and offer ashtrays to smokers so they do not drop a cigarette on the carpet. These and other similar problems do occur and can happen at any time. Even if someone would not drop a cigarette on a floor, a caterer must have the staff trained to anticipate this type of guest behavior.

As in all catering situations, the caterer must anticipate each guest's needs. If, while catering a stand-up party, a guest has an empty plate, a staff member must be trained to immediately relieve the guest of this soiled plate and fork. If the guest has an empty glass, does it need to be refilled or retrieved? Do the ashtrays need to be replaced with clean ones?

Disadvantages of Social Catering

There are some disadvantages of social catering. One disadvantage may be the caterer's limited capabilities to satisfy the often unrealistic demands of the client. Sometimes, without fault of the caterer, it may be impossible to satisfy a client. Therefore, it is important for the caterer to research and understand the customer's needs before accepting a job. A social caterer must be selective and realistic as to what can be accomplished based on the capabilities of the client's home.

When planning a social event to be held in a client's home, a caterer will need to seek the following information.

1. What is the purpose of the social event? Is the event an intimate dinner for 10–12 people or a cocktail party for 35–40 people?

2. What can be supplied by the caterer or the client?

3. Will the caterer require bartenders and adequate bar supplies? In most situations, the customer must supply their own liquor.

4. Will the caterer's insurance provide adequate protection for the staff as well as the guests? Did the caterer consider the legality of liquor liability? Will the homeowner have special insurance coverage for their own party?

5. Has the client made any last minute, out-of-the-ordinary special requests? If so, this is an opportunity for the caterer to generate incremental revenue. Sometimes, as the event approaches, a client, in their need to impress their guests, will have last-minute, panic requests to ensure the success of their event.

6. Are the details of the contract specifically spelled out (see Chapter 12)? A common request made by a client is for the celebration to continue beyond the contracted agreement.

What happens when the client requests an additional two hours for the event? A caterer must be prepared for these requests by having this spelled out in advance in the language of the contract. A contingency plan must be established so when this request is made, the caterer can implement the request. Basically, if the caterer extends the celebration, overtime charges will be assessed. The client must understand the pricing formula used to calculate the final bill. Overtime charges may also generate additional revenues and hidden profits for the caterer.

A caterer must understand the human nature of the client. The successful caterer should consider studying consumer behavior as it relates to the event and their request of services. Caterers may be bombarded with additional requests during the execution of the event. Make sure the specific details are spelled out and agreed upon by the client and the caterer in the contract. A caterer must refrain from deviating from the contract, especially if this action will incur a loss of revenue. This introduces *Ingredient for Success 6: "Never confuse being a nice person with being an astute business person."*

Summary

The process of selecting a caterer is influenced by multiple factors. A positive reputation may give a competitive advantage in the market. Both referrals and positive word-of-mouth advertising provide excellent opportunities for new business. Working to define the customer based on similar needs helps the caterer develop the market. Researching each job can help to selectively create a preferred customer list that may eliminate undesirable clients.

The professional caterer can work at either an on-premise or off-premise site, in a corporate or social environment. The corporate segment provides financial security, long-lasting relationships, and the challenge of designing creative events. Social catering, primarily held in the client's home, is a distinctive field having its own characteristics. Formulating individualized, simple plans that consider the environment, budget, and available resources are ingredients for success. Building a trusting relationship with the corporate or social client ensures long-term prosperity.

Review Questions

Brief Answers

1. Identify and discuss features that distinguish corporate catering from social catering.

2. Describe some common attributes that a client may use to select a caterer.

3. Discuss why reputation is one of the most important attributes of a successful caterer.

4. Define *referral*.

5. Discuss why *word-of-mouth* is one of the most powerful advertising techniques for the successful caterer.

6. Identify examples of *unanticipated inconveniences* a caterer may confront.

7. Discuss some types of *hidden costs* the caterer may experience when catering at an off-premise location.

8. Explain how experience will prepare a caterer for the challenges of business.

9. Define a *primary caterer* and *secondary caterer*.

10. What are the advantages of catering in the corporate sector?

11. Discuss how creativity can provide a caterer with a business edge in the corporate sector.

12. Discuss the role a caterer can play in catering for an amusement park.

13. Discuss the distinct characteristics found in catering in the social sector.

14. Discuss the challenges of catering in a client's home.

15. Discuss the following Ingredients for Success and explain what these mean to you.

    Ingredient for Success 1: "Every customer served at the event is a possible referral."

Ingredient for Success 2: "We cannot be all things to all people."

Ingredient for Success 3: "Research every job."

Ingredient for Success 4: "Build a relationship of trust."

Ingredient for Success 5: "Everything must be 100%, 100% of the time."

Ingredient for Success 6: "Never confuse being a nice person with being an astute business person."

Multiple Choice

Select the single best answer for each question.

1. This form of catering identifies a clientele consisting of business accounts.
   a. corporate catering
   b. social catering
   c. health care catering
   d. independent caterer
   e. primary caterer

2. A caterer who handles approximately seventy-five percent of a client's business is called:
   a. off-premise caterer
   b. secondary caterer
   c. corporate caterer
   d. social caterer
   e. primary caterer

3. The distinguishing facet of this type of catering is that the event is held in the client's home.
   a. secondary catering
   b. primary catering
   c. corporate catering
   d. social catering
   e. nonprofit catering

True or False

Read each of the following statements and determine if it is true or false.

1. Positive *word-of-mouth* advertising is often considered a very powerful way to promote a caterer.

2. One of the most important considerations a client faces in the decision-making process of selecting a caterer is the caterer's reputation.

3. The distinguishing feature of social catering is that the event is held at the corporate client's place of business.

Putting It All Together

Visit an independent caterer. Discuss the catering manager's responsibilities. Why would a customer select your services as a caterer for their function? What unanticipated inconveniences have you experienced as a caterer and how did you handle them? Write a short report summarizing your visit.

Chapter Three

Establishing the Right Kind of Catering for You

Objectives

After studying this chapter, you should be able to:

◆ Discuss a caterer's market.

◆ Explain market segments and relate how a caterer must identify them.

◆ Explain the major considerations when carving out a niche.

◆ Identify why personal characteristics are a key to success.

◆ Discuss mission statements and how they guide the caterer in the decision making process.

◆ Explain a strategic vision.

◆ Discuss and identify the elements of the strategic planning tool SWOT analysis (Strengths, Weaknesses, Opportunities, and Threats).

◆ Explain primary and secondary caterers.

◆ Discuss corporate and social catering.

◆ Discuss on-premise and off-premise catering.

49

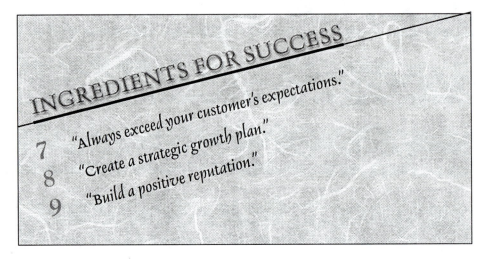

INGREDIENTS FOR SUCCESS

7   "Always exceed your customer's expectations."

8   "Create a strategic growth plan."

9   "Build a positive reputation."

Establishing the right kind of catering to strategically fit a specific market niche is an important decision for a caterer to make. This decision must be made before the first contract is negotiated to execute the first function.

◆ THE CATERING MARKET

A **caterer's market** is the group of all customers in a geographic service area who have unmet *needs*, *wants*, or *demands* requiring food and beverage service. It is extremely difficult and unreasonable to expect one caterer to service the entire market-range of current and potential customers in need or want of food, beverage, and related services. Remember *Ingredient for Success 2: "We cannot be all things to all people."*

"Carving the Market"

The caterer must carve or **segment** the whole market of customers into smaller pieces or niches. Segmenting the whole market into niches requires the caterer to identify customers with similar needs or wants and group them together. This enables the caterer to decide how to best build the business to satisfy that specific group.

To help the caterer identify the specific niche to pursue, a fundamental exercise would be to invest serious time answering a few key questions (Figure 3–1). By answering these key questions, a caterer will better understand the relationship between their strengths and the market's opportunities.

KEY QUESTIONS USED TO IDENTIFY A MARKET NICHE

1. What kind of catering can be executed right now?
2. What kind of food and service can be provided right now to meet and exceed the customer's expectations?
3. Is the caterer comfortable with specializing in chicken, steak, roast beef, prime rib, or pasta?
4. What quality standards can be created and maintained in both food and service?
5. What price-range will the caterer charge?
6. How many days will the caterer want to work each week?
7. How many hours each day will the caterer want to work?
8. What kind of food preparation skills does the caterer have now?
9. Will the menu be a specialized, *limited-menu* or will it be a *broad-line menu*?
10. What are the caterer's culinary skills and their relationship to menu design?
11. What kind of equipment does the caterer have?
12. What negotiating skills does the caterer have?
13. What is the caterer's knowledge regarding food and service sanitation standards?
14. Who will assist the caterer in these functions?
15. What is the skill level of the staff?
16. What kind of personnel demands will the caterer have to confront?
17. How large or small does the caterer want to be?
18. How fast or slow does the caterer want to grow?
19. How will the caterer evolve after the business has grown in three-to-five years?
20. How will the caterer evolve after the business has grown in ten years?

Figure 3-1 *Key questions used to identify a market niche.*

The purpose of answering these questions is twofold. First, a careful analysis enables the caterer to define who they are today. Second, the answers will provide the caterer with an understanding of what kind of professional development will be needed to provide continuous improvement in operations.

The answers to these questions will also help to establish a *business growth plan.* Remember **Ingredient for Success 2: "We cannot be all things to all people."** Caterers will only be able to effectively communicate their missions to prospective customers and to inaugurate the process of continuous improvement when they are comfortable with their own skills and abilities.

◆ WHO IS THE CATERER?

How caterers define who they are begins with an analysis of their capabilities as a caterer and how they can satisfy customers' needs and wants. This is a starting point to establish the right kind of catering business.

One challenge is to identify the market niche the caterer is most comfortable servicing (Figure 3–2). This niche will determine the customers' wants and needs to be satisfied by the caterer's business. Issues important to the caterer include:

1. Do they specialize only in on-premise catering?

2. Will the caterer specialize in off-premise catering?

3. Will the caterer attempt to position the business as both an on- and off-premise catering operation?

4. Will the caterer be able to compete in the social market?

5. Can the caterer satisfy the needs of a corporate account?

6. Will the caterer try to satisfy the needs of both corporate and social catering customers?

Figure 3-2 *Caterers must determine the type of clientele they are most comfortable servicing.*

◆ MISSION STATEMENT OR PURPOSE

One prerequisite for competitiveness in the marketplace is the ability for a caterer to confidently communicate the mission, or purpose, of the business to potential clients. The company's mission is written in a statement which defines the sole purpose of why the caterer is in business. The **mission statement** identifies who the caterer is and communicates what the caterer can do for all potential customers.

This statement of purpose is the foundation of the organization. The mission statement answers the question, "Why am I in business today?" It may also reflect what the caterer plans to become. As a management tool, it guides the caterer's decision-making process. The mission statement permits the business to remain on-course while pursuing its market niche by establishing a strategic business plan. It will describe the type of business including current customers, types of catering functions, where the events will be executed, and how to solve the current needs of the present customers. It also positions the caterer in relation to the competition, by defining it as a corporate caterer, social caterer, or an on-premise or off-premise caterer. By addressing these key issues, the caterer will formulate a concept and effectively communicate this concept.

Importance of the Mission Statement

The mission statement is the caterer's guiding light. Every action publicly displayed by the business should evolve from the mission statement. A mission statement helps communicate who and what a caterer is to the **stakeholders**—employees, suppliers, clients, guests, community, neighbors, competitors, government agencies, and others who have a direct relationship with the business. It is important for the caterer to share expectations and long-term plans with the community.

A mission statement is important for a number of reasons. First, the mission statement is important for the internal organization. It reflects the company's culture. A company's culture is a reflection of its core beliefs, values, and history. Employees need to know where the organization is now and where it wants to be in the future. Second, the mission statement positions the business independently from the competition. It separates the caterer selling rotisserie chicken from the local fire hall that is preparing stuffed cabbage and fried chicken. It helps to set the business apart from its competition by communicating how the business is better, different, and more professional.

There are many niches in the catering market. The lower priced caterers serve the market niche whose needs may demand macaroni and cheese, cabbage rolls, and chicken for approximately $5.00 per person. Caterers decide in advance if they want to be part of that segment or a caterer serving speciality foods like steak, ribs, or gourmet foods.

The mission of the operation will validate the caterer's market position, define competitors, identify what they can do, and how they do it. The mission statement will guide the caterer in all decisions, help to exceed the competition,

TIPS FROM THE TRADE

It happened back sixty years ago, so I am not sure how it transformed. One thing that is difficult to do in catering is to operate both a catering facility and an à la carte restaurant out of the same facility. Sometimes there are problems and conflicts, such as duplication of staff. We actually operated that way for many years. However, in the mid-1980s we shut down the à la carte restaurant within the catering facility and concentrated 100% on catering. It was one of the best moves we ever made. This helped us focus on what we did best at the time. We did not have the duplication of staff and we had the predictability that leads to a profitable operation. Caterers can predict the operations because they know what is coming in and what parties are booked. When you are an à la carte restaurant, you do not know what is going to come through the door. So it is hard to do both, be a caterer and run the à la carte restaurant. Also, customers get a mixed message. Customers do not know if you are a caterer or if you are a restaurant. When we made that separation, it helped our business tremendously.

Marty Horn
President/CEO
FOODgalaxy.com
Parsippany, NJ

allow them to function more economically, and help provide better service, to become the caterer of choice. A strong mission statement is like the Pied Piper's magic flute. When people know the caterer is responsible for an event, and they hear the caterer's name, it attracts them to the event because of their expectations. This drives **Ingredient for Success 7: "Always exceed your customer's expectations."**

Personal Reasons

A mission statement is more than simply *having a business and making money*. Although a caterer may cite various reasons for creating a business, these reasons are strictly individual and personal in nature, and often reflect their unique catalysts for the business. Start-up businesses can surge from many different directions.

A caterer will start a business for many different reasons including personal passion and individual desires, personal commitments, the belief that it can be done better than someone else, a means to create a respectable living through sufficient profits, and the desire to start a family business. Although personal reasons may drive the motivation to become a caterer, profit resulting from executing catering events will become the focus of a successful business. Good profits will be the desired outcome, but should not be the sole reason for being in business.

◆ GROWING THE BUSINESS

Knowing how to grow a business is an important skill. Growing a business must be strategically planned in advance. Controlled growth requires a caterer to understand successful business concepts and how they relate to their own situation.

Controlling growth is important to the fiscal health of the caterer's business. To formulate a **business growth plan**, a review of the following questions may help.

1. What is the projected five-year gross sales figure?
2. What techniques will best describe how to satisfy current customers' needs?
3. How will you describe any desire to diversify into a new market niche?
4. How will new customers be attracted?
5. Who will identify these needs, wants, and demands?
6. What is the strategy regarding menu mix and new product development?
7. How will new menu items and specialities be introduced?
8. How will efficient and effective multiple catering events be executed on a daily, weekly, or monthly agenda?
9. How will sustainable trends, rather than short-lived fads, be identified?

Professional Growth

The progressive professional growth of the catering organization must be a well-crafted part of this plan. This takes careful, patient planning. For example, a caterer can only maximize on-premise sales by allowing the facility and staff to efficiently and effectively operate at full-capacity. Therefore, the professional caterer must creatively plan financial and personal growth to develop an incrementally better organization every year.

Controlled growth is a management quandary. One dilemma a caterer must prevent is uncontrollable, exponential growth. Growing too fast can financially hurt the caterer. This can happen when a caterer accepts too many functions that need execution in a short period of time without sufficient staff or supplies.

Unfortunately, this dilemma is experienced by many caterers at least once in their career. Without a growth-control plan, every caterer will, at one time or another, experience the dilemma of accepting more responsibility than can be effectively and efficiently controlled. Planning for prosperous growth leads to *Ingredient for Success 8: "Create a strategic growth plan."*

The following illustration describes how a caterer can fall into this type of problem. A caterer may successfully manage $5,000 in gross sales per week. Believing the company can handle an increase to $7,000 per week, additional jobs are taken the following week. However, if the caterer's volume breaking point is in the range of $5,500–$6,000, problems emerge. The caterer cannot handle the increase of $2,000 because the facility and personnel have been *stretched* too far, and it does not work out. Instead of generating the expected incremental profit on the additional sales, the caterer will lose money because of uncontrollable circumstances resulting from the lack of an adequate facility and staff.

Strategic Vision

A **strategic vision** is future looking. It is important because it creates a long-term vision for the caterer. This strategy helps the caterer to envision where the business is headed and what kind of demand will exert pressure on the organization. A long-term vision will project growth over the next ten years. Anticipated concerns include seeking answers to the kind of professional development and special training the caterer needs to reach this proposed concept and what additional internal resources are needed by the caterer to attain this goal.

SWOT Analysis

A technique called **SWOT analysis** is a strategic management tool caterers use to match their business strengths to market opportunities. SWOT is an acronym that stands for identifying internal *strengths* and *weaknesses*, and the external *opportunities* and *threats*. This excellent tool is used to empower the caterer to interpret an overall business position. Using this information, the caterer can best match strengths to a specific niche in the competitive catering market.

SWOT analysis will lead to the identification of competitive strategies the caterer can use. Does the caterer have the internal strengths to pursue a strategy geared to catering on-premise, or only off-premise functions? Does the SWOT analysis reveal the caterer is best suited for social catering? Can the caterer compete successfully in the corporate catering segment?

Strengths

Strengths are identified as internal attributes, skills, characteristics, or assets that a caterer possesses which provide an enviable position of exceptional competitiveness in the market. A strength creates a tactical, defensible, competitive position for the caterer to use as an offensive or defensive weapon. This position makes it difficult for other caterers to compete in the market. Figure 3–3 provides an outline of a caterer's tangible and intangible internal strengths.

STRENGTHS OF A CATERER

1. Quality food—Set and maintain high standards for the food and ingredients. In catering, the ability to please diverse palates is a trademark of a successful caterer.

2. Unique food—Is the food different from other caterers? What is the caterer's **signature menu item** or what entree item is the caterer known for (Figure 3–4)?

3. Excellence—There are many average caterers. ***Ingredient for Success 7*** states: ***"Always exceed your customer's expectations."*** Strive to provide better-than-average food and services to guests. Gear strengths to meet and exceed customer satisfaction beyond the food and service. If the function is a social event in someone's home, provide valet parking and entertain the guests. If it is a corporate function, offer to present their awards or prizes for them. If it is a wedding, provide additional related services, such as cake, limousines, tuxedo rental, band or DJ, and bridal supplies. If children are involved, entertain them. If serving a buffet, strive to make it memorable beyond the food and different from the competition.

4. Ambition—The internal drive, intensity, and desire to become the best possible caterer is an intangible strength. Never be happy with mediocrity. Establish performance standards that stretch the organization's capabilities. In the catering field, a work ethic that demands focus is required. A successful caterer cannot be lazy.

5. Passion—The intense emotional drive of excelling as a caterer. Embrace the challenges of working with foods that are created differently, better tasting, more attractively presented, and served more professionally than the competition.

6. Personality—A caterer's good communication skills, the ability to work well with the public, and to understand people contribute to successful catering. A caterer must possess a strong personality, and sell himself, the team, the concept, and the organization.

7. Human Resources—The specialized skill, expertise, or training to work with others. Is the staff prepared to service the guest better than the next caterer? Is the staff competent at carving beef? Does the staff have special skills to execute the event? For example, never ask the dishwasher to put on a clean shirt, then hand him a carving knife and have him positioned to serve—especially if he has never seen a side of beef before. If the staff is extremely loyal to the organization, they will go beyond what is required of them.

8. Commitment to the process of continuous learning—The process of learning is a journey. This journey includes both formal training and self education. It helps to join local and national organizations; attend seminars; and read books on cooking, management, self development, and stress release. Always strive to learn something new. Support the process of education by developing an ongoing training program that requires everyone in the organization to learn.

(continued)

Figure 3–3 *Strengths of a caterer.*

9. Assets—Does a caterer have an incomparable banquet hall or location? Do they have specialized assets, such their own refrigerated trucks, chafing dishes, or insulated transportation boxes for either hot or cold food and other equipment?
10. Creativity—How is the caterer more creative than others? This business strength is important in the field of catering because there are constant changes in themes based on dissimilar celebrations and needs of the guests.
11. Logistics—The ability to successfully work in different off-premise locations is a significant strength for a caterer.

Figure 3-3 *Strengths of a caterer (continued).*

Figure 3-4 *Signature items help a caterer stand out from the competition.*

Weaknesses

Weaknesses are identified as those internal areas that can limit a caterer's ability to compete successfully in the industry. The strengths listed previously in this chapter could be viewed as weaknesses if a caterer, who does not possess them, competes against one who does.

A caterer can identify an internal weakness as (1) those tasks they do not execute well or (2) those done deficiently as compared to other caterers in their industry. Weaknesses include lack of physical endurance; lack of culinary, technical, or management skills; and lack of specialized equipment or other tangible or intangible assets.

Lack of physical endurance, or the required effort to complete a job, is one major weakness that can prevent a caterer from becoming successful. The entire staff needs stamina and energy to follow a job from beginning to completion. Planning, implementation, execution, and follow-up must be properly managed at each stage of the operation. Generally, long, odd hours are required in the catering industry. Working late and doing what it takes to make the event a success is the norm rather than the exception in catering. A typical event may consume twelve or more strenuous hours for a caterer. During this time, numerous demands can weigh upon a caterer. Can the caterer financially do the job? Is the caterer able to endure long hours of relentless stress? How will this stress affect a caterer's overall health? If the caterer cannot manage the event from the formulation through the implementation stages, it may not be a success unless a competent manager is put in place.

Another weakness is when the caterer is expected to fully participate in the event with the freedom of an invited guest. The caterer is separate from the event and cannot comfortably socialize, even though the guest may interpret this lack of participation in a negative way.

Lack of specialized knowledge can be a weakness. Either the lack of management training or culinary techniques can create a potential problem when trying to compete. The lack of competencies in culinary skills can limit a menu as compared to some competitors. This may result in losing potential clients by being unable to satisfy their needs.

Other weaknesses that may prevent a caterer from success include:

1. labor difficulties
2. last minute stock-outs by purveyors on food items that are needed for the event
3. insufficient operating capital
4. unreasonable lease agreements
5. excessive long-term debt
6. excessive payroll
7. unrealistic general overhead such as mortgage or rent payments, utilities, equipment payments, repairs, and maintenance
8. insufficient knowledge in the areas of food production, air-conditioning, and refrigeration repairs
9. uncontrollable temper or emotional instability
10. inability to provide leadership, especially in emergency situations (Figure 3–5)
11. poor communication skills
12. lack of attention to details
13. failure to solve problems
14. lack of accounting and financial skills; inability to be cost-efficient and profitable
15. over promising and under achieving; telling the client what they want to hear to get the job
16. Fear of taking risks

Figure 3–5 *Adequate staffing and effective leadership make last minute room changes a breeze.*

Opportunities

Opportunities are identified as those external, controllable, future catering events that best match the caterers' competitive strengths and which enable him or her to meet and exceed guest expectations. Opportunities reveal themselves as potential, profitable-growth zones. A caterer can identify those growth areas and pursue them as part of their overall business plan.

Another precious opportunity caterers have is **Ingredient for Success 9: "Build a positive reputation."** Caterers' reputations always precede them in the marketplace. At all costs, every caterer strives to continually build and cultivate a positive reputation. As in other industries, a prerequisite of success is the favorable reputation. At any given event, employees may not perform up to standards or mistakes may be made. If there are delays, explain them. It is the best policy for the caterer to always tell the customer the truth, and never lie about anything.

The caterer has other opportunities including the event itself. A caterer designs each event to the specifications of the client. The caterer controls the design—it is the caterer's creation based on serving the needs of the customer.

The opportunity to work with the newest foods and products in the marketplace is another opportunity the caterer experiences. Often, the caterer is the first to receive a new food item from the purveyor or food broker. The purveyor's distributor sales representative will field-test new products through a caterer to determine their popularity.

A caterer will also have the opportunity to work with other caterers and their staffs on certain events. An astute caterer can observe these competitors, glean new ideas, and gain an understanding of their strengths and weaknesses.

Opportunities appear in the market in many different ways. The following illustrate opportunities for a caterer.

1. business location of the facilities

2. potential economic growth

3. physical layout of the facility to support catering functions

4. adequate parking area clearly marked and lighted

5. ownership of the professional food production equipment

6. lack of competition

7. ownership of the facility and equipment

8. hours of operation and days of the week available to cater functions

9. recognition of sustainable trends

TIPS FROM THE TRADE

Jardine's Catering was hired to prepare charcoal-barbeque chicken at a location along a small creek on the client's farm. When the catering team arrived, they set up and filled the charcoal pits, readying them. When they attempted to light the charcoal, an immediate problem emerged. The charcoal would briefly ignite, but would soon extinguish itself. The area surrounding the creek, where the charcoal pits were built, was earlier filled with ashes by the client to absorb any moisture in the ground. The ashes were wet. The charcoal was drawing the moisture off of the ashes, making it impossible for the charcoal to burn. Immediately, a runner was dispatched and returned with 10 gallons of diesel fuel. This fuel was poured on the surrounding ground and ignited. The water in the ashes was burned off and the ground dried. Because of this delay, the food was one-half hour late, but Jardine's kept the client aware of the problem. The client was very grateful for the open communication and everything went well.

Bill Jardine
Jardine's Farm Restaurant & Catering
Sarver, PA

Threats

Threats are identified as those external elements which can cause a potential loss for a caterer. Government regulation and increased changes in the interest rates are uncontrollable threats confronting a caterer. A decrease in the demographics of the area, losses in gross sales, market share, and profitability are major business concerns. Some reasons for these business losses include the entry of new competitors; substitute products; and the relocation, downsizing, or shutdown of corporate customers.

Figure 3-6 *Can a new fish-fry restaurant pose a competitive threat to an upscale seafood restaurant and caterer?*

Competition is a major threat to the survival of a successful caterer. Competitive rivalry among caterers is a dynamic function of the business environment. The threat of new businesses entering in a local market is always a concern because of the lack of insurmountable barriers preventing it. The low cost of entering a segment of the catering market means it is relatively inexpensive for someone to start a catering business. There is no type of specialized technology or privileged information barring one from becoming a caterer. However, a positive reputation, a caterer's skills and abilities, client loyalty, and the buying power or economies of scale in their operation are some barriers new competitors may have to overcome.

Knowing the competition and where it exists will help a caterer develop effective strategies to confront any new competitive threat (Figure 3–6). Conducting frequent surveillance activities to monitor the competition will help a caterer gain strategic information on what others are currently doing.

A caterer's own lack of certain skills and abilities can be a threat. Movement or shutdown of corporations in the caterer's market area is a threat to the business. Another threat may be competition in the market niche. When trying to compete in the low-end segment of the catering market, it is very difficult to remain successful and profitable. See Figure 3–7 for a list of potential threats.

THREATS CONFRONTING A CATERER

1. Competition—Caterers must be aware of all competitors, especially those in the same target market. They must monitor and analyze the competition on a continuous basis to understand their strengths and weaknesses. What are their strategies? What do they charge? Where is their location? Do they have any special features? What is their purchasing power? What is their promotional and marketing expertise?

2. Target market or communities—Who are the customers? Are they price sensitive? What are the demographic variables such as age, income, gender, occupation, marital status, and ethnic background?

3. Offering to cater functions for a new market niche without enough analysis—Is the market niche growing? How fast is it growing? What economic and social factors will be influencing the market?

4. Is the client unhappy?—Once the function is running and in place, the happiness of a client is directly correlated to the caterer.

5. Future competition—Will new caterers enter the market? What weakness may be exploited by the competition to steal a share of the market?

6. Human resources—Does a shortage of properly trained, skilled workers exist? Lack of cooperation between members of the service staff and food production employees portrays unprofessionalism.

7. Inadequate equipment—Poor layout and design of production area and a shortage of small wares and equipment are common.

8. Poor management structure—Ineffective scheduling or a lack of planning, organizing, and controlling can result in a poorly executed event.

9. Inappropriate lease—Excessive rent or mortgage payments and/or lack of credit can cripple cash flow and profits.

10. Staff does not care about customer needs.

11. Lack of a plan for sanitation—Poor procedural follow up can cause a food borne outbreak and hospitalize guests.

Figure 3-7 *Threats confronting a caterer.*

Summary

To establish the right kind of catering, an accurate understanding of the caterer's strengths and a precise customer profile based on the identification of unmet needs, wants, and demands is required. To effectively communicate these strengths to the market, a mission statement is created to define the caterer's purpose. Strategically growing the business allows for the proper mix of financial and personal activities correlated to its long-term success. One strategic management tool used to match business strengths to market opportunities is SWOT analysis. SWOT is an acronym for identifying internal strengths and weaknesses, and external opportunities and threats.

Review Questions

Brief Answers

1. Briefly discuss why it is important for a caterer to understand the market.

2. Explain what is meant by a caterer *carving the market*. Provide examples to support your answer.

3. What are the key questions a caterer must answer to determine the market niche most favorable for them to pursue?

4. Why must caterers first understand their capabilities before they can effectively satisfy a customer's needs?

5. Explain the six purposes of a mission statement.

6. Who are stakeholders and why must a caterer respect them?

7. What is a strategic vision? Why is it important for a caterer to create a strategic vision for the business?

8. Describe the management tool SWOT analysis. How can a caterer use this tool to gain a competitive advantage in the market?

9. Give examples of the types of strengths, weaknesses, opportunities, and threats a caterer may have.

10. Discuss the following Ingredients for Success and explain what these mean to you.

    Ingredient for Success 7: "Always exceed your customer's expectations."

    Ingredient for Success 8: "Create a strategic growth plan."

    Ingredient for Success 9: "Build a relationship of trust."

Multiple Choice

Select the single best answer for each question.

1. Which one of the following reasons explains why a mission statement is important for a caterer?
   a. It guides the decision-making process.
   b. It communicates to the customer the type of business the caterer will become.
   c. It plays a minor role in the creation of a strategic business plan.
   d. It is the first step in understanding who the customers are in the market.
   e. All of the above.

2. The ___ is the group of all customers in a caterer's geographic service area who have an unmet need or want requiring the service of food and beverage.
   a. corporate client
   b. primary client
   c. on-premise client
   d. market
   e. social client

3. The ___ is future looking, creates a long-term direction for the caterer, and helps to answer the type of professional development and special training needed by the caterer.
   a. SWOT analysis
   b. mission statement
   c. strategic vision
   d. primary caterer
   e. secondary caterer

True or False

Read each of the following statements and determine if it is true or false.

1. A strategic vision helps the caterer answer the question, "Where is the business currently going?"

2. SWOT analysis is a catering-industry-specific acronym that means Sweat, Work, and Overtime—something every caterer will do sometime in their career.

3. Threats in the competitive marketplace are identified as those external elements which can cause some business loss for the caterer.

Putting It All Together

Search on the Internet for catering companies. Find if they have a mission statement. Review these mission statements against the criteria discussed in Chapter 3. Does the mission statement describe the catering company? What can you deduce from the mission statement?

<table>
<tr><td>

Chapter
Four

</td><td>

Choosing
Your
Client

</td></tr>
</table>

<table>
<tr><td>

Key Terms

</td><td>

Objectives

</td></tr>
<tr><td>

customer base

prospecting strategies

needs

wants

demands

relationships

life cycle of customer events

professional sales staff

upgrading the event

proposal

</td><td>

After studying this chapter, you should be able to:

◆ Explain how a caterer can build a solid customer base using specific prospecting strategies.

◆ Explain the details of a catering proposal.

◆ Explain why the planned growth of a catering company is achieved through a conscientious building of satisfied customers and the accomplishment of a caterer's financial objectives.

◆ Explain why a caterer may refuse to work for a particular client.

◆ Define the difference between a client's needs, wants, and demands.

</td></tr>
</table>

INGREDIENTS FOR SUCCESS

10 "Customer satisfaction grows your business."

11 "Understand why the customer has selected the caterer—what are the expectations?"

12 "To establish a long-term relationship with a customer and work, as frequently as possible, with each client one-on-one."

13 "Presentations are important—create special, unusual, personable, and impressive competitive proposals."

The creation of a solid **customer base** upon which to draw current and potential clients necessary to support a catering operation now and in the future, is one of the most important business tasks a caterer must faithfully perform. This task is a natural extension flowing from the caterer's established mission statement, as discussed in Chapter 3.

◆ CREATING A CUSTOMER BASE

Creating a solid customer base and attracting new customers is a continuous building process for the caterer. There are many good customers available in the market to build a solid base of support, however caterers must understand their capabilities. They must know the production capacity of the kitchen, understand the current skill level of the employees, and strictly adhere to the financial goals of the organization. They must also be able to accommodate the menu requirements such as providing a low-scale or upscale menu, servicing social or corporate events, and on-premise or off-premise functions.

Prospecting Strategies

A number of considerations must be examined when building a solid customer base. How can the caterer best accomplish the task of building a sustainable customer base? The caterer can begin by formulating a prospecting plan to complement the goals of the organization. Based on this plan (see the business plan, marketing section, in Chapter 6), a caterer can derive assorted **prospecting strategies** to communicate information to potential clients.

The caterer must fully understand how skills are used to meet and exceed customers' expectations. Since building sales depends largely on the number of people who buy the product, the proper place to begin a market analysis is with people. Therefore, a starting point is to understand the needs, wants, and demands of the customer.

Needs, Wants, and Demands

Customer **needs** can be very complex. A human need is a feeling of deprivation for something. Basic human physical needs include food, clothing, and safety. Customers have social needs as well. To fulfill a social need, the client may have an affiliation with an association or a group. The caterer must recognize the client has esteem needs as well. Prestige, recognition, and self-expression are esteem needs a caterer must satisfy.

Clients will package their basic needs into **wants**. A client's wants are always evolving. These wants are defined by the level of sophistication of the client. The caterer's challenge is to understand the difference between what the client *needs* and what the client *wants*. The caterer offers a combination of food and service to solve the client's basic issue.

When clients approach a caterer, they will have unlimited wants, but their budget and limited resources will constrain them. Clients will select the caterer who can provide the most satisfaction based on their budget. A client's *wants* become a client's **demands** when they are backed by financial resources and buying power.

The customer is the most important individual to the organization, as they are providing the funds for the service. Satisfying customers is the basic goal of any caterer. Every satisfied customer will sing the caterer's praise and recommend the services to others. However, this is far from a simple exercise.

Many caterers are very successful because they know how to exceed the explicit and implied needs, wants, and demands of their customers. They understand who the customer is and the characteristics of the target market by completing a market analysis (Figure 4–1).

A caterer often has the opportunity to work with the customer soon after the conception of the customer's idea. The real challenge is to translate their idea—the needs, wants, and demands—into a package. The caterer will bundle a package of complementary tangible products and intangible services to execute based on the client's budget. This introduces *Ingredient for Success 10: "Customer satisfaction grows your business."*

Understanding customer needs, wants, and demands enables the caterer to recommend to each client a winning combination of service and food. Carefully

---

Understanding the Customer

Demographics:　　　Age, level of income, gender, marital status, family composition, ethnic background, education level.

Lifestyle:　　　Family status, extracurricular activities, media preferences, professional and personal organizational affiliations, political affiliation.

Geographic Area:　　　Location; urban, suburban, rural, city. Region or neighborhood; residential, business, downtown.

Psychographics:　　　Status-seeking, trend-setting, liberal, conservative.

Decision Making:　　　Price, quality, brand name, reputation, location, speciality.

Sources of Market Data
1. Up-to-date census data
2. Current popularity trends
3. Regional or county planning commissions
4. Banks and newspapers

Sources of New Customer Prospects
1. Customers—direct contact
2. Phone books (local)
3. Employee survey
   —preplanned
   —regularly scheduled
   —conducted often
   —short and to the point
   —summarized and evaluated by management

Figure 4-1 *Market analysis.*

listening to the customer is the first step. Listen to hear not only what is being requested by the customer, but what the customer is implying in the request. This is the greatest challenge. Successful caterers listen, listen, and listen.

Translating a customer's message is vital. Adequately composing the right combination of food and service to exceed these needs, wants, and demands is the challenge. To ensure success, the caterer responds by asking the customer clarifying questions. These questions help the caterer translate the customer's requests to produce a synergetic combination of results which exceed the customer's expectations.

Each and every customer has a basic need: They need a caterer. All clients are also in need of good food, good service, professional conduct, and value. Complicating this fact, each customer brings his/her unique wants and desires to the caterer.

It is important to know a client's needs or be able to make suggestions. Each client has an idea as to what the caterer should be able to produce. Often caterers are asked to provide wild and unusual tasks. It is common to get challenging requests from particular ethnic groups, such as a European group who requests half authentic German and half American cuisine at an event.

TIPS FROM THE TRADE

Jardine's catered a wedding for a couple who requested half authentic Indian and American cuisine. First, we had to convince the couple that half of the wedding party would only eat Indian food and the other half would only eat American food, but the guests would probably eat some of each. Then, we recommended that they bring in an authentic Indian chef to prepare the food, but Jardine's, as the caterer, would serve it. This arrangement worked quite well. We made sure the chef was reliable, dependable, and had the food delivered on time, meeting everyone's expectations and demands. Other times a caterer will run into situations where clients have all kinds of unusual ideas, prompting the following polite response, "Sorry, we cannot produce that in our facility."

Bill Jardine
Jardine's Farm Restaurant & Catering
Sarver, PA

Customer Contact

In providing a general atmosphere conducive to sales of special functions, one important thing to remember is that the prospective buyer must be put in a positive frame of mind. One key is having a professional-looking office with comfortable furniture. This will help to elicit a positive attitude from the prospect. Trying to do business in a hallway or seated at a party table in an empty banquet hall only invites sales resistance. Avoid using the main dining room because constant interruptions and noise are likely to occur in this area. Remember to keep the conversation private. A buyer may have special requests and may not be completely at ease if there are people with no direct concern present. This is especially true when discussing financial matters. Common courtesy is to offer a cup of coffee, tea, or soft drink. Keep a refill readily available to avoid a lag in the conversation and to keep the conversation focused on the business at hand.

The total sales atmosphere must be one in which the prospect feels he or she is being helped. The caterer must convey that the decisions being made are in the best interests of the function and the guests. However, the customer may not always be right. Few people fully understand the logistics of planning an event. This is where the professional caterer must make the buyer feel his or her interests are paramount to the success of the event.

Customer Solicitation

The actual solicitation of the function starts with the initial contact between the buyer and the seller. This contract may be initiated by either. The seller (catering manager), using marketing information gathered earlier, may make it a practice to review articles in the local newspaper, seeking out information about prominent people and their families in society columns. These are the prospects (buyers). To keep a record of progress, the catering manager fills out a solicitation form, listing information pertinent to the prospect and to the event which might be scheduled. This includes the name of the individual; address; phone number; the type of occasion; whether or not the person involved has ever used the party facilities before; and when, where, and by whom, previous functions were booked. This is all information directly relevant to the solicitation of the sale.

Once the solicitor has determined that the person is a prospective buyer, the prospect is called, offered congratulations on the happy occasion, and invited to make use of the facilities to celebrate the event. It may be a wedding or a retirement party. Any occasion calling for a group celebration provides the catering manager with an opportunity to offer the services of the facility. Oral solicitation may be written out in advance by the manager and the administrative staff asked to do the actual calling, using the outline as a guide. Whoever calls, the basic idea behind the call is to make the initial contact, offer the service, and make an appointment for the prospect to visit the facility to discuss the details.

Reputation

The best method, of course, is to have the customer approach the caterer. This is when the caterer's reputation becomes most important. Reputation is a great way to attract new customers. This is especially important in corporate catering. Many high-profile companies operate on a limited budget, which is something a caterer must know. **Relationships** and the emergence of trust become important, as the president of one company will often recommend their caterer to others. Trust and reputation imply a level of quality the customer knows the caterer can deliver.

Current Customers

When a satisfied guest is pleased with the menu, food, and service, this customer becomes a prospect as a future catering customer. These customers enjoy the menu selections and signature items exclusively prepared and served by the caterer at their event. Many small restaurants have grown into catering companies driven by satisfied customers. This is a natural outgrowth of the restaurant.

At one time, Jardine's Catering would cater events at a local steel company's park which had a swimming pool, a picnic area, and an entertainment section. The park was established for use by the families of the steel company employees.

Several years after we catered events at this location, a call came from a company having an employee satisfaction dinner and wanted us to cater a steak dinner for them. At the first meeting with the company's representative responsible for the event we asked, "Why did you contact Jardine's? How did you find out about us?" This information was always requested of our new customers. This is **Ingredient for Success 11: "Understand why the customer has selected the caterer—what are the expectations?"** His reply was, "Our superintendent said to call Jardine's Catering and make sure they could cater this event."

After the event the superintendent came over, introduced himself, and said, "I'm glad that you could do our job. I enjoyed the steak just as much as I did when I was going to college." Our manager's reply was, "Well, how did you taste our steaks when you were going to college?" This superintendent was a lifeguard at the steel company's park and so when we catered there all the park's employees were also fed. Here is an example of a residual effect: Fifteen years later, Jardine's was contacted for a catering event because a lifeguard who was fed remembered how good the food and service were.

Whether to feed the workers is an important consideration when catering an event, especially in an off-premise facility. Jardine's previously catered at a facility rented by the customer. The hall would bring in six to eight of their own people to assist the caterer including bartenders, clean up crew, and coat room attendants. Not all caterers feed employees, but our policy was to always feed the workers. To compensate for this, we would always prepare food at an additional 3% over the guaranteed number given by the client. We fed the guests, other employees working the event, and then, our own staff.

Bill Jardine
Jardine's Farm Restaurant & Catering
Sarver, PA

Service Organizations

Membership in many of the community service organizations is a great way to meet people in the community. Becoming a member in community service organizations such as the local Chamber of Commerce, the Lion's Club, or Rotary Club provides great networking opportunities. This is another strategy for a caterer to meet potential clients.

Iron Bridge Inn provides service on a local basis for clubs, organizations, and leagues such as golf leagues and women's groups. These specific customers have made special requests including asking our restaurant to provide them with equipment, products, services, and sometimes employees. We have the facilities and the equipment to service such requests and will cater events generating income from $200–$2000. Catering has built customer appreciation, creates a great public relations opportunity, and is always providing an advertisement for the restaurant. It creates a favorable community response, especially when we provide our services for a charitable event, and helps us in our promotion of the restaurant. Catering is ideal for our research and development process and in some cases, we first introduce our newer menu items during events. We will use these new products as test samples at catering events to ascertain their popularity through customer response. If we are happy with our results, then we will incorporate them into our restaurant's menu.

The catering menu is created as a result of our guests requesting our basics. People come into the restaurant, look at our hard copy menu and select three items. They may pick a chicken entree, a beef entree, and a pasta dish for their party. If our guests have something special they would like us to make for them, such as traditional picnic foods, then we will package it for them, wrap it all up, and send it out.

We may price catering events differently. We usually have a 60–70% markup on the restaurant menu items. As for pricing a catering function, it depends on whether the function is held on- or off-premise. If the event is held off-premise, then the markup percentage is a little lower, set approximately between 30–40%. We do this simply because of the labor factor. Once we ship it out of the restaurant, we only have to deliver it to our clients. It is usually sent prepared ready-to-go and our client will set it up, serve it, and clean up after the event. If the event is on-premise, then we use the standard restaurant markup.

We are fortunate enough to have 8–10 golf courses within a 10–15 mile radius around the restaurant. We have catered golf outings in our back room for 40–50 guests. We shut the back room down and have it available only for them. We offer a set menu and give them a set amount of time and it seems to work very well. We do not take reservations at the restaurant so, we tell the golf leagues they can use the room during our slow periods, from 3:00–4:00. But they must be finished by 4:15 p.m. so we can prepare for our dinner service.

One of the best outcomes of our catering services is that it has built for us a loyal customer base who greatly appreciates our extra effort.

Dan Miller
Manager
Springfield Restaurant Group
Mercer, PA

Making New Customers

Personal attention and interaction with a prospective client is another positive strategy to build a customer base. At times, the caterer will personally call on clients. If the caterer is interested in catering for a particular client, this is an excellent way to introduce the business to the prospective client and explain how they can best meet their needs. Then they can ask for the opportunity to submit a proposal for their banquet and catering events.

A caterer can find new customers by reading the local newspaper. One efficient strategy many caterers have successfully employed for years is to pay careful attention to articles and announcements in the local newspaper. News announcements describing future community events, reunions, and engagements are excellent leads to new business.

When caterers read of an engagement, they send the prospective bride a sincere congratulatory letter. This letter would include an invitation for the couple to visit their catering facility/restaurant for a complimentary dinner or special treat. Upon the presentation of the congratulatory letter, the staff would know they are a newly engaged couple and would serve the couple with great fanfare. The letter might also include an invitation to meet with the caterer's professional staff for a consultation, even if the couple had already selected another caterer, at no obligation or cost.

As a result of successfully implementing these strategies, a caterer can service a **life cycle of customer events**. A client's lifetime may include events such as bridal showers, wedding receptions, anniversaries, birthdays, baby showers, births, baptisms, proms, sports banquets, graduations, college, marriage, and the cycle will repeat. It is even common for loyal customers to request the caterer to prepare the food served at their funerals.

Food-Tasting Events

Create an opportunity to speak one-on-one with the customers and potential clients during your slower sales periods. Invite them to attend a customer recognition dinner or a special taste-testing event to sample foods and signature items (Figure 4–2) featured on the catering menu.

For example, a caterer will invite clients and potential customers to a semi-annually-featured food feast. At this event, numerous stations are set up offering samples of their speciality and featured signature items. A caterer creates an environment to showcase special food items. An assortment of hors d'oeuvres, dessert items, breads, and beverages are provided (Figure 4–3).

Customers appreciate and anticipate attending this type of annual event. They are able to sample their favorite foods and are afforded the opportunity to sample new or exotic items being first introduced or field-tested for possible inclusion on the menu. Although the purpose of these events is to entertain customers, they may evolve into a wonderful selling tool and will become very popular with the customers who appreciate the opportunity to sample foods and interact with

Figure 4-2 *Featuring signature items at a taste-testing event helps build new clientele.*

other guests. An on-premise caterer can hold these events in his/her facility. An off-premise caterer could rent a facility or negotiate with the owner of a fabulous facility to sponsor the event in their hall.

This introduces ***Ingredient for Success 12: "To establish a long-term relationship with a customer and work, as frequently as possible, with each client one-on-one."***

Figure 4-3 *A variety of hors d'oeuvres and foods should be provided at a taste-testing event.*

Publicity

Advertising means a caterer will pay to have information placed into the media. *Publicity* is free media exposure. A caterer may exchange catering functions for free air time on the radio or television, or adspace in newspapers and magazines. Donations, special fund-raising activities, and community service may work as a press release to gain free publicity with the appropriate news media.

Planning how to publicize catering services requires considerable forethought by the catering manager. The obvious way to publicize these services is through the menu. Tasteful arrangement of menu selections on durable, yet colorful stock, printed legibly and relating directly to the type of function it is meant to supplement or to the general theme of the event, will do much to influence the decisions of the potential buyer.

Menus should be printed in warm colors. Soft earthy tones, such as browns, oranges, reds, golds, and yellow colors are relaxing to the eye and important considerations. Complement the ink colors to the paper stock. These are very effective sales tools. However, since it is often difficult to get the menu to the prospective buyer in advance of the personal interview, the caterer must seek additional ways of publicizing the goods and services he or she wants to sell.

A few well-chosen words printed on the regular menus will help to reach a broader market. Some menus may even include a flyer outlining banquet and party offerings. Posters and flyers placed in strategic locations may serve as a communication tool to remind potential clients of additional services that are available.

Publicity can also involve a recently presented event. Follow-up articles on a certain type of event, like a wedding, published in the newspaper, or presented orally as a society news item on a radio broadcast, can be a doubly effective way of getting the attention of those individuals in need of catering.

Advertising

Advertising catering services differs from publicizing them. Advertising requires a considerably larger expenditure of funds and should be budgeted in advance. A caterer should allocate a portion of the operating capital specifically for the purpose of promoting and soliciting business. Obviously, the best exposure is a satisfied customer who had an agreeable dining experience, but even this must be supplemented by an aggressive sales program.

A sales program may consist of a catchy and brilliantly illustrated advertisement placed in the newspaper at designated times. A well-placed advertisement at the entrance to the catering facility, or an effectively worded advertisement on the radio, may entice a prospect to investigate the possibility of holding a future function at the establishment. Since funds are being used to promote this activity, each manager should make every effort to provide some follow-up action, to determine the impact of the program on the prospect, and proven cost-effectiveness.

Closing the Sale

No sales transaction is complete until the sale is closed and the customer has signed the contract (Chapter 12). A mutual agreement between buyer and seller must be consummated. For the protection of both parties, a detailed document signifying this accord must be drawn up and signed by the caterer and the client. Managers should then use a check list to track the preparation of the event (Figure 4–4).

MANAGER'S CHECK LIST
(check when action is completed)

Advance Preparations

_____ Contract and scheduling of meeting
_____ Staffing and scheduling of employees
_____ Special functions sheet filled out
_____ Departmental instruction sheets
_____ Time of meeting
_____ Special setup instructions
_____ Meeting room ready
_____ Setup team ready

Logistics

_____ Tables and seating space
_____ Platform for speakers, tables, and chairs
_____ Visual aids and accessories
_____ Tables for handouts and demonstration
_____ Coffee break schedule
_____ Location and equipment for coffee break
_____ Billing for coffee break
_____ Luncheon arrangements
_____ Billing for luncheon
_____ Pre-registration needs
_____ Cocktail party arrangement
_____ Cocktail party billing
_____ Coat room arrangements
_____ Lighting, heat, and air conditioning
_____ Greeting of guests
_____ Receipt of advance shipping material—storage area
_____ Information for incoming guests

During the Meeting

_____ Employee skills and attitudes
_____ Delegation of tasks
_____ Quality of service

Figure 4–4 *Manager's checklist.*

Remember, the basic principle behind the scheduling of a special function is the satisfaction of the customer. This includes being satisfied with the costs as well as the production of the event. Before closing a sale, the good catering manager always ensures that the prospect is completely satisfied with the arrangements as outlined. After the event, following up immediately with a letter thanking the client and offering to be of service at future events is good business practice. If the event might be scheduled again, make a note of this fact for future reference.

Business Cards

The use of business cards by the caterer and the staff is another effective prospecting strategy. Employees should be instructed to distribute the organization's business cards to all interested guests attending a function if approved by the client. Remember to use common sense when handing out business cards. This is a very good way to leave a guest with a little reminder of the caterer for future reference. Make a goal to hand out five business cards per day.

Portfolio

The use of an attractive, professionally designed and maintained portfolio will communicate a strong visual message (Figure 4–5). The caterer may make arrangements to offer food and related services to the professional photographer covering the function in return for taking pictures of the food, layout, decorations, and employees. Otherwise, the investment in a quality, 35mm or digital

Figure 4-5 *Maintaining a professional portfolio of special events creates a strong visual message.*

Figure 4-6 *Photographs of previous catering functions help showcase your services.*

camera will give the caterer a means to document events for a portfolio. Many potential clients enjoy the opportunity to see previous catering functions executed by the caterer (Figure 4–6).

Telephone Directory and Yellow Pages

Yellow pages are a common but effective means of advertising the catering business. Many people in need of food and service will first search the local yellow pages to find a caterer in the area. Advertising in the yellow pages depends on the caterer's budget and the market.

Professional Sales Staff

Planned growth of a catering company is achieved through a conscientious building of satisfied customers and by the accomplishment of a caterer's financial objectives. Implementation of a **professional sales staff** is another method used by a caterer to achieve these business objectives. Often, the caterer is so busy with current projects they do not have the necessary time to invest in prospecting for new clients to grow future business.

The inclusion of additional sales staff, primarily working in the field, must be based on need and budgetary requirements. One advantage of this staff is the potential for an immediate and constant presence in the caterer's market niche. Most larger facilities, such as hotel operations, employ professional sales people to increase business.

PROFESSIONAL SALES STAFF FUNCTIONS

1. Communicate the caterer's capabilities
2. Provide information
3. Meet with clients one-on-one
4. Give tours of the caterer's operation
5. Design brochures
6. Pursue leads to new business opportunities
7. Design a logo
8. Formulation and implementation of the prospecting plan
9. Plan the marketing budget
10. Elevate developmental signature recipes

Figure 4-7 *Professional sales staff functions.*

The mission of a professional sales staff is to have a direct connection with the market, to help recognize potential clientele. Specifically, their task is to unlock new business doors. A specialized sales staff can provide a caterer with a dependable commitment to a marketing plan. Elements such as obtaining market-specific research, coordinating a public relations campaign, coordinating promotional tie-ins with suppliers, and composing caterer-generated communication messages are just some of the many responsibilities a caterer can authorize (Figure 4–7).

◆ NEVER STOP LEARNING

An informed, educated caterer is prepared to exceed the expanding needs of the consumer in the competitive catering industry. Continuous research of the marketplace provides the caterer with a flow of new information on the rapidly evolving industry. This vigilant attention to the marketplace provides information to help the caterer make decisions regarding emerging market trends, advanced packaging, new products, and updated government regulations in such areas as sanitation and human resources.

There are always new products being introduced by the processors. Twenty-five years ago caterers made all their own hors d'oeuvres, requiring many hours of intense labor. Now, professionally made frozen hors d'oeuvres are available as thaw-and-serve or heat-and-serve items. The major point of this example is to always be aware of the continuous development and introduction of new foods and new ideas.

As trends emerge and create continuous change, the successful caterer must adapt to those changes. A caterer must constantly be looking for trends, such as the popular portabella mushroom. Today it is acceptable to serve a portabella mushroom salad with a dinner, however, about five years ago this would not have been acceptable to the client. Approximately 2,000 pounds of portabella mushrooms were sold in the United States about ten years ago. Today, more than 40 million pounds of portabella mushrooms are projected to be sold.

Why has this market skyrocketed? Portabella mushrooms are easy to handle and prepare. It has become a popular food because it can be served in a variety of ways, including mushroom lasagna or a mushroom salad.

✦ UPGRADING THE EVENT

It is important to understand a customer's needs for many reasons. The caterer wants to plan an event which completely satisfies all of the client's expectations. A caterer can guide the client in their decision-making process by offering professional suggestions, especially by recommending upgraded elements of the total package.

Suggesting upgraded elements when meeting with the client enables the caterer to use experience and expertise to enhance the package and exceed a guest's basic needs. It means the enhancement of food and service by tweaking the plan originally suggested by the client. Upgrading sometimes offers upscaled alternatives for similar prices to create a super value for the customer's budget.

Upgrading the event can also mean a caterer suggests specific bridal shops, florists, limousine companies, photographers, and others who can help *professionalize* the event. This reciprocal arrangement can also help a caterer find new customers as these local business people will also send inquiring customers to the caterer.

The client expects the professional caterer to use expertise when discussing the delivery and showmanship of food and service. Professional suggestions are offered to enhance a client's perception of value. Suggestions range from a simple menu addition to the inclusion of additional service personnel. If a client wants to have a champagne toast for the bridal party, the caterer can suggest wine be served to the guests instead. This would be cheaper than serving champagne, tweak the event, and incrementally increase revenue. Suggesting ice cream be served with the wedding cake during the reception may add only a slight cost to the menu, but provides added features to make the event special.

A customer will initiate the first contact with a caterer. The caterer's purpose is to suggest the right combination of food and service at their specific price. However, every contact a caterer has with a potential client does not automatically guarantee a customer. A caterer must be aware of the customer, know the customer, and understand how the customer reacts to suggestions.

◆ HOW THE CATERER PROVIDES PROTECTION

Caterers learn from experience which customers they are not comfortable working with on events. One strategy is for the caterer to ask the potential client for a list of caterers in the past five years with whom they have worked. A caterer can then call these individuals as references.

One great advantage in the catering business is the caterer can be very selective about the client. It is not like a restaurant operation where the doors are open and everyone who enters is your customer. This way, the caterer can build a relationship with clientele the organization is proud to work with and feels comfortable with, and can avoid *undesirables*.

The caterer always has the option of declining work. This is accomplished rather politely, without offending anyone, and without having to say, "Look, I do not want to do work for you." A caterer will say they already have too many events booked during that week or their selected date has already been promised.

In social catering, the caterer must know the income level of the client. Can they afford to have the five-dollar-per-person event or the ten-dollar-per-person affair? Maybe there's a neighborhood party going on and everyone is contributing to the event. The client decides to have it catered but only wants to spend $5.00 or $6.00 a person. At this price, the caterer has a limited budget to include fixed costs, labor costs, and the cost of food. Therefore, it will be very difficult to give the customer much satisfaction for this price.

The caterer must also protect the profit margin. At this point, the caterer must ask, "Is the profit margin adequate to cover all the costs?" "Can the job be done satisfactorily?" "Can the combined expectations of the caterer and the customer be met?" Although there are caterers who will cater events for $5.00 per person, these events are very difficult to profit from. Look for the next niche up. Research the market. What jobs can the caterer execute which will meet and exceed customer expectations and achieve satisfactory profit returns?

Undesirables

A caterer gets most customers through referrals. These prospective clients know the caterer's reputation but the caterer may not know the client. It is therefore important to complete a background check before accepting a client as a customer, to determine if the prospective client has the ability to meet the financial obligations. Caterers must know if their clients are financially stable.

There may be a number of reasons for a caterer to reject an inquiry from a potential customer or refuse to work with a particular client. The location may be poor or the lack of adequate facilities may be a problem. Some people are very difficult to work with, especially in social catering. Some clients are moaners, complainers, or nitpickers. The more difficult the client, the more difficult it is to satisfy them. These clients are always demanding more than the caterer can afford to provide, or they try to create obligations and expectations the caterer cannot meet.

A group may be historically unruly and a caterer may simply refuse business with this client after the first bad experience.

◆ PROPOSALS

A **proposal** is a communication tool used to effectively inform and educate the prospective client of everything the caterer can do for them during the particular event. The written proposal must communicate how the caterer intends to eliminate the client's concern about the implementation and successful execution of their function. It must realistically communicate how the caterer can exceed their needs.

The proposal is a detailed document. It must list everything the caterer will do. Every detail, from the beginning of the event to its concluding activity, either at the caterer's facility or at an off-premise facility, must be stated. The proposal communicates to the client a first-impression image of the caterer, and information it provides is used by the customer when choosing a caterer.

Length and Complexity

Proposals vary in both length and complexity. The format may be a standard form or can be personally designed and written for each client. However, before creating a proposal to present to the prospective client, the caterer must know the needs, desires, and special requests of the client. It must be clear what the client is looking for and what kind of a budget the client is working with on this project. Is the client offering the caterer $12.00, $15.00, or $20.00? Price is important. The caterer will have to submit a competitive offer which may be compared to other caterers bidding on the event. If a chicken dinner is requested, the caterer cannot propose $30.00, and if a steak dinner is needed, a $5.00 proposal is also not feasible.

It is important for the caterer to know which costs are involved in each event. A caterer must have control over operations and know their fixed costs, food costs, and labor costs. Understanding costs is important so the caterer can prepare a competitive proposal that works to everyone's advantage.

Basic Proposal

The basic proposal will spell out in detail everything to be done by the caterer. A proposal is prepared for a variety of reasons. It becomes a planning tool that benefits both the caterer and the client. Each knows precisely what will be done and what is included for the set fee. Nothing is assumed.

A caterer should attempt to create an individual proposal for each client based on their needs. Depending on the type of catering event, a proposal can be very brief—merely listing the things the caterer is going to do. If catering an event for fifteen hundred people, the proposal would become very detailed and lengthy. All services provided by the caterer should be addressed in the proposal including:

- ◈ Will an attendant park the guest's cars?
- ◈ Will the caterer entertain the children?
- ◈ Will the caterer provide entertainment?
- ◈ Will the caterer provide snacks?

These and similar concerns can be addressed in the proposal.

The proposal will be similar in descriptive detail to the way the final draft of the contract (Chapter 12) is explicitly written. The information in Figure 4–8 will help a caterer prepare a well-written, descriptive proposal.

Proposal

Organization's Name_____ Client's Name_____

Day _____ Date _____ (function's day & date of execution)

DEADLINE OR DUE DATE

Purpose of Function_____ Theme _____

Function_____ (wedding, birthday, picnic, family reunion)

Address_____ Direction/Location_____

City_____ State/Zip _____

Phone_____ Fax_____

E-mail_____

Method of Payment_____ (cash, credit card, check, barter, other)

Party making the payment_____(e.g., wedding—bride/groom's family,

   social event—Elizabeth 50% + Samantha 50%, celebration—Stephen 100%)

Uniform Requirements

Wait staff_____ Food Production_____ Beverage Service_____ Other_____

Special Request_____ (e.g.,Tammie's birthday, Bill & Joyce's anniversary)

Starting and Ending Time_____ (exact starting and ending time)

Location_____ (exact location of function, directions)

Approximate Number of Guests_____ (best estimate, based on historical data)

Minimum Number Expected_____ (minimum guest count for this event)

*Final guarantee number will be charged unless adjusted prior to 1:00 P.M. on

_____ (last day for guest to adjust final count without penalty)

(continued)

Figure 4-8 *Proposal basics.*

Menu Requirements (All menu details as agreed upon with client)

Price Per Guest: $ (_____) (If quote per person, amount specified in this contract)

All food and beverage subject to (_____%) sales tax and (_____%) service charge.

Entree and Sides_____ (exact menu, portion size)

Service Style_____ (explicit description of service responsibilities)

Beverage Service_____ (nonalcoholic and alcoholic beverages and service)

Set up Requirements_____ (any special requests, floor plan, and seating chart)

Chefs—a flat $(_____) labor charge will be assessed for each Chef required for buffet-line carving stations.

Other Services

Linen and Napkins _____

Skirting Requirements _____

Style of Plateware _____

Style of Silverware _____

Style of Glassware _____

Table Requirements _____

Chair Requirements _____

Tent Requirements _____

Audiovisual _____

Florist _____

Photographer _____

Special Decorations and Service (e.g., ice sculptures, hand-carved centerpieces, individualized flower arrangements, and thematic decorations).

_____
_____
_____
_____
_____

Security _____

Valet Parking_____ Time_____ Guests_____

Entertainment _____

Weather Forecast _____ Update_____

Figure 4-8 *Proposal basics (continued).*

A famous ethnic orchestra was creating an annual fund-raising event and Jardine's Catering was invited to submit a proposal. Rather than send a traditional proposal by mail, the catering staff was motivated to create a special and unusual proposal. We wanted to excite the fund-raising committee by demonstrating through the proposal that we were the best caterer for the event. The proposal itself became a formal presentation. We created a sample of foods from the menu being presented to the committee. We packaged the items in a basket which was sent to the committee as part of the proposal. Our creativity and imagination provided a competitive edge other caterers found hard to match.

The catering staff used innovation and expertise to create a professional, personable, and memorable presentation. The baker made a variety of special rolls and breads, baked a miniature apple pie, and carved, in the crust of the pie, the initials of the organization. An American flag suspended on a stick was placed into the pie. The chef prepared a variety of signature sauces and included those in the basket as samples. To complement the food, a bottle of wine and four wine glasses were placed in the basket along with samples of the proposed linens, napkins, plates, and silverware.

To create a sense of urgency and importance, a professional messenger service delivered the basket of food and the traditional written proposal to the committee. Because of this very impressive way the proposal was submitted, Jardine's was awarded the contract. Over the years, we successfully replicated this method many times with success.

Bill Jardine
Jardine's Farm Restaurant & Catering
Sarver, PA

Submitting a Proposal

Creativity and imagination will help deliver a competitive edge when presenting a proposal. To impress the prospective client, a caterer should personally hand deliver the proposal. Remember, other caterers are bidding on this same event. This leads us to **Ingredient for Success 13: "Presentations are important—create special, unusual, personable, and impressive competitive proposals."**

Basket presentations are a unique idea to present a proposal that projects a very powerful image to the customer. Another competitive strategy to secure a contract from a client is to invite the committee to sample the food. At this sampling, provide a variety of the food considered for the event. One final suggestion is the use of a video. Having a professional video available to communicate the mission of the caterer offers an extra addition to any proposal. Remember, the caterer must always create new and exciting methods to stimulate a prospective client because sometimes the caterer gets the job, and sometimes not.

TIPS FROM THE TRADE

The only limitation to presenting unique proposals is your imagination. Proposals can be done on regular paper without any fancy presentation. They can be done on theme paper with special matching binders or created on CD-ROM with pictures to illustrate what the event would look like. The delivery of the proposal is dependent on the client's needs. If there is a formal presentation, the proposal should reflect this. If the proposal is being sent to the client it can be accompanied by freshly baked cookies, gourmet coffee, or popcorn. Knowing your client's likes and dislikes will give clues to what will impress them. The revenue generated by the event will determine how elaborate the presentation of the proposal should be. Again, your imagination is your only limitation in this area.

Michelle Albright Lennox
Catering/Convention Services Manager
Hyatt Orlando
Kissimmee, FL

Summary

The creation of a satisfied, sustainable customer base from which to draw current and potential clients necessary to support a catering operation now and in the future is one of the most important business tasks a caterer must faithfully perform. Creating such a base is accomplished by translating unmet customer needs, wants, and demands into a package of tangible goods and intangible services. Implementing prospecting strategies, such as linking current customers with new prospects, contacting community service organizations, reading local newspaper articles, sponsoring food tasting events, and using advertising methods and publicity will lead to the discovery of new customers.

To effectively inform and educate the prospective client of what the caterer can do during a particular event, a detailed proposal is drafted. The proposal will vary in length and complexity, but it will be similar in descriptive detail to the way the final draft of the contract is explicitly written.

Review Questions

Brief Answers

1. Discuss why creating a solid customer base by attracting new customers is a continuous building process for a caterer.

2. Describe why it is important to understand customer needs before one begins to build a foundation consisting of a solid customer base.

3. Discuss why it is a challenge for a caterer to translate customer needs into a package of tangible products and intangible services the caterer must implement to exceed a customer's desires.

4. Identify five needs all customers have when seeking a caterer.

5. Identify and discuss prospecting strategies a caterer may use to find new clients.

6. Discuss why membership in community organizations is a great way for a caterer to meet prospective customers.

7. Describe what is meant by the term *life-cycle of customer events*.

8. Identify and discuss challenges that a caterer might face attracting customers during their slower-sales time of the year. List two prospecting strategies a caterer can use to attract interested clients during this slower-sales period.

9. Identify and explain two strategies a caterer must employ when planning the growth of the catering company.

10. Why is the implementation of a professional sales staff important to the success of a caterer?

11. Discuss the importance of continued education for a caterer and how this helps in the identification of industry trends and changing customer needs.

12. Discuss how a caterer can use a variety of techniques to protect them against undesirable clients.

Multiple Choice

Select the single best answer for each question.

1. This catering tool is used by the caterer to communicate and inform prospective clients what will be provided during an event.
   a. proposal
   b. budget
   c. upgrading the event
   d. contract
   e. prospecting strategies

2. The advantage of a professional sales staff to the caterer is the:
   a. immediate presence in the marketplace.
   b. constant presence in the marketplace as a reminder to potential clients.
   c. identification of potential clients who are in need of service.
   d. communicating information regarding the caterer's abilities.
   e. All of the above are advantages experienced by the caterer.

3. The purpose of a caterer reading the daily local newspaper is to:
   a. keep current with national events
   b. understand local politics and upcoming elections
   c. identify local community events and recent engagements
   d. clip coupons
   e. None of the above are valid reasons.

True or False

Read each of the following statements and determine if it is true or false.

1. The planned growth of a catering company is achieved only by satisfying customers' needs.

2. An educated, informed caterer is prepared to exceed the always changing needs of the client in the competitive catering industry.

3. One advantage a caterer has over the traditional restauranteur is the ability to select their clients.

Putting It All Together

You are hired as a consultant to assist a local start-up catering company in your area. Your task is to develop and present a detailed prospectus plan for them to use in acquiring new clients for their business. Write a prospecting plan and prepare a sample proposal.

PART TWO

The Catering Operation

91

Chapter Five

The Seven Functions of Catering

Key Terms

Objectives

After studying this chapter, you should be able to:

◆ Introduce the seven key catering functions.

◆ Explain why planning is first and influences the other six functions.

◆ Explain the symbiotic relationship of the seven functions.

◆ Explain why a caterer must manage resources to exceed customer expectations and meet organizational goals.

◆ Gain an appreciation for the organizing effort required to execute a catering event.

◆ Explain why a successful catering effort is the outcome of a strenuous journey demanding a dedicated individual.

INGREDIENTS FOR SUCCESS

14 "The closer the caterer gets to the event, the more difficult the event becomes."

15 "Every observable action exhibited by the caterer emulates from the public mission statement."

16 "Accurate forecasting of market trends and changes in food prices are keys to establishing correct pricing and meeting preestablished financial objectives."

17 "Cost control procedures are created for the acquisition of timely information to equip the caterer with the data to scrutinize controllable costs and make appropriate operational decisions."

This chapter provides a brief synopsis of the key components that occur in every catering business.

All caterers including corporate, social, on-premise, or off-premise, need to have a solid understanding of the following seven fundamental catering functions. The mastery of these seven functions helps to ensure real success. These are the fundamental catering management functions: (1) formulating the strategic plan for the event; (2) executing the operational tasks; (3) organizing resources; (4) matching equipment needs to the requirements of the food and service; (5) implementing the plan; (6) controlling the event by use of financial tools and predetermined standards; and (7) obtaining insurance coverage and ensuring all legal concerns are covered by a contract.

◆ FIRST FUNCTION: PLANNING— THE BASIC CATERING MANAGEMENT FUNCTION

The first step after the acceptance of the proposal is for a caterer to begin **formulating** a comprehensive plan for the event. After the mutual acceptance of

Figure 5-1 *An effective menu evolves from a solid catering plan and mission statement.*

the proposal, the date of its execution may actually vary from a few days to several months. It is reasonable to have events booked one-to-five years in advance of the actual date of execution. But whatever the period of time, one fact is true: *"The closer the caterer gets to the event, the more difficult the event becomes."* This is *Ingredient for Success 14.*

Planning is a basic catering-management function. All plans should flow from the caterer's mission statement. Therefore, always remember *Ingredient for Success 15: "Every observable action exhibited by the caterer evolves from the public mission statement."* The successful caterer formulates and implements a plan based on competitive strategies deduced from the mission statement (Figure 5–1).

Purpose of a Catering Plan

A catering plan serves many purposes. One purpose of a plan is to ensure the caterer's future. A **strategic plan** is established to guide the entire catering operation over the long term, 3–5 years into the future. It attempts to position the organization on a path of success. A second type of plan, a **tactical plan**, is specifically created to guide the caterer in a much shorter time frame. A tactical plan creates a forceful focus on each event. Whereas a strategic plan stretches over a long time frame, a tactical plan is specific to the event. A strategic plan requires modification and rejuvenation as forces in the caterer's market shape and reshape it. Since it is over a longer time period, it is much broader and more general in its design. A tactical plan, on the other hand, has a much shorter life span, requires precise detail, and execution.

A plan enables the caterer to establish achievable **objectives**. Stated objectives flow directly from the mission statement. Objectives are established to serve as benchmarks to measure progress. A caterer can use these benchmarks to compare the actual performance against a predetermined target. This organizational progress can be specified in its strategic plan, or it can be established for each event as measured against a tactical plan. A caterer may create objectives that are beyond the believable accomplishment of the team to stretch the organization to greater levels.

Common organizational objectives may include the measurement of guest satisfaction, attainment of financial goals, human resource development, greater staff productivity levels, increase in market share, and positive organizational growth. For the specific event, tactical objectives might include guest satisfaction, event preparation, familiarity of location, handling guest count, menu item production, preparing the team, and obtaining the required equipment.

Finally, a plan is a blueprint or map. This powerful tool, when properly used by the caterer, keeps everyone in the organization on the right route. A plan helps to minimize unexpected surprises. It attempts to eliminate uncertainties by creating a supportive organizational environment.

One technique caterers use is known as the *Swiss Cheese Approach*. A caterer will break the master plan into smaller, more manageable segments—Swiss Cheese It! For example, a one-year-in-advance-event plan can be segmented into the following time lines: a six-month plan, ninety-day, sixty-day, thirty-day, two-week, one-week, four-day, two-day, the day before, and right down to the day of the event. Once the plan is created, the staff will execute each element guided by the leadership and management of the caterer.

Time-Line Planning

Formulation of a plan for a catering event must include all principal players responsible for executing the event. These would include the catering manager, the chef or food and beverage manager, the buyer or purchasing agent, and the service manager. These key personnel must meet during the early planning stages to discuss the date, month, day, and time of the activity. Often they will be able to offer advice on management of conflicting events. For the event to become successful and profitable, they must be consulted from the beginning.

The chef or food and beverage manager is responsible for the menu, recipe development, beverages and service, recipe costing, menu pricing, determining production needs, staffing needs, and scheduling of employees. The service manager is responsible for all service staffing needs, table setups, food and beverage service, and scheduling employees. The buyer or purchasing agent is responsible for researching the availability of each menu item and its cost. Following are two examples of a planning time line.

Food Production Planning Time Line

Event Minus 75 Days. In planning the menu for the event, it is necessary for the catering manager to fully inform the chef or food manager of the overall theme and objectives. If plans call for the function to become a regular part of the calendar of annual events, food production supervisors must know this in order to recommend compatible menu selections. It will be important to also provide alternative menu selections so that the event will not become prosaic or monotonous to the guests.

The catering manager should, in planning, allow a minimum of two or three weeks for the back-of-the-house staff to research menu selections, the product market, methods of procurement, appropriate recipes, and for recipe development.

The chef will, during the planning stage, be concerned primarily with the menu and its development, including the nutritional balance, taste, color, texture, plate coverage, and presentation. The chef will research the relative popularity of the menu items, the availability of ingredients to produce the menu, and know the relationship between the menu and the type of equipment needed for production. Recipes must be selected that will meet the needs and wants of those attending the event. Ingredient costs and production hours are forecasted by the chef based on the event's *budget* (money available for their purchase).

Finally, the chef must decide exactly how many employees are needed to produce the menu. The menu will determine the culinary expertise required of each employee in the food production area. All of these activities must be discussed in detail before a final decision is made to proceed with the event.

The buyer or purchasing agent must have a list of specific items needed to produce the menu. At this time, the purchasing agent will research the product market to ascertain product availability and cost. The purchasing agent will make recommendations on what items must be ordered in advance, their forecasted market price, and which products may not be available. The purchasing expert should suggest comparable substitutes that can be procured to meet production needs.

Event Minus 45 Days. At this point, the caterer will have a good idea of what products are available on the market and their relative costs. This is a good time to meet with the chef and finalize the menu. Recipe selections are discussed at this meeting, along with alternatives, especially if the menu is to be repeated or if products discussed at the first meeting are not available.

At this meeting, the chef, using an appropriate staffing guide, should be able to provide the caterer with an accurate description of personnel needed to produce the selected menus. Food costs should also be discussed. A reasonable selling price might be finalized. This selling price must be compatible with the predetermined profit objectives established by the caterer.

It is during this time that the chef or food manager meets to formulate the production plan with key production personnel in the kitchen. The chef discusses the function with the production team. Objectives, the menu, and staffing requirements are addressed. In addition to the menu, a production schedule is prepared. This worksheet details the menu items, recipes, special production needs, and preparation procedures. Responsibility and accountability will be delegated and recorded on the production schedule. A copy of this worksheet is posted on a bulletin board in the production area.

The purchasing agent can be present at this meeting to provide information on product availability, suppliers, special handling needs, and the dates and times of expected deliveries. A service supervisor should also be present to coordinate staffing requirements with the food production department.

Event Minus 30 Days. One month before the event, the chef or food manager will verify the menu. All required products should be inventoried or readily attainable on short notice. Copies of the finalized menu, individual worksheets, and standardized recipes are distributed to key personnel including production personnel, salad-makers, bakers, and all those directly involved in the production process. Delegation of individual responsibility for each menu item and its production will be verified.

Event Minus 15 Days. During this period, the chef or food manager checks with the purchasing agent to ensure inventory is in order. All staffing and work schedules are rechecked. Assurance is made that no positions of responsibility have been overlooked, usually due to illness or employee turnover. A thorough, final verification of all equipment needed to produce and serve the food on the menu is completed. Finally, coordination between the kitchen and other departments who provide support during the implementation of the event is completed.

Event Minus 7 Days. One week before the event, the caterer schedules another meeting. All department supervisors must attend. At this meeting, the purchasing agent reports on action taken for the procurement of ingredients and products. The chef or food manager will:

1. advise the attendees of any menu or production changes made since the last meeting.

2. brief the entire team on the production plan.

3. explain the function, its objectives, and the staffing requirements.

4. brief the team on the finalized menu, production techniques, and the finalized production schedule. This worksheet will detail the menu items, recipes, special production requests, preparation procedures, and delegated responsibility.

5. describe the details of plate arrangement for each course, including portion size, garnishes, and extras (appetizers, hot breads, beverages, etc.).

6. explain if the event requires any special arrangements (such as a buffet or salad bar in the dining room). The plan will be outlined at this time and responsibility will be discussed.

Event Minus 1 Day. The production schedule checklist (Figure 5–2) outlines the responsibility of the chef or food manager twenty-four hours in advance of the event.

Early on the day of the function, the chef or food manager should meet with the following kitchen personnel to review details of production: cooks, salad-makers and bakers, food service workers, warewashers, and janitorial (cleanup) workers.

At this meeting, all details of production and kitchen service must be explained and final responsibility delegated. Provision must be made for keeping accurate records (guest counts, *scatter sheets*, sensitive item inventories, sanitation procedures, customer comments, and production records). During the event, the chef, food manager, or responsible delegate, assumes a position to inspect all food leaving the production area to ensure quality service.

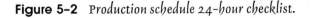

Production Schedule

	Menu	_____
	Standardized Recipes	_____
	Inventory	_____
	Food Issues	_____
KITCHEN		
	Food Cost	_____
	Staffing	_____
	Production	_____
	Portion Control	_____
	Plate Arrangement	_____
	Dining Service	_____
OTHER		
	Bar/Wine Service	_____
DEPARTMENTS		
	Reservations	_____
	Coordinate w/ Catering Manager	_____

Figure 5-2 *Production schedule 24-hour checklist.*

At the conclusion of food production, the chef or food manager should ensure that arrangements have been made for the proper handling and storage of leftovers, once they have been accounted for. A quick check of the garbage can (to see how much and what items have been returned uneaten) and of china and glass breakage during the meal can be effective means of controlling costs and adding profit to future events.

Event Plus One Day. This is the time for the caterer to make sure all records for the event are complete. This includes a final report describing the event and recommended changes in menu, production, and service for future events.

Staffing Planning Time Line

At the initial organizational meeting, where the purpose of the function is discussed, some consideration must be given to the staffing needs for the event. Department supervisors should submit preliminary figures on staffing requirements and forecasted labor costs.

Event Minus 75 Days. Staffing requirements should include the food production area, service and/or dining room, bar setup, and cleanup crews. The caterer should also give consideration at this time to any additional people needed for the event, who might not be employees of the operation but are hired on a temporary, one-time basis.

Event Minus 30 Days. All staffing needs should be finalized at least one month in advance of the function. At this time, managers must give consideration to special training requirements for employees who will assist at the event. Accountability and responsibility for employee training is delegated to the appropriate supervisors at this meeting.

Event Minus 14 Days. Two weeks prior to the event, the caterer reviews predetermined staffing requirements. A list of available, substitute employees should be made. This handy reference sheet will be valuable if assigned employees become ill or are otherwise unable to work.

The caterer should review and approve all department work schedules before they are posted. This is done to determine that the right personnel are scheduled (skill-level, regular, part-time, and intermittent). This helps control the cost of labor for the event. Once the schedules have been reviewed and approved by the caterer, they are posted in a visible location in the production area where the employees of the department can see them. Intermittent employees should be contacted by phone or e-mail.

Event Minus 7 Days. Seven days before the event, the caterer should be able to answer the following questions.

1. How many employees are scheduled for the event?
2. How many can assist in more than one job?
3. How much training was required?
4. Has training been completed?
5. Who will supervise in each department during the event?
6. Are backup employees and supervisors available?
7. What are the total labor costs by department?

Day of Event. At least one hour before the function starts, the caterer may require department supervisors to submit a report (orally or in writing) that all staffing requirements have been met and that employees are at their stations ready to assume their duties.

Event Plus One Day. One day after the event, all department supervisors submit an after-action report to inform the caterer how staffing requirements were met and how the work progressed during the function. This information, along with total labor costs, will assist the caterer in projecting needs for future events. It will also help to improve the quality of service.

◆ SECOND FUNCTION: OPERATIONS— EXECUTION OF TASKS

Once the caterer has identified and broken down a customer's needs and wants, it becomes easier to assign specific tasks to exceed their objectives (Figure 5–3). A successful caterer can interpret customer needs and wants but the real challenge is to translate each customer objective into a specific, **operational task**.

Figure 5–3
Thorough planning, control, and flow of operations help produce a desired outcome that exceeds customer objectives.

The caterer develops the plan with the organizational team. Every detail of the event is written down. Each detail is reviewed and assigned as a task. This list of operations, specific to the event, includes both the tasks and steps for executing them. Next, these individual tasks are *bundled* together. By identifying and bundling all similar tasks, the caterer can assign or **delegate** each **bundle of tasks** to the appropriate employee for *execution*. **Execution of tasks** involves the employee carrying out these predetermined goals. All tasks must be identified, bundled, delegated, and executed to exceed customer satisfaction. This procedure enables the caterer to identify and *operationalize* predetermined and intangible customer needs into achievable elements of a plan. Gearing up the catering team to execute these tasks identifies the third fundamental catering function—organizing resources.

◈ THIRD FUNCTION: ORGANIZING THE EVENT

Organizing is the process of formally *structuring* the organization so each assigned task can efficiently and effectively attain the stated objective. A purpose of a formal structure is for the distribution, maximum utilization, monitoring, and control of scarce resources by the caterer. The caterer will organize *human resources, capital resources,* and *financial resources* to accomplish stated objectives (Figure 5–4).

Human resources include the skill level, knowledge-base, experience level, and maturity level (length of service) of employees. The tasks of recruitment, selection, training, retainment, and advancement of the employees are critical to building a reliable and effective staff.

Figure 5-4 *Controlling inventory through the proper management of ordering, shipping, and receiving procedures is a crucial part of organizing.*

CATERERS' FINANCIAL CONCERNS

1. What are the financial estimates for the event?

2. How much is this event actually going to cost?

3. How much money is guaranteed in the deposit? Is it a 50% deposit? If it is a corporate account, will the bill for the deposit be mailed?

4. How and when will the final payment be made?

5. What are the payment terms? Is credit extended? Are the terms 10 days, 15 days or 30 days after the event?

Figure 5–5 *Caterers' financial concerns.*

Capital resources include the facility, equipment, land, and inventories of raw materials (food, beverage, and other supplies) managed by the caterer to exceed customer expectations.

Financial resources deal with the management, distribution, acquisition, control, and investment of money. These resources are managed as they flow through the catering operation. They are used to produce desired financial returns. Financial resources include the caterer's personal financial investment and the ability to secure capital from lending institutions. Monitoring the organization's financial resources is an important management task.

Caterers may have certain financial concerns as illustrated in Figure 5–5. If it is a social client, the caterer may require full payment on the day the contract is signed. If the event is booked one year in advance, a 10% deposit might be required. At thirty days before, a payment of 50% is due, and finally, seven days before the event, full payment is expected, except for any overcharges experienced during the day of the event. *Ingredient for Success 16* explains the importance of being aware of financial concerns: *"Accurate forecasting of market trends and changes in food prices are keys to establishing correct pricing and meeting preestablished financial objectives."*

◆ FOURTH FUNCTION: EQUIPMENT

Equipment needs are based on the menu, service requirements, type and location of the event, and special needs of the client (Figure 5–6). A common first question for the caterer is, "What equipment is needed for this event and how will it be handled?" Figure 5–7 includes some common questions that must be asked to determine the equipment needs for a function.

Figure 5-6 *Proper equipment is essential for safe hot and cold food production.*

DETERMINING EQUIPMENT NEEDS

1. Will the event be held on-premise or off-premise?
2. If the event is held off-premise, is refrigeration needed?
3. How will the cold and hot food be kept at temperatures required to minimize bacterial growth?
4. How will the hot and cold food be safely transported ?
5. What kind of serving equipment is needed for the event?

Figure 5-7 *Determining equipment needs.*

◆ FIFTH FUNCTION: IMPLEMENTING

Implementing the plan requires direct communication with the team leaders. Communication with the kitchen manager, service or dining room manager, office personnel, and purchasing manager is necessary for the team to know exactly what is required for implementation and execution of the plan.

The kitchen staff must review and bundle each task required to produce each menu item. The service staff needs to review and bundle its tasks relative to the type and style of service (Figure 5–8). For example, "How and where will the food be served?" "What type of service is required?" "Are linen and china needed?" "Will the food be served using disposables?" "Will the guests be seated and require table service?" "Will buffet style service be used at the event?"

As the event draws closer, the implementation of the plan by the staff becomes increasingly important. Finalizing schedules, identifying staff members accountable for executing each task, and review of procedures prepares the staff for successful implementation of the plan.

Figure 5-8 *Determining linen and service needs are important parts of implementing the plan.*

Subplan

A caterer will bundle tasks from each subsystem and add these elements together to create a master plan. Each catering function is implemented by its own executable subplan. Therefore, the event's master plan is built by the contribution of each subsystem.

◆ SIXTH FUNCTION: CONTROLLING

Controlling the organization's resources is perhaps one of the most important catering management tasks. Control in all facets of the catering operation is needed. The controlling function is built into the master plan through the contribution of each subplan.

The caterer must develop and implement internal and external control procedures into the management of the catering system. Control of food, beverages, and labor costs, including salaries, wages, and employee benefits is an extremely important catering management task (Figure 5–9).

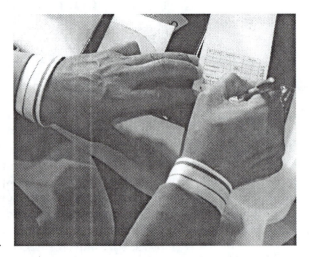

Figure 5-9 *Uncontrolled costs filter down to the end user resulting in lost business.*

Labor costs are either classified as direct or indirect costs. Direct labor costs are those employee costs that are directly involved in the production and service of the food. Food production personnel who prepare the food for an event are considered direct costs to that event. Indirect costs are those labor costs required to support the catering business such as administrative expenses.

Direct labor costs and food costs are usually bundled and called **prime costs**. *Ingredient for Success 17* explains the major reason why a caterer will create cost control procedures. *"Cost control procedures are created for the acquisition of timely information to equip the caterer with the data to scrutinize controllable costs to make appropriate operational decisions."*

◈ SEVENTH FUNCTION: UNDERSTANDING INSURANCE AND LEGAL ISSUES

No amount of planning can rectify the damages resulting from insufficient insurance coverage. Caterers must know their legal responsibilities to their patrons, employees, and to protect their own investment. Insurance plans should cover equipment, personnel, and guests at both on-premise and off-premise events.

Ensuring that the basics are covered is an essential step in protecting one's livelihood (Figure 5–10). But, how can caterers protect themselves from unforeseen events? Establishing a crisis team can help address immediate, unforeseen disasters and crises that may occur through no fault of their own.

Creating a similar safety management team can help troubleshoot **legal concerns**—particularly at off-premise events that pose their own unique blend of challenges. The team should be responsible for conducting routine safety checks of the staff, equipment, and procedures to ensure proper compliance with HACCP standards.

Figure 5-10 *Caterers should safeguard their assets with proper legal and insurance coverage.*

Above all, the caterer should never perform a function without a well-written, signed contract in place. The contract is the final document for determining liability. A contract should spell out basic stipulations for the event including the number of guests; the date, time, and location of the event; and other agreed-upon specifics to be carried out. It should also include provisions for refunds, cancellations, charges for increases or decreases in the number of guests, and the caterer's level of responsibility in the event of unforeseen occurrences.

Though contracts are officially binding, they offer peace of mind to both the caterer and the client by providing a clear document of exactly what is to be carried out at the given event.

Summary

Seven key fundamental catering functions that occur in every successful catering business are: (1) formulating the strategic plan for the event: (2) executing the operational tasks; (3) organizing resources; (4) matching equipment needs to the requirements of the food and service; (5) implementing the plan; (6) controlling the event by use of financial tools and predetermined standards; and (7) obtaining insurance coverage and ensuring all legal concerns are covered by a contract. These functions will be explained in detail in Chapters 6–12.

Review Questions

Brief Answers

1. Identify and define the seven fundamental catering functions.
2. Explain why a caterer's plan must flow from the mission statement.
3. Identify and discuss the three basic purposes of a catering plan.
4. Discuss the difference between a caterer's strategic plan and tactical plan.
5. What is the basic catering management function?
6. Summarize Ingredients for Success 13–16.
7. Describe the process in which a caterer turns plans into operational tasks.
8. Discuss how a caterer would use benchmarks in establishing objectives.
9. In your own words, explain how a caterer's plan is similar to a road map.
10. Discuss how a caterer will bundle tasks.

11. Define *organizing*. What is its primary purpose?

12. List the four resources a caterer will organize to accomplish stated catering objectives.

13. List the prime costs.

Multiple Choice

Select the single best answer for each question.

1. The basic catering management function is:
   a. organizing for the event.
   b. execution of operational tasks.
   c. formulating the plan.
   d. implementation of the plan.
   e. controlling the event.

2. These resources are primarily managed by a caterer to produce a desired financial return and exceed customer expectations.
   a. human resources
   b. capital resources
   c. financial resources
   d. scarce resources
   e. raw materials

3. This procedure enables the caterer to identify and operationalize predetermined, intangible customer needs and wants into achievable elements of a plan.
   a. planning
   b. organizing
   c. controlling
   d. implementation of the plan
   e. execution of operational tasks

True or False

Read each of the following statements and determine if it is true or false.

1. A successful caterer can interpret customer needs and wants but the real challenge is to translate each customer objective into a specific, operational task.

2. Financial resources include the facility, equipment, land, and inventories of raw materials (food, beverage, and nonfood supplies) managed by the caterer to exceed customer expectations.

3. The purpose of a formal structure is for the distribution, maximum utilization, monitoring, and control of scarce resources by the caterer.

Putting It All Together

Discuss the how the caterer utilizes the seven fundamental catering functions when planning a theme-based, sit-down dinner. The fundamental catering management challenge is to explain how each function interacts: (1) formulating the plan for the event; (2) executing the operational tasks; (3) organizing resources; (4) matching equipment needs to the requirements of the food and service; (5) implementing the plan; (6) controlling the event by use of financial tools and predetermined standards; and (7) insurance coverage and all *legal* issues for a Mardi Gras Festival. Be creative and use your imagination. This event will be for 300 people at an on-premise facility. Using the fundamental tasks, offer decorating suggestions, plan a menu to offer a choice of two entrees, a starch, two vegetables, salad, beverage, and dessert.

Chapter Six

Planning— The Basic Catering Management Function

Key Terms

Objectives

After studying this chapter, you should be able to:

◆ Describe why planning is the first catering management function.
◆ Explain how a plan provides guidance.
◆ Explain how a caterer prepares for an event.
◆ Show the planning sequence all caterers must follow regardless of the event.
◆ Explain how to formulate a catering plan.
◆ Describe why a menu is one of the important elements of a catering plan.
◆ Describe why a catering plan is complex.
◆ Provide examples of how caterers plan, how they construct a business plan and a hazardous analysis critical control plan.
◆ Describe how caterers transform objectives into operational tasks.
◆ Explain how a catering plan is implemented.
◆ Discuss why catering plans have to be flexible.
◆ Explain why budgetary constraints guide the formulation of a plan.
◆ Explain why catering management control features must be built into the plan.
◆ Explain why training needs of employees must be integrated into the catering plan.
◆ Explain why barriers may cause catering plans to fail.

INGREDIENTS FOR SUCCESS

18 "Strategies emerge as an outcome of planning."

19 "The longer the length of time between booking the event and its implementation date, the better opportunity a caterer has to create a detailed plan."

20 "To satisfy customer needs, the caterer must overproduce to exceed customer expectations."

21 "Outside suppliers are as important as a caterer's own key personnel."

The caterer and the client have agreed to the proposal. A contract has been discussed and signed. Now, the caterer must take the mutually-agreed-upon data contained in the proposal and make it come to life. This chapter addresses how a caterer builds an event-specific plan based on the client interview, the proposal and the contract. There will be a discussion of how a caterer begins the planning function; weaves specific details into a plan; and uses the plan to communicate, coordinate, and delegate task responsibilities to team members.

◆ PLANNING—THE BASIC CATERING MANAGEMENT FUNCTION

Planning is the first of the seven catering management functions. **Formulating** a plan is a beginning point to the successful execution of a catering event. Planning can be very hectic at times, but a well-formulated plan will serve the caterer well. A successful caterer is one who is well organized through planning.

Success evolves over time as the caterer becomes more adapted to the planning function. Keeping multiple events organized and straight requires a successful caterer to be well focused and organized. Each event must have an independent **subplan** based on client needs and the caterer's strategic plan. It is a challenge to bundle events due to individual expectations.

The best caterers are always thinking about their upcoming events. Experienced caterers are concerned with the following questions: What is going to happen? How is it going to happen? Where is it going to happen? When is it going to happen? The most successful caterers make sure it happens—as planned.

If organizational skills are not a strength of the caterer, a key team member who possesses exceptional organizational skills is needed. Details are critically important. Even the smallest detail must be discussed and outlined as attention to the minute details is what every customer expects.

Planning Provides Guidance

First, the plan is a **blueprint**. It becomes the outline for the event. Second, a plan provides guidance; it establishes direction for the catering team. Third, a plan identifies each course of action required to accomplish predetermined **objectives**. An objective is the goal or main purpose of the plan. Fourth, a plan is used to generate strategies to execute the elements of the plan. Strategies enable the caterer to accomplish objectives. *Ingredient for Success 18 states:* *"Strategies emerge as an outcome of planning."*

The caterer must have an idea of what will be done under any circumstances. **"What if" scenarios** should be added to the plan. For example, what if a client needs to have barbequed steaks prepared over live charcoal and the weather is 10°F below zero? A caterer must compensate for the temperature. How will the cooked steaks be stored until they are served? Likewise, what if the temperature is 95°F hot, and extremely humid? What adjustments must be made to compensate for the heat? The caterer must consider the employees' needs while working over the hot pits. Will the customers enjoy the meal in the sweltering heat at an outside event? One innovative way a caterer solved the heat problem was by hiring a local company, that manufactured portable air-conditioning units, to install a unit inside a tent. This air-conditioned tent provided a suitable environment for both the guests and the employees.

This innovative idea can create a profitable situation for the caterer by charging an extra 10–15% commission on the rental fee for the air-conditioning unit.

Getting Ready to Plan

Once the proposal has been accepted, the caterer begins the creation of an event-specific plan. *Ingredient for Success 19 states: "The longer the length of time between booking the event and its implementation date, the better opportunity a caterer has to create a detailed plan."*

At this initial meeting, discussion with the key staff members focuses on generating event-specific guidelines or objectives for the event. The objectives are built based on the interpreted customer needs and wants and are then reflected in the *budget*.

What does the customer want? Remember *Ingredient for Success 2: "We cannot be all things to all people."* Objectives are also based upon the caterer's financial and professional needs. When a caterer is doing a job for $50.00 per plate, the amount of planning is certainly different from the planning for the $12.00- or $15.00-per-plate event. Obviously, a caterer has more leverage to be creative for the $50.00-per-plate event.

The plan and its delivery to the customer should reflect the cost of the event. The plan for a client requesting a display of fresh-cut roses, as the table's centerpiece, and linen table clothes is much different from the plan using paper table clothes and plastic utensils. These are factors that affect the catering plan.

All details in the plan flow from the customer's preconceived understanding of what the caterer can do and the caterer's understanding of these expectations. The caterer must write the plan to include when it will be done, how it will be done, how much it will cost, and the potential profit.

Managing the event is a multitask process. Although every caterer develops a personal style for completing the job, all caterers follow a typical planning sequence. Basic planning is almost the same for each job. What is the caterer going to do? How is the caterer going to do it to the best of his or her ability so the client receives the utmost satisfaction for his or her dollar?

Planning Sequence

The planning sequence (Figure 6–1) always includes a review of the mission statement. This important exercise keeps the caterer focused on the stated purpose of the organization. To remain true to the purpose, every action taken by the caterer must mirror and flow from the organization's mission statement. If actions deviate from this statement, it signals that the purpose of the operation has changed and it is time to reevaluate the mission.

◆ FORMULATING A CATERING PLAN

Formulating a catering plan requires the knowledge of certain elements before the planning can begin. These elements are the same whether a caterer is planning a small or large event. Five required elements that must be identified before any plan can be created are budget, menu, location, number of guests, and labor

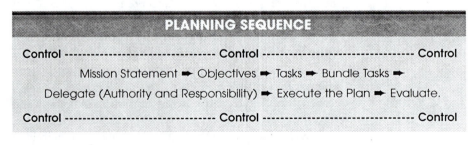

Figure 6-1 Planning sequence.

requirements. Other concerns include the decorations; floral arrangements; service style; and type of china, silverware, and table cloths.

The caterer transforms the initial catering proposal into a multitude of objectives or **benchmarks** that give life to the proposal as a plan emerges. The main purpose of an objective is to guide the caterer through the process. Every event is different; therefore, each event is driven by its own set of objectives. However, there are two required objectives caterers establish for all events: **financial objectives** and **customer-satisfaction objectives**, based on the client's needs and wants.

Budget

During the initial planning process, financial objectives are important. To create financial objectives for an event, a caterer will start with a budget. The **budget** is a financial plan used to set the parameters for each event. Each event will have its own budget that reflects the needs of the client. It is critical to establish the client's budget early in the process. The client could be looking for a low-end event, an upscale event, or something nestled in between.

A budget is a tactical, single-event, management tool used to explain how resources will be acquired (revenue or gross sales), and how these will be consumed in the operation of the business (expenses) to arrive at a predetermined profit for the specific event. Therefore, a budget also functions as a financial plan. This budget plan will provide answers to help design the blueprint of the catering plan (Figure 6–2) to execute the function.

EVENT PLAN BLUEPRINT

1. What is the profit objective for this event?
2. Will the client be able to pay the caterer? Will the client accept the quoted price that is needed by the caterer to meet the predetermined profit objective?
3. What is the cost of labor?
4. What are the food and production costs?
5. What additional equipment and subsequent rental costs are needed for this event?
6. What transportation is needed for this function? What is the expense?
7. What insurance coverage is required? Is there any additional coverage or expense?
8. What are the indirect, fixed costs, or overhead expenses?
9. Will any additional hidden expenses specific to this event be incurred?

Figure 6–2 *Building the blueprint for the event plan: The basic questions.*

The budget plan is further broken down into departmental plans. Each event is assigned its own objectives based on the budget plan. The kitchen manager will submit a budget detailing the number of hours consumed in production, transportation, serving, and cleanup tasks. An alternative is for the kitchen manager to establish production standards of hours based on 100 meals. Other budgeted items may include the cost of implementing a marketing plan.

Caterers' costs are less when they use their own facility because there are no transportation costs. Transportation costs can be excessive based on the distance and amount of time required for travel. Remember, from the employee departure time until their return, they will be on the payroll.

A well-constructed budget is an important part of the catering management control plan. A budget guides the caterer before the function as a control tool, and after the function as an accountability to make comparisons between the budgeted standard and the actual cost incurred in the execution of the event. It is used to evaluate the effective and efficient utilization of organizational resources by the caterer in the execution of the operation.

◆ THE MENU: A TACTICAL PLAN

The **menu** is the single most important factor contained in the overall catering plan. The caterer must create budgetary objectives based on the menu. Caterers construct menus with special attention to satisfying perceived client needs, staff skills, seasonal availability of food, quality and relative cost of food, cost of labor, predetermined profit margins, nutritional needs of the client, presentation and service style, and kitchen production capabilities.

Menu Format

A caterer will select one of three basic formats when presenting a menu to the client. First, a caterer will construct a new menu based solely on the needs, wants, and demands of the client. After the client has been interviewed, the caterer will build a menu to match the client's tastes and budget. This technique is time consuming because it often requires market research to ascertain product availability and costs. However, greater customer satisfaction is achieved when a caterer creates a menu based on the client's needs, wants, demands, and budget. One important advantage a caterer has when designing a menu for a client is the ability to set the selling price based on the needs, wants, and demands of that client.

A caterer will set the selling price on a customer-by-customer basis (Chapter 11). A caterer must know how the psychology of the set price affects the customer's perception of value. One customer might believe a menu priced at $10.00 per person infers poor value and would be much happier to pay the caterer $20.00 for the same menu. This reflects the *price versus value relationship*. On the other hand, another customer might be more conservative and accept the economical value of $10.00 with great enthusiasm.

A client, Scott, may be planning a wedding reception. He wishes to spend approximately $20.00 per plate and wants to serve a stuffed chicken breast as the main entree. During the initial interview, the caterer can *upscale* the event by suggesting Chicken Cordon Bleu. Or, the caterer can suggest two entrees, a smaller stuffed chicken breast and a small steak on the side for $5.00 more per person.

By reducing the cost of the chicken and increasing the cost per plate by $5.00, the caterer can include the cost of the steak. The customer will perceive this as a much more elegant event. The addition of the steak will help the customer's perception with the guests and increase the caterer's profit margin.

Although this method is an excellent way to increase customer satisfaction, one disadvantage may be an increase of production time in the kitchen. This example illustrates why the caterer must interview the customer. By interviewing the customer, a caterer can determine a client's budget and whether the menu can be upgraded. Always remember that each client has certain desires and tastes. Therefore, even though a caterer is trying to maximize income and build profit structure from the event, customer satisfaction is still the most important consideration.

Standardized Menu

Caterers will create a series of **standardized menus**, offering a variety food, beverages and service styles. These menus may be presented to each client regardless of the client's specific needs. These may exist as standard menu "A," "B," "C," "D," "E," and "F." The client selects the menu with the best fit to their needs and price range and is not usually permitted to substitute items.

A caterer can use a standard menu format to penetrate the low-end market niche. Using a standard menu format will permit a caterer to adapt a small production facility, lack of available skilled labor, and minimal production equipment to successfully exceed a client's needs. A standardized menu format can offer a choice between only two vegetables, two salads, two potatoes, and a limited variety of simple entrees. However, by offering a lower cost menu, the caterer must generate a higher volume of sales to make sufficient profit margins.

The advantages for the caterer having a standardized menu are simplification of inventory, a limited menu based on the skill level of the staff and the layout of the kitchen, predetermined costs and contribution to profit margins.

The disadvantages of working with a standardized catering menu include the possible lack of creativity, working on a tight budget, and a predetermined profit margin. When creating individual menus, the caterer has the ability to increase the profit margins much easier than with a standardized menu.

Master Menu

Caterers can also use another method of menu planning. Some caterers provide a **master menu** from which the client can select food and beverage items. This method permits the client to create their own menu based on their budget.

The caterer will present a variety of menu selections from a master menu, similar to an a la carte menu. The highest price the customer begins with may be a selection of the roast beef entree at a base price of $10.00. Stuffed chicken breast or roast chicken may start at $7.50. Then, as the customer selects additional items from the menu, the base price will increase. Add-ons include options for starches, vegetables, salads, beverages, and dessert items.

This type of menu has advantages for the caterer. The caterer has preselected a familiar menu of items his staff can competently produce using the kitchen and production facilities. This can eliminate customers requesting a rare ethnic dish the caterer is not trained to produce.

Complexity of the Plan

The complexity of the plan grows when the size of the event increases. First, the logistics for executing a catering event for 7,000 are different from an event for 100 people. Much more detail is required to ensure the event runs smoothly. When serving an event for 7,000 instead of 100, the menu must be simplified.

◆ PLANNING FOR A CATERING EVENT

To formulate a successful plan, all caterers must identify objectives, which are derived from identified customer needs and wants. The caterer must know what the customers expect by discussing events with them. The customer usually has an idea that the caterer must execute. To do this, a caterer must overproduce—focusing on the little things that can be added within budget to make the event look more elegant and exceed a customer's expectations. *Ingredient for Success 20: "To satisfy customer needs, the caterer must overproduce to exceed customer expectations."*

The caterer is similar to an artist. Every event is a new creation—different and better and exceeding customer expectations. Creativity is a skill resulting from a caterer's experience, and when combined with the skill of interpreting customer needs, it helps a caterer to plan a successful catering event. However, remember *Ingredient for Success 2: "We cannot be all things to all people."* This must apply to each and every potential customer.

A caterer can do little things beyond the customer's expectations to increase the success rate of an event. Simple but effective techniques such as the addition of extra frills and decorative touches on a buffet table can add eye appeal (Figure 6–3).

A caterer can enhance the attractiveness of a buffet line by serving foods from different height levels. Because customers are accustomed to being served from the same level on a buffet table, new heights create a depth and new field of vision as the eye focuses on the presentation of the food. Varying heights contribute to the overall objective of exceeding a customer's perception of value.

Figure 6-3 *Extra frills and special touches add appeal to an event.*

The human eye is in constant motion, scanning items in the environment. Adding floral arrangements, also set at varying heights, is another added feature. A caterer can use different types and styles of vessels to hold food on a buffet table enhancing the overall artistic presentation of the food.

Colors also attract the eye. Using different colored table cloths coordinated with the color of the food can accent the items. Planned use of different swatches of colored cloth placed beneath certain bowls can highlight the appearance of those items. These accent pieces are used to make the buffet more attractive than a plain buffet.

Planned presentation of the food on the buffet line brings organization to the event. Using a silver bowl instead of a glass bowl can enhance the presentation. A fluted dish instead of a simple round dish can be enough to please a guest. Mirrors placed beneath a certain food will enhance it. All of these simple techniques will help to create an overwhelming degree of satisfaction for the guest.

Objectives Become Operational Tasks

Objectives are translated into **operational tasks,** which are those singular activities that must be executed to accomplish an objective. Each individual task from turning on the light in the morning to turning it off at the end of the event must be organized and bundled together. All common tasks should be bundled to create a *job.* Since the caterer cannot physically do every task, this step enables the caterer to identify the approximate number of employees required to execute each job for an event. This task facilitates employee scheduling, contributes to identifiable and controllable labor and its related costs, and leads to the creation of a budget for the event.

Delegation

Each bundled task is delegated to a management team member, who then assigns those jobs to employees. This is why successful caterers have good, reliable, trusted people on staff. Appropriate levels of responsibility and authority must be delegated to each team member. Even though each task is delegated to a member of the staff, the caterer must exercise management control techniques to ensure the intricate details of the plan are being implemented and the objectives are being accomplished by the employee. Common catering management control techniques used to produce results are a combination of management team meetings and one-on-one interaction with key people.

If an event is scheduled one year in advance, a caterer will establish a timeline sequence of one year, 90 days, 60 days, 25 days, and so on until the event is completed (see example in Chapter 5). Following this time line, a caterer can implement control techniques to ensure the plan is being implemented by the staff, that everyone accomplishes their own objectives relative to the overall plan, and that every member does their own job.

The caterer may follow up with questions like: Is the team member responsible for the purchasing function doing the job? Has someone received prices from the suppliers on the major food items on the menu? Have the menu plan's food and beverage needs been discussed with suppliers? Have the suppliers of either the tent rentals or china been contacted?

Planning will alert a caterer to the necessity of acquiring rental items in advance. This is especially true when planning for seasonal events. If an event is booked in February for July, a tentative order with the supplier should be placed in February. This permits the caterer to have the flexibility to adjust the order. If a tent is needed to cover an area of 5,000 square feet, only a specialized rental company will most likely handle this type of tent. The caterer must know where to find such a tent and its approximate rental cost. Understanding costs are important so when the caterer meets with the client, reliable prices can be quoted. *Ingredient for Success 21 states: "Outside suppliers are as important as a caterer's own key personnel."*

A caterer may establish monthly meetings during the first six months before the event. Then, bimonthly meetings can be scheduled from six months to 90 days before the event. Weekly team meetings should be established 90 days before the event. This gives the staff a chance to share information. The team member in charge of purchasing food has to know what the wait staff will do. The team member responsible for transporting the food to the off-premise site must know when the food will be ready, what the holding time is, and if equipment is available to keep it cold and hot. The service personnel must be there to disburse the food when it arrives.

Implementation of the Plan

Putting the plan into action, the process of implementing each piece of the plan into the day-to-day activities, becomes the next step for the caterer. This requires a caterer to have all schedules for the event finalized. A key catering management task is the careful coordination of the front-of-the-house and back-of-the-house activities (see Chapter 7).

Post Event Meetings

When the event is over, performance evaluation based on predetermined objectives closes the planning sequence (Figure 6–1). The management staff must meet and discuss issues focusing on continuous improvement in all phases of the planning cycle and event implementation. Caterers seek answers to such questions as: What could have been done to improve all aspects of the operation? How could the implementation of the event have been made easier? What could have been done more efficiently to help save money, cut costs, or increase customer satisfaction?

TIPS FROM THE TRADE

While having a flexible event plan is nice, it is not always possible with the high volume of business we do. Rather, we, as the banquet department, must remain flexible in accommodating any groups' needs. We have learned, through experience, to anticipate probable last minute needs, such as additional AV equipment and added seating. One precaution we take is to prepare and seat for five percent more than requested by the group. Often, groups will put their guaranteed number lower than they actually are. By being prepared to handle an additional five percent above the guaranteed number, we save a lot of last minute frustrations.

Jeremy Engle
Banquet Manager
Beaver Run Resort & Conference Center
Breckenridge, CO

Flexibility of Plans

Plans must be made so they are flexible. Details laid out in a plan provide guidance and direction, however, flexibility is important because clients often change details before the day of the event. A caterer must anticipate changes and have contingency plans set to respond quickly as the details of the event change.

TIPS FROM THE TRADE

Jardine's Catering agreed to cater an event for 1,500 people. Six days prior to the event, it blossomed to 6,500 people. Because of the increase, the catering team went into a top-priority mode of immediate plan revision. Team meetings were held twice a day to keep everyone informed. Time constraints were prioritized and plans were revised to provide food and service for 6,500 guests. It also was necessary for the team to build the new infrastructure to support the implementation of the event. Team members were mobilized and sent scrambling to acquire additional equipment and extra staff. Increased communication with the suppliers became another priority. This communication guaranteed the right amount of food, at the best possible price, adhering to specifications, and delivery in time for this event.

Bill Jardine
Jardine's Farm Restaurant & Catering
Sarver, PA

Control Features

During the development of a plan, care must be taken by the caterer to build in control features. Controlling costs using catering management techniques will help achieve predetermined budgetary objectives regarding food, beverages and labor.

A caterer will depend on some type of standard or measurement as a relative point of reference to compare actual costs against a predetermined cost standard. Controls set standards to be used by a caterer in different ways. A standard is used in the selection of approved suppliers who provide the highest quality products at a competitive price. Control of labor and its related costs are also an integral part of achieving budgetary objectives. Proper scheduling and cross-training ensure catering employees are doing their jobs during a catering event.

Staff and Planning

Most caterers work with a relatively small management staff. Many operate with three to five key management personnel, who work together to build a catering plan. They will also lead the employees who are executing the tasks at the event.

Key personnel must be trained so they have an understanding of how the caterer wants the tasks completed. It is important for the caterer to have access to trained personnel. This is especially important in areas where a caterer may experience seasonal variations in business. Often, catering itself is seasonal business. Catering is not usually prevalent in some areas during the winter months. A caterer will place employees on temporary layoff status immediately after the holiday season. Some of these people will seek other, more permanent jobs.

Figure 6-4 *Coordinating uniforms present a polished, professional look and help guests identify service staff.*

When the caterer begins to gear up again in March or April, the staff may need to be replenished. This begins the cycle of continuous training for both new and returning employees. Continuous training for all staff members contributes to a successful organization.

Employees are the ambassadors of the catering company. Often, a client will interact with a caterer's employees at the actual event. The employee must be professional, look professional, act professional, and be pleasant and personable to all guests (Figure 6–4). The training and education of each employee is a must. Even the servers must know what type of food is being served so they can be prepared to answer guest questions and to help them navigate through the buffet line.

◆ BARRIERS TO PLANNING

What type of *barriers* must a caterer overcome to create and implement a successful catering plan? There are always barriers that will challenge the caterer, however, there are two basic barriers that will affect all caterers sometime in their career.

Operational Barriers

Barriers which interfere with the tangible elements of production or implementation of the event are called **operational barriers**. These can prevent the successful implementation of a plan.

Operational barriers disrupt the physical elements of an event. Human error and accidents are common operational barriers. At an off-premise event, if cooked vegetables fall when being pulled from storage, they cannot be used. How can the caterer handle this? The vegetables are already on the menu. Can the caterer call back to the facility and have more vegetables sent? Or, must the caterer spread food out in a different order or format to give the appearance of more food than is present?

Other operational barriers deal with time. In the production of the food, has the caterer adequately planned enough time to get the food prepared? If equipped with electric convection ovens, how will the product get cooked in the event of a power failure? One solution is to have propane or natural gas ovens available. Can the food be prepared at another location and heated on site at the event?

Natural disasters can create barriers to the plan. Storms, lightening, floods, and blizzards will disrupt even the best made plans, however, there is little the caterer can do in many of these situations.

Human Resource or Communication Barriers

The second type of barriers are **human resource** or **communication barriers**. Human error, unfortunately, is the biggest barrier against effective communication. Employees just "forget" elements of a well-thought plan. Usually, employees forget equipment, food, and other staff members, and this list can be endless.

Lack of communication among members of the catering team is always dangerous to the proper formulation and implementation of a plan. Human nature may cause certain employees to add their own procedures to a task, which is potentially dangerous. It must be strictly enforced through policies and rules that all standard operating procedures are followed and not permitted to be changed on a whim of whomever is on the job. As long as the standard operating procedures deliver optimal value to the client, they are to be maintained.

The caterer can create many solutions to these types of barriers by using their own creativity and experience, and knowing where the local convenience store is located relative to the catering site. Convenience stores offer ice, soft drinks, small wares, and other items to satisfy endless needs.

◆ BUSINESS PLAN
(Adapted with permission of Bruce Frankel, virtualrestaurant.com)

A business plan is one of the best types of plans any caterer can formulate. A business plan is a plan of action that serves many purposes. A caterer can use the business plan as a tool to implement the strategic plan and establish short-term organizational goals. It is the central strategy for the development of the business. It will create a focused vision for long-term success.

Virtual Restaurant gives prospective restaurateurs a chance to see probable outcomes of their business assumptions. Through the use of Internet technology, this service is offered easily and inexpensively.

Purposes of a Business Plan

1. The plan provides internal direction for the organization. It sets the direction for the organization.

2. It communicates to stakeholders the intended growth of the company.

3. This plan discloses the organization's financial goals. Financial goals are explained by exhibits of the statement of income, balance sheet, and cash flow statements. These exhibits are extremely important when courting potential investors. Financial analysts will rigorously examine this document to ascertain if the business and associated risk, as explained in the plan, is worthy of investment.

4. The plan presents the overall vision for the business. It communicates the concept, business philosophy, and ideas.

Writing a business plan will take research, self-examination, and the ability to communicate to all stakeholders. The formulation of the business plan is an exercise to conceptualize the entire catering business. A clear and crisp writing style is recommended. Before writing the details of the plan, select a format, or use the outline of a successful business plan.

Front Section of the Business Plan

See Appendix C for a sample business plan courtesy of <u>virtualrestaurant.com</u>. Each business plan has a front section and a back section. The front section of the plan includes the cover page, executive summary, and table of contents. The back section of the business plan includes the body or the specifics of the catering business and the appendices.

Cover Page

The cover page of the business plan should include the caterer's name, business name, address, phone number, fax number, e-mail address, and the date the report was completed.

Table of Contents

Since most business plans are longer than five pages, accurate identification of the major sections and their appropriate page numbers must be given.

Executive Summary

This executive summary is best written last. It is a recap and summary of the major points from all the other sections. The executive summary can well be the most important section of the plan, since most investors or stakeholders lack the time to read the report in its entirety. It should be no longer than three pages and be written in a clear and convincing style. Refer to the individual sections for reference and use the following format as a guide.

Body of the Business Plan

This section of the report will be the bulk of the business plan. This section may take a significant amount of research, self-reflection, and time to complete.

Company Description

This section includes the name, type of catering business, its location, legal status (business form), startup or continuing, date founded, and menu description. A detailed description of the menu(s) will communicate the level of professionalism, culinary skill level, equipment demands, staffing requirement, and price structure. Include a detailed section explaining how the menus have been developed and tested.

Writing the Business Plan Company Description Section

Mission Statement
> Nature and philosophy of the business
> Quality, price, service, customer relationships, management style, employee relations
> Corporate style, image
> Social and community image
> Growth and profitability goals

Company Name(s)
> Brand or trade names associated with products
> Subsidiary companies (e.g., a catering division)

Legal Form of the Business
> Corporation? "C" or "S"? In what state(s) is it incorporated?
> Who owns the company? How many shares outstanding? Other major shareholders?
> Partnership? Limited partners? Share amount?

Management
> President, officers, key management, and advisory personnel

Location
> Main place of business, offices or headquarters, branch locations

Stage of Development
> When company was founded
> Milestones reached so far
> Phase of development—idea stage (no product finalized), startup (early stages of operations), expansion, established, reworking
> Where are you within your phase? Has the product been tested, lease signed, suppliers arranged, staff hired, etc.?

Financial and Personnel Status
> Stage of previous and/or present funding
> Present financial state and obligations. Past performance if applicable
> Size of work force or anticipated increase

Patents and Licenses
> Trademarks, patents, licenses, copyrights—secured or pending

Industry Analysis

This section describes the general catering industry, discusses the economic characteristics of the industry, and assesses the present condition, future potential, and any factors such as trends that may determine them. What are the key success factors that make this industry attractive? What are the factors that make this industry unattractive? Are there any special issues, such as government regulations, or special problems common to this industry?

Key successful factors are those identifiable elements in the catering industry that make an individual caterer successful. These factors may include a specialized culinary skill, the ability to consistently produce quality food using signature recipes at a low cost, a favorable reputation, a convenient and beautiful banquet facility, and access to an appropriate and skilled labor supply. To sustain a competitive advantage against other caterers, a significant level of competence must be attained in these elements.

Writing the Business Plan Industry Analysis Section

General Information
Economic Sector—Food Service
The Catering and Restaurant Industry
Size and Growth Rate of the Industry
> Rate of expansion. How it compares with GNP growth
> How your specific sector might be different (corporate catering may be growing while off-premise social catering service is declining)
> Predicted trends and the strategic opportunities they offer (low-fat cooking is becoming more popular)

Sensitivity to Economic Cycles and Seasonality
> How national economic trends (recession, inflation) impact your business

How local industry (a large company you depend on for business) affects your situation

How seasonal variations in business affect your cash flow

Regulation

How local and national regulations affect your business (inspection standards, smoking regulations, wage and tax changes)

Financial Norms and Patterns

Terms with vendors, customers, the capital market

Standard markup of products

Inventory par levels

Profit expectations, etc.

(see also Income Statement Showing Industry Averages in the Financial section)

Products and Related Services

This section describes the menu, food production capabilities, and style of service the caterer will produce. A competitive review of other caterers' food and service is provided. Explain how the caterer will respond to emerging trends and evolving customer needs.

Writing the Business Plan Food and Service Section

Description of the Products

General concepts

Specific menu items

Production methods (costs, labor)

How the products (menu) change

Stage of development of the products

How the products compare to competitors

Any special value or aspect about the products (patent, etc.)

Product liability considerations

Description of the Services

The special services offered (take-out, delivery, meals-for-a-week)

How they help the business and create competitive advantage

Future Plans and Developments

How the products and services change to meet changing market demands

Are there any products or services planned for future implementation? When?

The Target Market

This section describes how the caterer will select the customer based on demographics, geographics, **psychographic segmentation** (lifestyle, social class, and personality characteristics), buying sensitivity, and market size. The target market or the set of all clients who share these identified characteristics will be served by the caterer.

Writing the Business Plan Target Market Section

Who exactly will be buying your food and service?

Demographics

      Age, income range, gender, occupations, marital status, family status, ethnic groups, education, sophistication, home or auto owner, etc.

Geographics

      Area served—neighborhood, city, region

      Density—urban, suburban, rural

      Nature of the location—downtown, business, shopping, residential

      Transportation—how will they get to the store?

Lifestyle

      Family status, family size, family life cycle

      Hobbies, sports, entertainment interests, social events

      Television, radio, magazines, and other media preferences

      Race

      Nationality

      Political and other organizational affiliation

      Occupation

      Education

      Religion

Psychographics

      Status-seeking or trend-setting?

      Socially or environmentally conscious?

      Free-spending or conservative?

      Practical or fun-seeking?

Buying Factors and Sensitivity

      Price, quality, brand name, service, reputation

      Special product features, advertising, packaging

      Location, facility design, ambiance, sanitation

      Nature or quantity of other customers

Market Size and Trends

      How big is the target market?

      How fast is it growing?

      Where is the market heading?

      What economic and social factors will be influencing the market?

      How will the market's needs be changing and why?

Strategic Opportunities

      In what ways do you plan to use your understanding of the market to your advantage?

Marketing Plan and Sales Strategy

This section includes how the caterer will promote the company image by sending a message to the potential client. This message that the caterer will convey through all marketing vehicles should be clear and consistent and must reflect the general corporate style and its mission. The image can be conveyed directly (description of products, pricing, services, etc.), or indirectly (suggestive design elements, logos, uniforms). A well-conceived marketing campaign will be used in both a complimentary and appropriate way.

Writing the Business Plan Marketing Plan Section

Think about what the customer wants
> How does the product meet their basic needs?
> How much does price matter?
> How about ease and convenience of purchase?
> How does the product make the customer feel—about themselves and the company?

Marketing Vehicles
What are the ways you will reach potential customers?
> Brochures, flyers, leaflets
> Print media—newspapers, magazines, specialty publications, Yellow Pages
> Broadcast media/electronic—television, radio, computer (Internet), movie theaters
> Specialties—packaging, T-shirts, etc.
> Hotel—In-house publications, video guides, concierge relations, services
> Direct mail, coupons, mailing list, Val-pak
> Promotions, credit card discount programs
> Signs—on stores, billboards, trains, cabs, blimps
> Trade shows, networking
> Point-of-sale devices, promotions, and employee practices
> Sampling
> Public relations (PR)—as a communication service media solicitor and event planner. PR is free, may create awareness of the caterer by potential clients, and may enhance a caterer's reputation.
> Charity events

Marketing Tactics and Strategy
> Mix of marketing vehicles you will use, and how they will be coordinated
> Will the campaign be divided into different phases? (pre-opening, opening, etc.)
> Creative or unique techniques you will be using
> Your marketing goals and methods of monitoring them

Marketing Budget

> What is the budget for all phases of the marketing effort?

Sales

> Training of employees involved in sales—waitstaff
> Catering or special function salesperson

The Competition

The competition section focuses on the competitors who are aiming at the same target market. Categorize the competition (off-premise, on-premise, corporate, or social caterers). List the competitors in each category.

Writing the Business Plan Competition Section

Competitive Advantages and Comparative Evaluation (for the caterer and the direct competitors).

Objective

> Price (and hidden costs), credit policies
> Location
> Quality
> Special product features
> Image/style/perceived value
> Service (and special service features), customer relations, social image

Internal

> Financial strength, volume purchasing power
> Marketing and promotional program and budget
> Operational advantages, strategic partnerships
> Company morale—personnel motivation, commitment, productivity

Market Share and Distribution

> How is the market distributed?
> Do any one or two companies dominate the market?
> How will you obtain sufficient market share?

Future Competition

> How and why will new competitors enter the market?
> How long will that take?
> What factors would prevent new competition from market entry? (secret recipes)

Strategic Opportunities

> How can you use your competitive advantages to exploit opportunities in the marketplace?

Operations

This section explains the day-to-day functions of the catering business. Focus on the aspects of the operation that are more important to the overall success and that will provide a competitive edge or innovative advantage.

Writing the Business Plan Operations Section

Facilities

> Location—addresses, parking, floor plans, etc.
> Lease—terms, length, important details
> Improvements—plans, funding, budget
> Key success factors—expansion potential, proximity to market, unique aspects, expertise and adaptation of technology (see Chapter 14), quality customer service, access to financial capital, facility design and location, signature recipes, low-cost production.

Production

> Process—how are the products created? stages, flow, efficiency
> Labor—kinds and numbers of workers, costs, part-time
> Productivity—how do you increase productivity without reducing quality?
> Suppliers—who are the major vendors?
> Capacity—how much work/volume can the present facilities handle?
> Quality Control—inspections, testing, training, incentive rewards

Cost Controls

> Inventory—forms, systems (computer), practices
> Food and beverage—check systems, management practices, training, periodic inventory
> General—management, inventory

Administrative and Financial Controls

> Bookkeeping systems and policies (payments, billing)
> Accounting systems (report intervals)
> Sales systems (computer)

Customer Service

> Service attitudes and policies
> Complaint process and reconciliation
> Feedback mechanisms

Other Operational Issues

> Safety and health (staff and customers)
> Insurance and legal
> Licenses and permits

Environmental concerns and practices

Management and Organization

This section has a biographical summary of the management team. Carefully written, this may be one of the most important sections of the plan. The educational and professional work experiences will introduce and explain who the most important people are in the catering operation and why. People are the most important resource a catering company will have. A complete narrative of the founder, president, chef, dining room manager, general manager, production manager, and catering manager must include their experience, successes, education, strengths, and weaknesses.

Writing the Business Plan Management and Organization Section

Compensation and Incentives
>How will you motivate and retain key personnel? (salary, bonuses, commissions, profit sharing, equity, stock options)

Board of Directors and Advisory Committee
>>For corporations, a Board of Directors is a legal requirement. An advisory committee is a less formal way of avoiding the cost of a formal Board.
>>Small caterers don't really need either and instead get advice and information as they need it from various sources.

Consultants, Professionals, and Other Specialists. Explain how each may contribute to the caterer's short- and long-term development.
>>Management, financial, or marketing consultants
>>Attorneys, accountants
>>Industry specialists
>>Architects and design consultants

Key Management to be added
>>If there is a key position that is not yet filled, explain your plans to do so.
>>Describe the job and the profile, compensation, and qualifications of the prospects.

Management Structure and Style
>>Outline of the lines of authority. Include a flow chart in the appendix
>>Describe the management style. Management style should reflect and support the general corporate style (from the mission statement)
>>Include any innovative or unusual aspects of management style that would impact growth or give a competitive advantage

Financial Data and Projections

All the decisions from each of the previous sections of the business plan have financial outcomes. Forecasts to best determine accurate numbers must be made. The caterer must gather, sort, and report an accurate financial position. This accurate financial data will determine the present position and current progress of the business, and will unveil probable new decisions about the future. For startup ventures, a reliable set of projected financial statements will offer meaningful information to help make many important decisions. It is perhaps the best (if not the most realistic) way to "see into the future."

Writing the Business Plan Financial Data and Projections Section

This section of the business plan requires that you
>Consult your accountant and your attorney

Be conservative and honest

Use standard industry forms and formats

Forms to Include

Sources of capital and debt service

Use of funding and start-up costs

Menu price and function cost calculations (optional)

Sales calculation

Payroll calculation

Detail of expenses worksheets

Income statement (1–5 years)

Monthly or quarterly cash flow statement (1–3 years)

Amortization and depreciation schedule

Balance sheet

Assumption Sheet

If you have not clearly stated basic assumptions in the above sheets, make a separate page with information such as sales volume, payroll rates, food costs, and financing costs.

Break-Even Analysis

How much income must be earned to pay fixed expenses?

Long-Term Development and Exit Plan

The caterer must describe what the ultimate destination for this business is and how the catering business will look at the different intervals along the way including the short- and long-term goals. What is the long-term vision for the company and the caterer? If the caterer is preparing this business plan to seek investment, then this section should tell investors how much money they can make and when and how they can get it.

Writing the Business Plan Long-Term Development and Exit Plan Section

Goals—What long-term vision is held for the company and the caterer?

Lifestyle provider—good, stable, reliable income

Innovator—creative, new, different products and services

Quality—reputation for excellence

Expanding and growth—market domination, large company, big bucks

Niche leader—doing only one thing, but doing it well

Specifically, where the company will be in the market in terms of sales, units, employees, etc., in the next year, 3 years, 5 years, etc.

Strategies—how will the goals be reached?

Market penetration

Promotion—increase business by marketing of current products and services

Expansion—add new products and/or new units

Other strategies

Milestones—As the company progresses toward the goals, find a way to mark and communicate the progress

List the short-term and long-term goals and the dates they are expected to be accomplished

Short-term goals

    Financing secured, lease signed, catering manager hired

    Catering business opened

    Projected sales level reached

    Second catering unit planned; second catering unit opened

Risk Evaluation—Outlining risks shows the investor that the caterer is not naively optimistic in planning

    Market acceptance, changing demographics

    New competition, new customer tastes

    Management performance, payroll costs

    Regulatory, licensing issues

Exit Plan—How and when will it end?

    Sale—to individuals

    Acquisition—by another company

    Buy-out—by stockholders or employees

    Go public—stock traded publicly

    Franchise—sell concept, receive royalties

    Hand down—to family?

    Close

Appendix

The appendix is the place for supporting documents and information. The items in the appendix should only confirm, reinforce, or elaborate on the major ideas and facts already stated in the main plan. Many people don't even read the appendix, so include all essential items in the plan itself. If the appendix seems too long, put it in a separate binder.

Suggested Appendix Items for the Business Plan

Menus

Resumés and financial statements of key people

Lease and other location information (pictures)

Marketing information (logo, dummy ads, packaging)

Supporting media information (newspaper articles, etc.)

Budgets and schedules, and analysis (equipment lists, project charts, flow chart)

Design or construction information (floor plan, renderings)

Contracts, trademarks

Bank loans, financial statements

Market research studies (bibliography)

◆ HAZARDOUS ANALYSIS AND CRITICAL CONTROL POINT PLAN

(Adapted from the 1999 FDA Model Food Code)

The most important type of plans a caterer must formulate and implement is a detailed set of action plans designed to keep the food they are serving safe, unadulterated, and wholesome. The single most important guarantee any caterer can imply to a client is the serving of honestly presented food free of bacterial, physical, or chemical contaminants.

Bacterial contaminants cause foodborne illness. These include pathogenic microorganisms such as bacteria, viruses, parasites, fungi, and toxins found especially in fish and plants. Physical contaminants are any foreign material introduced into the food. Metal shavings spewed from a dull blade on a can opener and toothpicks left in food are examples. Accidental spills of cleaning agents into food, pesticides, preservatives, and food additives are examples of possible chemical contaminants.

Monitoring and controlling food as it flows through the catering operation is a key catering management technique in the protection and assurance of serving safe food. Specific monitoring and controlling techniques built into the caterer's food tracking system as it flows through receiving, storage, preparation, cooking, holding, serving, cooling, and reheating is vital.

This monitoring and controlling of food as it moves through the operation is a growing concern for all caterers. The consumer expects safe food and the government demands it. There is absolutely no excuse for anything less than serving food free from bacterial, physical, or chemical contamination.

To insure food is wholesome, each and every caterer must formulate, implement, and monitor a specific plan of action individually designed to meet their needs. This individualized plan of action is called **Hazard Analysis and Critical Control Point (HACCP) plan**. A HACCP plan is a written document that delineates the formal procedures for following the Hazard Analysis Critical Control Point principles developed by The National Advisory Committee on Microbiological Criteria for Foods.

HACCP is a prevention-based, food safety plan. It is a system that identifies, monitors, and prevents or eliminates specific foodborne hazards—biological, chemical, or physical properties—that can adversely affect the safety of the food. HACCP is designed to prevent the occurrence of potential food safety problems. It represents an important food protection tool. This hazard analysis serves as the basis for establishing **critical control points (CCPs)**, which identify those points in the process that must be controlled to ensure the safety of the food. **Monitoring** and **verification steps** are included in the system, again, to ensure that potential risks are controlled. The hazard analysis, critical control points, **critical limits**, and monitoring and verification steps are documented in a HACCP plan. Seven principles have been developed to provide guidance on the development of an effective HACCP plan.

A review of the following terms and definitions will help clarify the seven principles.

◈ *Acceptable level* means the presence of a hazard which does not pose the likelihood of causing an unacceptable health risk.

◈ *Control point* means any point in a specific food system at which loss of control does not lead to an unacceptable health risk.

◈ *Critical control point,* as defined in the Food Code, means a point at which loss of control may result in an unacceptable health risk.

◈ *Critical limit,* as defined in the Food Code, means the maximum or minimum value to which a physical, biological, or chemical parameter must be controlled at a critical control point to minimize the risk that the identified food safety hazard may occur.

◈ *Deviation* means failure to meet a required critical limit for a critical control point.

◈ *HACCP plan,* as defined in the Food Code, means a written document that delineates the formal procedures for following the HACCP principles developed by The National Advisory Committee on Microbiological Criteria for Foods.

◈ *Hazard,* as defined in the Food Code, means a biological, chemical, or physical property that may cause an unacceptable consumer health risk.

◈ *Monitoring* means a planned sequence of observations or measurements of critical limits designed to produce an accurate record and intended to ensure that the critical limit maintains product safety. Continuous monitoring means an uninterrupted record of data.

◈ *Preventive measure* means an action to exclude, destroy, eliminate, or reduce a hazard and prevent recontamination through effective means.

◈ *Risk* means an estimate of the likely occurrence of a hazard.

◈ *Sensitive ingredient* means any ingredient historically associated with a known microbiological hazard that causes or contributes to production of a potentially hazardous food as defined in the Food Code.

◈ *Verification* means methods, procedures, and tests used to determine if the HACCP system in use is in compliance with the HACCP plan.

History

The application of HACCP to food production was pioneered by the Pillsbury Company with the cooperation and participation of the National Aeronautic and Space Administration (NASA), Natick Laboratories of the U.S. Army, and the U.S. Air Force Space Laboratory Project Group. Application of the system in the early 1960s provided food safety recommendations for the U.S. space program. The final product for NASA had an almost 100% assurance against contamination by bacterial and viral pathogens, toxins, and chemical or physical hazards. These hazards could cause illness or injury to astronauts while in space. HACCP provided a preventive system for producing safe food that had universal application.

In the succeeding years, the HACCP system has been recognized worldwide as an effective system of controls. The system has undergone considerable analysis, refinement, and testing, and is widely accepted in the U.S. and internationally.

Advantages of HACCP

The Food and Drug Administration is recommending the implementation of HACCP in catering establishments. It is the most effective and efficient way to ensure that food products are safe and wholesome. A properly designed HACCP system will:

1. delegate the caterer as the final party responsible for ensuring the safety of the food they serve.

2. provide continuous self-inspection through the monitoring, controlling, and prevention of food-related problems. Traditional inspection procedures by regulatory agencies are relatively resource-intensive and inefficient.

3. establish critical limits and identify critical control points and monitoring procedures. A critical item, if in a noncompliance, is more likely than other violations to contribute to food contamination, illness, or environmental health hazard. Critical limit means the maximum or minimum value to which a physical, biological, or a chemical parameter must be controlled at a critical control point to minimize the risk that the identified food safety hazard may occur. Critical control point means the last step, point, or procedure in a specific food system where the caterer can intervene to prevent, control or eliminate an unacceptable health risk.

4. create records that document adherence of operational procedures to rational, scientifically-based data.

5. organize a preventive process rather than a reactive reflex to a periodic regulatory "snapshot" inspection.

6. integrate HACCP-based procedure into daily employee and staff standard operating procedures. Management reinforcements of HACCP techniques and employee training are key factors to successful implementation.

7. make the system self-perpetuating so as not to rely on periodic facility inspections by regulatory agencies.

8. allow the regulatory agency to better determine a caterer's level of compliance by reviewing records and other documentation to verify that the HACCP is working.

To effectively create a HACCP plan, a team should be assembled to work on formulating this plan. Members of an HACCP team may include the catering manager, food production manager, service manager, service and production employees, supplier and/or equipment representatives, members of the local regulatory agencies and the professional pest control operator. Team members should be selected according to their ability to:

1. establish a clear mission and obtainable goals.

2. delegate responsibilities, authority, and assign accountability.

3. be cohesive when challenging each other but congenial when working together.

4. be familiar with the caterer's operation and their customers' needs, wants, and demands.

5. know of the specific production processes and service styles used by the caterer.

6. possess a basic understanding of microbiology.

7. understand how contamination occurs and know appropriate personal hygiene standards.

The implementation of HACCP principles continues to evolve. HACCP principles change as new menu items, recipes, food production, and service procedures are developed within the organization; as they are mandated by the individual state or the Food and Drug Administration; and as hazards and their control measures are more clearly defined by scientists.

To meet the challenges, caterers must keep themselves currently informed of these ongoing developments. Sources of information that can be particularly helpful include trade publications issued by the food industry, professional organizations, the Food and Drug Administration's Web site (www.fda.gov), and continuing education programs. Food safety training sponsored by the National Restaurant Association, and through colleges and universities, are also excellent resources.

SEVEN PRINCIPLES OF HACCP

The National Advisory Committee on Microbiological Criteria for Foods (NACMCF), which developed HACCP principles, was established in 1988. Its members include officials from several federal agencies including the Food and

Drug Administration, Centers for Disease Control and Prevention, Food Safety Inspection Service, Agricultural Research Service, National Marine Fisheries Service, and U.S. Army. The NACMCF also has national experts from academia, state government, consumer groups, and the food industry.

The NACMCF has developed seven widely accepted HACCP principles that explain this process in great detail. To prepare an effective HACCP plan these principles must be followed. Further, a comprehensive review of a HACCP plan must include consideration of these principles:

Principle 1: Hazard analysis

Principle 2: Identify the critical control points (CCP) in food production

Principle 3: Establish critical limits for preventative measures

Principle 4: Establish procedures to monitor CCPs: observations and measurements

Principle 5: Establish the corrective action to be taken when monitoring shows that a critical limit has been exceeded

Principle 6: Establish procedures to verify that the HACCP system is working

Principle 7: Establish effective record keeping systems that document the HACCP system

Principle 1: Hazard Analysis

The hazard analysis process accomplishes three purposes.

1. Identifies potential hazards by surveying menus and recipe files

2. Provides a risk basis for which a biological, chemical, or physical property may cause an unacceptable consumer health risk

3. Leads to development of preventive measures. These may include designing a specific process or a substitute product to ensure or improve food safety.

The first step in the development of a HACCP plan is the identification of hazards associated with the product. A hazard may be a biological, chemical, or physical property that can cause a food to be unsafe. The analysis of hazards requires the assessment of two factors with respect to any identified hazard, i.e., the likelihood that the hazard will occur and the severity if it does occur. Hazard analysis also involves the establishment of preventive measures for control. A HACCP plan does not have to include any hazards that involve low risk and that are not likely to occur. The HACCP plan will include all *potentially hazardous* foods.

Potentially hazardous food means a food that meets the following criteria:

1. natural or synthetic that requires temperature control because it is in a form capable of supporting the rapid and progressive growth of microorganisms.

2. a food that has a pH 4.6 or below when measured at 75°F (24°C)

3. a food with a water activity (a_w value of) 0.85 or higher

4. a food of animal origin that is raw or heat-treated

5. a food of plant origin that is heat-treated or consists of raw seed sprouts, cut melons, or garlic-in-oil mixtures that support bacterial growth.

Potentially hazardous foods do not include an air-cooled hard-boiled egg with shell intact, or a food in unopened, hermetically sealed containers. Nor do they include foods that are commercially processed to achieve and maintain commercial sterility under conditions of nonrefrigerated storage and distribution.

To be effectively addressed, hazards must be such that their prevention, elimination, or reduction to acceptable levels is attained. Numerous issues have to be considered during hazard analysis. These relate to factors such as ingredients, processing, distribution, and the intended use of the product. These issues include whether a food contains **sensitive ingredients** that can create microbiological, chemical, or physical hazards; or whether the lack of sanitation practices that are used can introduce these hazards to the food that is being prepared or processed. An example is whether the finished food will be reheated by the caterer and if it will be consumed off the premises. Even factors beyond the immediate control of the caterer must be considered. How will the food be treated if taken out by the consumer? How will it be consumed? These factors must be considered because they could influence how food should be prepared or processed in the catering operation.

Flow Diagram

The common path that food follows through the operation is known as the *flow of food*. A flow diagram (Figure 6–5) will display each step in the process from receiving, storage, preparation, and holding to sale, and service. This flow chart forms the foundation for applying the seven principles and will be used to determine the CCPs. The significant hazards associated with each step in the flow diagram should be listed along with preventative measures proposed to control the hazards.

The flow diagram should be constructed by a HACCP team. This team must have the knowledge and expertise of the product, process, and likely hazards associated with the caterer's production system and menus. The HACCP team must accurately construct a flow chart for each potentially hazardous food depicted on the caterer's menus.

Biological Hazards

Foodborne biological hazards include bacterial, viral, and parasitic organisms. These organisms are commonly associated with the food handlers and with raw products entering the catering operation. Many of these pathogens occur naturally in the environment where foods are grown or are carried on the skin, hands,

HACCP INSPECTION DATA FLOW DIAGRAM

EST. NAME: PERMIT NO.:   INSPECTOR:

DATE: TIME IN: AM / PM   TIME OUT: AM/ PM

Record all observations below - transfer violations to Inspection Report

FOOD TEMPERATURES / TIMES / OTHER CRITICAL LIMITS

Use Additional Forms If Necessary

FOOD	1	CRITICAL LIMIT	2	CRITICAL LIMIT	3	CRITICAL LIMIT	4	CRITICAL LIMIT
STEP								
A. SOURCE								
B. STORAGE								
C. PREP BEFORE COOK								
D. COOK								
E. PREP AFTER COOK								
F. HOT/COLD HOLD								
G. DISPLAY/ SERVICE								
H. COOL								
I. REHEAT								

OTHER FOOD TEMPERATURES OBSERVED   Use steps from above for location

FOOD	TEMP.	STEP	FOOD	TEMP.	STEP	FOOD	TEMP.	STEP

Figure 6-5 HACCP inspection data flow diagram. (Adapted from the 1999 FDA Model Food Code.)

or nose and throat of the food handler. Preventative measures include cooking to final cooking temperatures and following HACCP cooling, distribution, and storage procedures (Figure 6–6).

Bacteria cause the majority of reported foodborne disease outbreaks and cases. A foodborne disease outbreak means the occurrence of two or more cases of a similar illness resulting from the ingestion of a common food.

Because many of these disease-causing bacteria occur naturally in the environment where foods are grown, the caterer can expect a certain level of these pathogens with some raw foods. Poultry products may be contaminated with the salmonella bacteria which may already be present at the time the product is received by the caterer. Therefore, it is imperative to establish and follow HACCP recommended temperatures as this food item flows through the operation. Improper temperature abuse, such as improper hot or cold holding temperatures, can create favorable environmental conditions for bacteria. This will create unhealthful conditions causing rapid and progressive growth of bacteria. Likewise, cooked food, which has been subject to bacterial cross-contamination, often provides a fertile environment for the rapid and progressive growth of this bacteria.

Viruses can be foodborne, waterborne, or transmitted from a person or animal. Unlike bacteria, a virus cannot multiply outside of a living cell. Hepatitis A

Figure 6-6 *Fans and air-conditioning units are available to help maintain proper holding temperatures.*

and Norwalk viruses are examples of viral hazards associated with ready-to-eat foods.

Parasites are most often animal host-specific and can include humans in their life cycles. Parasitic infections are commonly associated with undercooking meat products or cross-contamination of ready-to-eat food. Fishborne parasites in products that are intended to be eaten raw, marinated, or partially cooked can be killed by effective freezing techniques.

Chemical Hazards

Chemical hazards in foods should be considered during a hazard analysis. Chemical contaminants may be naturally occurring or may be added during the processing of food. Harmful chemicals at very high levels have been associated with acute cases of foodborne illnesses and can be responsible for chronic illness at lower levels.

Physical Hazards

Illness and injury can result from hard, foreign objects in food. These physical hazards can result from contamination and/or poor procedures. Physical contamination may happen at many points in the food chain, from harvest to consumer, including those within the catering establishment. Physical contaminants include glass, wood, toothpicks, stones, metal fragments, band-aids, pieces of bone, packaging material, pins, and jewelry.

Determining the Level of Risk

The potential significance or **risk** of each hazard should be assessed by considering its likelihood of occurrence and severity. The estimate of risk for a hazard occurring is based upon a combination of experience, specialized data, and technical information. **Severity** is the degree of seriousness of the consequences of a hazard if it were to become an actuality.

Hazard identification, in conjunction with risk estimation, provides a rational basis for determining which hazards are significant. Hazard identification must be addressed in the HACCP plan. To determine risk during the hazard analysis, safety concerns must be differentiated from quality concerns. A food safety hazard is a biological, chemical, or physical property that may cause a food to be unsafe. There may be differences of opinion, even among experts, as to the risk of a hazard. The caterer must rely upon the expert opinion published in peer-reviewed literature or from experts who actively assist in the development of the HACCP plan. The hazards must at least include those that are commonly associated with a specific product. If a hazard that is commonly associated is dismissed from the plan, the basis for rejecting it must be clearly stated in the hazard analysis so that it is understood and agreed to by the regulatory authority reviewing the HACCP plan.

Hazard Analysis Process

This point in hazard analysis consists of asking a series of questions which are appropriate to each step in the flow diagram. The hazard analysis should question the effect of a variety of factors upon the safety of the food (Figure 6–7). These factors include the ingredients, procedures for the preparation of the food, microbial contents of the food, facility design, equipment design, food packaging, sanitation practices, employee health and hygiene, storage conditions, food's intended use and the intended consumer.

HAZARD ANALYSIS FOOD SAFETY FACTORS

1. Does the food contain any sensitive ingredients that are likely to present microbiological hazards, chemical hazards, or physical hazards?
2. Physical characteristics and composition (e.g., pH, types of acids, fermentable carbohydrate, water activity, preservatives) of the food during and after preparation can cause or prevent a hazard.
    - Which intrinsic factors of the food must be controlled in order to ensure food safety?
    - Does the food permit survival or multiplication of pathogens and/or toxin formation in the food before or during preparation?
    - Will the food permit survival or multiplication of pathogens and/or toxin formation during subsequent steps of preparation, storage, or consumer possession?
    - Are there other similar products in the marketplace? What has been the safety record for these products?

Procedures for the Preparation of Food

1. Does the preparation procedure or process include a controllable step that destroys pathogens or their toxins? Consider both vegetative cells and spores.
2. Is the product subject to cross-contamination between the preparation step (e.g., cooking) and packaging?

Microbial Content of the Food

1. Is the food commercially sterile (i.e., low-acid canned food)?
2. Is it likely that the food will contain viable spore-forming or nonspore forming pathogens?
3. What is the normal microbial content of the food stored under proper conditions?
4. Does the microbial population change during the time the food is stored before consumption?
5. Does that change in microbial population alter the safety of the food?

(continued)

Figure 6-7 *Hazard analysis food safety factors. (Adapted from the 1999 FDA Model Food Code.)*

Facility Design

1. Does the layout of the facility provide an adequate separation of raw materials from ready-to-eat foods?
2. Is positive air pressure maintained in product packaging areas? Is this essential for product safety?
3. Is the traffic pattern for people and moving equipment a potentially significant source of contamination?

Equipment Design

1. Will the equipment provide the time/temperature control that is necessary for safe food?
2. Is the equipment properly sized for the volume of food that will be prepared?
3. Can the equipment be sufficiently controlled so that the variation in performance will be within the tolerances required to produce a safe food?
4. Is the equipment reliable or is it prone to frequent breakdowns?
5. Is the equipment designed so that it can be cleaned and sanitized?
6. Is there a chance for product contamination with hazardous substances, e.g., glass?
7. What product safety devices such as time/temperature integrators are used to enhance consumer safety?

Packaging

1. Does the method of packaging affect the multiplication of microbial pathogens and/or the formation of toxins?
2. Is the packaging material resistant to damage, thereby preventing the entrance of microbial contamination?
3. Is the package clearly labeled "Keep Refrigerated" if this is required for safety?
4. Does the package include instructions for the safe handling and preparation of the food by the consumer?
5. Are tamper-evident packaging features used?
6. Is each package legibly and accurately coded to indicate a production lot?
7. Is each package properly labeled?

Sanitation Practices

1. Will the sanitation practices by the employees impact upon the safety of the food that is being prepared?
2. Can the facility be cleaned and sanitized to permit the safe handling of food?
3. Is it possible to provide sanitary conditions consistently and adequately to ensure safe foods?

(continued)

Figure 6-7 *Hazard analysis food safety factors (continued). (Adapted from the 1999 FDA Model Food Code.)*

Employee Health, Hygiene, and Education

1. Can employee health or personal hygiene practices impact the safety of the food being prepared?
2. Do the employees understand the food preparation process and the factors they must control to ensure safe foods?
3. Will the employees inform management of a problem which could impact food safety?

Conditions of Food Storage

1. What is the likelihood that the food will be improperly stored at the wrong temperature?
2. Would storage at improper temperatures lead to unsafe food caused by bacterial contamination?

Food's Intended Use

1. Will the food be heated by the consumer?
2. Will food be left over after service?

An Intended Consumer

1. Is the food intended for the general public (i.e., a population that does not have an increased risk of becoming ill because of it)?
2. Is the food intended for consumption by a population with increased susceptibility to illness (i.e., infants, the elderly, the infirm, and immuno-compromised individuals)?

Figure 6-7 *Hazard analysis food safety factors (continued). (Adapted from the 1999 FDA Model Food Code.)*

Developing Preventive Measures

The preventive measures' procedure identifies the steps in the process at which hazards can be controlled.

After identifying the hazards, the caterer must then consider what preventive measures, if any, can be applied for each hazard. Preventive measures are physical, chemical, or other factors that can be used to control an identified health hazard. More than one preventive measure may be required to control a specific hazard and more than one hazard may be controlled by a specified preventive measure. For example, if a HACCP team were to conduct a hazard analysis for the preparation of hamburgers from frozen beef patties, bacteria on the incoming raw meat would be identified as a potential hazard. Cooking is a preventive measure which can be used to eliminate this hazard.

Principle 2: Identify the Critical Control Points (CCPs) in Food Preparation

A CCP is a point, step, or procedure at which control can be applied and a food safety hazard can be prevented, eliminated, or reduced to acceptable levels. Points in food preparation that may be CCPs include cooking, chilling, specific sanitation procedures, product formulation control, prevention of cross-contamination, and certain aspects of employee and environmental hygiene. Cooking that must occur at a specific temperature and for a specified time in order to destroy microbiological pathogens is a critical control point. Likewise, refrigeration or the adjustment of a food's pH are CCPs. The pH must be adjusted to a level necessary to prevent hazardous microorganisms from multiplying or toxins from forming in the food.

Many points in food preparation may be considered control points, but very few are actually critical control points. A control point is any point, step, or procedure at which biological, physical, or chemical factors can be controlled. Concerns that do not impact food safety may be addressed at control points; however, since these control points do not relate to food safety, they are not included in the HACCP plan.

Different caterers preparing the same food can differ in the risk of hazards and the points, steps, or procedures which are CCPs. This can be due to differences in layout, equipment, selection of ingredients, or the process that is used at each facility. Generic HACCP plans can serve as useful guides; however, it is essential that the unique conditions within each caterer's facility be considered during the development of a HACCP plan.

CCPs must be carefully developed and documented. In addition, they must be used only for purposes of product safety. The following decision tree (Figure 6–8) is helpful in verifying which of the food preparation steps should be designated as CCPs.

Principle 3: Establish Critical Limits for Preventive Measures (Associated with Each Identified CCP)

This step involves establishing a criterion that must be met for each preventive measure associated with a CCP. Critical limits can be thought of as safety boundaries for each CCP and may be set for temperature, time, physical dimensions, a_w, pH, and available chlorine. Critical limits may be derived from sources such as regulatory standards and guidelines (FDA Model Food Code), scientific literature, experimental studies, and consultation with experts.

When establishing critical limits, they should be specific to the caterer's operation: appropriate for the kind of food normally prepared and the type of production equipment used. The critical limits should also be easy for the employees to implement and for management to monitor.

Critical Limit

A critical limit is defined as a criterion that must be met for each preventive measure associated with a CCP. Each CCP will have one or more preventive measures that must be properly controlled to ensure prevention, elimination, or

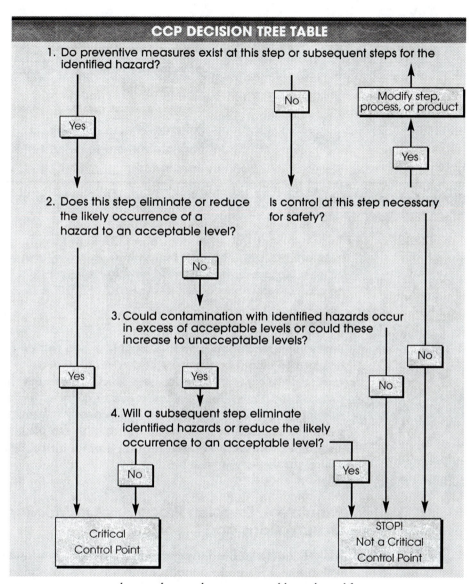

Figure 6-8 *Critical control point decision tree table.* (*Adapted from* NACMCF.)

reduction of hazards to acceptable levels.   The food establishment is responsible for using competent authorities to validate that the critical limits chosen will control the identified hazard.

Target Level

In some cases, variables involved in food preparation may require certain target levels to ensure that critical limits are not exceeded. A preventive measure and critical limit may be an internal product temperature of 160°F (71°C) during one

Process Step	CCP	Critical Limits
Cooking	YES	Minimum internal temperature of patty: 155°F/ 68°C
		Broiler temperature: _____ °F/ _____ °C
		Time: rate of heating/cooling
		(i.e., conveyer belt speed in): min/cm: _____ ft/min
		Patty thickness: _____ in /cm _____
		Patty composition: e.g., % Fat, % Filler
		Oven humidity: _____ % RH

Figure 6-9 *Critical control points and critical limits for a ground beef patty. (Adapted from the 1999 FDA Model Food Code.)*

stage of a process. The oven temperature, however, may be 160°F (71°C); thus an oven target temperature would have to be greater than 165°F (74°C) so that no product receives a cook of less than 160°F (71°C).

Application Example

An example for Principle 3 is the cooking of beef patties. The process should be designed to eliminate the most heat-resistant vegetative pathogen that could reasonably be expected to be in the product. Criteria may be required for factors such as temperature, time, and meat patty thickness. Technical development of the appropriate critical limits requires accurate information on the probable maximum numbers of these microorganisms in the meat and their heat resistance. The relationship between the CCP and its critical limits for the meat patty example is shown in Figure 6–9.

Principle 4: Establish Procedures to Monitor CCPs: Observations and Measurements

Monitoring is a planned sequence of observations or measurements used to assess whether a CCP is under control or to produce an accurate record for use in future verification procedures. There are three main purposes for monitoring.

1. It tracks the system's operation so that a trend toward a loss of control can be recognized and corrective action can be taken to bring the process back into control before a deviation occurs.

2. It indicates when loss of control and a deviation have actually occurred, and corrective action must be taken.

3. It provides written documentation for use in verification of the HACCP plan. Examples of monitoring measurements include visual observations, temperatures, time constraints, pH levels, and water activity.

Continuous Monitoring

An unsafe food may result if a process is not properly controlled or a deviation occurs. Because of the potentially serious consequences of a critical defect, monitoring procedures must be effective.

Continuous monitoring is always preferred, and is possible with many types of physical and chemical methods. The temperature and time for an institutional cook-chill operation can be recorded continuously on temperature recording charts. If the temperature falls below the scheduled temperature or the time is insufficient, as recorded on the chart, the batch must be recorded as a process deviation and reprocessed or discarded.

Instrumentation used by the food establishment for measuring critical limits must be carefully calibrated for accuracy. Records of calibrations must be maintained as a part of the HACCP plan documentation.

Monitoring Procedures

When it is not possible to monitor a critical limit on a continuous basis, it is necessary to establish that the monitoring interval will be reliable enough to indicate that the hazard is under control. Statistically designed data collection or sampling systems lend themselves to this purpose. When statistical process control is used, it is important to recognize that violations of critical limits must not occur. If a temperature of 155°F (68°C) or higher is required for product safety, the minimum temperature of the product may be set at a target that is above this temperature to compensate for variation.

Most monitoring procedures for CCPs will need to be done rapidly because the time frame between food preparation and consumption does not allow for lengthy analytical testing. Microbiological testing is seldom effective for monitoring CCPs because of its time-consuming nature. Therefore, physical and chemical measurements are preferred because they may be done rapidly and can indicate whether microbiological control is occurring.

Assignment of responsibility for monitoring is an important consideration for each CCP within the operation. Specific assignments will depend on the number of CCPs, preventive measures, and the complexity of monitoring. The most appropriate employees for such assignments are often directly associated with the operation, such as the caterer, chefs, and departmental supervisors.

Individuals monitoring CCPs must be trained in the monitoring technique, completely understand the purpose and importance of monitoring, and be unbiased in monitoring and reporting so that monitoring is accurately recorded. The designated individuals must have ready access to the CCP being monitored and to the calibrated instrumentation designated in the HACCP plan.

The person responsible for monitoring is also responsible for recording if the catering operation produces a product that does not meet critical limits to ensure that immediate corrective action can be taken. All records and documents associated with CCP monitoring must be signed or initialed by the person doing the monitoring.

Random checks may be useful in supplementing the monitoring of certain CCPs. They may be used to check incoming ingredients, serve as a check for compliance where ingredients are recertified as meeting certain standards, and assess factors such as equipment. Random checks are also advisable for monitoring environmental factors such as airborne contamination and cleaning and sanitizing gloves.

Principle 5: Establish the Corrective Action to Be Taken when Monitoring Shows that a Critical Limit Has Been Exceeded

Purpose of a Corrective Action Plan

Although the HACCP system is intended to prevent deviations from occurring, perfection is rarely, if ever, achievable. Thus, there must be a corrective action plan in place to:

1. determine the disposition of any food that was produced when a deviation was occurring.

2. correct the cause of the deviation and ensure that the critical control point is under control.

3. maintain records of corrective actions.

Aspects of the Corrective Action Plan

Because of the variations in CCPs for different catering operations and the diversity of possible deviations, specific corrective action plans must be developed for each CCP. The actions must demonstrate that the CCP has been brought under control. Individuals who have a thorough understanding of the operation, product, and HACCP must be assigned responsibility for taking corrective action. Corrective action procedures must be documented in the HACCP plan.

Food establishments covered by the Food Code will usually be concerned with food which has a limited shelf life and distribution. A primary focus for the application of this HACCP principle will be on the correction of the procedure or condition which led to the noncompliance. More frequent monitoring may be temporarily required to ensure that the deviation from the established critical limit is not continuing when the operation is resumed.

Principle 6: Establish Procedures to Verify that the HACCP System is Working

The first phase of the process is the scientific or technical verification that critical limits at CCPs are satisfactory. This can be complex and may require intensive involvement of highly skilled professionals from a variety of disciplines capable of doing focused studies and analyses. A review of the critical limits is necessary to verify that the limits are adequate to control the hazards that are likely to occur.

The second phase of verification ensures that the facility's HACCP plan is functioning effectively. A functioning HACCP system requires little end-product sampling, since appropriate safeguards are built in early in the food preparation. Therefore, rather than relying on end-product sampling, a caterer will rely on frequent reviews of their HACCP plan, verification that the HACCP plan is being correctly followed, review of CCP records, and determinations that appropriate risk management decisions and product dispositions are made when preparation deviations occur.

The third phase consists of documented, periodic revalidations, independent of audits or other verification procedures, that must be performed to ensure the accuracy of the HACCP plan. Revalidations are performed by a HACCP team on a regular basis and/or whenever significant product, preparation, or packaging changes require modification of the HACCP plan. The revalidation includes a documented on-site review and verification of all flow diagrams and CCPs in the HACCP plan. The HACCP team modifies the HACCP plan as necessary.

The fourth phase of verification deals with the regulatory agency's responsibility and actions to ensure that the establishment's HACCP system is functioning satisfactorily. Figure 6–10 provides examples to help the caterer with the verification part of the HACCP plan.

Training and Knowledge

Training and knowledge are very important in making HACCP plan successful in any food establishment. HACCP works best when it is integrated into each employee's normal duties rather than added as something extra.

Focus and Objective. The depth and breadth of training will depend on the particular employee's responsibilities within the establishment. Management or supervisory individuals will need a deeper understanding of the HACCP process because they are responsible for proper plan implementation and routine monitoring of CCPs such as product cooking temperatures and cooling times (Figures 6–11 and 6–12). The training plan should be specific to the establishment's operation rather than attempt to develop HACCP expertise for broad application.

The food employees' training should provide an overview of HACCP's prevention philosophy while focusing on the specifics of the employees' normal functions. The CCPs such as proper hand washing and use of utensils or gloves for working with ready-to-eat food should be stressed. The use of recipes or Standard Operating Procedures (SOPs), which include the critical limits of cooking times and temperatures, with a final cooking time and temperature measurement step, should be included.

VERIFYING A HACCP PLAN

Activities

1. Establishment of appropriate verification inspection schedules
2. Review of the HACCP plan
3. Review of CCP records
4. Review of deviations and their resolution, including the disposition of food
5. Visual inspections of operations to observe if CCPs are under control
6. Random sample collection and analysis
7. Review of critical limits to verify that they are adequate to control hazards
8. Review of written record of verification inspections which certifies compliance with the HACCP plan or deviations from the plan, and the corrective actions taken
9. Validation of the HACCP plan, including on-site review and verification of flow diagrams and CCPs
10. Review of modifications of the HACCP plan

Verification Inspections should be conducted:

1. routinely or on an unannounced basis, to ensure that selected CCPs are under control.
2. when it is determined that intensive coverage of a specific food is needed because of new information concerning food safety.
3. when foods prepared at the establishment have been implicated as a vehicle of foodborne disease.
4. when requested on a consultative basis, and resources allow accommodating the request.
5. when established criteria have not been met.
6. to verify that changes have been implemented correctly after a HACCP has been modified.

Information on a Verification Report should include:

1. existence of a HACCP plan and the person(s) responsible for administering and updating it.
2. the status of records associated with CCP monitoring.
3. direct monitoring data of the CCP while in operation.
4. certification that monitoring equipment is properly calibrated and in working order.
5. deviations and corrective actions.
6. any samples analyzed, using physical, chemical, microbiological, or organoleptic methods, to verify that CCPs are under control.
7. modifications to the HACCP plan.
8. training and knowledge of individuals responsible for monitoring CCPs.

Figure 6-10 Verifying a HACCP plan. (Adapted from the 1999 FDA Model Food Code.)

MINIMUM COOKING FOOD TEMPERATURES AND HOLDING TIMES

Food	Minimum Temperature	Minimum Holding Time
Unpasteurized shell eggs prepared for immediate service	145°F (63°C)	15 Seconds
Commercially-raised game animals		
Fish, pork, and meat		
Unpasteurized shell eggs not prepared for immediate service	158°F (70°C)	< 1 second
Exotic species of game animals	155°F (68°C)	15 seconds
Comminuted fish and meats	150°F (66°C)	1 minute
Injected meats	145°F (63°C)	3 minutes
Poultry; stuffed fish; stuffed meat; stuffed pasta; stuffed poultry; stuffing containing fish, meat, or poultry; wild game animals	165°F (74°C)	15 seconds
Food cooked in a microwave oven	165°F (74°C)	and hold for 2 minutes after removing from microwave oven

Figure 6-11 *Minimum cooking food temperatures and holding times. (Adapted from the* 1999 *FDA Model Food Code.)*

MINIMUM FOOD TEMPERATURES AND HOLDING TIMES FOR REHEATING FOODS FOR HOT HOLDING

Food	Minimum Temp	Minimum Holding Time at the Specified Temp	Maximum Time to Reach Minimum Temp
Food that is cooked, cooled, and reheated	165°F (74°C)	15 seconds	2 hours
Food that is reheated in a microwave oven	165°F (74°C)	and hold for 2 min. after removing from microwave oven	2 hours
Food that is taken from a commercially processed, hermetically sealed container or intact package	140°F (60°C)	No time specified	2 hours

Figure 6-12 *Minimum food temperatures and holding times for reheating food for hot holding. (Adapted from the* 1999 *FDA Model Food Code.)*

For all employees, the fundamental training goal should be to make them proficient in the specific tasks which the HACCP plan requires them to perform. This includes the development of a level of competency in their decision making about the implementation of proper corrective actions when monitoring reveals violation of the critical limit (Figure 6–13). The training should also include the proper completion and maintenance of any records specified in the establishment's plan.

FOOD ESTABLISHMENT INSPECTION REPORT

ESTABLISHMENT:	**PERMIT NUMBER:**	**DATE:**	
ADDRESS:	**CITY:**	**STATE:**	**ZIP:**
PERSON IN CHARGE/TITLE:		**TELEPHONE:**	
INSPECTOR:			
INSPECTION TYPE: ROUTINE	FOLLOW-UP	COMPLAINT	OTHER:	TIME:

Critical (X)	Repeat (X)	Code Reference	Violation Description / Remarks / Corrections

Figure 6-13 *Food establishment inspection report. (Adapted from the 1999 FDA Model Food Code.)*

Reinforcement

Training reinforcement is also needed for continued motivation of the food establishment employees. Some examples might include:

1. a HACCP video training program such as the Pennsylvania Department of Environmental Regulation's *Foodborne Illness: It's Your Business*.

2. changing reminders about HACCP critical limits such as "HAND-WASHING PAYS BIG DIVIDENDS" printed on employees' time cards or checks.

3. work station reminders such as pictorials on how and when to take food temperatures.

Every time there is a change in a product or food operation within the establishment, the HACCP training needs should be evaluated. When a food establishment substitutes a frozen seafood product for a fresh one, proper thawing critical limits should be taught and then monitored for implementation. The employees should be made sensitive to how the changes will affect food safety.

The HACCP plan should include a feedback loop for employees to suggest what additional training is needed. All employees should be made a part of the continuous food safety improvement cycle because the old statement is very true: "The customer's health is in their hands." This helps maintain their active awareness and involvement in the importance of each job to the safety of the food provided by their establishment.

Principle 7: Establish Effective Record-Keeping Systems that Document the HACCP System

This principle requires the preparation and maintenance of a written HACCP plan by the caterer. The plan must detail the hazards of each individual or categorical product covered by the plan. It must clearly identify the CCPs and critical limits for each CCP. CCP monitoring and record-keeping procedures must be shown in the establishment's HACCP plan. HACCP implementation strategy should be provided as a part of the caterer's documentation.

Record Keeping

Principle #7 requires the maintenance of records generated during the operation of the plan. The record-keeping procedure ultimately makes the system work. One conclusion of a study of HACCP performed by the U.S. Department of Commerce is that correcting a problem without record keeping almost guarantees that problems will recur. The requirement to record events at CCPs on a regular basis ensures that preventive monitoring is occurring in a systematic way.

Unusual occurrences that are discovered as CCPs are monitored, or that otherwise come to light, must be corrected and recorded immediately with notation of the corrective action taken.

The level of sophistication of the record keeping necessary for the caterer is dependent on the complexity of the food preparation operation. A *sous vidé* process or cook-chill operation for a large institution would require more record keeping than a limited menu, cook-serve operation. The simplest, effective, record-keeping system—that lends itself well to integration within the existing operation—is best.

Contents of the Plan and Records

The approved HACCP plan and associated records must be on file at the catering operation. Generally, the following items are examples of supporting documentation that can be included in the total HACCP system.

Supporting Documentation for a HACCP Plan

(Adapted from the 1999 FDA Model Food Code.)

1. listing of the HACCP team and assigned responsibilities
2. description of the product and its intended use
3. flow diagram of food preparation indicating CCPs
4. hazards associated with each CCP and preventive measures
5. critical limits
6. monitoring system
7. corrective action plans for deviations from critical limits
8. procedures for verification of HACCP system
9. record-keeping procedures

Summary

HACCP is a systematic approach that dramatically improves the level of food safety. The NACMCF has developed the seven HACCP principles discussed, and the FDA recommends the implementation of a HACCP system throughout the food industry.

An effective national food safety program from food production to consumer is enhanced by the implementation of HACCP. The statistics from foodborne surveillance reveal that retail level food establishments can have a significant impact on the health of consumers.

Implementation of HACCP programs by food establishments profoundly enhances their role in the protection of public health beyond the traditional emphasis on facility and equipment design, maintenance, and adherence to the principles of sanitation, good manufacturing, and food preparation practices. The education and training of all personnel are critical to the success and effectiveness of any HACCP program. The Food Code stresses the application to HACCP principles and the knowledge and responsibilities of establishment management and employees.

Specific HACCP plans for products prepared and sold by retail food establishments should be developed and implemented for optimal food safety management. HACCP systems are recommended for use as a tool for regulatory inspections. The regulatory official should incorporate procedures in the inspection process that ensure record reviews and active monitoring.

Because the catering industry is composed of large, small, corporate, and independent establishments, the level of food safety expertise varies widely and is not necessarily linked to either size or affiliation. Regardless of the size and sophistication of the establishment, a HACCP plan for safe food preparation and sales needs to be designed, implemented, and verified.

Studies have shown that a significant level of illness and mortality from foodborne disease in institutional feeding operations such as hospitals, nursing homes, and prisons is related to preventable causes. For populations that may be more vulnerable to foodborne disease, the FDA and the NACMCF recommend that HACCP systems be immediately implemented by establishments and institutions preparing foods for these susceptible individuals.

Catering establishments have the primary responsibility for food safety. The development and implementation of HACCP programs is a reliable and responsible step to help ensure the safety of food offered for consumption.

Review Questions

Brief Answers

1. Explain why the planning function is the first catering management task.

2. Explain why successful caterers are well focused and organized.

3. Discuss the four basic questions experienced caterers always think about when planning for their future events.

4. Discuss why a budget is a key factor when a caterer is formulating a catering plan.

5. Identify the basic menu formats used by a caterer. Explain the advantages and disadvantages of each format. What factors would influence a caterer's decision to use each format?

6. Discuss why each catering event is driven by its own set of objectives. Identify two common objectives which all caterers must address regardless of the event.

7. Why is a budget considered a financial plan? Explain how a budget guides a caterer when formulating a plan. What information or elements does a budget provide for the caterer?

8. Explain why the catering menu is the single most important factor in the formulation of the overall catering plan.

9. Explain what is meant by the term *overproducing* when discussing customer satisfaction.

10. Define *operational tasks*. Why is it important for a caterer to identify all operational tasks when formulating a plan.

11. Explain why a caterer holds post-event team meetings. Discuss what kind of information a caterer would seek at this meeting.

12. Explain why catering plans must be flexible.

13. Explain the following Ingredients for Success and what they mean to you.

Ingredient for Success 18: "Strategies emerge as an outcome of planning."

Ingredient for Success 19: "The longer the length of time between booking the event and its implementation date, the better opportunity a caterer has to create a detailed plan."

Ingredient for Success 20: "To satisfy customer needs, the caterer must overproduce to exceed customer expectations."

Ingredient for Success 21: "Outside suppliers are as important as a caterer's own key personnel."

Multiple Choice

Select the single best answer for each question.

1. Barriers that interfere with the tangible elements of the implementation of a catering event are called:
   a. communication barriers
   b. human resource barriers
   c. operational barriers
   d. intangible barriers
   e. governmental barriers

2. The first catering management function is _____ .
   a. controlling the budget
   b. creating "what if" scenarios
   c. building an event-specific menu
   d. formulation of a catering plan
   e. implementation of the catering plan

3. Which of the following is an advantage of having a standardized catering menu?
   a. excessive inventory
   b. limited menu selections
   c. complex kitchen layout
   d. uncontrollable costs
   e. lower profit margins

True or False

Read each of the following statements and determine if it is true or false.

1. A catering plan provides direction and identifies each course of action required to accomplish predetermined objectives.

2. The longer the length of time between booking the event and its implementation date, the better opportunity a caterer has to create a detailed plan.

3. The planning sequence will always begin with a review of the caterer's mission statement.

Putting It All Together

You are the owner of the Allegheny Catering Company. The Allegheny Catering Company is located on the beautiful Allegheny Mountain Range situated around the Allegheny River, all nestled in the Allegheny National Forest in Northwestern Pennsylvania.

Your market niche services corporate clientele who seek outdoor adventure activities year-round—activities such as fishing, hunting, horseback riding, boating, and hiking the forest and streams within the Allegheny National Forest.

The Allegheny Catering Company has been contacted by Slugger Computer International Distribution (SCID) to cater an event for twenty-five company personnel. These guests will be attending an adventure-theme management training program. The program will last four days and include adventure-based theme training.

On the evening of the fifth day, a graduation ceremony will be held for the twenty-five participants. The location of the graduation ceremony and catering site is a plateau off a mountainous trail two miles inside the Allegheny National Forest. The only available natural resource at your disposal is potable spring water. Everything else must be brought to the site by either horseback or all-terrain vehicles.

Your task is to formulate a functional HACCP plan to serve each of the twenty-five people the following menu:

> a fresh garden salad with choice of three dressings
>
> one – 1/2 barbeque chicken
>
> one – 6-ounce New York Strip steak
>
> one – 60-count baked potato
>
> one – 4-inch ear of sweet corn on the cob
>
> a sundae ice cream bar offering a minimum of three toppings
>
> a selection of at least four beverages—two nonalcoholic

The steak and chicken will be the only food prepared at the site. Food will be served at 12:00 P.M. on a Saturday in October. The event is being held in the autumn to take advantage of the colorful leaves prevalent during this time of the year.

Chapter Seven

Operations— Execution of Tasks

Key Terms

operations
front-of-the-house
back-of-the-house
physical, mechanical, and
financial catering activities
menu development
recipe
standardized recipe
recipe development
recipe research
field testing
signature recipe
base recipe
scratch foods
convenience foods
principal
speed scratch cooking
branded menu items
plate presentation
flow of food
staffing
scheduling
work production schedule
employee work schedule

Objectives

After studying this chapter, you should be able to:

◆ Describe a caterer's operation.
◆ Explain elements of the front-of-the-house operations
◆ Explain elements of the back-of-the house operations.
◆ Describe operational tasks.
◆ Explain how to formulate a recipe.
◆ Describe how critical the *flow of food* through the operations is to operations.
◆ Describe a standardized recipe.
◆ Provide examples of how caterers can create new recipes.
◆ Describe how caterers transform customer needs into signature recipes.
◆ Explain how a caterer can utilize convenience foods.
◆ Discuss why a caterer will use branded foods on the menu.
◆ Explain why a catering menu offers several advantages over a standard restaurant menu.
◆ Explain why a caterer must build management control features into the plan.
◆ Explain the catering management task of scheduling and staffing.

161

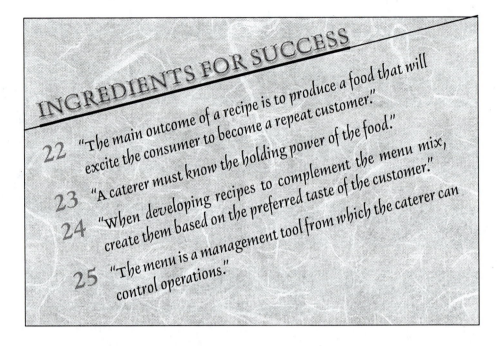

INGREDIENTS FOR SUCCESS

22 "The main outcome of a recipe is to produce a food that will excite the consumer to become a repeat customer."

23 "A caterer must know the holding power of the food."

24 "When developing recipes to complement the menu mix, create them based on the preferred taste of the customer."

25 "The menu is a management tool from which the caterer can control operations."

◆ OPERATIONS

A term used to describe the task of implementing and executing the daily elements of a catering plan is called **operations**. The second function of catering represents the transformation of the plan into the mechanical component of the catering business. The catering operation involves all activities outlined in the plan which require *front-of-the-house* and *back-of-the-house* execution.

Front-of-the-House

Front-of-the-house activities are those customer-driven service tasks designed to please the guest primarily in the dining area. These guest service activities are extremely visible to the guest. Guest service is the major focus and receives full attention in the front-of-the-house. The front-of-the-house is where customer expectations and a caterer's performance meet. At this intersection, a customer decides if their total experience, based on the combination of the food and service, meets their expectations. It can occur in the dining room, banquet room, or in the client's own home during an off-premise function (Figure 7–1).

The type of service provided depends on the catering event. Common types of service found in catering operations, as discussed in Chapter 10, include American Service, French Service, Russian Service, Self Service, and Buffet Service.

Figure 7-1 *Front-of-the-house activities should be customer-driven and aimed to please.*

Figure 7-2 *Buffet service is one example where customers may witness some back-of-the-house activities.*

Back-of-the-House

Back-of-the-house activities are not generally witnessed by the customer (Figure 7–2). These include the **physical, mechanical,** and **financial catering activities.** The physical activities include hands-on logistical tasks such as handling deliveries; purchasing, storing, preparing, and transporting food; and using proper sanitation procedures (Figure 7–3). Mechanical activities revolve around the equipment—its efficient and effective use and maintenance. Financial activities involve back-of-the-house management techniques which lead to accomplishing predetermined profit objectives by controlling food and labor costs.

Figure 7-3 *Food preparation is usually a back-of-the-house activity.*

Intangible ideas and elements of the plan become reality in the operations stage. This is where a caterer follows the blueprint to satisfy customer needs and event objectives. This is where the job gets done!

◆ OPERATIONAL TASKS

Operational tasks are a direct function of the type of catering event being implemented. Operational tasks depend on the customer and the food being prepared. Once the customer has been determined, the caterer begins the first task of operations—developing customer-approved menus.

The term *operation* is a term used to describe many interrelated activities. This term is used to simplify the assortment of activities every caterer performs for an event. Operational activities include recipes research, recipe development, scheduling production, defining customer service issues, preparation, transportation, and clean up.

The task of researching recipes follows a common path. A caterer will develop and field test recipes, create signature recipes, decide on either scratch foods or convenience foods, set and control portion size, and use brand name items.

Menu development defines the function of a menu, forecasting, pricing strategies, and item popularity and mix. Production and service are concerned with the type and layout of equipment, scheduling, employee skill level, flow of food, and sanitation. Purchasing tasks are an integral component of operations and will be discussed in Chapter 8.

◈ FLOW OF FOOD

Understanding how food moves through the operation is important. This knowledge will help a caterer effectively coordinate many numerous operational tasks that must be performed to create a finished product. The informed caterer can make better operational decisions regarding recipe development, sanitation, scheduling, receiving, storage, preparation, transportation and service of hot and cold prepared foods, storage of leftover food, reheating, and clean up. *Flow of food* as it relates to the organizing function is discussed in Chapter 8.

◈ RECIPES

A **recipe** is a plan or formula used to describe the preparation of a certain food. A **standardized recipe** is a more specific plan that results in a standard operating procedure (SOP). This SOP communicates how a caterer expects to use exact ingredients to prepare a certain food. This food will deliver a consistent quality, exact yield, and portion size each time it is produced. Caterers use standardized recipes to ensure product consistency, control costs, control quality, prevent foodborne illness, and to achieve financial objectives. A standardized recipe implies a fit between the recipe, consumer needs, kitchen layout and equipment, employee skill level, and the caterer's needs.

A standardized recipe provides the flexibility of having the item prepared the same way each time, regardless of who prepares it. A standardized recipe helps deter the desire of kitchen personnel from using their own cooking style and ensures the item will be produced each time to a predetermined standard. An outcome of production is for the efficient and effective utilization of the equipment, by a skilled employee, to prepare quality food, from a standardized recipe. When served, the food must meet these standards every time.

A caterer will strive to become famous for a certain food. Clients request certain speciality foods. These requests are usually based on their preference for the taste, texture, form, temperature, tenderness, and eye appeal of the item. Therefore, the challenge is to make the item the same way each time it is featured at an event.

A standardized recipe communicates standard information. Because even the smallest change will affect the outcome of a recipe, every detail must be included. Providing information such as length of cooking time, type of heat used, and temperature setting will help ensure a consistent product. A recipe should communicate the following standard information: a common recipe name, yield, exact number of portions and their size, exact measurements of ingredients listed in order of use, equipment needed to produce it, specific directions for its preparation, recommended cooking times, critical control points (CCP) for proper handling, and directions for plating, storing, sanitizing, and clean up.

Recipe Development

A caterer is always searching for new recipes used to support unique and different foods. ***"The main outcome of a recipe is to produce a food that will excite the consumer to become a repeat customer." (Ingredient for Success 22).*** Caterers develop recipes in response to changing consumer trends and tastes. **Recipe development** is a continuous task required to support services offered to the customer. Recipes are researched before, during, and after events.

Developing recipes is a direct result of a caterer's love of food, experience, and the basic knowledge of food preparation. **Recipe research** begins by seeking answers to the following questions: What type of event is being planned? What kind of food should be prepared? What are the capabilities of the caterer and staff? What kind of production equipment is available? What are the service requirements? Is service speed required for 1000 people or is it an elaborate feast for 75 guests? Recipes will vary based on the needs of the client and the guests.

TIPS FROM THE TRADE

I believe when you are developing a dessert portfolio, you must understand what the menu is, even before you go into desserts. If your menu is more of a homestyle, with stick-to-your ribs, full-of-flavor, large portions, then that is how I approach tying in a dessert.

I have worked for many years in fine-dining accounts. This experience has enabled me to develop new dessert recipes. I also read many chef magazines that identify current dessert trends and specific dessert items being served at fine-dining establishments. I am very involved in the chef market so I keep abreast of these developments. A concept called *trickle down* plays an important role in our industry. Trickle-down theory says what happens in fine dining usually ends up in casual dining three-to-five years later. So, I take my past experience in fine dining and apply it to creating signature desserts. For instance, I enjoy using some of the more exotic fruits, such as passion fruit, in new dessert recipes. I developed an apple-raspberry crisp for a Texas-style steakhouse company and threw passion fruit into the dessert. The customers absolutely loved it. It has become one of their best sellers.

I believe one key to creating a great signature dessert recipe is to marry something that is pretentious with something that isn't. The trick is to create a blend of flavors that you can play around with so it works out well.

Kenneth P. Darling
Executive Pastry Chef
Heidi's Gourmet Desserts
Tucker (Atlanta), GA

Recipe Creation

The most effective way to create new recipes is to start with a few items. Work the recipes until they are developed to the satisfaction of the caterer and consumer. New recipes can be found by reading cook books and newspapers, searching the Internet, trying new restaurants on vacation, dining in a competitor's restaurant, or even attending a competitor's catered event.

Developing a standardized recipe to compliment the existing menu mix requires a certain caution against its immediate use. Sometimes a terrific recipe will not work after it has been increased to serve 100 people. Careful adjustment of seasoning and salt are always a concern.

Experimentation with new food will require it to be adapted to the caterer's menu. Often, changing a seasoning, or adding, or eliminating an ingredient will make it fit. An exceptional caterer will know what products will adapt to the menu mix.

New Recipes

New recipes should be prepared at least six times and field tested before being introduced into the market.

Field testing can be done on friends, customers, family, or employees. Always have the catering employees sample all menu items, but understand, the employees may be biased in their opinion. These individuals may be selected using the following preselection criteria as a guide.

1. Testers must consume a majority of their meals outside of the home.

2. Testers should be comfortable with eating a wide variety of food.

3. The caterer must select a good gender mix.

4. The caterer should identify the preferred age of the customer.

New recipes must be proven to withstand the rigors of catering. ***Ingredient for Success 23*** states: ***"A caterer must know the holding power of the food."*** In other words, will the food be able to withstand storage at 140°F on a steam table, without deteriorating? Will the quality level remain the same after being held for six hours, as it was immediately after production? These criteria are used to evaluate new recipes before they can be used in the field. A caterer cannot use a hollandaise sauce that will break down in half an hour for a catering job that requires a two-hour hold time.

Discovery

Searching for new and different types of food and recipes to expand the catering menu is an active process. Creative food ideas can be discovered while dining in restaurants or attending catered functions.

While dining in a restaurant while on vacation in California, I asked a waiter to recommend a dessert. The waiter suggested the restaurant's most popular dessert, the Mississippi Mudpie. After sampling this excellent dessert, I asked for the recipe, but was denied. So, I returned to the restaurant the next night and only ordered the mudpie. Dissecting and eating it slowly, I identified a mixture of common ingredients and scribbled notes for myself on a napkin. Returning home, I used these notes to create a working mudpie recipe. After a few weeks of experimentation, I tested the dessert and a Mississippi Mudpie recipe was finalized.

That was how Jardine's created our own version of a Mississippi Mudpie. Of course it was based on the original and it was developed so our customers would also enjoy it. The ingredients included an Oreo® cookie crust, butter for stabilization, and French vanilla ice cream slightly flavored with coffee. Refrozen, this pie was covered with a fudge topping and toasted almond slices. It was served topped with whipped cream. The Mississippi Mudpie became our second best selling dessert of all time—a true signature menu item frequently requested by customers.

Bill Jardine
Jardine's Farm Restaurant & Catering
Sarver, PA

Signature Recipes

A **signature recipe** is a menu item unique to a specific caterer. It may have an added *twist* or *tweak*, such as a certain salad featuring a different taste or a steak, seafood, or a chicken dish made using a unique seasoning or marinade.

Many caterers began their catering life with a basic menu. A caterer may feature a charcoal-roasted chicken. To differentiate this product from similar products made by other caterers, a basting-sauce recipe of water, vinegar and oil enhances the flavor, helping the chicken remain moist at a 165°F internal temperature, and leaving it with a golden, sunshine-brown appearance when finished.

Next, a caterer creates a recipe to compliment the chicken. Working from a basic barbeque sauce recipe, a caterer can create his own signature sauce. Many caterers will perfect and develop recipes during their traditionally slower winter months. To create a standardized recipe, it is recommended to keep meticulous notes documenting the following details: ingredients, measurements, ratios and cost, preparation procedures, cooking times and temperatures, storage conditions, shelf life, portion size, and yields.

The result of this effort is a barbeque sauce offering a rich, fresh tomato flavor seasoned with a unique combination of spices and herbs. A caterer will use this first sauce as a **base recipe**, later creating other sauces by adjusting the mix of ingredients. While the first sauce, or base recipe, featured a rich, fresh-tomato flavor, by adding a mix of ingredients, such as apple butter and coffee to the original base sauce, a caterer can create a second sauce with a smokey, hickory-style flavor.

These two examples show the development of a standardized recipe, how a caterer differentiates a basic menu item to produce a customer-requested food that becomes the foundation of the menu mix, the creation of a unique signature flavor to enhance a basic menu item, how a caterer creates a new base recipe which can be featured in multiple menu items, and the meticulous attention to detail required when creating a standardized recipe.

The signature barbeque sauce may permit the caterer to expand the menu mix. A caterer can offer a variety of food selections, including chicken and charcoal-roasted barbeque pork, ribs, and pork loins. Remember one important factor and *Ingredient for Success 24: "When developing recipes to complement the menu mix, create them based on the preferred taste of the customer."*

Employee Suggestions

In many instances, staff and employees will offer recipes to the caterer. Be careful to follow the same rigid testing procedures, and adhere to the same established criteria with these recipes. Often, an employee will make a recommendation for a recipe based on preference, believing he or she has developed something unique. Remember, the recipe must meet the taste and needs of the consumer and preferences will vary from location to location throughout the country. Manufacturers of prepared salad dressing, for example, blend different flavors and sell them under the same label in each section of the country because of the taste differences of people in various locations.

Ingredients

When developing recipes, the quality of *ingredients* used in the recipe will affect its outcome. Cheapest is not always the best. Although the purchasing task will be discussed in a later chapter, using the highest quality ingredients will contribute to a quality menu item.

The level of quality is determined by the purpose of the menu item. Knowing the relationship between different foods on the market is important. Always inspect the item for its quality whether it is frozen, fresh, canned, or dehydrated. Since the caterer has the option of selecting from many items in the market, first research how these items fit the menu.

Always purchase the best product at the best possible price for its intended purpose. If two hundred, seven-ounce, boneless, skinless, chicken breasts are needed for an upcoming event, a caterer must research the market to find the best product. One purveyor may have a boneless, skinless, chicken breast on sale, but they are a random pack. A random pack is packaged without a standard, uniform size. Therefore, the chicken breasts may range from six to seven-and-one-half ounces. The caterer is confronted with options if he orders this item: either accept and try to use the randomly packed chicken breasts or reject the chicken and find another source.

◆ RECIPE ADJUSTMENT

It is often necessary for a caterer to adjust standardized recipes. A standard recipe produces a standard yield designed to produce a specific amount of food. This yield, or standard, is expressed in portion size, volume, or weight. Sometimes, the yield from a standard recipe may need to be adjusted. (See Appendix B for a listing of standard recipe weights, measures, and abbreviations.) Yields may need adjustment to fit the capacity of the production or cooking equipment, to alter portion sizes, or to match the number of guests attending an event.

One method a caterer can use to adjust a recipe's yield is the conversion factor method, which uses a conversion factor (CF) to adjust all of the ingredients in a standardized recipe (Figure 7–4). This conversion factor is multiplied by each ingredient in the recipe to calculate the adjusted amount.

Step 1: Begin with the known yield of the standardized recipe. Divide the desired yield by the known yield to obtain the conversion factor.

Remember: New yield divided by old yield = conversion factor (CF)

Step 2: Convert ingredients to weight, if possible.

Step 3: Multiply each ingredient in the original recipe by the conversion factor.

Step 4: Multiply the original total weight of ingredients by the conversion factor (CF).

Use common sense when adjusting a recipe. Spices, salt, garlic or sugar may not be increased or decreased at the same rate as other ingredients.

A standardized recipe's portion size may need to be adjusted, depending on the needs of the client (Figure 7–5). Portion sizes may differ when catering an event for a group of senior citizens, a group of teenagers, or catering the recognition banquet for a senior high school football team.

To change the portion size of a given recipe:

Step 1: Determine total yield of the standardized recipe. Multiply the number of portions by the portion size.

Portions x Portion Size = Total Old Yield

Step 2: Determine the total yield desired. Multiply the desired number of portions by the new portion size.

Desired Portions x Desired Portion Size = Total New Yield

Step 3: Calculate the conversion factor. Divide the new yield by the old yield to get the conversion factor.

Total New Yield divided by Total Old Yield = Conversion Factor

Step 4: Multiply each ingredient by the conversion factor.

Conversion Factor x Old Quantity = New Quantity

BEEF STROGANOFF

Yield 10 portions, portion size is 6 oz
Adjust yield to 25 portions at 4 oz

Ingredients	Amount
Clarified butter	2 oz
Oil	2 oz
Onions	4 oz
Mushrooms	8 oz
White wine	2 oz
Tomato paste	1 oz
Mustard	2 tsp
Demiglaze	1 1/2 pt
Sour cream	1 1/4 cup
Beef tenderloin tips	2 1/2 lbs E.P.*

CONVERSION FACTOR

10 portions at 6 oz = 60 oz is old yield
25 portions at 4 oz = 100 oz is new yield
100 oz divided by 60 oz equals 1.67 conversion factor

Ingredients	Amount	Conversion factor = 1.67
Clarified butter	2 oz	3.34 oz
Oil	2 oz	3.34 oz
Onions	4 oz	6.68 oz
Mushrooms	8 oz	13.68 oz
White wine	2 oz	3.34 oz
Tomato paste	1 oz	1.67 oz
Demiglaze	1 1/2 pt (24 fl oz)	40.08 fl oz = 1qt (32 fl oz) + 8.08 fl oz
Sour cream	1 1/4 cup (8 oz, 2 oz)	16.7 oz
Beef tenderloin tips	2 1/2 lbs E.P.*	4 lb, 10.22 E.P oz.

*E.P. is edible portion. Edible portion is trimmed of all fat, cut into tips, and has a yield of 90%.

Figure 7-4 *Standardized recipe: Yield adjustment using a conversion factor.*

CHICKEN BREAST ROMANO

Yield 10 portions

Portion Size is one chicken breast, 4 oz

Ingredients	Amount
Flour	3 oz
Salt	1 tsp
White pepper	1/2 tsp
Eggs	4 ea
Romano cheese	3 oz
Boneless, skinless chicken breasts	10 ea
Butter	4 oz

CONVERSION FACTOR

Yield 10 portions - adjust to 65 portions

Portion Size is one chicken breast, 4 oz

Ingredients	Amount	Conversion factor = 6.5
Flour	3 oz	19.5 oz = 1 lb. 3.5 oz
Salt	1 tsp	6.5 tsp = 2 Tbsp, 1/2 tsp or to taste
White pepper	1/2 tsp	3.25 tsp = 1 Tbsp, 1/4 tsp or to taste
Eggs	4 ea.	26 eggs = 2 dozen + 2 eggs
Parmesan cheese	3 oz	19.5 oz = 1 lb, 3.5 oz
Milk	1 fl. oz	6.5 fl oz
Boneless, skinless chicken breasts	10 ea.	65 = 5 dozen + 5 breasts
Butter	4 oz	26 oz = 1 - pt = 16 fl oz, 1 cup = 8 fl oz, 4 tbsp = 2 fl oz

Conversion factor (CF) new yield 65 divided by old yield 10 equals 6.5

Figure 7–5 *Standardized recipe: Portion adjustment using a conversion factor.*

◆ CONVENIENCE FOODS

While researching recipes and developing the menu, caterers often complement scratch foods with the use of value-added or convenience foods. **Scratch foods** are the menu items prepared by the staff using standardized recipes. **Convenience foods** are products that are manufactured by a **principal**, or manufacturer, and delivered to the caterer in a *ready-to-eat* or *ready-to-cook* form by a purveyor.

One of the first convenience items accepted by the catering industry was hors d'oeuvres—very small pieces of food usually consumed in one bite. Because of their small size and composition, they require skilled labor to prepare them. Often, they are very expensive to make because ingredients, such as puff pastry or phyllo (very thin sheets of dough), can be difficult to handle.

Caterers have become famous for creating their own scratch, signature hors d'oeurves. A caterer might fill a certain kind of a mushroom cap with a delicate crab and sausage meat. This item may not be available in a prepared form, so customers may request it. This popular item becomes a competitive advantage for the caterer to offer.

Some popular hors d'oeuvre items can be purchased already prepared and frozen, requiring only a few minutes of roasting time in the oven. For example, take fresh chicken livers, place a water chestnut in the center, and wrap bacon around it. This labor intense item is now purchased fully prepared and ready to serve.

Many of the world's largest food service companies or principals manufacture a variety of prepared, heat-and-serve, frozen entree items. These products are used by caterers throughout the world. Customers accept these products because of their high and consistent quality. Often, consumers may not realize they are eating a convenience item because of its high quality.

Frozen entrees are widely known and used for their versatility in the catering industry. Caterers, upscale hotels, white table cloth restaurants, and others in the food service segment rely on these items to supplement their menu mix. Many operators will serve the item right from its pan. Other operators may season it with spices or add crumbled bread crumbs to slightly alter its appearance. As a result of these minor alterations, the consumer is led to believe the product is the caterer's own signature scratch menu item. Convenience items provide the caterer with several advantages and disadvantages.

Advantages of Convenience Foods

1. The quality of the finished product remains consistent each time it is prepared.

2. Precise serving costs, based on exact food costs and portion size per container or case, are easily determined.

3. These foods provide easy expansion of the menu without the added increase of ingredients, storage facilities, cost of control, and employee skill levels to produce.

4. Features include some reductions in handling of bulk ingredients and the elimination of "waste" by overproduction.

5. Convenience items are available immediately, on demand (minus production time) as needed by the caterer.

6. A caterer can reduce the cost of skilled labor by using convenience foods.

Disadvantages of Convenience Foods

1. The cost of the item may be higher than the cost of preparing it from scratch.

2. Nutritional values may be elevated. Many convenience foods have higher levels of sodium and monosodium glutamate than scratch-prepared foods. (Make sure the consumer is not restricted in their diet based on these and other ingredients.)

3. Storage facilities may not be adequate to store these frozen convenience foods.

A caterer can locate convenience foods by asking their distributor's sales representative (DSR) or their local Food Broker. Caterers should also attend local distributor-sponsored food shows as well as the National Restaurant Association's annual trade show in Chicago, Illinois each May.

◈ SPEED SCRATCH COOKING

Foods that are made from scratch and are finished off in the caterer's kitchen may be referred to as speed scratch cooking. **Speed scratch cooking** has little preparation, provides excellent quality, and lowers labor costs because less preparation is involved. Speed scratch cooking offers the caterer some of the following strategic advantages.

1. lower inventories

2. less equipment in the kitchen

3. fewer employees

4. less waste

5. less preparation and cleanup

6. better consistency

7. meets and exceeds the customers' expectations

For example, some seafood products, such as shrimp cocktail, can be purchased precooked and individually portioned with just as much flavor and consistency as starting with a raw product and paying somebody to prepare it. Another example is a prime rib. This is a fully cooked, heat-and-serve product that provides the caterer with exact portion costs and extremely high yields.

◈ BRANDED MENU ITEMS

Caterers use brand names to identify certain food items on their menus. One reason is because the consumer recognizes perceived quality levels in certain names. Even though the caterer is not preparing this item homemade (from scratch), the value of using a branded food will satisfy a client's tastes. **Branded menu items** most often used by a caterer include frozen desserts. There are many great frozen cheesecakes in the market. The use of a branded cheesecake on the menu is an excellent example of how a client will recognize and perceive a quality product. Cheesecakes are not difficult, but expensive to prepare, are labor intensive, and lack consistent quality.

Caterers may use branded menu items because the principal will pay to have their name placed on the menu. The most popular branded nonalcoholic beverages are carbonated beverages. A caterer would not list just "cola" on the menu, but might add the logo of a particular brand.

Most companies do promotional work. They help caterers by providing glasses, equipment, or supplies. Caterers can use this to their advantage.

TIPS FROM THE TRADE

Jardine's was once a popular vendor at many county fairs. We would prepare charcoal-roasted, barbeque chicken and serve carbonated *brand* X as the soft drink. The vice president of the carbonated beverage *brand* Z syrup division was having dinner at our place on the fairground. The VP asked: "Why don't you use *brand* Z cola?" We had a very nice conversation and he asked me about the rented tent I was using at the fair. We could seat one hundred twenty people under this tent at one time. The VP asked, "Would you be interested in switching products if I provided a tent?" Of course I was interested and we signed a contract right on the spot. Within a week, he had sent me a new tent. This new tent had the same seating capacity as the one we were renting. However, this new tent had a *brand* Z cola banner which encircled the outside of the tent. I switched to *brand* Z and used it for the next few years, mainly because the *brand* Z tent saved our operation quite a bit of money.

Bill Jardine
Jardine's Farm Restaurant & Catering
Sarver, PA

◆ MENUS

Standardized recipes are developed based on the needs of the consumer and the caterer. These recipes are bundled together and marketed by the caterer's menu. *Ingredient for Success 25* states: ***"The menu is a management tool from which the caterer can control operations."***

Advantages of a Catering Menu verses a Restaurant Menu

A catering menu differs from a restaurant menu by providing distinct advantages. Management control is the single greatest advantage offered to the caterer. Unlike a restaurateur, the caterer does not have to forecast future sales. A caterer is not required to make "best guess" customer counts or base food production on menu item popularity trends. Caterers do not have to perform these tasks because each event is planned in advance.

The catering menu is created based on guaranteed customer counts. Once the catering menu is created, the management function of control and execution becomes predictable. Most *unknowns* that challenge the restaurateur are eliminated. This gives a caterer greater control over the production process and the inputs of raw materials and labor.

If a client guarantees three hundred fifty guests, the caterer can be operationally prepared for the event. The caterer will know, in advance, the exact number of guests, the menu, what levels of inventory will be carried, the exact portion size per guest, the amount of food to purchase, cost of the food, the production schedule, service requirements, labor costs, and the expected profit based on the negotiated price (Figure 7–6). The client will have paid in advance for this function. This same scenario can be a gamble for a restaurateur. If a restaurateur has forecast and prepared for three hundred fifty people on a Saturday night and suddenly, unexpected inclement weather, such as a snow storm or a tornado hits, and only twenty-five people show up, the night will be a financial disaster.

Figure 7-6 *Food production is calculated based on a guaranteed event.*

TIPS FROM THE TRADE

Mayfair Farms is located in West Orange, New Jersey. My grandfather started it in 1943 as an à la carte restaurant and later added a banquet room. Over the years we built three more banquet rooms on the property. Catering is an extremely profitable operation. A standalone, traditional, à la carte restaurant may have a profit margin at best of 10 percent. The profit margin in catering may be as high as 25 percent. I have a steakhouse where the food cost ranges from 31 to 32 percent. My catering facility has a food cost of 16 percent. Because you sell parties at a higher price than you do in the à la carte restaurant, catering is a tremendously profitable operation when you can hit the critical mass of parties. If you can cater enough parties, you can have a very profitable opportunity.

Marty Horn
President &CEO
FOODgalaxy.com
Parsippany, NJ

A Communication Tool

One basic function of a catering menu is a tool to communicate, in writing, what the caterer can provide in food and service, the value and quality of the food, and service mix based on its price.

How does the caterer plan a menu and who is involved? How does a caterer find the right menu item for each job?

First, a caterer must have certain capabilities. This begins with a properly equipped kitchen capable of producing what the customer wants. The caterer must meet with the customer before the menu is planned. A wedding is the most important day for a potential bride and groom who are planning this wonderful day. A caterer probably would not plan the same menu for a wedding that would also be used for a picnic, although caterers have done picnics for weddings. After meeting with the bride and groom, the caterer would build a menu based on the needs and wants of the customer.

The caterer must consider the kind of food being prepared, its service presentation, **plate presentation** and color mix (Figure 7–7). A plate presentation of mashed potatoes and a roasted, stuffed chicken breast with steamed cauliflower would not appear to be appetizing because of its lack of color. Plate presentation must be attractive and colorful, and the food must taste good.

If planning a buffet menu, it must be attractive and have eye appeal. Eye appeal is important since a customer first "eats" with their eyes before they "eat" with their mouth.

A caterer will always be involved with people in need of different types of foods. Because of this, a caterer must always remember, when building a menu, to answer this question: "Does the kitchen staff have the skill level and equipment

Figure 7-7 *Plate presentation should be colorful and attractively arranged to be eye-appealing to the guests.*

to produce what the customer wants?" Suppose one day the caterer meets with a bride and groom planning their wedding reception. The next day a meeting is held with the CEO of a manufacturing company who needs lunch served in the board room during a board of directors meeting. Can the caterer meet the needs of the bride and groom and create what the CEO requests with current staff and kitchen capabilities?

If the caterer is not capable of meeting this CEO's needs respond by saying, "I am not capable of producing that, but I can prepare this item, which I believe you would be much happier with overall." A caterer must be aware of the customer's needs but the customer must understand the caterer's capabilities. Remember, since the caterer is meeting with the client, he has already earned this client's trust.

Flow of Food

Another basic function of the catering menu is to determine production and the **flow of food** through the operation. Production includes budgeting and scheduling, determining what can be produced, understanding how fast it can be produced, requiring the proper equipment, and matching the skill level of the personnel to the menu. A caterer must only offer clients what the production staff can produce.

Production begins with the creation of a labor budget to determine the number of labor hours or labor dollars that will be allocated to the kitchen. This budget includes the predetermined gross income and profit objectives and how the kitchen can help to accomplish them.

Scheduling

The menu becomes a management tool in production scheduling by answering the following questions.

- How quickly must the food be prepared?
- What ability does the staff have to get the food out?
- How long does it take to prepare each item?
- Who will do the prep work?
- Who will do the finish work?
- Where will the food be held after it is finished?
- What is the capacity of the equipment?
- Can all of the food be cooked at once?
- How will the production be allocated to utilize the equipment?
- Does the food have to be batch cooked and stored?
- Is there any need to precook the food?
- Will anything be cooked the day before the event?
- Will anything need to be cooked two days before the event?
- How will precooked food be stored?
- Will any food be stored in an insulated container?
- After cooking, will the food be frozen or stored in a refrigerator?
- Will the food need to be reheated just minutes or hours before the event?

Staffing

Detailed in the catering plan is each task to be performed to accomplish all predetermined objectives as set for each event. Once these tasks have been identified, they are bundled and delegated to an employee. This catering management task is accomplished through an effective and efficient exercise of staffing and scheduling based on the menu selected by the client.

Staffing is the caterer's task of identifying a suitable number of employees required for an event, while **scheduling** balances that number of employees against the given volume of work.

Employee Skill Levels

A caterer can have all types of skill levels in a kitchen. These can range from employing individuals with cognitive delay to do routine jobs, such as salad preparation to certified culinary professionals, such as a chef. A production staff includes pantry, prep, and butcher work, preparing sauces, roasting, and sautéing. Each employee must be continually trained to appropriately contribute to the organization and to avoid the high cost of poor planning, estimating, or food production.

Work Production Schedule

Scheduling food production begins with the menu. This catering management task helps control food costs. A **work production schedule** is created for a standardized recipe to communicate the following information: recipe number, recipe name, yields, exact number of portions, portion size in exact measurement, and specific handling instructions. Handling instructions will describe the approximate preparation time, where to store the food immediately after it is cooked, if the food needs to be transported, when and where the food will be served. Special emphasis should be placed on proper handling procedures to ensure against the contamination of foodborne illness.

Employee Work Schedule

Scheduling employees is a catering management task that helps control labor costs. A caterer will design an **employee work schedule** based on the amount of work determined by an event's production schedule. When constructing the employee work schedule, careful attention must be paid to the capacity of the equipment and distribution of an equalized work load among the employees throughout the time leading up to the event. Each employee should know their responsibilities and the length of time to complete each task. Explicit instructions describing what everyone will do with the food when they are finished preparing it, how they will get the food to the event, and how it will be served are distributed to each employee.

The first step in scheduling is to identify each recipe and the tasks needed to produce it. Coordinating the menu, equipment, skill level, preparation needs, and production time is critical because tasks will vary depending upon the food category. Successful employee scheduling requires production knowledge of the following categories: appetizers; sandwiches and hors d'oeuvres, sauces, stocks, and soups; salads and salad dressings; fruits and vegetables; red meat; poultry; fish, shellfish; bakeshop (cakes, icing, yeast breads, pies and pastries, quick breads) and desserts; eggs, milk and cheese; cereals, and beverages.

◈ FOOD PREPARATION

Proper food preparation includes many factors to be considered by a caterer. What type of vegetable will a caterer use? Vegetables are a concern because a caterer must factor the total holding time on the buffet line at 140°F storage in an insulated container. Fresh green peas, for example, may need to be refreshed every twenty minutes. If green peas are prepared and held for two hours, the peas will disintegrate into a mass of dark green mush. A solid vegetable, such as a carrot, green bean, or corn will hold much better over time. A caterer must plan production, preparation, and storage time when considering a vegetable.

Preparation of meat also takes careful planning. For example, when will the roast beef need to be placed in the convection ovens? How long will it need until it is finished? Is there a sauce, au jour or gravy? Will the roast beef be sliced during the function on a buffet line or will it be sliced before the event? Understand the production capacity of the equipment, especially for outdoor events (Figure 7–8).

The caterer may have multiple functions scheduled at the same time. Review of each menu will identify which tasks can be bundled and which items can be produced together. If a salad is a common item found on each menu, salad production is scheduled to produce enough salad for all events. Then it is separated into smaller quantities for each job.

Figure 7-8 *Outdoor production often involves complex requests like this mass barbecue pit to accommodate large numbers.*

A knowledgeable caterer must make realistic decisions when creating a production schedule. Can a steamer be used during the critical hours right before service? Must the food be prepared before service and held in storage? Because fresh carrots take longer to cook than canned carrots, will it be necessary to precook and finish them right before service? Should the potatoes be baked three-fourths of the way and finished right before service? Can the production facilities handle preparing fresh mashed potatoes? Is a fresh mashed potato, or a frozen mashed potato which requires only a few minutes of preparation, a better choice?

A production schedule and the event menu must be coordinated. Purchasing the right type of food, such as raw carrots verses canned carrots, will affect the production schedule. This includes scheduling the equipment for the entire production line, from planning to final refrigeration. The production schedule must deliver the correct quantity of food at the right time. This happens when the caterer produces tested, standardized recipes. Signature foods are a good example.

Developing a competency and comfort level from the staff, producing the same food, using standard menus, leads to a strong learning and experience curve. Producing a consistent, quality product demanded by the clientele is a strategic advantage for a caterer. Not only will the production personnel learn how to execute their tasks more efficiently, but they will be in a better position to offer suggestions of how to incrementally improve the overall production system.

Innovation and creativity become important factors in food preparation. Employees offering innovative ideas on improving production, redesigning work flow, and streamlining work stations contribute to reducing costs and increasing customer value. Such production tips (Figure 7–9) sometimes present a challenge for the caterer to reward and retain these innovative employees.

FOOD PRODUCTION TIPS

1. Get everything assembled before production begins—*mise en place.* This includes equipment, utensils, recipes, and ingredients.

2. Become familiar with the recipe or instructions.

3. Let the equipment do the work. Use attachments to their fullest advantage.

4. Save time by using the correct tools. Measure using large containers; 1 quart, for example instead of 4 cups.

5. Use scales for measuring ingredients instead of volume measures to be more accurate.

(continued)

Figure 7-9 *Food production tips.*

6. To measure honey or other sticky substances, first grease the measuring cup.

7. Arrange working materials so there is no break in movement or waste in motion.

8. If a steam-jacketed kettle does not come with its own measuring stick, have one made. If the kettle does come with a measuring stick, check for accuracy.

9. Cook food in serving pans when possible. The food will be more attractive when served, it will stay warm longer, and it will save pans, washing, and labor.

10. Grind raisins before putting them in sweet roll dough or cookies.

11. Raisins coated with melted shortening will go through the food chopper without sticking.

12. Put several slices of dry bread through the grinder after grinding food. It will be easier to clean.

13. Place soiled pans, especially those having baked-on cheese or spaghetti, into the stack steamer for five to ten minutes. This will help loosen the baked-on food and promote easier cleaning.

14. Turn a stool upside down to hold round bottom bowls, such as those for a salad or a mixer.

15. To grate or cube cheddar cheese, place it into plastic bags and freeze. Thaw as needed. Record weight and date.

16. Small frozen chunks of cheese may be grated without sticking to a vertical cutter mixer or food cutter blades.

17. Use a dry vegetable brush for removing cheese from a grater before washing it. This also works well for lemon and orange rind.

18. Apply a thin coat of butter to the cut surface of cheese to prevent drying out during refrigeration.

19. When opening eggs, have a pan ready in which to drop the shells.

20. Break eggs into a small funnel to separate the whites from the yolks.

21. If a whole egg will spin like a top, it is hard-cooked.

22. Do not over-mix meat mixtures. Over-mixing toughens the product.

23. Meats brown more quickly if the salt is not added at first. Salt draws the juices which prevents browning.

24. Portion ground meat with a scoop on an 18" x 26" baking pan. Cover with waxed paper and place a second 18" x 26" baking pan on top. Push gently to flatten meat patties, Your second pan is ready for filling. Handle small batches and keep food out of the danger zone.

(continued)

Figure 7-9 *Food production tips (continued).*

25. Layer hamburger patties between sheets of foil or waxed paper in a sheet pan. Use three layers maximum with strips of foil or waxed paper for best results. Keep out of the food danger zone.

26. Refrigerated storage of bread quickens the staling process.

27. Freeze bread if it is to be held over one day.

28. Freezing will not restore freshness to stale bread.

29. Unbaked bread can be frozen satisfactorily for up to two weeks.

30. Whip butter before spreading. It will spread faster and easier and it offers better flavor than when melted.

31. Grind butter with filling for sandwiches.

32. A small amount of peanut oil may be added to peanut butter to improve the spreading consistency.

33. Sandwiches made before serving time may be kept palatable by placing a clean, sanitized damp towel on the bottom of a flat pan. Cover each layer with waxed paper, stacking the sandwiches carefully. Cover the top layer with a damp towel.

34. Rolls for hot sandwiches should be heated by placing them in a pre-heated oven or stack steamer. Protect them from drying out by using a sanitary damp towel for the oven or plastic wrap for the steamer.

35. Butter adds flavor and palatability. It may be used on all sandwiches except hoagies and barbeques.

36. For easy separation of cheese or meat slices, alternate corners when stacking the slices.

37. When heating milk in a steam-jacketed kettle, coat the inside with butter to prevent milk deposits and scorching. This will make the cleaning job easier.

38. When whipping cream or dry milk, chill the bowl, beater, and cream. The cream will whip in half the time. Should the cream seem too thin to whip, place the chilled dish in a pan of hot water and then whip.

39. If coring lettuce for immediate use, hit the core end on the table.

40. In preparing lettuce, remove core. Let the water run through the core hole into the lettuce to loosen and separate the leaves. Washing in portable water also removes insects, dirt and other contaminants.

41. When using flavored gelatin for molded salads or desserts, heat only enough liquid to dissolve the gelatin. To hasten the congealing, use ice water to make up the total amount of liquid.

42. Do not mix freshly cut tomatoes or cucumbers into combination salads until ready to serve. The acid from these vegetables will tend to wilt the other vegetables in the salad.

(continued)

Figure 7-9 *Food production tips (continued).*

43. Add salad dressings to salad immediately before serving. Salad dressing added before service will cause the salad to wilt and become unattractive.
44. Always keep salads refrigerated and serve them on well chilled bowls or plates.
45. Scald oranges before peeling. Use a perforated steam table pan, one layer deep for two to four minutes in a steamer or put them through a dishmachine on the rinse cycle. Chill immediately in cold water.
46. When chopping apples, the first step is to use the corer and sectioner, then chop.
47. To prevent browning of apples or bananas, dip into an anti-oxidant or citrus fruit juice. Do not allow them to stand in this solution as softening occurs.
48. Use a slicer to slice melons.
49. Pink applesauce is made by adding one-half cup of dry strawberry gelatin to each number 10 can of applesauce.
50. Flavored gelatin sprinkled over a custard dessert adds flavor and serves as a garnish—use to decorate cookies too.
51. Pears can be tinted quickly by sprinkling with dry flavored gelatin.
52. Banana chunks dipped in anti-oxidant and rolled in peanuts makes an attractive dessert.
53. To chop onions without crying, put in hot water for 5 minutes. Cut into quarters to chop.
54. Time is saved in skinning onions by slicing off root and top ends and quartering the onions before skinning them.
55. Cut potatoes into serving size when eyeing to handle each potato only once.
56. Half a cup of dried parsley flakes and a quarter cup of paprika adds something different to scalloped potatoes when mixed with two and one-half gallons of white sauce.
57. To chop parsley, freeze it first.
58. Season green beans with chopped chives, butter, salt, pepper, and a dash of nutmeg.

Figure 7-9 *Food production tips (continued).*

Summary

The term used to describe the activity of implementing and executing the daily elements of a catering plan is called *operations*. Elements of operations occur in both the front-of-the-house and back-of-the-house. Front-of-the-house activities are those customer-driven, service tasks designed to please the guest primarily in the dining area. Back-of-the-house activities are not generally witnessed by the customer and include the physical, mechanical, and financial elements. Operational tasks are a direct function of the type of catering event being implemented. These include recipe research, recipe development, menu creation, scheduling production, defining customer service issues, preparation, transportation, and clean up.

Review Questions

Brief Answers

1. Describe what is meant by a caterer's *operation*.
2. Explain the components found in the front-of-the-house operations.
3. Explain the components found in the back-of-the-house operations.
4. Describe a caterer's *operational tasks*.
5. Explain how caterers may formulate recipes.
6. Why is the concept *flow of food* important to a caterer?
7. Describe a *standardized recipe*.
8. Provide examples of how caterers can create new recipes.
9. Describe how a caterer can transform customer needs into signature recipes.
10. Explain how a caterer can utilize convenience foods.
11. Discuss why a caterer will use branded menu items.
12. Explain the advantages a catering menu provides over a standard restaurant menu.
13. Explain why elements of catering management control features must be built into the plan.
14. Explain the catering management task of scheduling and staffing.
15. Explain what the following Ingredients for Success mean to you.

    Ingredient for Success 22: "*The main outcome of a recipe is to produce a food that will excite the consumer to become a repeat customer.*"

    Ingredient for Success 23: "*A caterer must know the holding power of the food.*"

    Ingredient for Success 24: "*When developing recipes to complement the menu mix, create them based on the preferred taste of the customer.*"

    Ingredient for Success 25: "*The menu is a management tool from which the caterer can control operations.*"

Multiple Choice

Select the single best answer for each question.

1. Catering management activities include the physical activities and "hands-on" logistical tasks of handling food, preparation of food and the transportation of food. These activities take place in:

   a. the front-of-the-house

   b. the back-of-the-house

   c. an off-premise location

   d. social catering

   e. corporate catering

2. A signature recipe is described as:

   a. a food unique to the caterer

   b. a common food prepared by every caterer

   c. a consistently difficult food to produce

   d. a food requiring "field-testing" before implementation on the menu

   e. a food considered low quality

3. Which of the following is an advantage of using a convenience food item?

   a. excessive inventory

   b. limited menu selections

   c. consistent quality

   d. uncontrollable costs

   e. lower profit margins

True or False

Read each of the following statements and determine if it is true or false.

1. Caterers will use brand names to identify certain food items on their menus.

2. Standardized recipes are developed based on the needs of the consumer and the caterer.

3. The production task begins with the creation of a labor budget to determine the number of labor hours or labor dollars that will be allocated to the kitchen.

Putting It All Together

Visit an independent caterer or the catering department of a hotel, health care facility, college/university, military base, or restaurant known for catering. Ask the catering manager how they use standardized recipes. Ask them to describe their signature foods and how they developed their recipes. Ask how their customers describe their signature menu items. Identify and discuss the mix of menu items and how each one complements the mission of the organization. Write a short report summarizing your visit.

Chapter Eight

Organizing the Event

Key Terms

organizing function

formal structure

specifications

supplier sales representatives

distributor sales representatives (DSRs)

territory sales managers

merchandising associates

distributors

specialty distributor

specialty wholesaler

broadline distributor

food broker

manufacturer's agents

wholesale clubs

retail grocery store

ordering

receiving

storage

Objectives

After studying this chapter, you should be able to:

◆ Describe why organizing is the third catering management function.

◆ Explain how organizing helps accomplish the plan.

◆ Explain how a caterer organizes for an event.

◆ Explain specifications.

◆ Explain the main goal of purchasing.

◆ Provide examples of common purchasing policies.

◆ Describe basic purchasing needs.

◆ Explain how to build a caterer and supplier relationship.

◆ Explain how a caterer can find a reliable supplier.

◆ Discuss why a caterer attends food shows.

◆ Describe a food broker, broadline purveyor, and manufacturer's agent.

◆ Explain why ordering is important to the purchasing function.

◆ Explain standard receiving procedures.

INGREDIENTS FOR SUCCESS

26 *"Structure is dependent on the mission of the organization."*

27 *"Every caterer should have at least two good suppliers, a principal supplier and a backup supplier."*

28 *"The supplier is only as dependable and responsible as the salesperson and the truck driver who delivers the food."*

29 *"Good receiving and planning provide the caterer with a major economical advantage. Good receiving principles provide control."*

◆ ORGANIZING

All caterers, corporate or social, on- or off-premise, need to have a solid grasp of the third catering function: organizing for the event.

The **organizing function** occurs within a supportive organizational structure. Created by the caterer, this formal structure centers on the organization's mission. *Ingredient for Success 26* states: *"Structure is dependent on the mission of the organization."*

Formal structure refers to the management design of the catering organization, which is designed to help allocate and control resources. A strong, but flexible formal structure must support the implementation of the caterer's evolving strategy, as outlined in the catering plan. It must be responsive to incremental and sudden changes occurring in the internal organization or external marketplace, thus permitting the caterer to adapt to each client's special needs.

When a catering plan is sprung into action, it is the organizing function that bolsters the staff's action to efficiently and effectively execute each task and attain the stated objectives.

Organizing Tasks

Building an organizational structure with the flexibility to support the implementation of multiple-event plans centers on the catering management task of organizing. The core organizing tasks for most caterers include creating the menu, developing recipes, writing specifications, ordering, receiving, issuing, producing, transporting, and service. These major tasks are further divided into individual activities. These individual activities then support each individual catering function plan (Figure 8–1).

Caterers use each of these tasks to implement the event plan, build management control features, and allocate resources. Catering management control techniques are discussed in Chapter 11.

Catering Management Tasks

Menu

The *menu* plays an important role because it is the foundation upon which everything revolves. As discussed in Chapter 7, **Ingredient for Success 25** states: ***"The menu is a management tool from which the caterer can control operations."*** The menu determines the type of food to be prepared, standardized recipe, flow of food, layout and capacity of equipment, size and type of storage facilities, and human resource requirements.

A caterer begins preparation with the menu.

1. What combination of foods has the customer selected for a menu?

2. What needs does the customer have and how can the caterer satisfy them?

3. Does the caterer understand and interpret these needs to procure the appropriate food?

Figure 8-1 *With careful organizing, even a monochromatic salad bar provides customer appeal.*

4. How many people are attending the event? This will determine the quantity of raw materials the caterer will need to purchase.

5. What additional resources are needed for this event?

Specifications

After a menu has been selected, the level of quality and service must be determined. Quality is defined by the menu and standardized recipes as outlined in the caterer's mission. An outcome of well-managed production is quality food from a standardized recipe, created by a skilled employee, using the most efficient and effective equipment available.

The customers' perception of quality is exhibited by the menu they have selected. The menu selection will identify the flavor, texture, form and temperature of the desired food, as well as control the portion size and mix of ingredients (Figure 8–2). By preplanning the menu, the caterer will have already considered eye-appeal; however, the service style will be another variable that influences the customers' perception of value. ***"The main outcome of a recipe is to produce a food that will excite the consumer to become a repeat customer"*** *(Ingredient for Success 22)*.

Caterers write **specifications** to ensure consistent preparation and presentation, exciting the consumer to become a repeat customer. Specifications are used in catering operations to communicate standards both within the organization and externally to the competitive marketplace. A specification is an exact narrative that explains what is needed. It is written to identify ingredients, level of preparation, and method of production. The specification will explicitly define the item's:

1. form.

2. texture.

3. temperature.

Figure 8-2 *The menu determines the portion size and mix of ingredients.*

4. color.

5. flavor.

6. unit size and its cost.

7. portion size.

8. purchase size.

9. common trade or industry name.

10. brand name required.

11. federal or trade grade.

12. place of origin.

13. variety.

14. size or count per package.

15. style of cut or package.

16. age or degree of ripeness.

17. type of package.

A specification includes all information necessary to produce the exact menu item. A precisely written specification controls quality, reduces costs, and keeps the information clear and concise. The specification establishes the caterer's acceptable standard to guarantee consistency of operations and to keep customers happy. For example, before purchasing a steak, a caterer must write a precise description of that item based on the needs of the client and caterer.

Specifications also are used to guarantee price. First, always purchase from a reputable, trusted, purveyor. Most sales representatives in the food industry work on a commission; therefore, some sales representatives may be motivated to overprice items to get a higher commission. Specifications work best when the caterer gives a copy of them to their purveyors. *Ingredient for Success 27: "Every caterer should have at least two good suppliers, a principal supplier and a backup supplier."*

◆ PURCHASING

The menu has been selected. Specifications have been written for each item. The exact quantity is determined (items required for the function minus inventory). The next task is to purchase the raw materials. The goal of purchasing is to procure the item in agreement with its specification, in the right amount, at the right time, at the right cost, and from the right supplier.

Before executing the actual purchasing task, however, a plan must be formulated. The purchasing plan outlines how the purchasing objective will be accomplished. The plan is written into a purchasing manual to guide organizational members through the purchasing task. The purchasing manual will include policies (general guidelines for employees to follow), procedures, (a description of how the task must be accomplished), and rules (to communicate precise behavior).

Policies, procedures, and rules support the purchasing function by encouraging consistent execution of the purchasing task. Caterers may write policies, procedures, and rules to guide behavior of those directly responsible and accountable for this task. Employees who may be accountable to the purchasing function are the buyer, receiving clerk, production manager, chef, catering manager, and owners. Common policies a caterer can establish to provide guidance may include:

1. accepting gifts.

2. making personal purchases.

3. accepting free samples.

4. setting hours for receiving sales people.

5. setting a time range for delivery of food.

6. acceptable substitutions of items by the purveyor.

The purchasing manual must include security procedures. Policies and standard operating procedures will describe security concerns such as when to unlock and open the back door, protecting against internal theft, etc. Frequent inspections by the caterer to monitor and reinforce procedures will help control this task.

Right Supplier

The right supplier will meet and exceed a caterer's needs as defined by the customer's needs, wants, and demands. Therefore, variables such as the caterer's mission; the organizational structure; the competitive market; and type, capacity, and layout of the production equipment will influence the supplier's ability to support the caterer.

Basic Purchasing Needs

Almost every caterer has the same basic purchasing needs. These needs exist regardless of individual needs.

Basic Purchasing Needs

1. Does the caterer have an acceptable comfort level with the supplier?

2. Does the supplier have an acceptable reputation?

3. Can the supplier provide the required brand?

4. Does the supplier carry an acceptable product line?

5. Is there an acceptable pricing policy? Will the purveyor negotiate in good faith?

6. Is an acceptable delivery schedule available with professional courtesy?

7. Are orders generally delivered on time?

8. Is the food of an acceptable quality level?

9. Does the supplier have an acceptable merchandise return policy?

10. How often are substitute products sent?

11. Does the supplier have an acceptable, professional support staff?

12. Is the supplier located in a convenient geographical location with a warehouse facility?

13. Is there a minimum dollar amount for the order to be delivered?

Every caterer has variable needs that a supplier must satisfy. If catering a small function, will the supplier deliver a small order? If catering a large function, can the purveyor meet the volume requirements? Is a purveyor's delivery schedule flexible?

It is common for a caterer to execute functions on a weekend, so delivery is sometimes needed on a Saturday or Sunday. It may be necessary to find a purveyor to deliver on a weekend. Some clients may contract for a two-day event, such as a corporate fund-raising activity or picnic. These events may exceed 10,000 guests each day. If catering this type of function, the caterer should arrange with a purveyor several weeks in advance to schedule weekend deliveries.

TIPS FROM THE TRADE

Due to the amount of specialty and last minute requests, it is very important that, as a caterer, we have established relationships with suppliers and vendors. The range of suppliers and vendors we deal with on a daily basis is very diverse, from electricians and phone companies to florists and specialty chocolates. At Hyatt we offer our customers our "Preferred List" of vendors. This list covers entertainment, florist, décor rental, audio visual, security, etc. The vendors who appear on this list know that they are always the first to be recommended by our managers; therefore, we expect their quality and service to be consistent, timely, creative, and to always exceed our guests expectations. These relationships are established through numerous trials of many products and services. At our hotel we have six managers. . .one bad experience with a particular vendor could quite possibly lose the referral of their product or service from our entire catering team.

Dianne Herzog
Catering Manager
Hyatt Orlando
Kissimmee, FL

Building a Supplier and Caterer Relationship

Building a relationship with a supplier based on trust may be one of the most important considerations for the caterer. Establishing professional relationships with suppliers should be encouraged. Actually, strong relationships between a distributor sales representative and the caterer create a team approach to purchasing by recruiting the sales representative to become a part of the caterer's team. *Ingredient for Success 28: "The supplier is only as dependable and responsible as the salesperson and the truck driver who delivers the food."*

Professional relationships contribute to a successful purchasing program. The caterer and purveyor jointly build a professional and ethical loyalty toward each other.

TIPS FROM THE TRADE

I have been catering for four and one-half years. I was in the restaurant business for ten years before that. The catering business I bought was about to go bankrupt and we were trying to revitalize it. I kept some of the same purveyors because of their outstanding service. I can probably get the same type of food from other purveyors, but my sales representative was awesome. He would come in and do everything he could to get an order. If I could not get an order in for the next day, he would grab it, put it in his car, and drop it off for me. That is why I stuck with them.

I have another purveyor that supplies my paper products, aluminum, pots and pans, and similar products. I could probably pay less if I went to a national broadline purveyor, but this representative comes into my facility twice a week and inventories all my paper goods and aluminum items that we send out on catering jobs. So, that is why I stick with that supplier.

Mark Sparacino
Chef/Catering Manager
Traveling Fare
River Forest, IL

Supplier Sales Representatives

Supplier sales representatives are called **distributor sales representatives (DSRs)** or **territory sales managers** or **merchandising associates**. DSRs make a sales call and take the physical order. They are the contact between the caterer and the distributor.

DSRs may have a pager number, telephone number, voice mail number, and an e-mail address. The DSR's job is to match their distributor's resources to the caterer's needs to devise solutions. They will be in the process of menu development, while searching for new recipes or involved in many other stages of preparation. The DSR may offer computer assistance, sponsor continuing education programs, and provide culinary training. They also keep the caterer informed of market changes, new products, market trends, competitive maneuvers, and industry "gossip."

Finding Suppliers

Often, the *supplier* will find the *caterer*. If a new catering business or an established caterer is seeking a supplier, "gossip" or "word" spreads quickly through the catering community. Everyone is alerted to a potentially new customer who has entered the market. Suppliers will quickly send sales representatives to the catering business.

A caterer sometimes actively seeks suppliers by asking for recommendations from other caterers; searching telephone books, trade journals, and magazines; attending seminars and conferences; and seeking advice from local associations. The Internet is also a useful tool.

A caterer can become very popular with a supplier's sales representative, especially if the caterer is a volume buyer. Always be courteous to each sales representative.

◈ MARKET INTERMEDIARIES

Purchasing food and supplies is accomplished through interaction with numerous market intermediaries involved in the distribution and delivery of food. The caterer may purchase from a purveyor, otherwise known as a *distributor*, a *wholesale club*, or a *retail grocery store*. The caterer may also interact with a *food broker* and a *manufacturer's agent*.

The caterer will most likely purchase from a purveyor, commonly known in the trade as a distributor. **Distributors** purchase directly from the principal (the manufacturer or the farmer). Distributors set up huge warehouses to handle large volumes of food and supplies, providing service to a predetermined geographical area. There are two basic types of distributors. One is called the speciality distributor and the second is classified as a broadline distributor.

A **speciality distributor** is used when a specific item is required by the caterer. Speciality distributors handle only one product or a limited inventory. They may specialize only in produce or seafood, carry only commercial food service equipment, or handle only detergents and chemical agents.

Bernard Food Industries, Inc., of Evanston, IL, is a **speciality wholesaler** not many caterers' may be familiar with. This product specialist is a direct sales company that manufactures their own brand name products and package private label items for the purveyor. They also operate a retail store on the Web at www.diet-shop.com. Bernard Food Industries, Inc. has recognized the needs of their customers who, for medical reasons, must restrict their intake of sugar, sodium, fat, cholesterol, or calories. The products they offer are the same high quality sold to restaurants, cruise ships, spas, and healthcare facilities nationwide.

CUSTOMER-RESPONSIVE POLICIES

1. Break up cases to permit a caterer to mix and match individual products at no additional cost to the buyer.
2. Provide samples of any product.
3. Sponsor product and cooking demonstrations.
4. Provide complete nutrient analysis on each item in a product line.
5. Provide diet cookbooks with complete, standardized recipes.
6. Make direct mail catalog available for individual consumers.

Figure 8-3 *Customer-responsive policies.*

These specialized products are offered on the Web so that individuals can conveniently maintain their dietary regimen while enjoying delectable foods which might otherwise be prohibited. Diet-Shoppe products also appeal to customers who wish to establish healthier eating patterns for their families. All products are labeled with complete nutritional information. Bernard Food Industries, Inc. is the first company to pioneer NutraSweet™ in cake mixes after it was approved by the Food and Drug Administration.

Bernard Food Industries' primary niche is for long-term care, assisted-living facilities, health care facilities, summer camps, institutional food service, correctional facilities, and school food service. Caterers who service these markets request Bernard's products when they must meet the nutrition requirements of specialized diets because they are customer driven (Figure 8–3).

Broadline Distributors

Broadline distributors are another type of distributor. A **broadline distributor** will stock a large variety of food, nonfood supplies, and equipment. It is common for a broadline distributor to stock in their warehouse between 7,000 and 20,000 different products. A broadline distributor is a speciality distributor and will "bundle" a number of specialized product lines, then warehouse them together (Figure 8–4).

Food Shows

A food show is an opportunity for a caterer to sample multiple product lines and individual items. These are purveyor or restaurant association sponsored. Most distributors will have a food show at least once a year. The principals' entry or booth fees, paid to the distributor for the right to participate in the food show, pays the expenses.

BROADLINE DISTRIBUTOR BUNDLED PRODUCT LINE

1. produce
2. meats
3. seafood
4. beverages
5. paper products and cleaning supplies
6. equipment
7. branded foods
8. dairy

Figure 8-4 *Broadline distributor bundled product line.*

The reason principals participate in distributor-held food shows are because of the buyers who attend. This captive audience is ready to buy. Each registered participant receives a color-coded badge to indicate the position of the participant. Badges are issued to reveal visitors who do not have purchasing authority, visitors who have recently selected the distributor as their supplier, visitors who are deciding if they want to use the supplier, those with purchasing power, and VIPs (Very Important People). The color of the badge helps each principal's representative at the show to quickly identify those visitors who have purchasing authority from those who lack purchasing power.

Distributors have *buying clubs* within their customer groups. These buying clubs may have names like the *Gold Club*, the *Silver Club*, and the *Bronze Club*. To become a member of one of these clubs, an annual payment of a specified dollar amount must be made to the distributor. Membership in some of these clubs denotes special customers who purchase very large volumes of products. These customers benefit from pricing formulas, based on the volume they purchase. The color of the badge worn by these customers will immediately identify a buyer who purchases a large volume of products.

Food shows are local, regional, and national. The largest trade show in the world, the National Restaurant Association Restaurant, Hotel-Motel Show is held each May at Chicago's McCormick Place.

Attending food and trade shows is important because it gives the caterer opportunity to meet the manufacturer's agent who sells to the distributor. They may meet the food service broker, who is the link between the principal and the distributor. Many times, the caterer's DSR, as well as the distributor's entire professional support staff, is available to provide personal attention.

The food show is usually held in a large convention hall or at a conference facility. The food broker will set up booths which display their principal's product lines. The smart caterer will work the show and create networking opportunities by navigating through the maze of booths to:

◆ sample a variety of new and different foods.

◆ gather information on new emerging trends, nutrition, and changing lifestyles.

◆ see new products and technology.

◆ meet and discuss business in a "low pressure" environment.

Another advantage of attending food shows is the financial incentive granted by the principals. Principals sometimes offer show allowances, which are price discounts that may extend six to eight weeks after the close of the show. The money saved per case may enable the caterer to achieve financial objectives. Caterers can purchase the same item at a reduced price, or a higher-priced, higher-quality item at a discounted price equal to the standard item's cost.

Principals may also offer sales promotions and incentives during the show. For example, a buyer will receive a discounted price per case. They will also issue "bonus bucks" per purchased case. The discounted savings are reflected at the time of purchase. The price is automatically adjusted on the invoice when the purveyor ships the product and the caterer takes ownership at delivery.

The bonus buck promotion is an additional incentive designed for the buyer to place an order at the show. Bonus bucks are issued when the buyer physically submits the order from the broker at the food show. These bonus bucks, which must be redeemed before the show ends, can be used to acquire different items such as prizes, as selected by the distributor; gift certificates from mail order catalogs, issued by the distributor; and equipment. The bonus buck value can be deducted from the balance of the invoice price. This additional reduction is granted when the caterer has taken delivery of all cases ordered..

Food Brokers

A **food broker** serves distinctive functions in the industry. First, the broker will bring the buyer and the seller together in the marketplace. Second, the broker may represent many different noncompeting product lines from noncompeting principles or manufacturers. Third, a food broker understands the attributes of each product line and communicates this information to the caterer. Fourth, the broker provides the principal with a national sales force. The broker is the principal's local sales representative.

Brokers serve a valuable role by understanding the local caterer's needs, wants, and demands and by communicating these to the principal. Brokers monitor trends and try to identify the future direction of the market. Acting as the principal's sales representative, the broker is also assigned as their representative to a distributor. The broker arranges for the distributor to stock and distribute the principal's product line in their assigned geographical area. However, the broker does not take title to the goods sold or set prices for the items they represent.

Brokers maintain an office, but will visit or *call-on* caterers to demonstrate their principal's product line. They will also teach caterers how to prepare the products. A broker may visit a caterer alone or *ride with* or *work with* a DSR from their assigned distributor. A caterer should be notified in advance by the DSR or by the broker to set an appointment.

Brokers conduct training programs to educate caterers about new ideas, products, culinary techniques, and bundling of product lines to build recipes. They also train DSRs. They are the channels used to relay information from the principal to the distributor. The brokerage firm will employ brokers based upon their need, number of principals, and size of geographical service area.

TIPS FROM THE TRADE

Catering is a fascinating field. The products that are used by caterers most frequently are what I will call the *upper-grade of products*. Caterers seem to use the rice products we call our long-grain and wild, or long-grain and wild-garden blend, at many weddings or other big feeding events. When people see wild rice on their plate, it gives a perception of "upper class" or upscale dining. The guest's perception is that they are receiving a higher grade of food. These products work very well for a caterer.

The cost of long-grain and wild rice is between 16 and 18 cents a serving, so it is fairly inexpensive. One advantage our rice delivers for the caterer is that it accents the plate very well when served with a protein. Regardless of whether the protein is beef, seafood, or poultry, our rice product line provides the caterer with many alternatives and allows flexibility when planning a menu for a client.

The products Uncle Ben's, Inc. are coming out with now seem to be targeting and dovetailing more to meet the needs of the caterer. We are introducing an entire line of organic pastas and sauces. These items are ideally suited for the catering industry because they offer a great appreciation for popular pesticide-free foods. This product line is not a usual item that a consumer can purchase in a grocery store.

Michael P. Simon, Jr.
Great Lakes Region Manager
MasterFoodServices™,
A Division of Uncle Ben's, Inc.
Houston, TX

Manufacturer's Agents

Caterers will have the opportunity to work with **manufacturers' agents** who are employed directly by the principal to represent their interests in a geographical area. A manufacturer's agent works exclusively for the one principal. This person functions as the account executive for the parent company, very similar to the food broker, but with more responsibility. They have direct responsibility for completing paperwork and accomplishing sales goals for each product with the distributors. They do not take title to the goods sold, nor do they issue invoices or set prices. A manufacturer's agent will meet with a caterer to demonstrate their product lines and help the caterer to achieve success in their business. A manufacturer's agent may also be called a *territory manager*.

There are two types of manufacturers' agents in the marketplace. One is the manufacturer's agent who has direct sales responsibilities. This person operates as an individual in the market and does not share their time with anyone else in the promotion and distribution of their company's product. The other type is a manufacturer's agent with broker responsibility who functions in the same way but has a network of brokers to support the individual's and principal's sales efforts.

Wholesale Clubs

Wholesale clubs are generally organized as very large warehouses that stock a variety of bulk foods, clothes, and equipment. A caterer can join these clubs for a membership fee, granting the privilege to purchase food and supplies at this warehouse. Wholesale clubs have both advantages and disadvantages (Figure 8–5).

Retail Grocery Store

Some caterers may use the **retail grocery store** to make purchases. Depending on the production needs and the menu selected, it might be good business to purchase

WHOLESALE CLUBS

Advantages
- ◆ They offer a competitive price for the purchase of bulk food items, non-food supplies and equipment.
- ◆ Many operate seven days a week, twenty-four hours per day.
- ◆ No minimum purchase is required.

Disadvantages
- ◆ They are "cash and carry" operations. Unless a credit card is used, the wholesale club does not extend credit.
- ◆ The caterer must physically shop at the club.
- ◆ They must get the items back to the operation using their own transportation.
- ◆ A membership fee is charged, usually on an annual basis.
- ◆ They lack professional support services, such as menu development, educational services, or computer assistance.

Figure 8–5 *Advantages and disadvantages of wholesale clubs.*

exactly what you need, in the right quantities, at the right price, in the grocery store. Often, the caterer can negotiate a deal with the owner of the grocery store to establish a fixed markup or better pricing formula than a consumer purchase.

◆ ORDERING

Ordering implies the caterer will secure the right amount and kind of raw materials needed to meet production and satisfy the client. Ordering requires an understanding of the menu, number of guaranteed guests, portion size, and standardized recipes. Other factors include the storage capabilities, inventory levels, yield, and production capabilities.

The ordering task can be further divided by activity. First, determine the correct quantity of raw materials. This is accomplished by identifying each item on the menu. Then, review each standardized recipe's ingredients, expected yield, and portion size. Multiply this information by the guaranteed number of guests. Once the exact amount is determined, subtract this from its inventory level. The difference between what is needed and the inventory level is the amount to order (Figure 8–6). The actual delivery of the order depends on the purveyor's delivery schedule in the area the caterer is located.

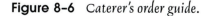

CATERER'S ORDER GUIDE
(Confidential)

Eff. Date:

Run Date:

Order Guide Number   Page:

Purveyor's Name & Address
Territory Manager & Phone Number
Deliver Instructions

Last Purchase Date	Product Number	Units/Each	Description	Line Number	Price

Figure 8-6 *Caterer's order guide.*

The second task is to place the order. The caterer will contact the purveyor with items to be delivered. The purchase order (Figure 8–7) lists the items to be ordered, terms, and delivery date. Each caterer must develop an ordering format based on their individual needs.

CATERING COMPANY PURCHASE ORDER

Purchase Order Number 00001

Order Date _____

Name of Catering Company _____ Address _____

Purchasing Agent _____ E-mail _____ Voice mail _____ Fax _____

Order Requested By _____ E-mail _____ Voice Mail _____ Fax _____

Authorized by _____ Date_____
(Signature)

SUPPLIER NAME

Address _____ Contact Person _____

E-mail _____ Voice mail _____ Fax _____

Please Ship

Required Delivery Date_____

Terms_____

Freight Charges FOB _____ COD (Amount) $ _____ Pre-paid _____

Special Instructions

Quantity Ordered	Pack Size/Description	Page No.	Lbs./Quantity Shipped	Unit Price	Extension

TOTAL $ _____

Copies to Purchasing___, Receiving__, Accounts Payable____, Purchase Request____

Figure 8-7 *Catering company Purchase Order.*

Portion Control

One of the most important catering management control tasks is the measurement of ingredients and portions in food production. A caterer will measure ingredients by number, volume, or weight. Standardized recipes are also written with ingredients stated as either weight or measure.

The use of a dipper (scoop) or ladle is primarily used to control the amount of food served, thus helping to control portions(Figure 8–8). These are excellent tools to standardize each guest's portion size, simplifying the purchasing task. The size of a dipper reflects how many portions one leveled dipper gives per quart. For example, a dipper number 6 delivers six scoops per quart. Ladles range in size, and are used to serve stews, soups, sauces, gravies, or dressings. Some of the most common size ladles, (Figure 8–9), range in size from one to eight ounces.

Purchasing the correct amount of food may challenge the caterer when there is a loss because of waste. Unless purchasing a convenience food, which offers a 100% yield, food may vary from it's *As-Purchased (A.P.)* form to its *Edible Portion (E.P.)* form, the amount of food the guest will consume.

The form and amount of food As Purchased (A.P.) may affect its E.P. yield. This depends on its storage environment, handling, method of preparation, and consumption form. Meat stored in refrigeration may lose weight as it ages because water will evaporate over an extended period of time. If the caterer cuts steaks from beef tenderloin, some loss of the product is expected because of the handling and processing. Also, cooking the steak will result in a loss of the product as it may shrink due to the loss of moisture and fat during the cooking process.

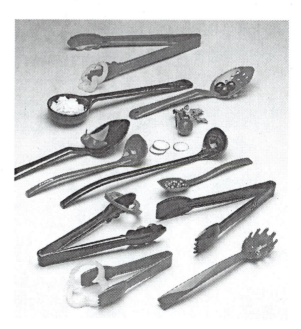

Figure 8-8 *Manufacturers provide an array of sizes for serving utensils to help control portion size and simplify purchasing.*

COMMON LADLE SIZES	
Dipper Number	**Approximate Weight**
6	6 oz
8	4–5 oz
10	3–4 oz
12	2 1/2–3 oz
16	2–21/4 oz
20	1 3/4–2 oz
24	1 1/2–1 3/4 oz
30	1–1 1/2 oz

Figure 8-9 *Common ladle sizes*

To purchase correctly, an accurate understanding of the relationship between A.P. and E.P. concepts must be comprehended.

1. **As-Purchased (A.P.).** This is amount of raw material purchased. It is in the form as delivered by the purveyor. The As-Purchased amount will always represent the original weight. It is the base, beginning weight; it always represents the total or 100%.

2. **Edible Portion (E.P.).** The Edible-Portion is the amount of food a caterer will expect the customer to consume. It is always less than the As-Purchased weight.

3. **As-Served (A.S.).** The As-Served weight represents the portion size a caterer will serve to the guest. It is always less than the As-Purchased weight.

4. **Waste (W).** Waste is the amount of product lost during its preparation and storage. Its removal delivers its As-Served or Edible-Portion weight. Waste *will always* be a part of the As-Purchased weight or part of the 100%.

5. **Waste Percentage (W%).** The waste percentage is the amount of waste expressed as a percentage. To calculate the waste percentage, divide the Edible-Portion weight by the As-Purchased weight and multiply by 100.

The following example of the AP/EP comparison using pistachio nuts helps clarify this concept.

A.P.: One pound (16 ounces) of pistachio nuts in the shell (As-Purchased). Remove the meat from the shell.

E.P.: One-half pound (8 ounces) of pistachio nuts without the shell (Edible-Portion).

The caterer must calculate the As-Purchased weight to meet the Edible-Portion needs. First, the caterer will multiply the Edible-Portion size by the customer count. This amount will be the total Edible-Portion weight required to serve each guest the correct portion amount. To further illustrate this concept, a caterer is serving 125 guests 4 ounces (E.P.) beef tenderloin. Therefore, 125 guests multiplied by 4 ounces equals 500 ounces or 31.25 pounds of E.P. weight. It is extremely important to control portion size. Each guest should be served only 4 ounces. If the guests are served more, the caterer will not have enough beef tenderloin.

The next step is for the caterer to calculate the As-Purchased weight. The A.P. calculation is important because the right amount of raw beef tenderloin must be procured. To calculate this amount, the caterer must know the yield of the beef tenderloin. Each caterer should calculate their own yield information using the same preparation and cooking techniques as stated in the recipe. It is recommended to conduct at least three tests to arrive at the yield. Although accurate records should always be kept by the production staff for reference, the yield can also be approximated using industry standards.

Using the beef tenderloin example, the caterer uses a yield of 90%. To calculate the A.P. amount, divide the E.P. weight by the yield. Therefore, 31 lbs. divided by 90% equals 34 lbs. 7 ounces. The caterer will purchase 35 pounds of beef tenderloin.

If the caterer begins with 35 lbs., and after cooking the beef tenderloin, found the ending weight is 31 lbs., the waste is 4 lbs. The waste percentage is calculated by dividing the ending weight by the beginning weight. In this case, 31 lbs. divided by 35 lbs. equals 89%. For reference and consistency, many caterers use a portion control form (Figure 8–10).

◈ RECEIVING

Receiving is a vital task that requires attention from all personnel. The fundamental task of receiving is to verify all deliveries against specifications and quantity; what has been delivered by a purveyor must match what has been ordered and paid for by the caterer. This leads to **Ingredient for Success 29: "Good receiving and planning provide the caterer with a major economical advantage. Good receiving principles provide control."**

Receiving is the first control point in the flow of food through a caterer's facility. Because it is the first step, careful attention paid to this task can reduce defects that may cause potential problems throughout the entire system. Therefore, it is important to formulate a well-researched receiving plan based on standard operating procedures and guided by policy (Figure 8–11).

The receiving area should be organized as part of the formal management structure. The caterer must implement some form of control and tracking system (Figures 8–12 and 8–13) to verify the actual receiving activities being executed for the benefit of the organization. First, separate all related purchasing and receiving responsibilities. A separate employee should be accountable for the act of buying, receiving, and paying of bills.

PORTION CONTROL FORM

Production Department Manager/Chef _____

Service Staff Manager _____

Function _____

Day of Function _____ Date of Function _____

Date of Production _____

Production Schedule Verified _____

Guaranteed Number _____ Percent Overage* _____ Total Portions _____

Menu Item	Recipe No.	Yield	Portion Size	Actual Yield	Portions Served	Difference	Waste	Variance + or -

*Percent overage is an approximate percent based on historical data, forecasting, and the educated guess. It is determined by including the calculation of potential employee mistakes (spilled food, less than 100% food E.P. yields), food for employee meals, bartender meals, and entertainer meals.

Figure 8-10 *Portion control form.*

STANDARD RECEIVING PROCEDURES

1. Immediately inspect each item against a copy of its specification and purchase order.
2. Know the quality standard against which all products will be compared.
3. Understand the purveyor's policies regarding a rejected delivery.
4. Understand the purveyor's policy for credit because of an overcharge.
5. Understand the purveyor's policy for issuing a request for credit/pickup.
6. Verify weights, count, and price by comparing the actual delivered item against the invoice and the specification.
7. Follow first-in, first-out procedures.
8. Write the delivery date and its price directly on the case or item to denote time and value.
9. Schedule deliveries during slower business hours.
10. Schedule enough employees to help put the order away.
11. Sponsor training to prepare receiving personnel in all phases of their job.
12. Keep the receiving area organized, clean, and sanitized.
13. Be prepared to randomly sample items to keep everyone honest.
14. Keep accurate receiving records each day.

Figure 8-11 *Standard receiving procedures.*

DAILY RECEIVING REPORT

Date _____

Employee _____

Purveyor	Invoice Number	Item Description	Unit Price	Amount Received	Total Cost	Receiving Temp. (CCP)	Accept/ Reject

Comments

Figure 8-12 *Daily Receiving Reports help track quantities and costs for billing reconciliation.*

Day _____   Date _____

Received by _____

Delivered by (Driver's Name) _____

Specification Adherence _____

Critical Control Points _____

Correct Weight _____

Correct Count _____

Correct Prices _____

Comments:

Figure 8-13 *Receiving Stamps provide vital records and contacts for resolving discrepancies.*

Trust is especially important in this activity. Separating these related tasks provides a safeguard against unethical behavior by any one person. Detailed records should be kept of all credit and return requests (Figures 8–14 and 8–15).

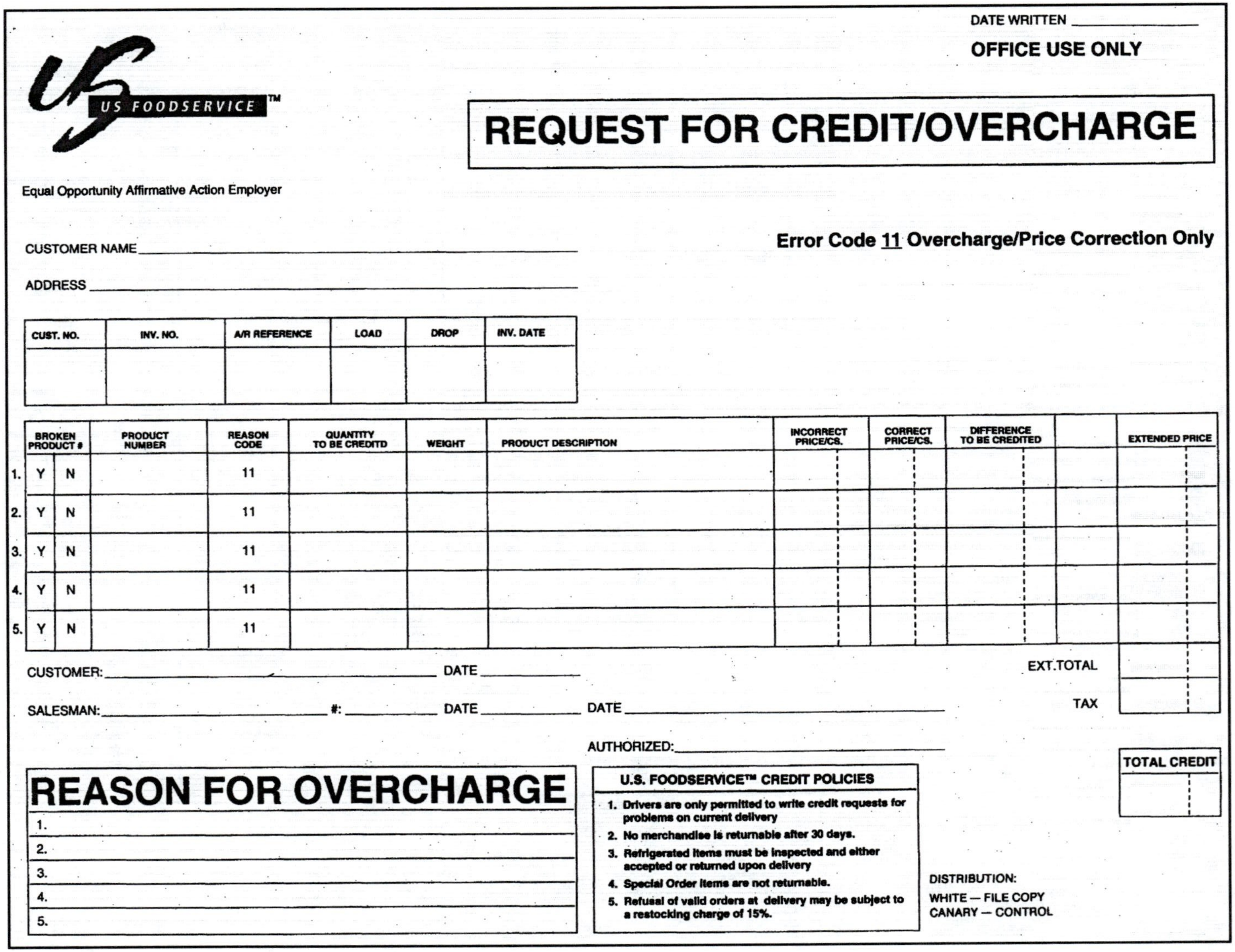

DATE WRITTEN ____________

OFFICE USE ONLY

US FOODSERVICE™

Equal Opportunity Affirmative Action Employer

REQUEST FOR CREDIT/OVERCHARGE

Error Code 11 Overcharge/Price Correction Only

CUSTOMER NAME ____________

ADDRESS ____________

CUST. NO.	INV. NO.	A/R REFERENCE	LOAD	DROP	INV. DATE

	BROKEN PRODUCT #		PRODUCT NUMBER	REASON CODE	QUANTITY TO BE CREDITD	WEIGHT	PRODUCT DESCRIPTION	INCORRECT PRICE/CS.	CORRECT PRICE/CS.	DIFFERENCE TO BE CREDITED		EXTENDED PRICE
1.	Y	N		11								
2.	Y	N		11								
3.	Y	N		11								
4.	Y	N		11								
5.	Y	N		11								

CUSTOMER: ____________ DATE ____________ EXT.TOTAL

SALESMAN: ____________ #: ____________ DATE ____________ DATE ____________ TAX

AUTHORIZED: ____________

TOTAL CREDIT

REASON FOR OVERCHARGE

1.

2.

3.

4.

5.

U.S. FOODSERVICE™ CREDIT POLICIES

1. Drivers are only permitted to write credit requests for problems on current delivery
2. No merchandise is returnable after 30 days.
3. Refrigerated items must be inspected and either accepted or returned upon delivery
4. Special Order items are not returnable.
5. Refusal of valid orders at delivery may be subject to a restocking charge of 15%.

DISTRIBUTION:
WHITE — FILE COPY
CANARY — CONTROL

Figure 8-14 *Credit/Overcharge request form.*

Figure 8-15 *Credit/Pickup request form.*

Receiving Fundamentals
(Adapted from the 1999 FDA Model Food Code)

The receiving area should be well lit. All acceptance of food should be done in an area that is near the delivery door. The storage areas, such as refrigeration, freezer, and dry storage room should be near the door also. The receiving area should be equipped with some common tools, which may include a scale, thermometer, can opener, razor knife, and permanent markers.

The thermometer may be the most important universal tool found in a catering operation. It is used by the receiving personnel to inspect items against their specification. The thermometer of choice should have a scale ranging from 0° to 222°F; accurate to +/- 2°F, numerically sealed, bimetallic with a five-inch stem, and having a two-inch sensing area.

The correct thermometer is used to ensure that the food being received by a caterer is at proper temperatures. All refrigerated, potentially-hazardous food must be received at a temperature of 41°F (5°C) or below. Upon receipt, all potentially-hazardous food should not exhibit any evidence of previous temperature abuse. If a food is labeled frozen and is shipped frozen by a food processing plant, it must be received from a supplier in the frozen state.

Potentially-hazardous food that is cooked to a specific temperature and received hot must be at a temperature of 140°F (60°C) or above. Always obtain food from reputable suppliers who comply with local, state, and federal laws.

◆ STORAGE CONTROL

The objective of **storage**, a major component of the purchasing process, is to maintain adequate space for perishable goods, dry goods, beverage, chemicals, and equipment. Organization of the storage area helps reduce clutter and prevents loss of merchandise (Figure 8–16). Frequent cleaning and sanitation eliminate potential insect and rodent infestation. Many establishments fail to recognize the potential loss through spoilage, pilferage, and theft. Spoilage can be prevented by ordering

Figure 8-16 *An organized storage area reduces clutter and pilferage.*

the correct amount, properly rotating stock, and having optimal environmental conditions. Adequate temperature and humidity help to maintain the quality of food. Pilferage is often referred to as inventory shrinkage or skimming. Pilferage is employee theft by stealing. Employees may also eat food without authorization.

If during the process of food production any food or ingredients are removed from their original packages and placed into working containers, always identify the food. Common ingredients such as cooking oils, flour, herbs, spices, and sugar are often transferred into appropriate storage containers. Always identify the food in their new containers with its common name. The date may be also added to the container. When the food or ingredient is easily and unmistakably recognized by an employee, such as with dry pasta or dry noodles, the common name of the food may not need to be identified on the container.

Always be on guard to prevent cross contamination. This can be accomplished by separating raw animal foods during storage, preparation, holding, and display (Figure 8–17).

HOW TO PROTECT FOODS FROM CROSS-CONTAMINATION

1. Protect raw, ready-to-eat food, including raw animal food such as fish for sushi or molluscan shellfish, or other food such as vegetables, from each other.
2. Protect cooked, ready-to-eat food from raw food. The exception, of course, is when they are combined as ingredients that will require cooking.
3. Clean and sanitize equipment and utensils used while displaying food.
4. Use separate equipment for each type of food.
5. Arrange each type of food in sanitized equipment so that cross-contamination is prevented.
6. Prepare each type of food at different times and in separate areas.
7. Store the food in packages, covered containers, or wrappings to prevent cross-contamination.
8. Clean hermetically-sealed containers of food of visible soil before opening.
9. Protect food containers, that are received packaged together in a case or overwrap, from cuts when the case or overwrap is opened.
10. Store damaged, spoiled, or recalled food being held in the food establishment away from other foods.
11. Separate unwashed fruits and vegetables from ready-to-eat food.
12. The following foods do not apply to the above principles.
    a. whole, uncut, raw fruits and vegetables, and nuts in the shell that require peeling or hulling before consumption
    b. primal cuts, quarters, or sides of raw meat or slab bacon that are hung on clean, sanitized hooks or placed on clean, sanitized racks
    c. whole, uncut, processed meat such as country hams and smoked or cured sausages that are placed on clean, sanitized racks

Figure 8-17 *Protecting foods from cross-contamination. (Adapted from the 1999 FDA Model Food Code.)*

Storage or Display of Food in Contact with Water or Ice

The caterer should not store packaged food in direct contact with ice or water if the food is subject to deterioration if the water enters its packaging or container.

Unpackaged food must not be stored in direct contact with undrained ice. However, whole, raw fruits or vegetables; cut, raw vegetables such as celery, carrot sticks, or cut potatoes; and tofu may be immersed in ice or water. Raw chicken and fish that are received immersed in ice in shipping containers may remain in that condition temporarily while awaiting preparation, display, service, or sale.

In-Use Utensils, Between-Use Storage

During any break in the food production process, all food preparation and dispensing utensils should be stored in a proper manner (Figure 8–18). Always use common sense when storing food and ingredients (Figures 8–19 and 8–20).

◆ INVENTORY MANAGEMENT

Inventory management is the key to protecting the physical assets for all events. Inventory control is the task of managing the amount of merchandise in the storage areas. Each caterer will need to maintain a minimum level of inventory, depending on the type of caterer. Proper management of inventory keeps the right amount in storage and prevents the over purchase of items, which may lead to problems such as spoilage, quality deterioration, theft, and pilferage.

UTENSIL STORAGE DURING PRODUCTION AND SERVICE

Food utensils should be stored:

1. in the food with their handles above the top of the food and the container.
2. in food that is not potentially hazardous with their handles above the top of the food within containers or equipment that can be closed, such as bins of sugar, flour, or cinnamon.
3. on a clean portion of the food preparation table or cooking equipment only if the in-use utensil and the food-contact surface are cleaned and sanitized at the acceptable frequency.
4. in running water of sufficient velocity to flush particles down the drain, especially when used with moist food such as ice cream or mashed potatoes.
5. in a clean, protected location if the utensils, such as ice scoops, are used only with a food that is not potentially hazardous.
6. in a water container if the water is maintained at a temperature of at least 140°F (60°C) and the container is cleaned frequently.

Figure 8-18 *Proper storage of food utensils during production and service.* (Adapted from the 1999 FDA Model Food Code.)

FOOD STORAGE PRINCIPLES

Food shall be protected from contamination by proper storage:
1. in a clean, dry location.
2. where it is not exposed to splash, dust, or other contamination.
3. at least 6 inches (15 cm) above the floor.
    a. Food in packages and working containers may be stored less than 6 inches (15 cm) above the floor on case lot handling equipment.
    b. Pressurized beverage containers, cased food in waterproof containers such as bottles or cans, and milk containers in plastic crates may be stored on a floor that is clean and not exposed to floor moisture.

Figure 8-19 *Food storage principles. (Adapted from the 1999 FDA Model Food Code.)*

PROHIBITED AREAS FOR FOOD STORAGE

Food may not be stored:
1. in locker rooms.
2. in toilet rooms.
3. in dressing rooms.
4. in garbage rooms.
5. in mechanical rooms.
6. under sewer lines that are not shielded to intercept potential drips
7. under leaking water lines, including leaking automatic fire sprinkler. heads, or under lines on which water has condensed.
8. under open stairwells.
9. under other sources of contamination.

Figure 8-20 *Food storage prohibited areas. (Adapted from the 1999 FDA Model Food Code.)*

Inventory is a financial investment for the caterer. Each item in the inventory should be marked with the date and its unit price when it is received. Pricing each item individually or by the pack, package, or case will alert every employee to the value (real cost) of the item. This is one method some caterers use to communicate the value of inventory.

The caterer will want to balance the investment of the inventory, or its stock levels against how fast it can be consumed in the operations. It does not make good business sense to tie up money into a large inventory. This is why inventory must be coordinated with production and forecasted against future functions. This will establish individual par levels, or the amount maintained in storage to be sufficient to meet the production needs without excessive money invested. A challenge of managing this inventory is to avoid stock-outs. A *stock-out* occurs when an item is depleted before the next order is delivered. Frequent stock-outs cause break downs in the production system by creating pauses in production. When a stock-out occurs, the caterer will have to send an employee to the store to purchase this item.

Inventory management also determines the amount of inventory consumed for each function or for a particular accounting period. This is accomplished by tracking all purchases. First, the dollar value of the beginning storeroom inventory is calculated. All purchases transferred to the storeroom are added (less any items that have been issued). The total should equal closing inventory. *Issues* represent items requisitioned from the store room. Direct issues are items sent immediately upon receipt by the caterer into the production system.

Another task of inventory management is the physical counting of each item to find out what is in storage. Physical inventories may be taken at the end of a function, end of a weekly accounting period, or at the end of the month. Appropriate inventory control alerts the caterer to shortages or other discrepancies that may occur in the catering system. One method to calculate the cost of sales is illustrated in Figure 8–21.

Inventory control affects the entire operation. The cost of food sold will emerge on the income statement (Chapter 11). This figure represents everything that was consumed in the production process, lost through waste or pilferage, and unauthorized consumption by employees. The challenge for the caterer is to interpret this cost of goods sold by determining if the value is higher or lower than the established standard.

Product and stock rotation are also vital. The process of rotating inventory should always be a main concern for a caterer. Organization of storage areas insures proper sanitation and distribution of all products from their designated areas. Properly placed inventory also provides accurate accounting of products for effective reordering techniques.

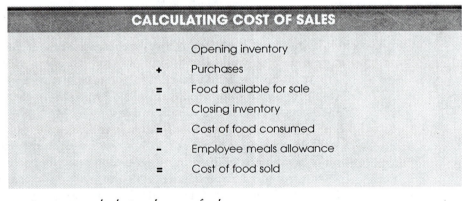

CALCULATING COST OF SALES

	Opening inventory
+	Purchases
=	Food available for sale
−	Closing inventory
=	Cost of food consumed
−	Employee meals allowance
=	Cost of food sold

Figure 8-21 *Calculating the cost of sales.*

The inventory turnover rate is calculated to find how quickly the entire stock level is being consumed or to determine how each individual item or category is being sold and replaced in storage. This rate will signal how effectively the caterer is managing the inventory. An inventory turnover rate is calculated using the cost of food sold and the average inventory rate. The average inventory rate is determined by adding the opening and closing inventories for the period and dividing by two. To calculate an inventory turnover rate, take the cost of food sold divided by average inventory cost.

Summary

The organizing function helps to accomplish the catering plan. Created by the caterer, this formal structure is designed to help allocate and control resources. A strong, but flexible, formal structure must support the implementation of the caterer's evolving strategy, as outlined in the catering plan. The core organizing tasks for most caterers include creating the menu, developing recipes, writing specifications, ordering, receiving, issuing, producing, transporting, and service.

Review Questions

Brief Answers

1. Describe why organizing is the third catering management function.
2. Explain how organizing helps accomplish the plan.
3. Explain how a caterer organizes an event.
4. Explain specifications.
5. Explain the main goal of purchasing.
6. Provide examples of common purchasing policies.
7. Describe how to build a caterer and supplier relationship.
8. Explain how a caterer can find a reliable supplier.
9. Discuss why a caterer attends food shows.
10. Describe the role of a food broker, broadline purveyor, and manufacturer's agent.
11. Explain why ordering is important to the purchasing function.
12. Explain standard receiving procedures.
13. Explain what the following Ingredients for Success mean to you.

    Ingredient for Success 26: "Structure is dependent on the mission of the organization."

    Ingredient for Success 27: "Every caterer should have at least two good suppliers, a principal supplier and a backup supplier."

Ingredient for Success 28: "The supplier is only as dependable and responsible as the salesperson and the truck driver who delivers the food"

Ingredient for Success 29: "Good receiving and planning provide the caterer with a major economical advantage. Good receiving principles provide control."

Multiple Choice

Select the single best answer for each question.

1. A(n) _____ refers to the management design of a catering operation.
   a. informal structure
   b. formal structure
   c. invisible structure
   d. intangible structure
   e. covert structure

2. Specifications are used in the catering operation to:
   a. confuse competition
   b. create "what if" scenario's
   c. communicate standards
   d. design a catering plan
   e. implement a catering plan

3. Which of the following is an advantage of attending a food show?
   a. sample a variety of different kinds of foods
   b. see new products and emerging technology
   c. network with other caterers
   d. secure financial incentives from manufacturer's agent
   e. all of the above are considered advantages

True or False

Read each of the following statements and determine if it is true or false.

1. A manufacturer's agent is employed directly by the principal to represent their interests in a geographical area.

2. The primary purpose of a food broker is to bring a buyer and a seller together in the marketplace.

3. All caterers have basic purchasing needs, regardless of the specific needs unique to their own operation.

Putting It All Together

Contact some representatives from the food distribution channel—a broadline purveyor, a speciality purveyor, a food broker, and a manufacturer's agent. Seek information to describe what their roles are in the distribution channel. Ask for information regarding the services they provide a caterer.

Chapter Nine | Equipment

Key Terms | Objectives

multitasking equipment

retherm

workstation

After studying this chapter, you should be able to:

◆ Describe equipment and design considerations.

◆ Explain how a caterer selects the type of utility to use as the energy source.

◆ Explain why the menu is a powerful tool used to determine the design and layout of workstations.

◆ Explain individual workstations, such as preparation, hot and cold food production, and final preparation needs.

◆ Explain how the caterer acquires equipment.

◆ Explain the appropriate methods and techniques a caterer must implement to prevent occurrences of foodborne illness.

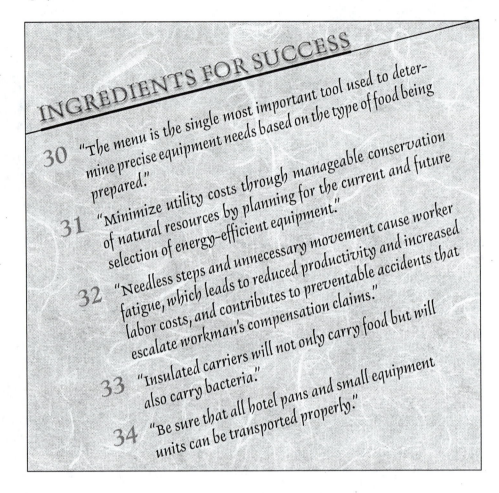

INGREDIENTS FOR SUCCESS

30 "The menu is the single most important tool used to determine precise equipment needs based on the type of food being prepared."

31 "Minimize utility costs through manageable conservation of natural resources by planning for the current and future selection of energy-efficient equipment."

32 "Needless steps and unnecessary movement cause worker fatigue, which leads to reduced productivity and increased labor costs, and contributes to preventable accidents that escalate workman's compensation claims."

33 "Insulated carriers will not only carry food but will also carry bacteria."

34 "Be sure that all hotel pans and small equipment units can be transported properly."

◆ EQUIPMENT AND DESIGN CONSIDERATIONS

In the catering operation, the challenge is for a caterer to efficiently and effectively design and equip the food production facility by maximizing spatial relationships and functionality, while minimizing capital investment through the selection of **multitasking equipment**. *"The menu is the single most important tool used to determine precise equipment needs based on the type of food being prepared." (Ingredient for Success 30).*

The fourth catering function involves identifying what furniture, fixtures, and equipment are needed to equip the facility. The answers to the following questions will help to identify the type of equipment needed.

1. What kind of menu will be produced? What type of equipment is required to produce the food, hold it, **retherm** it, transport it, serve it, and clean it?

2. Who is the target customer? Remember *Ingredient for Success 2: "We cannot be all things to all people."* If the focus is to cater breakfast functions, the type of equipment may be different from that required to prepare complete meals for dinner functions.

A caterer must first determine the mission of the organization and then set a strategic direction as the first step toward creating an effective menu. To adequately prepare the food production area, the caterer must understand the relationship between several key factors that shape, build, and can lead to the success of the catering business. These factors are always exerting either covert or overt pressure on the catering business. They demand attention, requiring the caterer to constantly monitor their business environment The following factors will influence the caterer's ability to adequately equip a food production system.

1. performance and functionality of design—simple to take apart and reassemble

2. maintenance, reliability, and warranty of equipment; availability and cost of replacement parts

3. employee skill level and relationship to the production needs of the menu

4. current and future equipment requirements based on customer needs, wants, and demands

5. application and development of new technology

6. government regulations, including HACCP procedures and safety features

7. competitors' adaptation of technology to reduce labor and utility costs

8. innovations in product design, aesthetics, components, and/or construction features

◈ UTILITIES

The decision to use either natural gas, electric, or a combination of both as the energy source to drive the equipment in the production area, is another factor that affects the purchase of equipment. While there are advantages and disadvantages for each kind of utility, the decision to use one or another may simply be a personal preference of the caterer or may be limited to availability at the facility.

◈ THE MENU

The menu is a powerful tool used to determine the design, layout, and equipment for the production and service area and each individual **workstation** created within the production area.

TIPS FROM THE TRADE

When Jardine's first opened, electric power was the only utility available at their location so there was no decision to be made. All of the production equipment purchased was powered by electricity. Because electricity is rather expensive when compared to natural gas, we were vigilant in creating a structured production schedule to minimize energy use and its cost. This production schedule eventually evolved into a bigger program which featured *energy conservation awareness training* for the employees.

Later, when natural gas became available, a decision was made to switch the equipment from electricity to natural gas because gas is less expensive. Using natural gas significantly reduced the operation's monthly utility costs.

This illustrates **Ingredient for Success 31: "Minimize utility costs through manageable conservation of natural resources by planning for the current and future selection of energy-efficient equipment."**

Bill Jardine
Jardine's Farm Restaurant & Catering
Sarver, PA

◆ WORKSTATIONS

Common workstations designated in a caterer's production facility are created by the menu with emphasis on time and motion studies. Understanding the flow of food and production tasks leads to carefully laid-out workstations. Carefully laid-out workstations minimize movement and needless steps (Figure 9–1).

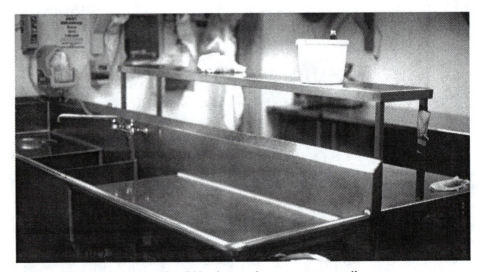

Figure 9-1 *Workstations should be designed to minimize needless steps.*

Ingredient for Success 32: "Needless steps and unnecessary movement cause worker fatigue, which leads to reduced productivity and increased labor costs, and contributes to preventable accidents that escalate workman's compensation claims."

Workstations are created using three basic dimensions: method of preparation, type of cooking method, and volume of food. These three dimensions determine the equipment and corresponding spatial requirements of a workstation.

Complexity of the menu, ranging from simple preparation skills to more complex culinary techniques requiring professionally trained chefs, will affect workstation design. The menu mix, including the use of convenience and scratch foods and the number of similar or different kinds of food, affects equipment needs and the menu complexity.

Workstations are usually organized by similar task. The designer must know how much baking the caterer will be doing, how much roasting space will be needed and what size range top is required based on the volume of food being produced at any one time.

By analyzing the menu, workstations can be planned. Common workstations in a typical catering operation are generally organized into one of the following categories based on similar production tasks: preparation, hot food production, cold food production, final preparation, warewashing, and transportation.

Preparation Area

The preparation area should be located near the storage areas. Some common types of equipment located in the preparation area include food mixers and attachments (flat beater, wire whip, dough arm, pastry knife), food slicers, food choppers, ovens, ranges, tilting braising pan, sinks, garbage disposal units, measuring tools (scales, ladles, scoops, volume measures), hand tools (serving spoons, hand whips, food turners, spatulas, tongs), kitchen cutlery, pots and pans, and refrigeration and freezer units.

Employee cleanliness and proper hygiene are most important in ensuring the preparation and service of food free from harmful bacteria. While preparing food, production employees should keep their fingernails trimmed, neatly filed, and maintained so the edges and surfaces are cleanable. When working with food, fingernail polish or artificial fingernails should never be worn. A simple wedding band is the only piece of jewelry that should be worn while preparing food.

When handling the food, all employees must follow appropriate food handling procedures. Always minimize the contact of raw food with bare hands. Never touch exposed, ready-to-eat foods with bare hands, except when washing fruits and vegetables. Use common sense when handling food. Use suitable clean and sanitized utensils such as deli tissue, spatulas, tongs, single-use gloves (Figure 9–2), and dispensing equipment.

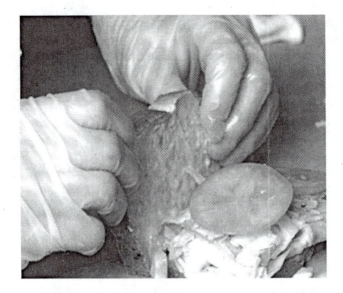

Figure 9-2
Gloves should be worn whenever handling exposed, ready-to-eat foods.

Every employee must be taught to wash their hands before engaging in food preparation and before handling clean equipment, utensils, or unwrapped single-serve and single-use articles. Hands must be washed whenever they might become contaminated. The 1999 FDA Model Food Code recommends handwashing:

1. immediately following the use of the bathroom.

2. after touching bare body parts.

3. after caring for or handling service animals or aquatic animals (molluscan shellfish or crustacea).

4. after touching soiled rags, utensils, or equipment.

5. after coughing, sneezing, using a handkerchief or disposable tissue, using tobacco, eating, or drinking.

6. during food preparation as necessary to prevent cross-contamination.

7. when switching between working with raw food and working with ready-to-eat food.

Hand washing techniques include washing the arms from the elbows down to the finger tips. Soap must be applied. The hands must be vigorously rubbed together for a minimum twenty seconds and thoroughly rinsed with clean water, then dried using a clean paper towel or hot-air dryer. Only an approved handwashing sink should be used, never a sink used for food preparation or a service sink used for the disposal of mop water.

Hygienic practices must also be followed to avoid cross-contamination from eating, drinking, or using tobacco products. An employee should only eat, drink, or use any form of tobacco in approved, designated areas to prevent contamination of exposed food, clean equipment, utensils, and linens.

APPROPRIATE USES OF GLOVES BY THE FOODHANDLER

1. Single-use gloves should be used for only one task, such as working with ready-to-eat food or with raw animal food, and for no other purpose. They should be discarded when damaged or soiled, or when interruptions occur in the operation.

2. Slash-resistant gloves that are used to protect the hands during operations requiring cutting should be used only in direct contact with food that is subsequently cooked, such as frozen food or a primal cut of meat.

3. Slash-resistant gloves that have a smooth, durable, and nonabsorbent outer surface, or single-use gloves, should be used with ready-to-eat food that will not subsequently be cooked.

4. Cloth gloves may not be used in direct contact with food unless the food is subsequently cooked, such as frozen food or a primal cut of meat.

Figure 9-3 *Appropriate uses of gloves by the foodhandler. (Adapted from the 1999 FDA Model Food Code.)*

All food production personnel must wear hair restraints. These include hats, hair coverings or nets, beard constraints, and clothing that covers body hair.

Use of Gloves

An effective technique to prevent foodborne illness is for employees to follow good personal hygiene procedures including proper and frequent washing of their hands. Proper handwashing, combined with appropriate use of gloves, will create an effective barrier against foodborne illness (Figure 9–3).

Hot Food Production

The hot food production area (Figure 9–4) may contain some of the following types of equipment: range, range oven, microwave oven, convection oven, combination convection oven/steamer otherwise known as a "combi oven" (which is extremely convenient and very popular, but expensive) fryers, broilers, griddles, tilting braising pan, steam jacketed-kettle, low or high pressure steamers, and refrigeration and freezer units. It is important to establish procedures to ensure final cooking temperatures are achieved (Figure 9–5).

Figure 9-4 *The hot food production area contains a variety of ovens so care must be used when handling food or equipment in this area.*

FINAL COOKING TEMPERATURES FOR SELECTED FOODS

1. Fruits and vegetables that are cooked for hot holding should be cooked to a temperature of 140°F (60°C).
2. Cooked and refrigerated food that is prepared for immediate service in response to an individual consumer order, such as a roast beef sandwich au jus, may be served at any temperature.
3. Potentially hazardous food that is cooked, cooled, and reheated for hot holding shall be reheated so that all parts of the food reach a temperature of at least 165°F (74°C) for 15 seconds within two hours.
4. Potentially hazardous food, reheated in a microwave oven for hot holding, shall be reheated so that all parts of the food reach a temperature of at least 165°F (74°C). The food should be rotated or stirred, covered, and allowed to stand covered for 2 minutes after reheating.
5. Ready-to-eat food taken from a commercially processed, hermetically sealed container, or an intact package from a food processing plant that is inspected by the food regulatory authority with jurisdiction over the plant, should be heated to a temperature of at least 140°F (60°C) for hot holding.

Figure 9-5 *Final cooking temperatures for selected foods. (Adapted from the 1999 FDA Model Food Code.)*

The Microwave Oven

Microwave ovens use microwaves, or "waves of energy," that are either reflected (metal), transferred (glass), or absorbed (food). Cooking food using a microwave oven is accomplished by setting an appropriate amount of time necessary for the waves to penetrate the food and cook it. Microwaves differ from conventional ovens in that conventional ovens use convection heat to cook food and rely more on the temperature inside of the oven. Because of this difference, cooking poultry, beef, lamb, and pork in a microwave will require a strict adherence to some basic principles (Figure 9–6).

Cold Food Production

Cold food production is called a *pantry* or *garde manger*. It is also known as the *pantry chef*. This includes the production of all cold foods such as appetizers, salads and salad dressings, cold appetizers, and some desserts. The important aspect of the garde manger station is to make sure cold foods are served cold, with a temperature range at or below 41°F (5°C).

As a professional caterer, the need for adequate plate service is most important. Most common preparation techniques include chilling of the china and refrigeration of raw materials, foods in process, and prepared foods. Common pieces of equipment found in cold food production are glass racks, chilled plates, ice machines, and refrigeration and freezer units. Transporting cold foods should be done as close to service as possible. A mistake professional caterers can make

STANDARD OPERATING PROCEDURES FOR THE MICROWAVE OVEN

1. Food should be arranged in such a manner as to allow for even penetration of the microwaves.
2. Because of uneven distribution of the microwaves, stirring will allow for more even distribution of heat. Rotating or rearranging foods from the center to the outside avoids overcooking some pieces and undercooking others.
3. Covering the food prevents it from splattering inside of the oven, and prevents heat and excessive moisture loss. The covering may be plastic wrap, a glass lid or plate, or waxed paper.
4. Food should be heated to a uniform temperature of at least 165°F (74°C).
5. Standing time, the length of time between when the item is removed from the microwave oven and when it is served, must be routinely utilized. Food should be covered and stand for at least two minutes for the temperature to stabilize. During this time, the food will continue to cook.

Figure 9–6 *Standard operating procedures for the microwave oven.*

when planning an event is to misjudge the amount of refrigeration and storage required for an event. For this reason, caterers should prepare themselves by providing some form of refrigeration or cooling techniques for each event. A common refrigeration technique is the rental or leasing of large refrigeration units that will be placed close to the event.

Raw fruits and vegetables handled in the cold food production area must always be thoroughly washed in water to remove soil and other contaminants. They must be washed before being cut, combined with other ingredients, cooked, served, or offered for human consumption in ready-to-eat form.

Final Preparation Area

The final preparation area should be located near the service area (on-premise location) or near the loading area to assemble for off-premise events. Transportation of most catered foods is accomplished by the use of insulated carriers that accommodate both hot and cold foods. A professional caterer should be aware of both the handling and storage capacities of the many available insulated carriers on the market today.

An important aspect in maintaining proper sanitation with insulated carriers is careful maintenance in relationship to cleanliness. The insulated carriers should be washed and sanitized before and after each event. A helpful reminder is *Ingredient for Success 33: "Insulated carriers will not only carry food but will also carry bacteria."*

Food Production Procedures

Proper food handling procedures during the preparation process helps ensure the quality of the food. It is every employee's responsibility to handle all food in a safe manner. Figure 9–7 lists proper thawing and cooling procedures for handling potentially hazardous food and details the appropriate cooling methods.

◆ STYLE OF SERVICE

The menu determines the design, layout, and equipment for the service area. Style of service may include buffet service, banquet service, French service, Russian service, or Family style service (see Chapter 10). Skill requirements of the production staff, number of personnel, and their cost of labor are determined by the desired style of service.

The intended service style will dictate how the caterer organizes the efficient and effective progression of raw materials as they flow through the production area. This includes easy access of all raw materials based on time and motion utilization needed to prepare the menu items.

THAWING POTENTIALLY HAZARDOUS FOODS

Thawing Procedures

1. Potentially hazardous frozen food that is slacked to moderate the temperature should be held under refrigeration that maintains the food temperature at 41°F (5°C) or less.
2. Potentially hazardous food should be thawed under refrigeration that maintains the food temperature at 41°F (5°C) or less.
3. Foods completely submerged under running water should be thawed:
   ◆ at a water temperature of 70°F (21°C) or below.
   ◆ with sufficient water velocity to agitate and float off loose particles in an overflow.
   ◆ for a period of time that does not allow thawed portions of ready-to-eat food to rise above 41°F (5°C).
   ◆ for a period of time that does not allow thawed portions of a raw animal food requiring cooking as specified or to be above 41°F (5°C) for more than 4 hours including:
      (a) the time the food is exposed to the running water and the time needed for preparation for cooking, or
      (b) the time it takes under refrigeration to lower the food temperature to 41°F (5°C).
4. Frozen food being thawed as part of a cooking process must be:
   ◆ cooked as specified following proper temperature guides.
   ◆ thawed in a microwave oven and immediately transferred to conventional cooking equipment, with no interruption in the process.
   ◆ thawed and prepared for immediate service in response to an individual consumer's order.

Cooling Procedures

1. Potentially hazardous cooked food should be cooled:
   ◆ within 2 hours, from 140°F (60°C) to 70°F (21°C).
   ◆ within 4 hours, from 70°F (21°C) to 41°F (5°C) or less.
2. Potentially hazardous food shall be cooled within 4 hours to 41°F (5°C) or less if prepared from ingredients at ambient temperature, such as reconstituted foods and canned tuna.
3. Except as specified, a potentially hazardous food, received in compliance with laws allowing a temperature above 41°F (5°C) during shipment from the supplier, shall be cooled within 4 hours to 41oF (5°C) or less, except for shell eggs if placed immediately upon their receipt in refrigerated equipment that is capable of maintaining food at 41°F (5°C) or less.

(continued)

Figure 9-7 *Proper thawing and cooling procedures and appropriate cooling methods for handling potentially hazardous food. (Adapted from the 1999 FDA Model Food Code.)*

Cooling Methods

Cooling shall be accomplished in accordance with the time and temperature criteria specified by using one or more of the following methods, based on the type of food being cooled.

1. Place the food in shallow pans.
2. Separate the food into smaller or thinner portions.
3. Use rapid cooling equipment.
4. Stir the food in a container placed in an ice water bath.

Figure 9-7 *Proper thawing and cooling procedures and appropriate cooling methods for handling potentially hazardous food (continued). (Adapted from the 1999 FDA Model Food Code.)*

Capacity needs of the production equipment are based on the menu items and subsequent volume of food produced to satisfy the number of guests.

The physical sizes of the storage areas (Figure 9–8) are influenced by the menu, projected number of guests, and the volume of food needed to be produced. Refrigeration and freezer storage are two areas a caterer must consider. Depending on the style of service, reach-in or walk-in refrigerators or freezers may be needed.

The Hazardous Analysis Critical Control Point Plan (see Chapter 6) will be developed based on the requested style, menu, equipment, and storage facilities.

Figure 9-8 *Required storage area space is determined by the menu, the projected number of guests, and the volume of food to be prepared.*

◆ OBTAINING EQUIPMENT

A caterer has a choice of purchasing or renting equipment. When purchasing either new or used equipment, a caterer should work with a reputable equipment dealer who will guarantee the equipment and manufacturers who offer special discounts or sales. A caterer can also attend food shows or trade shows and negotiate with the manufacturer's representatives who are displaying equipment at the show and purchase these "show models," usually at a discounted price. Attending used equipment auctions is another method of purchasing equipment.

A caterer may opt to rent equipment. There are professional rental services that will provide everything from a napkin to a refrigerated truck. Many caterers will supplement their equipment inventory with rented equipment. Some caterers decide to build an inventory of equipment based on frequency of use. If the equipment is a required element of every catering function, such as a chafing dish (Figure 9–9), the caterer will most likely invest in the item. In addition, a caterer may purchase equipment if they plan on catering a large annual function for the next five years. The caterer can then reduce the equipment expense by depreciating it over that time.

The decision to purchase or rent will be determined by the individual caterer's situation and location. Often, a caterer will purchase equipment needed to support the infrastructure of the business, such as ovens, refrigeration units, and other back-of-the-house equipment.

Figure 9–9 *Chafing dishes are essential for nearly every catering function to maintain proper heating temperatures.*

TIPS FROM THE TRADE

Holstein Manufacturing is a family run business with deep roots in Iowa. Our first grills and rotisseries were made to help promote Iowa's pork industry. Over the last 20 years, we have expanded our line of catering and food preparation equipment while adding many specialty products. At Holstein Manufacturing, it's our goal to continue meeting our customers' needs and expand the line of products we offer.

Catering is a growing business! Caterers who purchase our equipment service anywhere from 100 to 2,000 people at one time. They need bigger equipment to be able to cater the function and make it profitable for them. Efficiency and labor costs are the two big concerns for a caterer. With our bigger equipment, we can help the caterer cut labor costs and make production more efficient.

For those large cookouts, a 240 lb. live weight hog or seven 20 lb. roasts will be cooked and ready to eat in 7 hours or less! In addition, the chicken rotisserie with skewers will roast 72 whole birds in less than 2 hours. If the baskets are used, 64 chicken quarters and larger cuts of beef, pork, and fish can be roasted.

Our backyard barbeque equipment for patios is also a growing business. Leisure time has to be spent some way, and cooking good food is the way to use some of that time.

Bruce Schmidt
President/Owner
Holstein Manufacturing, Inc.
Holstein, Iowa

Advantages of Rental Equipment

1. No storage area is required for the equipment.

2. No maintenance of the equipment is needed.

3. Handling of the equipment is minimized—rental company may deliver and retrieve equipment.

4. Rental company may wash, sanitize, and repackage items.

5. Special equipment needs and their costs may be charged to the client.

6. No investment or capital expense is required for the equipment.

7. Security and inventory control may be tighter, as each item *must* be accounted for.

8. The caterer can "field-test" a variety of equipment before making a long-term investment by purchasing it.

Disadvantages of Rental Equipment

1. The equipment may not be maintained as well as the caterer would like it to be.

2. In the event of last minute requests, or the caterer forgetting to reserve the equipment, the rental company may be out of stock.

3. If a caterer loses a piece of rented equipment, a replacement charge will be incurred.

4. A caterer can build a reputation on having custom designed and elegant pieces of equipment. A caterer may have an inventory of specially designed plates, special roasting ovens, and so on.

5. Many caterers help each other during the catering season. Friends may lend equipment to each other. Therefore, owning the equipment gives the opportunity to lend it to friends or rent it to competitors.

6. Having to secure equipment from another source can be inconvenient.

Off-Premise Equipment Safety

How will the caterer transport the food (Figure 9–10)? How will the food be kept hot enough to prevent it from becoming unappetizing (Figure 9–11)? How will the caterer keep it hot enough to prevent an outbreak of foodborne illness? How will the caterer keep the food cold?

A major task for the off-premise caterer is keeping the food at the proper temperatures to avoid the growth of harmful bacteria and to make sure the food is either hot or cold for the customer. Every caterer needs to structure the event plan with detailed *HACCP procedures* (see Chapter 6), including directions detailing precise instructions on the selection and use of the right equipment (Figure 9–12a, b, c).

Figure 9–10 *Mobile catering trucks provide efficient transportation and proper heating/cooling temperatures for the preparation and storage of food.*

Figure 9-11
Canned fuel helps maintain proper serving temperatures for both on-and off-premise functions.

Figure 9-12 *The type of equipment needed to comply to HACCP procedures will vary depending on the event.*

Basic Large Equipment

The traditional pieces of reliable production equipment have been the standard workhorses of any kitchen. A range top (Figure 9–13) is one such piece of equipment, while a stove will provide for both cooking and/or sautéing. A deep fryer is another important piece of equipment available for preparation of many prefabricated products. Some food service companies today provide complete lines of prepared and frozen foods that are designed to be deep fried and transported immediately.

Another large piece of equipment is a pressureless steamer, which serves two purposes. The use of steam provides the caterer with the opportunity to not only cook, but to reheat foods prior to service.

Basic Small Equipment

Small equipment can make or break the service at any event. Necessary pieces of small equipment include knives, spatulas, sheet trays, and cookware. A variety of pots, frying pans, and hotel pans are major pieces used in all production kitchens. In addition, the caterer must be aware of the size and shape of all insulated transport carriers. *Ingredient for Success 34* states: ***"Be sure that all hotel pans and small equipment units can be transported properly."***

Cleaning and Sanitizing

Proper cleaning and sanitizing of all food equipment and utensils is required, especially if their surfaces come into contact with food. Proper procedures for both cleaning and sanitizing must be emphasized when handling these implements. Wash and rinse to clean; sanitize to reduce, remove, or eliminate any

Figure 9-13
This portable range top is easily transported to off-premise catering events.

Figure 9-14
Equipment storage areas should be clean and well-organized with adequate space and lighting.

harmful levels of bacteria. There are a number of acceptable procedures to do the job depending on what is being cleaned and sanitized.

◆ STORAGE OF EQUIPMENT

The maintenance of adequate storage facilities (Figure 9–14) for all equipment and utensils is a critical consideration. Cleaned and sanitized equipment and laundered linens, as well as any single-service and single-use articles, must always be stored at least 6 inches above the floor and away from a wall. This equipment should be either covered or inverted. Single-service and single-use articles should be stored in their original protective package. If not, make sure the storage provides protection from contamination. The equipment storage area must be clean, sanitary, dry, and well lighted. There are areas in a catering establishment that are not appropriate for the storage of equipment and utensils (Figure 9–15).

NON-APPROPRIATE EQUIPMENT STORAGE AREAS

1. employee locker rooms (except laundered linens or single-service and single-use articles that are packaged or contained in a cabinet)
2. bathrooms
3. garbage-storage rooms
4. mechanical rooms
5. under sewer lines that are not shielded to intercept potential drips
6. under leaking water lines, including leaking automatic fire sprinkler heads, or under lines on which water has condensed
7. under open stairwells
8. under other sources of potential contamination

Figure 9-15 *Non-appropriate equipment storage areas. (Adapted from the 1999 FDA Model Food Code.)*

Summary

The fourth catering function involves the ability of a caterer to efficiently and effectively design and equip the food production facility. It must always be remembered that *"The menu is the single most important tool used to determine precise equipment needs based on the type of food being prepared." (Ingredient for Success 30).* Factors that affect the selection of equipment include performance and functionality of design; the maintenance, reliability, and warranty of equipment; availability and cost of replacement parts; employee skill level and relationship to the production needs of the menu; current and future equipment requirements based on customer needs, wants, and demands; the application and development of new technology; government regulations, including HACCP procedures and safety features; competitors' adaptation of technology to reduce labor and utility costs; and innovations in product design, aesthetics, components, and/or construction features, all influence the selection of equipment for a food production system. Careful analysis of the preparation areas, the hot and cold food production areas and the type of utilities are other concerns for the caterer. Both basic large and small traditional pieces of equipment will require the caterer to research their capabilities and fit them into the food production system. A caterer has a choice of purchasing or renting equipment. The decision must be made by the individual caterer based on their needs and budget constraints. Finally, adherence to the Model Food Code must be maintained to ensure implementation of HACCP standards.

Review Questions

Brief Answers

1. Describe common equipment and production design considerations.

2. Explain how a caterer may select the type of utility to use as the energy source.

3. Explain why the menu is a powerful tool used to determine the design and layout of workstations.

4. Explain the type of equipment normally found in each of the following individual workstations; preparation, hot and cold food production, and final preparation.

5. Explain different ways a caterer acquires equipment.

6. Explain what the following Ingredients for Success mean to you.

Ingredient for Success 30: "*The menu is the single most important tool used to determine precise equipment needs based on the type of food being prepared.*"

Ingredient for Success 31: "*Minimize utility costs through manageable conservation of natural resources by planning for the current and future selection of energy-efficient equipment.*"

Ingredient for Success 32: "*Needless steps and unnecessary movement cause worker fatigue, which leads to reduced productivity and increased labor costs, and contributes to preventable accidents that escalate workman's compensation claims.*"

Ingredient for Success 33: "*Insulated carriers will not only carry food but will also carry bacteria.*"

Ingredient for Success 34: "*Be sure that all hotel pans and small equipment units can be transported properly.*"

Multiple Choice

Select the single best answer for each question.

1. Multitasking equipment provides which of the following advantages?
   a. maximizes spatial relationships
   b. maximizes capital investment
   c. decreases the functionality of the equipment
   d. increases movement and worker fatigue
   e. All of the above.

2. The organization of workstations is affected by:
   a. bundling similar tasks
   b. complexity of the menu
   c. employee skill level
   d. type of cooking method
   e. All of the above.

3. Which of the following is not considered a factor that influences the caterer's ability to adequately equip a food production system?
   a. employee skill level
   b. future equipment needs
   c. networking with other caterers
   d. government regulations
   e. competitive maneuvering

True or False

Read each of the following statements and determine if it is true or false.

1. The menu is a powerful tool used to determine the design, layout, and equipment of the food production area.

2. Common workstation design in a caterer's production area focuses on time and motion studies.

3. Purchasing the appropriate equipment is a vital task that requires attention by all personal.

Putting It All Together

Research the various rental companies a caterer may use to supplement equipment. Ask the rental company for a copy of their general terms, requirements, and policies. What are the most common types of equipment rented? What emerging trends exist regarding the kind of equipment rented? Find a rental dealer who will rent: staging, tables, chairs, silverware, linen, napkins, dance floors, trucks, refrigerated trucks, vans, trucks, and chafing dishes.

Chapter Ten

Implementing

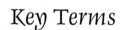

Key Terms

service

service standards

teamwork

informal structure

appropriate personnel

French service

Russian service

buffet service

American service

sit-down dinner

tabletop

small wares

undercloth (silencer, silence cloth)

overlay (napperon)

cover

family-style service

Objectives

After studying this chapter, you should be able to:

◆ Explain what service means to a caterer.

◆ Review the front-of-the-house service activities.

◆ Describe how the caterer can build a reputation based on service.

◆ Explain how caterers can build a professional service staff.

◆ Explain how caterers can use standards to define *service*. Provide examples of how a caterer can develop service standards to mirror the organization's mission statement.

◆ Describe an informal organizational structure and explain how it can affect employee morale.

◆ Explain and provide examples of what *appropriate personnel* means to the catering organization.

◆ List the attributes of appropriate service personnel.

◆ Explain the differences between informal and formal service styles used by caterers.

◆ Describe the defining characteristics of each service style.

◆ Explain how a tabletop is set.

◆ Explain how to purchase linen.

INGREDIENTS FOR SUCCESS

35   "The end result of the job relies on the entire staff working together—teamwork."

36   "Construct detailed diagrams of every buffet in advance."

37   "The more service given, and the better care taken of the customer through exceptional attention to detail, the happier the client will be and the more repeat business will be generated from that event."

38   "Consider every job a major production."

39   "A caterer's performance is a reflection of the business."

This chapter covers the importance of building a team-oriented service staff. An explanation of the common types of service approaches used by caterers will be discussed. Delivering consistent customer service geared to exceed a customer's needs is perhaps one of the most important missions of a catering business. Unfortunately, however, it is often the most lacking skill found in the catering industry. Although a formal description will be given to specifically define each type of service, most caterers will borrow and incorporate techniques from each style. These techniques are married together for the efficient and effective service of food and beverages required to exceed a guest's expectations.

◆ SERVICE

The delivery of **service** to the guest is a catering management task that is very important to the effective and efficient execution of an event. Because a caterer's reputation can be built on service, it is necessary to develop an effective recruiting and hiring strategy to complement service objectives.

To ensure consistent delivery of service, a caterer must define *service* as it applies to the mission of the operation. Remember **Ingredient for Success 2: "We cannot be all things to all people."** Even though a caterer cannot satisfy every need in the marketplace, setting a clear direction through the mission statement begins the ongoing process of maintaining a professional service staff. The maintenance and continuation of that staff is established by planning and setting service objectives.

What is *service* to the caterer, organization, employees, and client? A caterer has built and refined the back-of-the-house tasks—now the front-of-the-house needs definition so each employee understands his or her role in service delivery. For example, a guest was attending one of the many corporate-sponsored receptions during the National Restaurant Association's annual trade show. The reception was held in the grand ballroom of a fine service-oriented hotel in Chicago. Approximately 1,500 guests were in attendance. Having a carbonated beverage, appetizer plate, fork, and napkin in hand was a bit overwhelming. A little shuffling and the fork fell to the carpet. Before it could be retrieved, a member of the service team quickly responded. She not only picked up the fork, but smiling, simultaneously handed a clean one in its place. This is service!

A caterer needs to create obtainable, observable, and trainable **service standards** so each employee understands his or her role. To build a strong reputation, a caterer must have highly trained employees. This is one factor often lacking in the catering industry. To maintain highly trained employees, a key component of the catering mission plan should be continual training programs. Regardless of whether it is a small caterer with four or five employees, or a large employer with 175 employees, a caterer must plan to train for the effective and efficient delivery of service.

When planning the details of each event, the caterer must include specific training needs in each plan. Either a review or a new *training goal* needs to be implemented with the plan. This is true regardless of the style of service requested by the client.

Building Professional Service

Ingredient for Success 35 states: ***"The end result of the job relies on the entire staff working together—teamwork."*** **Teamwork** is an absolute requirement for the efficient and effective execution of any catering event. Implementation of the catering plan through teamwork happens successfully when the caterer has created and nurtured the *informal structure* of the organization.

The **informal structure** of a caterer's organization represents the relationships among the caterer's employees. Employee relationships occur regardless of the formal structure bound by policies, procedures, and rules, and are extremely important to the positive morale of the organization. The guest can observe or "feel" the positive or negative health emitting from the service staff during an event.

Since employees spend many hours together preparing and executing the event, the importance of a positive atmosphere, created through team-building to accomplish organizational goals, cannot be overemphasized.

To build a positive informal organization, a fundamental step is hiring **appropriate personnel**. A caterer can define what *appropriate personnel* means to the organization by creating personnel standards. This human resource standard will clearly define the type of personnel needed to accomplish the tasks identified by the caterer and the organization's mission.

A caterer must take tremendous care and time to recruit and hire the appropriate person to execute the right tasks. Characteristics of appropriate personnel include:

1. a positive, energetic attitude.

2. a spirit for teamwork.

3. a professional demeanor.

4. enthusiasm.

5. a sincere concern for the guests and their needs.

6. acceptance of responsibility.

7. acceptance of positive feedback on performance.

8. a commitment toward delivering consistent service.

9. a kind, friendly, courteous, trustworthy, and loyal personality.

10. an "ownership attitude."

11. nonstop smiling.

12. an ability for listening to understand.

13. respect for guests and their opinions—never arguing with a guest.

14. respectful speech including use of "Sir" and "Madam."

15. an understanding that the guest is the most important person at the event.

◆ CREATING AN EMPLOYEE-SUPPORTIVE CULTURE

The ability to attract and retain appropriate human resources is a great challenge to all catering professionals as well as to the entire hospitality industry. Scarcity of labor and the challenge of recruiting and retaining appropriate staff have been a concern to the hospitality industry since 1900. It was because of the need for a professionally trained employee, specifically a steward, that began the movement to create a training school in the United States. The idea of an academic program offering professional development and industry experience was one reason why the movement to establish a more formal educational system began.

The subsequent establishment of specific hotel and restaurant management programs later merged with many existing institutional management programs at America's colleges and universities. Whereas these offer some relief to the need for qualified personnel, the evolution and continued growth of the industry have kept appropriate employees in high demand.

The catering profession is one that requires long and difficult hours. Caterers usually work hard while others are enjoying the function. Holidays, weekends, summer festivals, and late nights may lead to displeased employees.

A challenge to the successful caterer is to attract employees who want to work these hours. Caterers need to find dedicated individuals who seek full-time or part-time work and must offer wages to complement their life styles. Parents of school-age children are often attracted to this schedule because they can work while their children are attending school. Other employees can be found at colleges, universities, and vocational-technical schools. Caterers find this pool of potential employees favorable.

College students seek the income and can work around their school schedules. Work experience, especially for students enrolled in departments of hospitality, business, or culinary arts is extremely valuable. These programs often require work-related experience as part of their graduation requirement and some require internship experience.

Vocational-technical schools grant students a flexible schedule. They are encouraged to seek employment and are permitted to leave school to work. Innovative training partnerships can be created between the educational facility and a caterer to benefit both the student and the caterer.

One way a caterer can build a great team is to formally structure the organization to be receptive of new ideas. This encourages employee participation. It must begin at the top, with the owner/caterer, and be a crucial component of the organization's mission.

One important component is to create an environment so all management personnel can accept this mission. Proper training of management and employees is critical. Basic training established to meet precise organizational goals must be part of the plan. Training techniques that arouse passion can help this process. Building an internal culture that rewards creativity and innovation; seeking employees who display courtesy, respect, and efficiency; and clearly defining each role in relationship to the entire operation contribute to an employee-supportive culture. Management's acceptance of employees' ideas will help create this culture. The organization must always strive for continued incremental improvement in all activities.

Long hours and demanding work are just one element of the catering adventure. One distinct advantage a catering operation does have over other traditional food service operations is the need for incessant creativity and innovation. This characteristic is a required element of the profession since consumers' needs are always evolving. Prospective clients challenge a caterer to create new and exciting themes, menus, and reasons for events. Unexpected situations challenge the caterer to instantaneously implement creative solutions. These challenges provide an opportunity for active employee participation in decision-making. What better ways to encourage employee creativity and motivation? Listening to the employee and supporting active employee participation during the planning and execution of an event will energize the staff. This aura of excitement will definitely be felt by the guest. Internal excitement becomes a magnet used to attract other innovative and creative personnel. Eventually, instead of the caterer trying to *find* an employee, innovative and creative personnel will gravitate toward the organization.

Job specifications and descriptions for the creative and innovative needs of the company should be written. Current employees should be encouraged to recommend friends and family who fit the needs of the company. Many caterers reward employees with incentives for recommending appropriate personnel.

◆ UNIFORMS

The caterer can further enhance a guest's perception of the professional service delivered through the use of a standardized uniform and dress code for the staff (Figure 10–1). A uniform should be designed to:

1. complement the mission of the organization.

2. complement the type of service being performed.

3. identify the employee as a member of the catering staff.

4. communicate to the guest what job task is being performed.

Figure 10-1
A standardized uniform and dress code enhances perception of the professional service delivered.

Uniforms can range from a black tuxedo to a clearly-defined, standard-style outfit unique to the caterer. A uniform standard will carefully define each component, from the hair style to polished shoes including some or all of the following:

1. Shirt—explain style, color, long or short sleeve, and material composition

2. Pants—explain style, color, and material composition

3. Belt—describe color and style

4. Shoes—describe the acceptable color, style, and cleanliness (clean and polished)

5. Tie—describe style and color

6. Hair and facial hair standards—describe acceptable length, style, grooming, and hygiene

7. Jewelry, make up, and appropriate scented perfumes or cologne regulations—describe appropriate make up, only a simple wedding band, and small earrings

8. Hygiene standards, bathing requirements, cleanliness of the uniform

9. Socks—describe style and color

10. Hat requirements

◈ TYPES OF SERVICE STYLES

There are several formal and informal styles of service. These service styles may be used in combination with each other, depending on the needs of the client and the type of event. Common types of events include private family functions; business or corporate functions; and community, group, and association functions. These include banquets, receptions, meetings, picnics, baptisms, bar mitzvahs, anniversaries, office parties, holiday parties, charitable events, and weddings.

It is best to maintain a written description of the various service methods the caterer is competent to handle. This list may include the type of function, the type of equipment needed to execute this event, and the various kinds of service provided in conjunction with each. This list can then become a handy reference when the caterer is meeting with the prospective client.

All catering operations have certain attributes commonly requested by customers. There will always be a great demand to use a facility for wedding receptions, dining-in functions, retirements, promotion dinners, and other events with similar needs. Each of these functions demands a special setting and a special menu. Other events may require several alternative settings and menus. An effective way for the catering manager to break down the list of functions is to base it on a common menu and staffing requirements.

A typical list, using this method, might look like this:

Type of Event	Service
Formal dinner	Formal table service
Informal dinner	American type service
Buffet dinner (smorgasbord)	Modified table service
Regular luncheon	American table service
Buffet luncheon	Modified table service
Brunch-style buffet	Minimal table service
Modified standup luncheon or tea	Buffet service
Pool-side or patio party	Bar and set-up service
Barbecue or cookout	Bar, set-up and clean-up service
Nationality (dinner or luncheon)	Formal American or buffet service

Once the type of function and service is decided upon with the prospective client, the caterer is in a position to offer a number of menu suggestions. These menu suggestions can be prepared and served in a manner most suitable to the client's needs and at the same time to best meet the caterer's profit objectives.

Formal styles of service include *French* and *Russian service*. The most common types of service used by caterers are the informal styles which include *buffet, American,* and *family-style service*.

French Service

French service is one of the most elaborate styles a caterer can perform for the guest. Preparing the food at table-side using *a gueridon* (a small table with wheels) and a *rechaud* (a pan set over a heating element) is the distinguishing characteristic of French service. This style of service is often reserved for the most intimate, smaller functions. French service requires expert specialization in handling the equipment, excellent culinary skills in preparing or finishing the food at table-side, and superior service skills when presenting the finished food to the guest. Many caterers would not execute this style of service because of its difficulty.

Although the traditional, classical French style of service requires an exceptionally trained, skilled staff and efficient coordination to use, many caterers adapted a modern approach to this style of service. For example, a major department store manager invited VIPs to a private recognition luncheon, held in their facility, as their way of saying thank you. These important guests were primarily elderly women who had spent a large amount of money each business quarter at the department store. The luncheon included a tremendous amount of personal attention from the department store employees and the women were given the first view of the newest clothing fashions received by the department store.

Because of the small, intimate size of the group, the caterer adopted the French service style of table-side cooking to provide each guest with more personalized attention. Based on the staff's capabilities, the caterer developed a service to fit the needs of the client and to completely satisfy their guests. It was a huge success. The menus were kept simple and elegant by using the caterer's signature recipes. Most of the food was prepared in advance at the caterer's facility and was finished table-side in front of the seated guests. The guests were most impressed with the quality of food and the exceptional attention they received from the staff.

Classical French service, similar to this, would be very difficult for banquets serving large numbers of people because of the increased staff and equipment that would be required.

Russian Service

Russian service is a very formal and elegant type of service. The distinguishing characteristic of Russian service is the unique presentation of food to the guest. Its elegance is derived from the use of silver serving platters, the skillful handling of the serving utensils, and the arrangement and presentation of the food.

Russian service requires the food to be arranged artistically in the kitchen on silver platters. The server carries this platter into the dining area and presents the food display for the guest's visual excitement. First, a hot plate is served. Next, the food is individually presented to each guest.

An advantage of this type of service is its beauty and speed. A waiter can quickly serve many guests while providing the perception of personalized attention. Using this type of service, a skilled waiter, trained in the service procedures, can easily maneuver around tables and through the dining room. However, this form of service does require skilled employees. Mastering the skill of handling the multiple, repetitive tasks involved in this serving style requires practice and time. Since the use of silver platters and fine serving utensils is required, this can be an expensive investment for a caterer. Once the silver serving utensils are purchased, a caterer must protect their investment. Caterers' may lose this equipment by theft. Unethical employees will steal it and unethical guests may take it home with them. Equipment is also lost when it is forgotten at off-premise locations or left in the back of rented trucks and other vehicles. The caterer should plan to count each piece at the conclusion of every event.

Buffet

Most caterers will offer buffet service. **Buffet service** is perhaps the most common type of service a caterer will execute both on- and off-premise. A distinguishing characteristic of buffet service is the customer's active participation in the service. The consumer supplements a caterer's service.

The guest is invited to the buffet table at a predetermined time and sequence based on the number of guests to be served. They will leave their seat and enter a line leading past an organized table of serving plates and a variety of food, garnishes, and artistic displays (Figure 10–2). The main difference between

Figure 10-2 *Buffet tables set for service.*

buffet and banquet style service is the customer's active participation in the service at a buffet. At a banquet, on the other hand, the guest remains seated and the serving staff serves everyone together at a predetermined starting time.

Buffet service requires a caterer and the staff to be very well organized. When serving buffet style, a key attribute of the service style is artistic creativity. It is important, whether it is the owner, spouse, cook, or member of the wait staff, to have someone on staff with artistic ability.

Since "consumers eat with their eyes as well as their stomachs," an attractive buffet, with artistic flare, is very important. A caterer should ask, "Does the buffet offer an appetizing appeal? Is the buffet well organized?" A caterer should always review the competitor's buffet when attending these functions.

Building a buffet to create an appetizing appeal begins with the menu. Menus can offer a variety of food. Based on a price scale, the menu can be built around a simple lower-cost option or a more elaborate, higher-cost option. It will depend on the customer's needs and budget. Is chicken, pasta, or beef requested by the guest or will prime rib and lobster Newburgh be served? What salads and side dishes will complete the menu? The final menu should include a variety of colors, textures, shapes, tastes, and an appealing appearance based on the approved budget.

Building a Buffet

Depending on the type of event, most buffets begin with selecting a plate. The size and type of plate will influence the amount of food a guest can select. At the buffet, it is most important to have all of the guests move in the same direction.

To help maintain and control its cost, temperature, and palatability, food on a buffet should be offered in the following sequence: salads and other cold foods; the lowest food-cost items on the menu; the side-dishes including breads and vegetables; then entrees from least expensive to most expensive. This is known as the *flow of food* concept in which the cold foods are set out first and the hot foods are placed toward the end of the buffet. This helps keep the hot food hotter, especially when the dining area is air conditioned and the plates are cool in temperature. If a large volume of guests is expected, the buffet line should be accessible from both sides. A separate table for both the dessert and beverage station should be used.

Important Accents

The element of display is an important attribute for a buffet (Figure 10–3). A variety of different colors should be included. Multiple green salads should never be placed together. Foods with bland colors, such as a mashed potato and an au gratin potato, should not be placed side-by-side. It is best to use foods that are visually appealing (Figure 10–4). Each item on the buffet should be complemented. Where will the item be placed on the buffet? What type of dish or bowl will the food be served from? Will the food be served from a chafing dish? What height-level will the food be served from? Making a diagram can help to answer these questions and create an attractive buffet. **Ingredient for Success 36: "Construct detailed diagrams of every buffet in advance."**

Food at a buffet should be served from different heights. Common props, such as empty milk crates, dish racks, and cardboard boxes, can be integrated into a buffet.

A mixture of mirrors and lighting enhances buffets. White lights can be placed beneath the buffet table. Colored flood lights are often used beneath the skirting on a buffet. Small lights can be strung around the under edge of the buffet table to highlight the skirting and make it appear more attractive.

Figure 10–3
Buffets should be varied and eye-catching with multiple foods and colors.

Figure 10-4
Presenting food on a Credites Tray creates eye appeal for a buffet.

The use of greens, ferns, flowers, edible flowers, and fresh herbs helps to make the buffet more attractive. Different size dishes and dollies also add to its appeal. If serving shrimp from the buffet, serve it using a bowl that looks like a huge scallop or use silver trays. Creativity and color enhance the buffet and make it more appealing (Figure 10–5).

The caterer must be organized. Since there are aspects common to all buffets, standard operating procedures (SOPs) to guide both the management staff and employees with the task of building the buffet can be created. See Figure 10–6 for SOP guidelines.

Figure 10-5
Creativity enhances a buffet.

STANDARD BUFFET OPERATING PROCEDURES

1. Themes—selection is based on numerous factors
   A. Nationality
   B. Country
      1. Regional
      2. District
   C. Sport
   D. Holiday
   E. Occasion
      1. Wedding
      2. Baby shower
   F. Seasonal
   G. Seafood
2. The Buffet Plan
   A. Menu creation
   B. Number of covers
   C. Price of covers
   D. Time of serving
   E. Location where the buffet tables are to be displayed
   F. Menu zoning arrangement—diagram the buffet in advance. Describe how to set it up.
   G. Number of serving lines. These are based on the number of covers and zones, recommended 100 guests per zone
   H. Number, size, and shape of tables
      1. Banquet table
         a. 6 feet x 30 inches
         b. 6 feet x 36 inches
         c. 8 feet x 30 inches
         d. 8 feet x 36 inches
      2. Round table
         a. 60 inches in diameter
         b. 72 inches in diameter
         c. 84 inches in diameter
      3. Half-round table is 60 inches in diameter
      4. Quarter-round table is 30 inches in diameter
      5. Serpentine
      6. Trapezoid has 30-inch sides and is 60-inches across
   I. Type and color of table cloths. Skirt the tables and add the lights or props.

(continued)

Figure 10–6 *Standard buffet operating procedures.*

J. Set the buffet with empty chafing dishes and empty bowls to help visualize the completed buffet.

K. Label each bowl and chafing dish using a note card with the name of the food item as it will appear on the buffet. This review will eliminate any potential confusion once the staff is ready to set the food. Light heat fuel one-half hour before service.

L. Nonedible pieces
   1. Ice carving
   2. Tallow
   3. Flower arrangement
   4. Fountain

M. Other concerns that might need to be added to enhance the theme or atmosphere.
   1. Buffet table shapes
      a. Factors that determine shape
         1. Number of serving lines
         2. Size and shape of the room
         3. Seating arrangement
         4. Preference of the guests
         5. Occasion
   2. Calculation of the buffet table size
      a. Skirting
         1. Straight skirt—allow one foot of material per foot of table.
         2. Pleated skirt—allow one yard of material per foot of table
   3. Zoning—to expedite service never exceed 100 covers per zone.
      a. Basic zone arrangement
         1. Appetizers
         2. Fish
         3. Poultry
         4. Meat—beef, game, and pork
         5. Salads
         6. Hot foods
      b. Plates indicate where zone starts
      c. Pastry and beverages should be on separate tables
   4. Food serving trays
      a. Types
         1. Silver
         2. Mirrors
         3. Plastic trays
         4. Cut crystal—bowls and trays

(continued)

Figure 10–6 *Standard buffet operating procedures (continued).*

5. Equipment and supplies needed
   a. Banquet tables
   b. Chafing dishes
   c. Heating fuel
   d. Extension cords
   e. Stands for plates and trays
   f. Salad bowls
   g. Utensils for serving food
   h. Heat lamps
6. Service Preparation Procedures
   a. Count clean and sanitized china, silverware, glassware, silverware for the buffet.
   b. Check all china and glassware for chips, cracks, and foreign material (food spots, lip stick).
   c. Check all silverware for spots, food particles, and tarnish.
   d. Handle with care and follow proper sanitation handling techniques. Only touch flatware by the handles and glassware by the stem.
   e. Inspect all linen and napkins for cleanliness, stains, and holes.
   f. Clean, sanitize and fill all sugar/artificial sweetener holders.

Figure 10–6 *Standard buffet operating procedures (continued).*

A buffet will vary, even if using standardized menus, since customers have their own needs. Based on these needs, clients may select different foods from the menu. A customer may select two starches from a group of six, and two entrees from a group of eight. Then, the customer may select two salads to complement those entrees from a group of ten. This makes each buffet a little different.

When planning a buffet, make sure to determine the staffing requirements, employee scheduling and food-quantity requirements. The challenge is to have enough food on hand. A rule of the thumb suggests that the last guest must have the same opportunity to select from the same variety of food as the first guest. The serving dishes may not be as full, but an adequate supply and variety should be on hand. There is nothing more disappointing to a customer than when they approach a buffet and it is empty or low on food. This is one clue the caterer is not well organized.

Key tasks of planning a buffet are determining portion size and calculating the approximate amount of food each customer will eat. Researching the most popular foods in an area will help a caterer determine how much each person may eat. If roast beef is the favorite, a caterer must plan to have more roast beef than chicken on the buffet, but if chicken is the favorite, more chicken should be prepared. Remember to attractively place the inexpensive foods first on the buffet line.

Figure 10-7 *An artistic buffet is one the guests will remember and rave about to their friends.*

Plan accordingly, and study the diagrams. Review the diagrams with the staff. Have beautiful serving utensils and attractive dishes. Organize the buffet and make it an artistic piece the customers will rave about (Figure 10–7).

Salads on a Buffet

When using a salad on a buffet, the choice of salad dressing can be limited. If a tossed salad is set on the buffet line, blue cheese dressing, French dressing, signature dressing, and a low-fat Italian are too many choices. Each guest may spend between 35 and 45 seconds to decide which dressing to use. If there are 150 people and each person takes one-half minute to decide on a choice of dressing, the caterer must calculate 75 minutes on the service line consumed by the guest just making a decision on the type of salad dressing. To save time at the buffet, the caterer might encourage the client to have a preset salad for each guest on the table.

Food Handling Tips

Although buffet service may be handled by a smaller staff of employees, without effective methods of portion control, food waste may negate savings in reduced payroll expense. Concern is on serving hot foods hot and cold foods cold. Key food handling tips include:

1. Keep all food out of the temperature danger zone, 41°–140°F (5°–60°C). Use only food service equipment that will keep this food out of the danger zone.
2. Assign responsibility to monitor the temperature of the food, using an appropriate thermometer, at 2-hour intervals.

3. Discard all food that has been held on a buffet line for a maximum period of four hours.

4. Always use appropriate serving utensils and have the handles facing the guests.

5. Use only hot holding equipment, such as chafing dishes, to hold hot food. Never use hot holding equipment to cook or reheat food. This is a violation of the Model Food Code, since it will permit the food to remain in the temperature danger zone too long.

6. Never add fresh food to prepared foods being held on the buffet line.

7. Never add raw foods to already cooked foods.

8. Assign the responsibility to an employee to keep the buffet line stocked with food, trays, china, silverware. Advise staff to keep the area clean and appealing for the duration of the service. Keep all the kitchen personnel advised as to the number of guests remaining in line, especially when replenishing food items.

9. A half-full container looks unappealing. Toward the end of the serving period, transfer food from large containers to smaller bowls to make the food more appealing.

10. If serving very expensive food items, assign an employee to serve these items.

11. Place emphasis on providing exceptional table service (coffee, tea, water, beverages, and personal attention) at all times.

12. Always protect the food on the buffet line by keeping it covered, or using sneeze guards or other similarly styled food shields.

13. Always provide clean plates and silverware for guests at the buffet line. Assist the guest by providing an employee stationed at the buffet line to monitor clean plate usage.

American Service

American service, often displayed as a **sit-down dinner,** can be a very elegant event. The caterer must be well organized and start with a good plan based on the menu decisions. What is the entree? Will the entree be served in courses? Is the staff trained so they know how they are going to serve it? What utensils do they need to serve the food? How many courses are planned? What time will the service begin? How much time will it take between courses? Is the table set the way the customer anticipates it to be done? The distinguishing characteristic of a sit-down dinner is that the food is arranged artistically on the plate before it is brought out.

The sit-down dinner is as important as the buffet. One advantage of the sit-down dinner is lower food costs than a buffet because the caterer will not have to over prepare. Remember, when offering a buffet, the caterer prepares enough food so the first and last guest have enough to eat.

Another advantage of planning a sit-down event is the caterer knows exactly how many guests will be served. This allows the caterer to calculate the exact portion-per-guest and the total amount of as-served food required for the event. A rule of thumb when calculating a sit-down dinner is to prepare 2–3% more than is required for the guaranteed number of guests. Once the food is purchased, production is set with the two or three percent overrun. The food is prepared, plated, and served to the guest. The guest will not come back for seconds or thirds as will happen on a buffet.

Again, building the menu for the guests begins with their needs. After the menu has been selected, the caterer must consider the entree. If the caterer is serving a stuffed chicken breast, chicken cordon bleu, a strip steak, or prime rib, complementary accompanying dishes must be selected.

When building a menu, color and variety are important. A chicken breast should not be served with mashed or scalloped potatoes and a steamed cauliflower. The lack of color will definitely affect the guests' opinion of the food. When serving something light, such as a stuffed chicken breast, it is recommended to add a medley of vegetables, a glazed carrot, or a fresh green bean in a mushroom sauce, or perhaps an au gratin or a red skinned potato. These combinations add color and make the plate of food attractive.

Caterers use garnishes to enhance the plate appearance. The use of an edible flower on the plate is an excellent example of a garnish. When plates are set down in front of the customers, they should look at the plates in awe. Imagine using the plate as the painter uses the canvas. The center of the plate is framed by its outside rim. Blending the right flavors, textures, colors, temperatures, and visual appeal can create a special art work. The goal is to excite the guests, have them talk about the artistic presentation, and appreciate the quality, flavor, and overall appeal of the food.

Tabletop

The social life of a caterer manifests itself during the process of delivering guest services. It is this interaction with a guest that publicly defines the caterer. Regardless of the event—be it simple, elaborate, ceremonious, religious, or joyous—the one common facet for each caterer is the guest's experience at the dining table.

How a caterer will be defined—that is, builds his or her reputation—will revolve around a guest's experience at the table. The flawless execution of the appropriate table service and the subsequent delivery of quality food are most important when building a caterer's reputation. Regardless of the professional care in the back-of-the-house during the food preparation and handling stage, nothing will compensate for poor arrangement and service experiences in the dining room. Therefore, from the table arrangement of the cloth, china, silver, and glass, to a precise portrait of the service, each detail builds to the standard against which the performance will be gauged.

A caterer must always make the tabletop attractive and the food must always have eye appeal to please the guests. Strong factors making the table arrangement elegant and attractive are well-laundered table cloths, and napkins that are neatly organized and properly sanitized, as well as spotless tableware.

The **tabletop** includes any items placed on the table that are needed by guests for their dining experience. Items include table cloths and napkins, otherwise known as napery; plateware or china, such as the service plate, dinner plate, salad plate, bread and butter plate, and soup bowls; flatware or "silverware," such as forks, spoons, and knives; and water and wine glasses, collectively called glassware.

A caterer can create *signature* plateware using a unique logo or their own trademark. This can help to distinguish the reputation of a caterer and customize the type of plateware used. Of course, the type of tabletop equipment will depend on the needs of the customer and the mission of the caterer.

Regardless of a caterer's mission, a concern is the maintenance of the tabletop accessories. One common problem is breakage or *chipping* of the glassware and plateware. This is always a concern when transporting equipment to off-premise catering sites. Proper packaging for safe transportation and handling not only protects the plateware and glassware, but will also protect the guests and employees.

Broken or chipped accessories can cause serious injury to guests. Improper lifting and handling of bulky items can lead to an employee injury. Broken glass and plates can seriously lacerate an employee's hands. When an accident happens, the employees' immediate response is to quickly clean the area. This sometimes happens without thought of personal safety, especially if the employee feels responsible for this action. Checking tabletop accessories before each event can help avoid this type of accident.

Linen. When setting a table, clean, stainless, and pressed table cloths without holes should always be used. The type of table cloth will depend on the client's needs. It can be linen, cotton, polyester, cotton and polyester blend, plastic, or paper. The location of the function, indoors or out, on- or off-premise; its purpose; and a customer's budget will affect this selection.

If table linen or cotton is being used, it is recommended to purchase or rent the highest quality a caterer can afford. If just beginning, it will be necessary to rent the table cloths and napkins. Prices are usually affixed per napkin and per table cloth. If renting napery, always request its specifications from the rental company. By knowing the specifications, a competent decision can be made as to whether it will meet a caterer's needs. Napery composed of linen, 100% combed cottons, polyester and cotton blends, or 100% polyester is available. Each one has its own distinct characteristics, strengths, and weaknesses.

Purchasing wisely is most important when deciding on napery. The caterer must understand a few common facts before ordering.

1. What is the purpose and how will the napery fit the mission of the organization? This is a strong consideration.

2. What are the needs of the caterer in relationship to the type of clientele and type of functions that will be catered?

3. What material or blend of material will be selected? Based on the type of material, what is the expected life of its service? How durable is it?

4. Will the napery be laundered in a commercial laundry or will it be handled on-premise by the caterer? If the linen is handled on-premise, the caterer may launder the napery in-house, requiring additional handling, such as folding and ironing.

5. What is the most appropriate color and style?

6. Are personalized or crested table linens necessary?

7. What is the cost of the table cloth?

8. What is the correct size needed?

9. What size table cloth is required to fit a round table?

10. What is the inventory requirement?

Mr. Chris Gowdy, Director of Marketing at Mount Vernon Mills, Inc., Riegel Consumer Products Division in Johnston, South Carolina, reminds the caterer that the accurate measurement of the table is necessary to correctly specify the corresponding table cloth size. This measurement is one of the most important specifications required, he says. To help his customers, Mr. Gowdy designed a very useful guide, the *Riegel Sales Reference Guide*. This guide provides step-by-step instructions explaining how to properly measure a table and match this measurement to the appropriate size table cloth (Figure 10–8).

Setting the Table

The needs of the client will direct a caterer's plan to deliver the maximum benefit in regard to the accessories required to set an appropriate table (Figure 10–9). Although standard rules guide a caterer in the proper etiquette of table setting and service, the needs of a client will customize the package for them. An informative review of basic guidelines and rules of etiquette to setting tables can be found at the Web site of Learn2 Set a Table at www.learn2.com/06/0608/0608.ph3, and at the Milliken Table Linen Web site at www.visatablecloth.com/html/main.htm. These two sites will contain information on standard place setting guidelines, formal place setting guidelines, napkin variations, and folding guides, as well as guides to purchasing napery.

HOW TO MEASURE SPECIAL SIZE TABLES

Square or Rectangular Table

1. Measure the table—i.e., 36 x 96 inches
2. Figure the amount of drop (or drape) you would like from the edge of the table. This is a matter of preference. Generally, the longer the drape, the more formal the service. A 9–12 inch drop is usually sufficient. A formal drop is 15 inches.
3. Double this drop number (i.e., 10 inches x 2 = 20 inches) and add this to the table width measurement (i.e., 36 inches + 20 inches = 56 inches).
4. Find the closest standard width fabric available (standard fabric widths are 45, 54, 64, 72, and 90 inches). Subtract the table width from the fabric width and divide by 2 to find the drop that width would give you:

$$54 \\ -35 \over 18 \div 2 = 9 \text{ inches drop} \qquad\qquad 64 \\ -36 \over 28 \div 2 = 14 \text{ inches drop}$$

5. Determine which of these drops is appropriate for you and add twice this drop amount to the length of the table.

   Example

$$9 \text{ drop} \\ \times 2 \over 18 + 96 \text{ (table length)} = 114" \qquad 14 \text{ drop} \\ \times 2 \over 28 + 96 \text{ (table length)} = 127"$$

6. The exact table cloth size for this 36 x 96 table is either 54 x 114 inches or 64 x 127 inches. Standard banquet lengths are 110, 120, or 126 inches, so the best choice for this table would be 64 x 126 inches or 54 x 120 inches. (Width drops and length drops do not necessarily have to be exactly the same—i.e., a 10 inch width drop or a 12 inch length drop is acceptable).

Tables

Height = 29 to 31 inches

Depth of each place setting (Measure from the edge of the table in front of the diner, toward the middle) = 14-inch minimum.

Place setting minimum width

Fine dining..............27 inches

Normal...................24 inches

Aisle minimum width

Occasional service.......30 inches

Regular service..............36 inches

Round Tables Using Square Cloths

1. Measure the diameter of the round table—i.e., 36 inches.
2. Subtract the table diameter from an appropriate square table cloth diagonal. (Use chart for standard squares' diagonals.)

(continued)

Figure 10–8 *Measuring tables for table cloths.*

Example

> 90.5 inches (diagonal of 64 x 64 inches)
> – 36   inches (table diameter)
> 54.5 inches + total point (corner of the table cloth) drop off table.

3. Divide this point drop by 2 to determine the drop off the table of all four corners.

Example

> 54.5 inches ÷ 2 = 27.25 inches drop

Note: This point should not exceed 28 inches since a standard table height is 30 inches. The drop on the sides of the table is determined the same as "A" above (i.e., 64 inches - 36 inches = 28 inches ÷ 2 = 14 inches drop).

Formula

Diagonal of cloth – Diameter of table ÷ 2 = Length of Drop of Points

Sizing Things Up

Here is a list of standard cloth sizes and the table shapes and sizes they fit.

Table Cloth Size	Table Shape	If Your Table Measures
54 x 54"	Square	28 x 28" to 30 x 30"
64 x 64"	Round	36 " diameter
54 x 72"	Rectangular	30 x 48"
64 x 64"	Square	36 x 36" to 40 x 40"
81 x 81"	Round	60" to 66" diameter
54 x 96"	Rectangular	30 x 72"
72 x 72"	Square	48 x 48" to 52 x 52"
90 x 90"	Round	72" diameter
64 x 96"	Rectangular	40 x 72"
64 x 120"	Rectangular	40 x 96"
64 x 144"	Rectangular	40 x 120"

Diagonals for Round Tables

Size	Diagonal
45 x 45"	63.6"
54 x 54"	76.4"
64 x 64"	90.5"
72 x 72"	101.8"
81 x 81"	114.6"
90 x 90"	127.3"

A round table with a diameter of 60 inches or 66 inches takes an 81 x 81-inch square table cloth.

(continued)

Figure 10-8 *Measuring tables for table cloths (continued).*

A round table with a diameter of 72 inches takes a 90 x 90-inch square table cloth.

Diameters of round tables
32" for 3 people
40" for 4 people
50" for 6 people
60" for 8 people
66" for 8–10 people
72" for 10 people

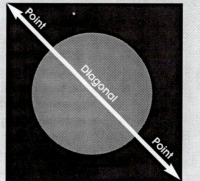

Figure 10-8 *Measuring tables for table cloths (continued).*

Creativity and artistic expression, communicated to a guest the moment they arrive at the table, help to create little details that make a lasting memory. The artistic expression derived from a flawless table is a powerful form of non-verbal communication. A guest's impression of the layout and design of the tabletop is part of the complete package that will help grow the reputation of a caterer.

The first step is to diagram, on paper, a precise cover or setting in advance of a function. Diagraming the table setting in advance allows time to conduct

Figure 10-9 A *conventional table setting arrangement.*

ample research, plan, and create a standard for all service employees. The standard shows the exact placement of each required dish, china, and small ware.

Small wares refers to sugar holders, salt and pepper shakers, ashtrays, pitchers, creamers, ice buckets, and compote dishes. A diagram allows for the careful matching of colors, table decorations, and napkins, and the coordination of center pieces with the menu and theme.

Careful planning creates a coordinated, synchronized, synergetic effect, tying together all of the individual components of an event, such as the tabletop accessories, menu, service, and decor. It causes a guest to focus attention toward a common point, the dining table, and more specifically, the center of the plate.

Everything must be neat, clean, and well organized before the task of setting a table begins. The first assignment is to cover the table using the correct-size **under cloth**, **silencer**, or **silence cloth** as it is sometimes called. Depending on the material composition and its design, a silence cloth may have elastic corners that permit it to hug or attach to the table. It may be made of flannel or plastic. If the under cloth does not have elastic corners, it should extend approximately five inches over each side of the table.

The use of a silence cloth serves many purposes.

1. It helps to prevent the table cloth from sliding on the table.

2. It helps to protect the table cloth from excessive wear and tear, extending its usable life.

3. It helps to protect the table surface from heat or dampness.

4. It makes the table cloth feel softer as it provides a cushion-effect.

5. It helps to silence noise caused by setting china, glassware and the movement of other tabletop implements.

6. It gives the table cloth a heavier look and brings out any pattern on the cloth.

When this thick silence cloth, or under cloth is smoothly in place, the table cloth is spread over it. The crease in the middle of the cloth should fit exactly in the middle of the table, with the crease of the cross-fold meeting precisely at the center. The correct size table cloth will hang evenly over the edges of the table. It should never touch the floor. When serving a dinner event, the overhang should drop between twelve and fifteen inches. When catering a luncheon event, the overhang should drop between eight and twelve inches. The chairs should be set away from the table in such a way as to prevent the bottom edge of the table cloth from touching a chair. Skirting may also be used to wrap the table, eliminating the overhang of a table cloth.

A feature some caterer's use to accent or protect the table cloth is called an **overlay** or **napperon**. The overlay or napperon is a small table cloth that covers the larger one. Overlays are used to accent the table cloth by using a different color combination. The overlay provides the caterer with another decorative feature or creative option. Its functional purpose is to protect the table cloth from stains, spills, and crumbs.

Next, the plates are put into position on the table. When possible, the distance between plates should be at least twenty inches. The standard *cover*, or individual guest space or position, is twenty-four inches wide with a depth measuring fifteen inches. This distance is measured by a caterer from the center of one plate to the center of the plate set parallel, or beside it. The plate is set one inch from the edge of the table. However, plates can be set as far away as two inches from the edge of the table.

It is very important for a caterer to position the plates precisely on a table (Figure 10–10). The position of the plate sets a mark or reference point for placement of the silverware. The bottom rim of the plate will be parallel and in precise alignment with the lower tips of the utensils' handles, and the lower edge of the napkin. Correct placement of the plates leads to a symmetrical and artistic tabletop.

A **cover** is the complete place setting for one guest at the start of a meal. This includes all the accessories required by one guest to dine. A complete place setting includes a service plate, flatware, napkin, and water glass. The name of this service plate has changed over the years. A service plate has been otherwise known as a *place plate, cover plate, show plate, base plate,* or *lay plate.*

A service plate is much more decorative than a dinner plate. It is slightly larger, approximately ten to eleven inches, or about one inch larger than a standard dinner plate. Its main purpose is for decoration. During formal service, the service plate is placed in advance of the meal and set in the center of each cover. It is set down approximately one or two inches from the edge of the table with

Figure 10-10 *Place setting.*

the pattern facing the guest. This ornate plate is used as the foundation on which the plates of the first course are placed. No food is ever set directly on a service plate. The service plate is removed and replaced by a caterer immediately before the first hot course or right after the soup is consumed.

Table Ornaments. Once care has been used to position the plates on a table, the center ornament should be set. A caterer may use center ornaments to complement the theme of an event. For example, a carousel horse set at each table can magnify a circus theme. At another event, the use of wild flowers in a simple but powerful arrangement communicate an atmosphere of an old-fashioned farm gathering.

Center ornaments are unlimited by a caterer's artistic expression and imagination. However, these are certainly limited by a client's budget (Figure 10–11). The most effective table ornaments are those created by the imagination of a caterer that are simple but unusual. Where other caterers may feature ice carvings as the main table ornament, signature ornaments may feature unusual and exotic flowers in appropriate arrangements. These may include an arrangement of flowers portraying a professional football player kicking a football. Unique table ornaments can be created using a combination of different items. Flowers, candles, and antique artifacts, such as tools, books, farming implements, post cards, pictures, and clothing may be used to provide an unforgettable experience.

The table decorations should always fit or complement the purpose of the event. This is why successful caterers create their own complete package based on the client's individual needs. It is another facet of the complete service mix that will differentiate a caterer from the competition.

Figure 10-11
Tabletop centerpiece ornament.

The table ornament should always be married to the theme. It is best to keep it simple and not over decorated. The caterer should not pile things together merely to cover space. Open space is an important component of the complete thematic package. The purpose should be understood and the ornament matched to the event. Is the event a formal function? Is it a ceremonious event? The facility, food, table cloth, napkins, and color schemes must be coordinated. The concept of height should be applied to the table ornament. Various heights can be used, but the view of the guests should not be obstructed. These guidelines must be reviewed often while formulating the plan of the event.

Flatware, Napery, and Glassware. After setting the table ornament, the flatware or silverware is set. The menu will determine the amount and kind of silverware required on the table. Is a cocktail fork, a salad fork, or an entree fork needed? Is a butter knife required? Is an entree knife needed? Perhaps a steak knife is required, especially if something needs to be cut, such as roast beef. Spoons will be placed next to the knife. Will a dessert spoon be needed? Maybe a spoon for iced tea or a soup spoon is needed as well.

To ensure an easy arrangement, it is important to imagine a grid or an imaginary template set on the table. This grid or template will guide the proper placement of flatware and accessories on the table and will create a symmetrical appearance. By following imaginary lines stretching out across the entire table, the caterer can achieve a well balanced tabletop (Figure 10–12).

Figure 10-12 *Proper table setting placement.*

Forks are placed to the immediate left of the service plate, on the grid so they are parallel with the plate. The tines of the forks are up. Knives are placed to the right of the plate with the cutting edge facing toward the plate. The knives must be parallel to each other and in alignment with the forks. The arrangement of the forks and knife is easy to remember. While eating, a guest will use the fork in the left hand and a knife in the right hand. The silverware will thus be parallel and in alignment.

Spoons are placed to the right of the knives, parallel, with the bowl facing up. If an oyster fork is needed, place this to the immediate right and parallel to the spoons. This small fork may also be placed on the oyster plate.

The amount of silverware is determined by the menu. Each menu item must either have its appropriate piece of silver placed at the cover or be brought in before the service of the course. The silverware should be set according to the sequence of its use. The first pieces to be used are placed farthest from the plate and the guest will work in toward the plate.

It is recommended to only place three forks. Two or three knives may be placed at a cover. This number does not include the butter knife or the oyster fork, if required. When dessert requires silverware, it can be set at the cover, immediately before service of the dessert, or be brought in on the dessert plate. If the dessert silverware is set at the cover, the spoon is placed above the fork.

The napkin can be set to the caterer's preference. If set to the left of the forks, its edge is kept parallel to the silverware, using the imaginary tabletop grid. If folded in a simple square, the napkin's open corner is placed in the lower position nearest the plate. Napkin selection should be based on the theme and budget of the event.

Will a paper napkin be sufficient, or must it be linen? Will the napkin be folded? If yes, what kind of fold will complement the event? What color napkin will be used? If white, what color table cloths will be used? Does the napkin match the color of the table cloth?

A subtle way to incrementally increase the profit of a function is to suggest colored linen and/or napkins to the client. Most linen companies will charge the same price for either white or colored linen. The caterer can possibly charge the client a few cents more, perhaps an incremental charge of fifty cents per person, for the use of colored linen.

Table settings need glassware. Is water and/or wine being served with the meal? Will one or two glasses be needed? Is a white wine glass or a red wine glass needed? Is a glass for champagne needed? If serving coffee or tea, will a cup and/or saucer be needed? These are needs which must be determined in advance and a plan prearranged to satisfy them.

Placement of the bread and butter plate is above the tips of the forks. It is laid on the grid so the plate sits on a line parallel to the water glass. The bread and butter knife is set on the plate, parallel to the edge of the table, with the cutting edge facing the guest, and the handle extending to the right. The knife can be placed on the right edge of the plate, blade facing left. It can be placed toward the area just inside of the plate, with the handle running parallel to the plate's right-outside edge. A caterer will set the water glass one inch above the tip of the knife, closest to the service plate.

When the cover is set, the grid will create a symmetrical arrangement on the tabletop.

Small Wares. The classical table setting requires a placement of salt and pepper dispensers between every two covers. If the table is set with eight or more guests, individual salt and pepper dispensers can be set at each corner of the table. If set at a small table, individual dispensers can be placed at the two corners. Following the guidelines of classical table service, the bread and butter plates and the salt and pepper dispensers are removed immediately after the salad course.

When a caterer uses a place card to assign a cover to a specific guest, these are placed above the service plate or at the top center of the cover. All covers should be set on the grid so they face directly opposite of each other.

Compote dishes are set at the tabletop to balance the table setting and hold either mints, nuts, or an assortment of both. They are usually set toward the end of a table and should range between two or four in number.

Candles are used by a caterer to create an ambiance, complement the theme, or balance the tabletop. Candlesticks or a candelabra can be used to enhance the table decorations. The height of the candle should correspond to the height of the holder. Tall candles should be used in a low holder and smaller candles in a tall holder. Etiquette requires the use of tall candles in formal functions. The candles are lit before the guests enter the dining room. They will remain lighted until the guests have departed, even if the candles have burned down to their sockets. When using candles, the caterer should check with the facility, in advance, to make sure there is not an *open-flame* policy.

Service

Diagrams of table settings will help the service staff. After diagraming the table settings, caterers meet with the wait staff and explain the details of the plan. To execute the plan, the service personnel must know specific details of the service.

1. What time will the food be ready for service?
2. Will runners bring the food out on trays?
3. Will tray jacks be used?
4. Will the service staff be responsible for retrieving the food from the distribution area without the runners and serve it themselves?

These service concerns hinge on the type of catering function. Service and customer care provide the groundwork for **Ingredient for Success 37: "The more service given, and the better care taken of the customer through exceptional attention to detail, the happier the client will be and the more repeat business will be generated from that event."**

A caterer always wants to exceed the customer's expectations. Remember, if catering an event for 350 people, make sure enough wait staff is scheduled to properly serve 350 guests. Customer service is just as important on a small job. If organizing an event for 35, 40, or 50 people, a caterer must overwhelm the customer with service.

If the wait staff is responsible for pouring beverages, such as water, coffee, or iced tea, standard operating procedures should be established based on the catering objectives and the function plan. If the consumer's glass is half-full, always refill it during the first half of the meal. Then, during the last half of the meal, ask the customer if they would prefer to have their glass refilled. This will standardize procedures and create continuity in the delivery of service.

Standard operating procedures will also help the caterer to prevent waste and breakage, and reduce beverage costs. It will help to reduce labor time spent clearing soiled cups from the tabletop. This overall savings is compounded over time when one considers how much time is lost while hassling with excessive beverages remaining in cups on the tabletop. It will also help to reduce beverage costs. Establish procedures to help the service staff with the little things such as ice, creamers, rolls, and butter. These are the individual decisions each caterer makes to differentiate them from the competition.

When serving cold beverages, it is important to have ice in all pitchers. Customers do not like warm "iced" tea or warm "ice" water. When serving coffee, serve it hot! Offer a choice between decaffeinated and regular. Creamers must also be served using pitchers or portion-control creamers. A six-month, unrefrigerated, shelf-stable, portion-control creamer is available that can eliminate the worry of serving spoiled cream. These portion-controlled creamers can be served from an attractive bowl placed directly on each table or served individually with the coffee.

Similar decisions are made when serving bread, rolls, and butter. The caterer can purchase foil-wrapped butter pats that look very elegant, or individual butter pats that are covered with a small piece of paper can be used. Little touches include serving the butter at room temperature. There is nothing more aggravating to a customer than placing butter on a nice, fresh roll or piece of bread and finding that the butter, having just been pulled from the refrigerator or freezer, is as hard as a rock and will not spread.

These are some examples of the little things taken into consideration in advance by a caterer to promote good customer service. The caterer must think, prepare, make notes, have charts, build checklists, and train the staff because each job is important and every job requires exceptional attention to even the smallest of details. ***Ingredient for Success 38: "Consider every job a major production."*** A caterer wants to project a proud, competent image either as the owner or as an employee of the organization. ***Catering Rule 39: "A caterer's performance is a reflection of the business."*** When the job is finished, the caterer wants to have rave reviews from the customers. A caterer should think of each job as the most important job they will ever do.

Preset Tableware

If tableware is preset, care must be taken to prevent its contamination. Recommended techniques include wrapping it, keeping it covered, or inverting it on the tabletop. Any unused exposed place settings will be removed when a consumer is seated. If it is not removed, it must be cleaned and sanitized before further use.

Clean Linens

All linens should be free from food residues and other soiling matter. Linens that do not come in direct contact with food should be laundered between events if they become wet, sticky, or visibly soiled. Linens and napkins that are used on the tabletop will be laundered between each use. Wet wiping cloths will be laundered daily. Dry wiping cloths will be laundered as necessary to prevent contamination of both food and serving utensils.

Soiled linens should be kept in clean, nonabsorbent containers. Clean, washable laundry bags are also acceptable as a storage container. Always handle soiled linen separately to prevent the cross-contamination of food, clean equipment, clean utensils, and single-service and single-use articles.

Linens and napkins may not be used in contact with food. However, they can be used as a liner in a container for the service of foods, such as breads, if they are replaced each time the container is refilled for a new consumer.

Laundry facilities on the premises of a catering establishment should be used only for the washing and drying of items used in the operation of the establishment. However, separate laundry facilities located on the premises for the purpose of general laundering, such as for institutions providing boarding and lodging, may also be used for laundering food establishment items.

Improper Use of Tableware

Caution must always be exercised when handling soiled tableware, either at their removal during a function or when cleaning after its completion. Proper techniques and an appropriate level of service staff must be used, and the cross-contamination of clean and sanitized pieces always avoided.

Soiled tableware cannot be reused by a consumer. This includes single-service articles, or tableware to provide second portions or refills. Consumers are not permitted to use their soiled tableware to obtain *seconds* from a buffet line or other food display area. A clean plate or utensil should always be used. Exceptions include the refilling of a consumer's drinking cup or container, which includes personal take-out beverage containers, such as thermally insulated bottles, nonspill coffee cups, and promotional beverage glasses. These can either be refilled by an employee or the consumer at a self-serve area. They must be refilled in such a manner as to prevent contact between the pouring utensil and the lip-contact area of the container.

A caterer cannot permit a take-home food container returned by the consumer to the caterer to be refilled with a potentially hazardous food.

Family-Style Service

Another form of service is called **family-style service**, where the food is delivered to the table in serving dishes or platters with enough quantity for each guest seated at the table. Family-style is considered self service. As the food is passed around the table, the guests help themselves.

Guests can be seated by 4, 6, 8, or 10 per table (Figure 10–13). Usually, at a family-style event, there are standard-set tables. It is very important to know how many people are seated at each table. If serving two entrees, such as breaded pork chops and oven-baked chicken to eight guests, ten pork chops are placed on a serving plate and ten pieces of chicken are placed on another serving plate, along with enough salad in a serving bowl and enough vegetables in their own bowls to serve eight people.

The serving dishes, platters, and bowls are placed directly on the table. No food is served by the wait staff to any guest. The customer likes this form of service because they are overwhelmed with the thought "I can have all that I want to eat." In reality, a caterer will use just slightly more food than if preplating the food as in the American style, for each guest.

The salad is delivered first, followed by the rolls, assorted breads, butter, and side dishes. Finally the main entree is delivered. The guests' beverages are kept filled with water, coffee, or wine. If the bottle of wine is left on the table and the guests are serving each other, empty bottles should be promptly removed.

Figure 10-13 *Family-style table setting.*

Remember, even with family-style, the more service a caterer can offer, the more impressive it is for the customer.

Family-style service offers some advantages for the caterer. Since the food is presented informally to the guests at the table on platters, the wait staff does not have to be highly trained in service techniques. Also, the speed of service is very fast. The food is neatly arranged per platter and delivered as is instead of requiring each portion to be individually placed on a plate for each guest. One concern with family-style service is the menu. Depending on the number of items being served, a careful determination of table space is necessary to make sure there is enough room.

Regardless of the type of service—buffet, sit-down, or family style—the staff must be aware of the needs of the guest. Careful attention and anticipation of the guests' needs is required. Especially important is the removal of the soiled plates and dishes. If serving multiple courses, the soiled dishes are removed as the new courses are served. The soup dish is removed when the salad is served, and the salad is removed when the entree is served. When finished with the entree, the entire table is cleared except for the coffee cup or beverage glass. Then the dessert is served. After dessert, everything is completely removed from the table.

The serving staff should always be alert to bussing opportunities. Since the entree, bread and butter, and salads are served in bowls and platters, extra dirty dishes will always appear on the table. These empty serving bowls and platters should be removed so the customers do not have any dirty dishes in front of them. There is nothing more unappealing for the customer than to be sitting at the table looking at dirty dishes for ten to fifteen minutes after finishing their meal.

◈ SERVICE GUIDELINES

Any unused, potentially hazardous food, returned by a consumer after it has been in their possession, may not be re-served or offered again by the caterer as food for human consumption.

However, a container of potentially nondangerous food may be re-served from one consumer to another if the food is dispensed so that it is protected from contamination, and the container is closed between uses, such as a narrow neck bottle containing ketchup, steak sauce, or wine. If the food remains in an unopened original package and is maintained in sound condition, such as crackers, salt, or pepper, it can be re-served to a consumer.

◈ ROOM ARRANGEMENT

The arrangement of tables is an important factor contributing to the success of the function. A caterer may use any number of arrangements, but it is important to create an environment suitable for the *purpose* of the function. Some common functions may include a business meeting, a wedding, and a social event. When planning the arrangement of a room, a caterer should research the following room layout considerations.

1. size or square footage of the room area
2. aisle space required for service personnel to navigate while serving the food
3. service area or wait stations, including soiled dish area
4. placement of the beverage stations, coffee stations, and portable bar
5. number of seats at each table
6. shape and size of a table
7. total number of guests
8. activity and flow of the guests
9. fire and safety codes in relation to the capacity of the room and the emergency exits

Many caterers, to help decide on the arrangement of the room, will create standard operating procedures designed to *standardize* each type of function. The term *banquet style* (Figure 10–14) is generally used to describe room setups for meal functions.

1. Use round tables (generally 66–72 inches round).
2. Sit eight to ten guests per table.
3. Tables are usually ten feet apart from center to center.
4. Place chairs a minimum of two feet from side walls.

Figures 10–15, 10–16, and 10–17 illustrate some of the most common meeting and dinner table arrangements.

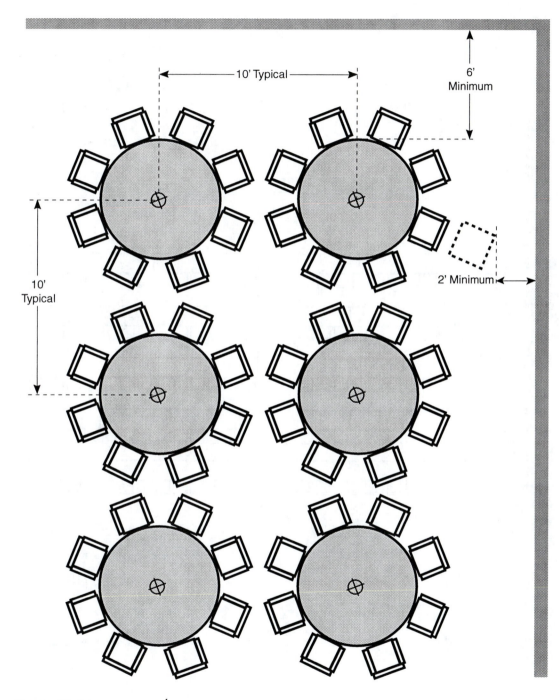

Figure 10-14 *Banquet-style setup.*

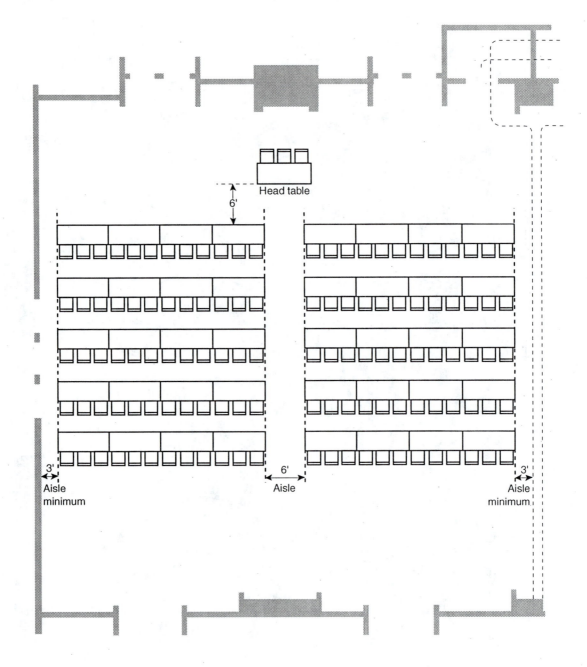

Head table

6'

3'
Aisle
minimum

6'
Aisle

3'
Aisle
minimum

Figure 10-15 *Schoolroom/classroom setup.*

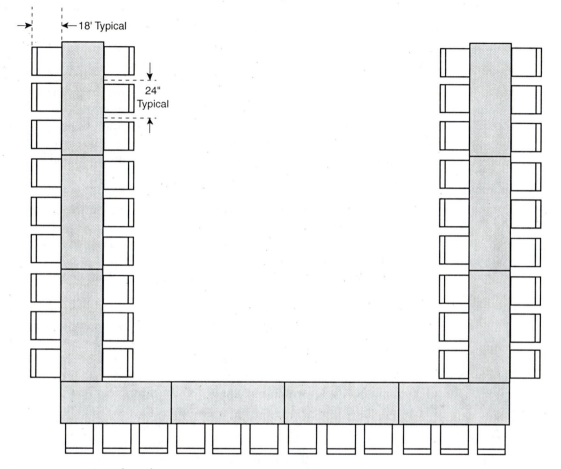

18' Typical

24"
Typical

Figure 10–16 *"U" shaped setup.*

Figure 10–17 *Board room setup.*

Summary

Delivering consistent customer service, geared to exceed a customer's needs, is perhaps the most important mission of a catering business. Successful caterers will define service based on their mission statement as to what it means to the catering operation. Service occurs in both the front-of-the-house and back-of-the-house activities. Many caterers will build their reputation by providing service to meet and exceed the needs of their clients. Understanding service leads to implementing an exceptional training program, to educate and build skills necessary to create a professional service staff comprised of appropriate personnel.

There are several formal and informal styles of service. These service styles may be used in combination with each other, depending on the needs of the client and the type of event. Common types of events include private family functions, business or corporate functions, and community, group, and association functions. These include banquets, receptions, meetings, picnics, baptisms, bar mitzvahs, anniversaries, office parties, holiday parties, charitable events, and weddings.

It is best to maintain a written description of the various service methods the caterer is competent to handle. This list may include the type of function, the type of equipment needed to execute this event, and the various kinds of service provided in conjunction with each. Formal styles of service include *French* and *Russian* service. The most common types of service used by caterers are the informal styles which include *buffet, American,* and *family-style service.* The needs of the client will direct a caterer's plan to deliver the maximum benefit in regard to the accessories required to set an appropriate table. Although standard rules guide a caterer in the proper etiquette of table setting and service, the needs of a client will customize the package. An informative review of basic guidelines and rules of etiquette to setting tables must be completed before the execution of each event. A review of information on standard place setting guidelines, formal place setting guidelines, napkin variations, and folding guides should be completed based on the event itself.

Review Questions

Brief Answers

1. Define the term *service* as it relates to catering management.

2. Discuss how service plays an important role in satisfying customers' needs at the front-of-the-house.

3. Explain how a customer is directly involved in the service activities of the caterer.

4. Explain how a caterer can build a reputation based on service.

5. Explain how a caterer can build a professional service staff.

6. Explain how caterers can use standards to define service. Provide examples of how a caterer can develop service standards to mirror the organization's mission statement.

7. Describe an informal organizational structure and explain how it can affect employee morale?

8. Explain and provide examples of what *appropriate personnel* means to the catering organization.

9. List some of the common attributes of *appropriate service personnel*.

10. Explain the differences between informal and formal service styles used by caterers.

11. Describe the defining characteristics of each service style.

12. Describe how teamwork plays an important role in satisfying customer objectives.

13. Explain what the following Ingredients for Success mean to you.

Ingredient for Success 35: "The end result of the job relies on the entire staff working together—teamwork."

Ingredient for Success 36: "Construct detailed diagrams of every buffet in advance."

Ingredient for Success 37: "The more service given, and the better care taken of the customer through exceptional attention to detail, the happier the client will be and the more repeat business will be generated from that event."

Ingredient for Success 38: "Consider every job a major production."

Ingredient for Success 39: "A caterer's performance is a reflection of the business."

Multiple Choice

Select the single best answer for each question.

1. This style of service is characterized by the use of table-side cooking using two pieces of equipment called a *rechaud* and a *gueridon*.

   a. Russian service

   b. American service

   c. buffet service

   d. French service

   e. family-style service

2. A distinguishing characteristic of _____ service is that the customer actively participates in supplying part of the service. The consumer supplements a caterer's service.

   a. Russian

   b. American

   c. buffet

   d. French

   e. family-style

3. _____ service has the food delivered to the table in serving dishes or platters with enough quantity for the number of guests seated at each table. The food is passed around the table with each guest serving themselves.

   a. Russian

   b. American

   c. buffet

   d. French

   e. family-style

True or False

Read each of the following statements and determine if it is true or false.

1. To ensure a consistent delivery of service, a caterer must define *service* as it applies to the mission of their operation.

2. Caterers can further enhance a guest's perception of the professional service delivered through the use of a standardized uniform for the staff.

3. It is disappointing to a customer to approach a buffet and find the caterer has run short of food and/or it is empty.

Putting It All Together

Interview local caterers. Ask them to describe the service styles they have used to serve their guests. What special training needs, requirements, or pieces of equipment did they need to obtain before executing the event? Ask them to describe how the service style satisfied the needs of the client. Is there any style of service which they would never use? Why? Detail your findings.

Chapter Eleven | Controlling

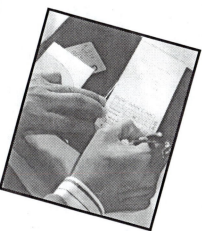

Key Terms

Objectives

After studying this chapter, you should be able to:

◆ Describe the catering management function of control and explain why it is needed.

◆ Describe why the control of an organization's resources is an important catering management task.

◆ Describe the process of control.

◆ Explain why the caterer must develop and implement both internal and external control features into the catering management system.

◆ Explain why the easiest task for most caterers to neglect, without an immediate penalty, is the control function.

◆ Explain why elements of control begin when the caterer designs specific internal techniques to direct an employee's behavior in accomplishing predetermined objectives.

◆ Explain why *controlling* has multiple meanings and serves multiple purposes.

◆ Explain why a caterer needs timely and relevant information to ensure appropriate business decisions.

◆ Explain why a caterer must be concerned with protecting the uninterrupted flow of cash into the organization.

◆ Define a formal payment policy and list its advantages.

(continued)

◆ Describe how a caterer arrives at a final price to charge the client for an event.

◆ Explain the relationship between financial goals and predetermined profit objectives.

◆ Explain why, if an event has experienced a financial loss, the caterer must very carefully study and review the circumstances that have contributed to this failure.

◆ Explain why it is important for a caterer to always be on the alert for unexpected price changes and hidden costs.

◆ Provide an example of how a caterer might misjudge, misquote, or inaccurately speculate on an event.

◆ Explain why the caterer must implement internal controls to protect the company's assets.

◆ Describe creative methods for earning revenue other than from food and beverage sales.

◆ Explain how membership in an appropriate organization or association benefits a caterer.

◆ Describe the balance sheet and the income statement.

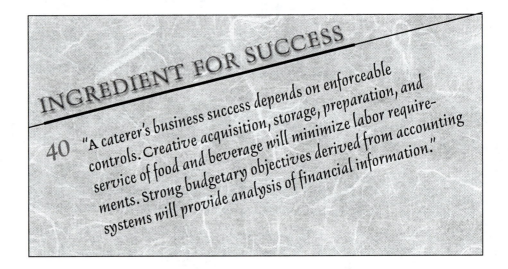

INGREDIENT FOR SUCCESS

40 "A caterer's business success depends on enforceable controls. Creative acquisition, storage, preparation, and service of food and beverage will minimize labor requirements. Strong budgetary objectives derived from accounting systems will provide analysis of financial information."

This chapter addresses the sixth catering management function—*controlling.* Catering managers establish control techniques to protect the financial interests of the organization. Comprehensive control techniques are accomplished by an astute caterer who knows that the most effective way to earn a profit is to first understand how and why a caterer may lose money. If a caterer understands how money may be drained from the organization, effective controls can be used to tighten operations.

This sixth catering management function must be an integral component of the whole organizational plan. The objective of building control techniques is for the survival of the business and the attainment of the organization's mission. This includes a detailed strategy of how the control techniques will be implemented into each event plan.

◆ CONTROL

Controlling the organization's resources is an important management task required to ensure the financial health of the business. Caterers create control techniques using financial tools and predetermined standards to accomplish the other catering management functions.

Control techniques must become a key component integrated into each of the other catering management functions to have a successful organization. Whether formulating or implementing the event plan, executing the operational tasks, or organizing resources, the ability to integrate fundamental catering management controls ensures the capability of comparing actual performance against planned objectives.

Both internal and external control features must be developed for the catering management system. Control of food (Figure 11–1), beverages and labor costs, including salaries, wages, and employee benefits; are examples of internal costs. Internal costs such as direct food and labor costs associated with producing the food are usually bundled and called **prime costs**.

Ingredient for Success 17, first introduced in Chapter 5, explains why a caterer needs to create cost control procedures. ***"Cost control procedures are***

Figure 11-1

Caterers must manage portion control based on the guaranteed number of guests and food costs.

created for the acquisition of timely information to equip the caterer with data to scrutinize controllable costs and make appropriate operational decisions."

According to *Ingredient for Success 40*, "*A caterer's business success depends on enforceable controls. Creative acquisition, storage, preparation, and service of food and beverage will minimize labor requirements. Strong budgetary objectives derived from accounting systems will provide analysis of financial information.*"

Lack of Control

Using effective catering management controls enables the caterer to evaluate key objectives regarding each event. Often, small catering businesses lack long-term sustained success because of neglecting to effectively execute the control function.

The caterer must assume the *jack-of-all-trades* approach and cannot always rely on a professionally trained management staff for input of specialized knowledge into the decision-making process. As a result, the caterer must personally execute each catering function. Since each catering function requires a commitment of time, certain elements may lack appropriate monitoring. Unfortunately, the *easiest* task for most caterers to neglect, without an immediate penalty, is the control function because control is, by nature, a task simultaneously done while every other element is in progress. But neglecting to enforce control procedures when executing operational tasks sends a negative message to the employees that could result in lost revenue.

Elements of Control

Elements of control begin when the caterer designs specific internal techniques to direct an employee's behavior in accomplishing predetermined objectives. Since the caterer bundles common tasks together and delegates these to an employee for execution, control techniques are required to guide the employee in the appropriate direction. Effective control techniques provide guidance without direct supervision.

Multiple Meanings

The sixth catering management function, **controlling**, has multiple meanings and serves multiple purposes. First, control means to establish standard operating procedures to ensure employees' proper execution of their tasks. These standard operating procedures set an appropriate amount of time to execute the task. Second, controlling means the establishment and timely implementation of predetermined objectives, derived from the mission of the organization. Third, control is a process used to integrate each independent catering management function into an achievable event plan. Fourth, control helps to protect a caterer's assets, including money, food, beverages, and equipment. Protection of a caterer's assets must be every employee's responsibility. Finally, control creates the efficient utilization of the caterer's assets to produce a product at a profitable price.

Process of Control

The process of control is the focus of **Ingredient for Success 17: "Cost control procedures are created for the acquisition of timely information to equip the caterer with data to scrutinize controllable costs and make appropriate operational decisions."** First, the caterer must have timely and relevant information to make appropriate decisions. These decisions must benefit the business and the client. Appropriate market information is critical when researching menus and establishing a fair market price to charge the client.

Second, the benefit of timely and relevant information helps to create achievable standards and operating procedures. For example, designing appropriate standard operating procedures, to implement a hazardous analysis critical control plan for an event, must be based on appropriate information.

Third, the caterer must monitor each event, comparing actual performance against predetermined objectives. Appropriate financial information to set and accomplish financial objectives is crucial to the immediate and sustained success of the catering operation. The only effective way to immediately correct defects in the system is to quickly eliminate problems by using appropriate information.

◆ CASH FLOW

A caterer must protect the uninterrupted flow of cash into the organization. **Cash flow** includes a client's series of payments made to the caterer for services. A **formal payment policy** is used to monitor the cash flow into the organization. A formal payment policy explains how the client will pay the caterer for the food and services rendered. Of special concern, however, is the caterer's need for a steady cash flow and to ensure that prompt payment is faithfully made.

Payment Policies

Forty years ago, it was common practice to invoice the client for the food and services rendered between two and four weeks after the event. As corporate catering grew, many caterers' payment policies evolved to accommodate corporate clients' financial payment policies. These policies often pay a caterer within 60 days after an event. Social clients soon began to adopt similar policies. They began to disburse their final payment between 45 and 90 days after the event. Unfortunately this type of payment policy can limit cash flow.

One control to ensure a prompt payment by the client is for a caterer to write a formal payment policy based on the financial needs and the mission of the catering operation. One example is the structured, client-payment policy, requiring the client to pay one-third of the total bill when the contract is signed. Payment of the next one-third is due immediately before or on the day of the event. The final one-third of the bill is due within 30 days after the event. This type of payment schedule is flexible and could be adapted depending upon the type of function and the client.

In today's market, successful caterers must create very structured payment policies to protect themselves against clients defaulting on their obligation to pay their bills. A caterer incurs certain pre-event expenses such as purchasing and preparing food, hiring and training the staff, and acquiring or renting equipment. These and other expenses negatively affect the caterer's financial position.

Payment policies can be written to cover these pre-event costs. At the signing of the contract, the caterer receives one-third of the money owed. Another one-third of the bill must be paid 45 to 30 days before the event. Finally, the last payment is made two weeks before the event. Written into the contract and spelled out in detail is a statement notifying the client that if the caterer incurs any additional costs, the client will be invoiced separately for them. This type of payment schedule is highly recommended as it:

1. ensures the caterer will receive prompt payment for services rendered.
2. guarantees a positive, steadier cash flow.
3. eliminates any unnecessary stress from the caterer worrying about when payment will be made.
4. helps to ensure the business's success.

More and more caterers are becoming successful because they have implemented a structured payment schedule that delivers a consistent, positive cash flow. This steady cash flow helps to eliminate financial worry and stress. An added bonus to a structured payment policy is that the customer must agree to it before hiring the caterer, and the caterer can make sure to get some money up front.

TIPS FROM THE TRADE

Hyatt has established corporate policies that dictate proper billing and collection procedures. We do have some flexibility when writing contracts depending on the amount of estimated charges. For instance, if the estimated amount is less than $1,000, I will require the estimated charges as a nonrefundable deposit. All invoices that will be paid by check, cash, or credit card must be prepaid 10 days prior to the actual function date. We do provide direct billing for accounts which will exceed $2,000 total. A direct bill application must be submitted 30 days in advance and is subject to the Hotel's approval.

Dianne Herzog
Catering Manager
Hyatt Orlando
Kissimmee, FL

◆ PRICING THE EVENT

How does a caterer determine the final price to charge the client for an event? There is no universal method used to derive a final price per event because caterers use different procedures to calculate costs. A caterer can charge each client a different price for the same menu based on the package, quality of food, and level of service. Each caterer calculates pricing formulas based on specific needs.

A caterer may decide to offer a one-price *total package* to the client. This package will include an option of selecting from a variety of menus that differ in price, according to the type of entree and style of service.

There are three basic methods to arrive at the price for any function. The first method is called the *cost-based pricing method*, the second is the *client-based pricing method,* and the third is *competitive-based pricing*. Two additional pricing strategies are called *market-skimming pricing* and *market-penetration pricing*.

If using the **cost-based pricing method**, the caterer will calculate the actual cost to produce the function and then add a predetermined markup to arrive at the client's cost.

The actual expense per event will vary depending on the menu, type of service, competition, market demands, special requests, and the time of year (e.g., Christmas, New Year's Eve, or Mother's Day). A caterer must first calculate the total cost of executing an event, set an achievable, fair, profit objective, and then verify that the client is capable of making the structured payment schedule.

Establishing the expenses for a function will determine how much the caterer must charge the client in order to meet the predetermined profit objective and exceed the guest's expectations. The actual mechanics of *crunching* the expense numbers for a final price may vary. There are different mathematical formulas a caterer can use to total the expenses, and arrive at a price to charge the client.

One important consideration in setting a price is to include overhead. **Overhead** is the cost of operating the catering business regardless of the type or number of functions executed. Overhead is a term used to describe indirect labor, utilities, indirect material cost, insurance, taxes, depreciation, and repairs and maintenance of equipment. These costs are indirectly related to the cost of executing a catering function. Remember that prime costs are direct labor and food costs incurred in executing a catering function.

A caterer must calculate or budget a total overhead cost for an operating period. Once determined, budgeted overhead costs can be allocated directly to each function. A dollar amount, or a percentage factor, used to allocate a partial cost of overhead, may be added to the direct cost of the event to determine the client's price.

The second basic pricing method is called the **client-based pricing method**, which uses the client's perception of the function's value as the foundation for setting the client's price. The caterer's costs may not directly influence final price. Rather than basing the client's cost on the direct food and labor cost, the caterer may use other perceived services from the complete package, such as valet parking or special linen requests, to adjust the price to the client's perception of value. Theoretically, the caterer can therefore charge every client a different price. Price is based on the client's perception of the value of food and related services, and their ability to pay.

The third method of pricing a function is the **competitive-based pricing method**. This method bases client cost on the comparative price as charged by the other caterers in the market. This price is not determined by direct costs or a client's perceived value. Rather, it is set by the market conditions and competitive *jockeying*.

The two additional pricing strategies are called *market-skimming pricing* and *market-penetration pricing*. A caterer implements a **market-skimming pricing strategy** by setting a very high price to *skim-off* the profits from the market. This may happen if there is only one type of specialized caterer in a market to service specialized needs. One disadvantage is that the large profits may attract competition into the market.

A caterer may use a **market-penetration pricing strategy** to gain a large market share by penetrating a new niche or market. Prices are initially set low, but must be compensated by high volume. Again, low price may attract competitors into the market.

Menu

Establishing the cost for the event begins with the menu. If the menu features one-half chicken, the caterer will realize a much different profit structure than if featuring a filet. The caterer will also have a much different profit structure if doing a breakfast event than if catering a sit-down dinner. Standardized recipe cost sheets (Figure 11–2) help establish menu costs.

Expenses

The caterer must understand what expenses will be incurred from executing the event. If the caterer is doing a breakfast for thirty-five people at an off-premise site located five miles away, calculating total costs for the event must include the cost of transportation and the cost of labor to get the food to the location.

One method used to determine the cost and price structure is to quote a flat price for the entire event (Figure 11–3). A flat price must cover all expenses including labor, preparation, and transportation of the food. Will the caterer drop-off the food at the location and leave? Can the caterer leave the equipment safely overnight and retrieve it the next morning? If not, will the crew be required to return immediately after the event to retrieve the equipment? Or, will the crew be required to stay at the event? If staying, will the crew provide services and clean the facility at the conclusion of the event? Or, will the client provide any services themselves, such as delivering the food, serving the guests, or cleaning up? All of these activities have an impact on the cost structure of an

STANDARDIZED RECIPE COST SHEET

Event_____

Date of Event _____ Time of Event _____

Week Number of Operation _____

Date Recipe Costed _____

Adjusted Date Recipe Costed _____

Date Approved _____

Catering Manager _____

Production Manager _____

INGREDIENTS	INGREDIENT COST		
Item	Amount	Unit Cost	Total Cost

Recipe Yield _____

Portion Size _____

Portion Cost _____

Total Recipe Cost _____

Recipe: Prepared by _____

HACCP Instructions Reviewed _____

Critical Control Points _____

Suggestions for Improvement _____

Production Process Defects _____

Recipe Number _____

Figure 11-2 *Standardized Recipe Cost Sheets help establish menu pricing.*

event. It is important for the client to understand the cost structure of even a simple menu offering coffee and donuts. A client must be willing and able to pay the price, even though some clients may be more interested in the service of providing the breakfast than the actual cost. On the other hand, a client may not want to pay more than $10.00 per person for a luncheon featuring a nice entree.

EVENT COST-PRICING WORKSHEET

Do Not Hang on the Bulletin Board!

Name of Event _____   Date of Event _____

Prepared By_____   Date Prepared _____

Contact Person _____   Number _____

E-mail _____

Time of Service _____ Service Duration _____ Location of Event _____

Guest Count _____ Price Per Person $ _____ Date Price Quoted _____ Initials _____

Revised Price and Reason for Revision:

$_____/_____ Date _____ Initials _____

	MENU ITEM	PORTION SIZE	PORTION COST*
Appetizer	_____	_____	$ _____
Entree I	_____	_____	$ _____
Entree II	_____	_____	$ _____
Starch	_____	_____	$ _____
Vegetable	_____	_____	$ _____
Salad	_____	_____	$ _____
Dressing(s)	_____	_____	$ _____
Bread	_____	_____	$ _____
Butter/Spread	_____	_____	$ _____
Dessert	_____	_____	$ _____
Beverages(s)	_____	_____	$ _____
Condiments	_____	_____	$ _____
Other	_____	_____	$ _____
	Total Raw Food Cost		$ _____
	Extra Production Costs, Etc.		$ _____
	Total Cost Per Person		$ _____

$_____ divided by _____ %   equals $ _____

Total Cost Per Person   Desired Food Cost Percent   =   Selling Price Per Person

Standard Markup Percent

* See Figure 11-2 for each individual recipe item.

Figure 11-3 An *Event Cost-Pricing Worksheet helps a caterer determine how much to charge a client for an event.*

Although the cost of the food would definitely be much higher for the luncheon than for the breakfast, the caterer would have the same expense of labor, transportation, and overall fixed expense for catering this event. These are some variables a caterer must think carefully about when calculating the price to charge a client for a catering function.

Each event must be reviewed on an individual basis. Menu prices will be based on different factors. A banquet menu is often priced according to the choice of an entree. If the entree selection offers a choice of stuffed pork chops or chicken breasts, the cost might be $15.00 per person. If the entree options include steak or prime rib, the cost per person might be $25.00. An option of either shrimp or a lobster would most likely be an even higher price.

Other Factors

There are other factors to consider that are not covered in the selling price (Figure 11–4). What are the number of hours required to execute the event? What is the cost of serving an appetizer? A different pricing formula is required when figuring the expense of serving an appetizer because the caterer must determine the type of appetizer and how many will be served to each person. Will soup be served? Will it be served with a salad? These details must be considered when setting the client's price.

TIPS FROM THE TRADE

I think all of us who have been in the catering business for a number of years have received, sometime during our career, a severe education in pricing an event. It is not good business to merely ask the questions, "Can I really afford to do that? Well, I want the job, am I willing to sacrifice?" That kind of reasoning does not pay the bills. You must always look at the financial structure of each event. A caterer should not do a job unless he can make money.

In addition, when bidding on a job against a caterer who offers lower quality work, always maintain a fair and reasonable price that includes the profit structure needed to successfully operate your business.

If you are ever bidding on an event, make sure you are comparing apples to apples, or oranges to oranges. If two or three caterers are bidding on the same event, make sure each is submitting a similar menu. When I bid on an event, I ask for specifics. Are we going to do a 14-ounce boneless New York strip steak with a one inch tail, graded USDA choice? What size baked potato are we using? Are we serving both butter and sour cream? If we are serving a tossed salad, what type of salad dressing are we using? The menu must be spelled out exactly so our quote is basically in the same ballpark with the other caterers. If I am purchasing higher quality ingredients than the other caterers, my costs might be higher, but at least we are pricing apples to apples and not apples to oranges.

Bill Jardine
Jardine's Farm Restaurant & Catering
Sarver, PA

SERVICE OR EQUIPMENT NOT COVERED IN "SELLING PRICE"

ITEM	TOTAL COST	PER PERSON COST
1. Table Top:		
(a) Special Linens and Napkins	$_____	$_____
(b) Centerpieces (candles, etc.)	$_____	$_____
(c) China, Flatware, Glassware	$_____	$_____
(d) Other	$_____	$_____
2. Tables, Chairs	$_____	$_____
3. Silver Trays, Chafing Dishes, etc.	$_____	$_____
4. Special Bar Equipment	$_____	$_____
5. Truck Rental	$_____	$_____
6. Miscellaneous Equipment	$_____	$_____
7. Facility Rental	$_____	$_____
8. Tent(s)	$_____	$_____
9. Cake(s), Pie(s), Cookie(s)	$_____	$_____
10. Truck Rental	$_____	$_____
11. Extra Personnel or Hours	$_____	$_____
(a) Server ____ hrs x $ ____* =	$_____	$_____
(b) Back-of-the-House ____ hrs x $ ____* =	$_____	$_____
(c) Truck Driver/Other Labor ___hrs x $ ____ =	$_____	$_____
(d) Employee Meals ____ x RFC $ ____ =	$_____	$_____
12. Other_____	$_____	$_____
13. Allocated Fixed Cost Factor or Amount	$_____	$_____
Sub Total	$_____	$_____
14. Add _____% of Sub Total for Admin. Cost	$_____	$_____
15. Bring forward Selling Price Per Person from the bottom of Figure 11–3.		$_____
Total Selling Price Per Person		$_____

* Preset Amount

Figure 11–4 *Worksheet to calculate service and equipment not covered in the "selling price."*

Each caterer establishes the selling price per event based on a per-person cost basis. To do this, the caterer must know exactly what the total costs for the event are including fixed costs, transportation costs, labor costs, and food costs.

Financial Goals

To attain the profit objectives set for the business, the caterer must set financial goals for each event. These goals may be different for each event, depending on the function. The caterer must understand the financial aspects of catering in order to make a profit.

TIPS FROM THE TRADE

We participated in an event called "The Taste of Honolulu." Many cities have these events to feature local cuisine. Attendees pay script and the idea is for the caterers and vendors to get their money back while featuring their signature foods.

Our booth was so popular that, by the end of the first day, we were nearly sold out of all our food. We prepared our food based on the promoter's forecast of what we would sell. After having spent the entire day working this event, we had to return to our facility, clean and sanitize everything, and begin production again. We produced one and one-half times more of what we had originally made because we sold it so quickly. We produced food almost the entire night to be ready for the next day. After working most of the night, we returned to the event with a four hour rest to start all over again.

I think the promoter had given us an accurate number as far as the number of people who came to the event. But the estimated number who would actually come to us and purchase our food was too low. There were actually three categories of vendors: those who did not have much of a line, those who had a long line because they were slow, and those who had a fairly long line but kept it moving. We were one of the vendors who had a constant line. We had so many workers that we were able to put the food out very quickly. In one respect, that was great. We were able to keep people moving through the line. But, in another respect, it was not so good because we sold all our food in the first day. When people see long lines, they often think, "Oh, that must be a good place because everyone is going there to eat." That might not necessarily be the case. It might really mean that it has slow service. Our booth had both good food and fast service. Unfortunately, that worked against us in one respect.

Henry Holthaus
Certified Executive Chef/Instructor
Culinary Institute of the Pacific
Honolulu, HI

Once the caterer becomes established and builds a clientele who knows the menus are priced fairly, the customer will return as long as the caterer continues to exceed their needs and provide good food and service. It takes a caterer time to build a reputation based on honesty, integrity, and a sense of customer loyalty. This kind of positive reputation is built on a foundation of mutual trust. Customers know that they will not be excessively charged or under served.

TIPS FROM THE TRADE

I had a first time event. Circumstances happened which were totally unforeseen. I was the prime vendor at a charitable event that lasted for a week. The organizers misjudged the amount of people they believed would be attending the event and, likewise, the amount of food that would be consumed. We lost a considerable amount of money because we purchased additional equipment to handle the event, thinking it would be a high-volume event. Our plan was to spread our costs over three years to make money on it. Well, in a week's time, I lost $10,000. This is a considerable amount of money for a caterer. You have to work a long time to make up that amount. These are the types of events that educate caterers very quickly. The ironic thing about this example was that about five years later, I was asking another caterer to describe some of his worst experiences. He started to tell me about this event they catered and lost "megabucks" on it. They lost between $8,000–$10,000 five years after I had done the same event. He apparently went into the event with the same plans as I had. Maybe if we both had been a little smarter, we would have researched it much better, talked with the caterer who had done the previous job, or had a little communication with other caterers, and made a decision not do it.

Bill Jardine
Jardine's Farm Restaurant & Catering
Sarver, PA

Extraneous Factors

A caterer must also be aware that at times, based on extraneous factors, the anticipated profits do not materialize. If an event has experienced a financial loss, the caterer must very carefully study and analyze it. What are the factors or the circumstances that led to this failure? How can they be avoided in the future?

What if the caterer quotes a menu price to a client who is negotiating the contract nine months in advance? Say the client wants a steak dinner for a corporate picnic. If the caterer is researching the price of a boneless strip loin in October, remember that the market price can change. The caterer must base the cost of the future event on the market price of the boneless strip loin in October. What happens if, in July, the meat market experiences a change in price? Instantly, the expense of a boneless strip loin increases by $2.00 per pound above the quoted price. If the expense has increased by $2.00, how can the caterer protect himself?

Contract Protection

One technique used to protect the caterer against unexpected price changes in the market and unforeseen circumstances, when negotiating with a client at least six months in advance, is the use of a contract. It is common to include a statement in the contract to protect the caterer and the client against this kind of change. Something similar to the following statement can be included. *This is an approximate price. The finalized price will be given (15 or 30) days before the event.* The caterer can then be assured of receiving a fair market price for the services rendered. If the price suddenly decreases, then savings can be passed on to the customer as well. Giving the customer a savings on the original price will definitely communicate the caterer's dedication to building a solid reputation based on honesty, integrity, and a sense of loyalty built on mutual trust.

Underlying Causes of Lost Revenue

When executing a catering event, one should always be on the alert for *hidden costs* that may suddenly reveal themselves and severely dilute the anticipated profit objectives. A caterer's insurance costs or expense of labor may have increased. Sometimes the caterer may just misjudge, misquote, or unsuccessfully speculate on an event.

TIPS FROM THE TRADE

I owned a barbeque restaurant on the island of Oahu. I bid on a job to be the exclusive caterer for the Sandy Beach Pro Am Surf Tour. This five-day event was a surfing tournament held on the island of Oahu, in Hawaii. The promoters told me this event would attract at least 2,000 people each day for five days. Therefore, I based the bid on 10,000 people. I came out with an original number that I believed was very fair to begin with. I projected approximately $2.00 per person per day collected from each participant. I was going to be the exclusive caterer at the site. No other vendor was permitted to set up. I thought a soda was going to be at least 75 cents and most people would be drinking soda.

After the tournament, the revenue from catering this event was 50 cents per person *total* throughout the five days. It was partially because the attendees were kids who did not have much money and complained about the prices (even though I sold nothing for more than $3.00). Also, across the street from this event, outside of the jurisdiction of the promoters, were lunch wagons, taking some sales away from me. This is an example of a caterer losing revenue because of a promoter who exaggerated the number and type of people expected at an event. Caterers must research each event to understand who their market is going to be. If the market represents a clientele 25-years of age and younger, calculate a very high cost per person.

These outdoor types of catering events offer special challenges to the caterer. You usually have to leave all of your equipment at the site. In this illustration, we left everything out on the beach. We camped right there to guard the equipment. We had people attempting to steal our food during the night. We had a crew member stand guard throughout the night, then get up early the next morning, take a cold shower out on the beach, and start all over again. I was up with the sun at 5:30 A.M. and working until the event was over at 6:00 P.M. The we would clean up, get everything together, feed the crew, and before I knew it, the time was 9:30 or 10:00 P.M.

Better research may have revealed some of the hidden costs incurred at this event, allowing me to provide a more accurate bid.

Henry Holthaus
Certified Executive Chef/Instructor
Culinary Institute of the Pacific
Honolulu, HI

◆ PROFESSIONAL SERVICE COMPANIES

The caterer needs to build a relationship with professional service companies such as photographers, florists, and rental companies. Professional service companies will return a set percentage of the client's cost to the caterer for just the referral. A caterer making a referral for a tent rental costing $4,000 may receive 10–15%. Commissions are a positive addition to the caterer's profit structure. If catering a wedding, negotiate with a cake baker (Figure 11–5) for a percentage of each referral. Other service companies will include entertainment, a photographer, limousine service, or any of a number of services offered to a bride, including wedding gowns and tuxedos.

All of these incidentals add to the function's profit structure. These are great ways to earn additional revenue to complement the food and beverage service.

Unethical Purchasing Behavior

One of the most important catering management tasks is the purchasing function. The caterer strives to build a positive relationship based on mutual trust with the suppliers.

Mutual trust means the distributor sales representative (DSR) will satisfy the caterer's needs. The DSR may reward the caterer's loyalty by giving bottom line pricing on all products. It is important, however, to establish a primary and a secondary supplier, or a backup distributor to keep everyone honest. Distributor sales representatives work on a commission and may get a little complacent. The caterer should always check distributor invoices for accurate pricing because a DSR may inflate prices to increase their commission.

Figure 11–5 *Caterers often recommend the services of a professional baker to supply the wedding cake for the event.*

The caterer must use internal controls to protect the company's assets. A trusted, ethical, and intelligent member of the team must be responsible for the purchasing function. The buyer has been formally granted a significant amount of position power in the organization and can legally bind the organization with suppliers through contracts. Some buyers may have the ability to spend a significant amount of the organization's money. Imagine the operating budget of a large caterer for food, beverage, equipment, and supplies.

Controls are important to help prevent or eliminate the opportunity for unethical behavior. A buyer can enter into an illegal arrangement with a supplier. This is called *collusion*. A kickback occurs whenever the buyer receives money for an illegal activity. A supplier may agree to reward a buyer with a personal kickback each time the buyer uses the supplier. Maybe a rental company agrees to pay the caterer 15% of each rental contract referred by this caterer to the supplier. In this case, maybe the catering company receives 10% and the individual buyer gets 5%. Caterers should avoid this type of unethical behavior by hiring buyers who can be trusted and who work to protect the company's assets.

TIPS FROM THE TRADE

A company approached me after I had one of my employees terminated. The representative from a meat company informed me how this employee had planned to make a deal for the summer catering season. The representative informed me that the individual wanted to cut a deal where the buyer would guarantee all of Jardine's business for a couple of beef items in exchange for a personal kickback of 10 cents per pound. I was thoroughly disgusted with the distributor for coming to me after the fact. I asked why he did not approach me when the employee first suggested the deal. I told the distributor I did not think it was fair that he kept this knowledge to himself without informing me.

Although this practice was prevalent in the past, I do not think it is as common today because more distributors refuse to engage in that kind of dishonest practice. But, there is always that *one* person, so each caterer must be vigilant by creating and enforcing good, internal control techniques.

Bill Jardine
Jardine's Farm Restaurant & Catering
Sarver, PA

Code of Ethics

Each caterer must write and live by a **code of ethics**, which is a formal statement written and communicated to each employee and each stakeholder. Stakeholders are the owner, employee, customer, supplier, competitor, and the community.

The purpose of the written code of ethics is to guide individual behavior. A written code of ethics will define acceptable behavior for everyone in an organization. Each person may have a different religious or philosophical view of everyday life, but a written code of ethics will help prevent any misunderstanding of professional conduct that may lead to personal gain. The caterer and the employee may be confronted each day with questions regarding their conduct and behavior. A written code of ethics may prevent harm done to others and help an employee to make the best behavioral decisions.

The code of ethics can be introduced during the recruitment and hiring stages. A written code of ethics may be integrated into every employee training program and should become part of each employee's job for it to work.

Just as a written code of ethics will guide individual conduct, it will also guide the entire organization. The caterer must communicate a standard of moral conduct. This standard will guide the entire organization in its decision-making process to accomplish its mission. The ethical standard will help to create an ethical environment.

Professional Associations

The *Tips from the Trade* in this text are situations that are experienced by real caterers. Because caterers often experience similar situations, memberships in professional organizations are recommended. Membership in a local catering organization, the National Association of Catering Executives, the National Restaurant Association, or the American Culinary Federation is important for networking with other professionals. They meet and discuss experiences: issues with clientele, problems they confront in their market, and creative solutions they have used to contribute to their success.

◈ THE FINANCIAL COMPONENT

The crucial financial concern of every caterer involves making decisions to acquire and employ resources to maximize the efficient and effective administration of the operation. Every caterer must forecast their short-term and long-term financial needs. The acquisition of funds from external sources to finance these business activities is one task of financial management. Monitoring and controlling those funds as they flow through the catering operation is another.

The fundamental purpose of financial management is to maximize shareholder or owner wealth; that is, wealth being measured by the current market price of the firm's common stock, or value of the operation. The goal is to create a healthy balance between risk and profitability. This balance teeters between achieving an optimal return on the owner's investment while averting unwarranted risk.

Financial management is a key concern of every catering operation. Key financial management activities include raising capital, building relationships with the suppliers of this capital, establishing a credit policy and installing an accounting and budgeting system.

The primary financial responsibility of a caterer is to secure funds and to allocate those funds to selected purposes within the operation. Where can the funds be obtained? What mix of funding is the most advantageous for the caterer? How will the funds be repaid? These are some basic questions that must be addressed by a caterer.

The caterer can secure external funds from financial markets. Two segments of the financial market are the money market and the capital market. If the maturity of the financial instrument matures in less than one year, it represents the money market. If the maturity of the financial instrument is more than one year, it represents the capital market.

The caterer will need to obtain external funding to build inventories, purchase new equipment, pursue projects, engage in new product development (signature items), and to assist in the management of the cash flow cycle.

The caterer can secure external funding in the form of financial assets of cash, stock, and debt. This is accomplished through what is commonly referred to as *equity* or *debt financing*. Equity financing is accomplished by raising funds through the issuance of stock, retained earnings, or funds generated from depreciation. Debt financing is the use of a borrowed amount that is owed within a definite payment schedule and/or due date.

Stock refers to common stock or ownership in an organization. Retained earnings are the profits generated by the firm that are reinvested in the organization. Depreciation is the process of amortizing or allocating the cost of an asset to the accounting period in which it is used to generate earnings for the caterer. Depreciation is an expense that is deducted from the generated revenue during the accounting period. It is not a cash payout by the caterer to an external source, but rather it is placed back into the operation for internal use.

Debt represents a promise to pay a specified amount plus interest to a creditor at an agreed upon future date. Government securities, corporate issues, and international instruments are other financial instruments that can be used to raise funds. Cash is issued by the U.S. Treasury as coins and paper currency.

Accounting Function

The role of the accounting function is to provide timely and accurate information enabling the caterer to make effective business decisions. The ability to analyze and interpret key financial reports is a technical skill of utmost importance. Effective business decisions made in a timely manner will better enable the caterer to improve the organization's financial position.

The purpose of an accounting system is to summarize and provide an accurate and complete report of all business transactions incurred by the caterer in the daily operation of the organization. This is accomplished using bookkeeping procedures. Bookkeeping leads to the function of an accountant. The function of an accountant is the evaluation and analysis of the data to create accurate and complete reports summarizing the business transactions.

These reports serve many different purposes. First, these financial reports are required by government agencies for tax reporting purposes. Second, these financial reports communicate the financial vitality of the operation to creditors and suppliers. If a caterer needs to obtain funding for a special project, or an advance of working capital to restart the business after a seasonal shutdown, the success of securing a short-term or long-term loan will be determined by these financial reports. If taking on a rather large function, the acquisition of food and supplies may necessitate a short-term loan or a line of credit from a bank to cover the initial cost. These reports provide the information a bank needs to approve a loan. Third, these financial reports are used to inform investors if and how the business has maximized their wealth, as measured by the current return on their investment or by the current value of the market share of common stock. Fourth, they provide an accurate and precise financial picture of the operation used by the caterer to make appropriate day-to-day operational business decisions and to enhance the success of the operation.

Accurate and complete reporting of all business transactions enables any owner to track the financial success of day-to-day business operations. Ownership of a catering operation may take one of the following basic forms: a sole proprietorship, partnership, or corporation. Depending on the form of ownership, the principal owners may not be actively involved in the day-to-day operational management decisions. The owner(s) or a board of directors may be established to represent the financial interests of the *silent owners*. This board will create a structure and delegate the day-to-day operation of the catering organization to a management team. While the management team will have the authority and responsibility to operate the catering firm, accurate and complete accounting reports will keep the absentee owners in touch. These reports will provide valuable information so the owners can access the effectiveness and efficiency of the management team in accomplishing all financial and operational objectives.

Financial Statements

The two key financial reports prepared from the accounting system to summarize and provide an accurate and complete report of the caterer's operation are called the *balance sheet* and the *income statement*. The **balance sheet** is a financial picture of what the organization is worth on a specific date, at the end of the month, or at a specific time during the year. The **income statement** reveals how well the operation is performing financially over a specific period of time.

Balance Sheet

The balance sheet is a picture of the financial condition of the business at a specific moment in time. The financial condition of a catering business will depend on:

1. amount of personal investment incurred by the owners.
2. the ability to obtain credit or borrowed capital.
3. the ability of the caterer to enter and compete in the market.
4. the location of the catering business and the local economic conditions.

Every balance sheet will have three main categories: the value of what the business owns (assets), how much the catering company owes its creditors (liabilities), and how much the caterer or owner is worth at a specific reference point in time (owner's equity). Owner's equity, or capital, is the amount of money or the investment made by the caterer to start the business.

Assets, liabilities, and owner's equity are listed by category according to their similarity. Assets include cash, accounts receivable, inventory, land, building, and equipment. Assets are further classified as either current assets or fixed assets. Current assets are cash, accounts receivable, inventory, and prepaid expenses. Assets are considered current when they can be consumed during a normal operating period, such as one fiscal year, although it can be any time period. One fiscal year is usually segmented by every three months, or quarter, of the year.

Current assets may be easily and quickly converted into cash. Accounts receivable represent accounts whose money will be collected in the near future. They are considered a current asset because a caterer can sell this account, called *factoring*, to a collection agency in return for cash. Inventory, or the raw materials a caterer uses to create a finished food item from a recipe, will be sold to a client in exchange for cash. Cash is then used to purchase the raw material to restock inventory. Prepaid expenses represent advanced payment made by a caterer for such needs as insurance premiums. Insurance coverage is needed during the current fiscal operating period or quarter.

Fixed assets are those that a caterer uses in the business over a longer period of time than one year. They are also called *plant assets*. These assets are used in the catering operation to produce food and assist in the delivery of service. Fixed assets include land, buildings, furniture, fixtures and equipment. Workstations designed with specific equipment, such as ovens, mixers, and slicers are considered fixed assets. These major fixed assets help the caterer to operate the business.

Caterers can increase the assets of the business by investing their own money into the business. Assets can be increased by securing a loan or receiving an extension of credit, such as when a purveyor delivers an order of food and extends the caterer fifteen days to pay the invoice. Loans can be secured from lending institutions or other investors, such as family members. Assets are increased when a caterer renders a service to a client in exchange for cash.

Liabilities and owner's equity form the *equities* side of a balance sheet. When the catering business receives cash, secures a loan, or an infusion of money from the caterer himself, these transactions increase the owner's equity. An owner can be either a sole proprietor, which means a single owner; a partnership, which means it is jointly owned by two or more individuals; incorporated, which basically means the catering business exists separately from its owners as granted by a charter issued by one of the fifty United States. The owner's equity in a corporation is called stockholders' equity.

Liabilities, like assets, are also classified by a time frame. Liabilities are either short or long term. Current liabilities are those that will be extinguished or paid during the normal operating period, usually one year. Current liabilities are usually incurred by a caterer securing current assets to be used in the execution of a catering event. If a caterer purchases food for an event having 1,500 guests, the cost of the food is classified as a current liability. It is expected that the caterer will pay the current liability or accounts payable from the revenue received from the client. Other current liabilities include utility bills, payroll taxes, and local property taxes.

Working capital is the excess of current assets minus current liabilities. Working capital is required for the caterer to execute the daily operations. Potential uses of working capital include:

1. the need to purchase and secure opening inventories.

2. paying for the startup costs at the beginning of a new catering season.

3. paying the caterer's first and last month's rent and utilities.

4. covering expenses during the time required for a new business to generate enough revenue to support full operation.

Long-term liabilities are those whose due date is longer than one year from the date of the balance sheet report. One such example is a mortgage incurred on the building, which may have a thirty-year due date.

The balance sheet will help identify the assets and liabilities at a given time (Figure 11–6). The balance sheet is best understood by the following accounting formula:

$$\text{assets} - \text{liabilities} = \text{the amount of owner's equity}$$

This balance sheet formula must meet the standard rules of mathematics, where each of the items found positioned on either side of the equal sign must balance.

The standard accounting formula is the format for the operating layout of the balanced sheet:

$$\text{assets} = \text{liabilities} + \text{owner's equity}$$

Notice in Figure 11–7 how both sides of the equation balance. Review the accounting equation using the numbers from the balance sheet to see how the equation balances. The balance sheet reveals valuable information about assets and equity (Figure 11–8).

Income Statement

The income statement (Figure 11–9) is a financial report that reveals how well a company is performing financially during a specific period of time. It summarizes the inward flow of operating revenue (sales) against the outward or potential flow of costs and expenses.

The format of an income statement will vary depending on the needs of the caterer. The basic formula of the income statement is the same:

$$\text{operating revenue} - \text{operating expenses} = \text{net income or loss}$$

Operating revenues, or net sales, result from a caterer receiving payment from a client for food and service provided. A caterer will incur expenses in the execution of a catering event that are usually grouped by similarity. *Cost of goods sold* represents the expense of the actual food and beverages used by a caterer to serve a client. Subtracting the operating revenue (generated from the sale of goods and their cost) from the net sales gives a *gross margin. Operating expenses* are those

THE CATERING COMPANY (NAME OF COMPANY)
BALANCE SHEET (TITLE OF REPORT)
DECEMBER 31, 2000 (DATE OR PERIOD OF REPORT)

ASSETS

Current Assets	
Cash	$ 13,000
Accounts Receivable	1,000
Inventory	2,000
Prepaid Expenses	1,000
Total Current Assets	17,000
Fixed Assets	
Land	10,000
Building	25,000
Less: Accumulated Depreciation*	– 5,000
Total Fixed Assets	30,000
TOTAL ASSETS	$47,000

LIABILITIES AND CAPITAL

Liabilities	
Current Liabilities	
Accounts Payable	3,000
Notes Payable	2,000
Accrued Liabilities	1,000
Total Current Liabilities	6,000
Long-Term Liabilities	10,000
Total Liabilities	16,000
Capital	
Billy Caterer	31,000
TOTAL LIABILITIES AND CAPITAL	$ 47,000

*Depreciation expense is the cost of the normal, physical wear and tear of a fixed asset over its limited and useful life. This cost is allocated to the various fiscal periods as depreciation expense.

Figure 11-6 *The balance sheet identifies the caterer's assets and liabilities at a given time.*

ACCOUNTING EQUATION

Assets	minus	Liabilities	equals	Owner's equity
$47,000	-	$ 16,000	=	$31,000

Figure 11-7 *Both sides of an accounting equation must be equal or "balanced."*

INFORMATION DERIVED FROM A BALANCE SHEET

On the asset side, a balance sheet will reveal the:
- amount of operating cash.
- amount of cash tied up in food inventory.
- investment in land and building.
- cash for any down payment on land and building.
- cost of furniture, fixtures, equipment, and utensils.
- cost of parking lots, driveways, lighting, and other improvements to the property.

The equities side of the balance sheet will show the:
- necessary short-term funds that must be borrowed.
- amount of payables.
- amount of long-term mortgages on building and land.
- type of business ownership—a proprietorship, partnership, or corporation.

Figure 11-8 *The balance sheet reveals valuable information regarding assets and equity.*

costs incurred by a caterer to operate the business. Controlled operating expenses are those directly influenced by the caterer. These include wages and salaries. Direct operating expenses are those expenses that are incurred by servicing the client. These may include laundry, napery, glassware, china, silverware, and licenses.

One very useful method for interpreting the income statement is to have each item listed by category, calculated as a percentage of sales. It is much easier to evaluate the financial status of the business by using percentages. A raw number by itself is meaningless. Figure 11–9 shows that the food cost for the Figure Skating Banquet is 19.95%. Is this a good percentage? Is it a bad percentage? How can it be interpreted?

THE CATERING COMPANY (NAME OF COMPANY)
INCOME STATEMENT (TITLE OF REPORT)
FIGURE SKATING BANQUET (EVENT)
APRIL 30, 2000 (DATE OR PERIOD OF REPORT)

Revenue (net sales)*	Dollars		Percentage
Food	$ 2,000	66.67	$2,000/3,000
Beverage	1,000	33.33	$1,000/3,000
Total Revenue	$ 3,000	100.0	
Cost of Goods Sold			
Food	$399	19.95	$ 399/2,000
Beverage	150	15.0	$ 150/1,000
Total Cost of Goods Sold	$ 1,140	38.0	$1,140/3,000
Gross Margin	$ 1,860	62.0	$1,860/3,000
Controllable Operating Expenses			
Payroll	$1050	35.0	$ 1050/3,000
Direct Operating Expenses	300	10.0	$ 300/3,000
Total Operating Expenses	$ 1350	45.0	$ 1350/3,000
Rent and Other Occupation Costs	$ 300	10.0	$ 300/3,000
Net Income	$ 210	7.0	$ 210/3,000

*Revenue or net sales in this example are generated by charging 200
guests $10.00 each for food and $5.00 each for beverages.

Figure 11-9 *Sample income statements are available for both public and competitive review analysis.*

The real value of a financial statement is the information derived from it by the caterer. Using percentages, a caterer can compare different events and time periods, as well as their own expenses against different caterers. Comparisons can also be made against industry standards. Financial organizations annually survey caterers to ascertain information regarding their operations and publish this information for public review. A caterer may compare their financial picture against these industry-average ratios.

A caterer must formulate a financial plan based on the mission statement that best suits their needs. The plan will guide the caterer in establishing the necessary financial objectives to meet financial and strategic goals.

The caterer must determine the cost of food and beverages used in the execution of each catering event. This is easily accomplished by keeping careful records of what items were actually consumed. It is necessary to take a physical inventory of every item stored in the business during the regular accounting period.

Summary

This chapter discussed controlling, the sixth catering management function. Catering managers establish control techniques to protect the financial interests of the organization. Comprehensive control techniques are implemented by an astute caterer who knows that the most effective way to earn a profit is to first understand how and why a catering business may lose money. If a caterer understands how money may be drained from the organization, effective controls can be used to tighten operations.

This sixth catering management function must be an integral component of the whole organizational plan. The objective of building control techniques is for the survival of the business and attainment of the organization's mission. This includes a detailed strategy of how the control techniques will be implemented into each event plan. Caterers create control techniques using financial tools and predetermined standards. Whether formulating or implementing the event plan, executing the operational tasks, or organizing resources, the ability to integrate fundamental catering management controls ensures the capability of comparing actual performance against planned objectives.

The elements of a plan of control will include the acquisition of timely and relevant information, securing an uninterrupted flow of cash, defining a formal payment policy, establishment of financial goals and predetermined profit objectives, and the knowledge that control functions are the easiest task for many caterers to neglect.

Review Questions

Brief Answers

1. Explain what *controlling* means to a caterer.
2. Describe why controlling the organization's resources is an important catering management task.

3. Explain why each catering function will require elements of managerial control.

4. Describe the process of control.

5. Explain why the caterer must develop and implement both internal and external control features into the catering management system.

6. Explain why the easiest task for most caterers to neglect, without an immediate penalty, is the control function.

7. Explain why elements of control begin when the caterer designs specific internal techniques to direct an employee's behavior in accomplishing predetermined objectives.

8. Explain why controlling has multiple meanings and serves multiple purposes.

9. Explain why a caterer needs timely and relevant information to make good business decisions.

10. Explain why a caterer must be concerned with protecting the uninterrupted flow of cash into the organization.

11. Define the formal payment policy and list several advantages.

12. Describe how a caterer arrives at a final price to charge the client for an event.

13. Explain the relationship between financial goals and predetermined profit objectives.

14. Explain why if an event has experienced a financial loss, the caterer must very carefully study and review the circumstances which contributed to this failure.

15. Explain how a caterer can protect himself against unexpected price changes in the market.

16. Explain why it is important for a caterer to always be on the alert for hidden costs.

17. Explain how the caterer might misjudge, misquote, or inaccurately speculate on an event.

18. Explain why the caterer must implement internal controls to protect the company's assets.

19. Describe three creative ways for the caterer to earn additional revenue other than from the traditional sale of food and beverage sales.

20. Describe how membership in an appropriate organization or association benefits a caterer.

21. Explain the following Ingredient for Success and what it means to you.

   Ingredient for Success 40: "A caterer's business success depends on enforceable controls. Creative acquisition, storage, preparation, and service of food and beverages will minimize labor requirements. Strong budgetary objectives derived from accounting systems will provide analysis of financial information."

Multiple Choice

Select the single best answer for each question.

1. The cost per catering event will vary depending on:
   a. menu
   b. type of service
   c. customer being served
   d. style of service
   e. all of the above

2. In today's market, _____ protects the caterer against clients defaulting on their obligation to pay their bills.
   a. budget control
   b. appropriate information
   c. structured payment policy
   d. membership in associations
   e. reputation

3. Which of the following best describes *controlling?*
   a. Controlling means to establish standard operating procedures to ensure an employee's proper execution of daily tasks while consuming an appropriate amount of time.
   b. Controlling means the establishment of predetermined objectives derived from the mission of the organization.
   c. Controlling is a process used to regulate and integrate each independent catering management function into an achievable event plan.
   d. Controlling refers to the efficient utilization of the caterer's assets to produce a need-satisfying product at a predetermined, profitable price.
   e. All of the above.

True or False

Read each of the following statements and determine if it is true or false.

1. Food and labor costs are usually bundled and are called prime costs.

2. The creation and implementation of control techniques by the use of financial tools and predetermined standards are the heart of this sixth catering management function.

3. Elements of control are completed when the caterer designs specific internal techniques to direct an employee's behavior in accomplishing predetermined objectives.

Putting It All Together

You are the owner of the Allegheny Catering Company, located on the beautiful Allegheny Mountain Range, near the Allegheny River, nestled in the Allegheny National Forest in northwestern Pennsylvania. Your market niche services a corporate clientele who seek year-round outdoor adventure activities such as hunting, horseback riding, and hiking in the forest. Other activities include fishing and boating on the streams near the Allegheny National Forest.

The Allegheny Catering Company has been contacted by Slugger Computer International Distribution (SCID) to cater an event for twenty-five company personnel. These guests will be attending an adventure-theme management training program that will last four days and include adventure-based theme training.

On the evening of the fifth day, a graduation ceremony will be held for the twenty-five participants. The location of the graduation ceremony and catering site is a plateau off a mountainous trail two miles inside the Allegheny National Forest. The only available natural resource at your disposal is potable spring water. Everything else must be brought to the site by either horseback or all-terrain vehicles.

Your task is to formulate a functional HACCP plan to serve each of the twenty-five people the following menu:

> a fresh garden salad with choice of three dressings
> one – 1/2 barbeque chicken
> one – 6-ounce New York Strip steak
> one – 60-count baked potato
> one – 4-inch ear of sweet corn on the cob
> a sundae ice cream bar offering a minimum of three toppings
> a selection of at least four beverages—two nonalcoholic

All food must be prepared at the site. Food will be served at 12:00 p.m. on a Saturday in October. The event is being held in the autumn to take advantage of the colorful leaves prevalent during this time of the year. Good luck!

Chapter Twelve | Understanding Insurance and Legal Issues

Key Terms | Objectives

After studying this chapter, you should be able to:

◆ Describe why insurance and legal concerns are important to the caterer.

◆ Explain intrinsic and extrinsic rewards.

◆ Explain why the caterer must develop and implement the right insurance and legal program.

◆ Explain how a caterer can avoid, transfer, or reduce risk.

◆ Explain the purpose of a crisis management team.

◆ Explain the purpose of a safety management team.

◆ Explain why a caterer needs to conduct frequent safety surveys.

◆ Explain the basic insurance coverage for property, liability, and workers' compensation.

◆ Explain personal and advertising coverage, fire damage liability, medical expense coverage, and automobile coverage.

◆ Explain why a caterer must create a contract that covers the basics.

INGREDIENT FOR SUCCESS

41 *"The creation and maintenance of the right insurance and legal package, based on the mission of the organization, will protect the caterer against any unpredictable crisis."*

There are definitely more challenges to managing a catering operation than the visible, concrete tasks of preparing food, serving the guests, and exceeding the visible and covert needs of the client. The ownership and management of a catering business will challenge and continuously test the caterer. Each subsequent success will create the feeling of great accomplishment and reward. Successful caterers experience a plethora of *intrinsic* and *extrinsic* rewards.

◆ REWARDS

Intrinsic rewards are those that the caterer experiences as a result of the successful implementation and execution of an event. A powerful feeling of achievement is created when the client, guests, and everyone involved *demand* to see the caterer and sing praise of how the Herculean tasks had just been accomplished. The positive reputation of a caterer is an intrinsic reward.

Extrinsic rewards are those that the caterer experiences outside of the event itself. The financial reward of executing a catering event is one example. When the event has been properly managed, a caterer can earn a comfortable salary and employ a staff which benefits the local community.

To protect the caterer's intrinsic and extrinsic rewards of a successful business, catering management decisions regarding insurance and legal issues must be made. *Ingredient for Success 41* states: *"The creation and maintenance of the right insurance and legal package, based on the mission of the organization, will protect the caterer against any unpredictable crisis."* Some basic information will be provided to assist the caterer in choosing the right *risk management* and *insurance program* for the organization and its mission.

◈ RISK MANAGEMENT

Any business is a risky venture and catering is no different. Some of the daily risks a caterer confronts are obvious, others are very subtle and may go unforeseen until it is too late. Some events can literally cripple and destroy a catering business. Suppose, for example, a caterer purchased and installed new deck convection ovens. Installed by the manufacturer, the lower-oven malfunctioned during the first week of its operation. Both ovens were destroyed and the entire building was seriously threatened. In this specific case, the manufacturer paid for all damages and replaced the ovens.

Here is another tragic scenario: A fire roars throughout the night destroying much of the caterer's building, equipment and inventory. These assets, having been the accumulation of one's life work, vanish in the night. Compound this scenario with the addition of a wedding scheduled for the next day. Consider the potential loss in terms of a caterer's assets, staff, reputation, as well as the client's decorations and belongings, placed in the building.

What can a caterer do, especially if the building, equipment, inventory, and other assets were destroyed? Imagine the enormity of the crisis as the potential profit and future earnings based on upcoming guaranteed events have suddenly disappeared. **Risk management** is the task of identifying these potential hazards and creating standard operating procedures to prevent their occurence.

Crisis Management Team

In this case, the caterer might cancel the wedding reception. An attempt to locate another facility could be made, but being personally overwhelmed with the magnitude of the situation, it might be impossible to expect a caterer to respond so quickly on their own. However, a well-organized catering business will anticipate a variety of potential crisis scenarios that might occur. In response to these potential problems, a caterer will create an internal *crisis management team*.

A **crisis management team** is a group of homogenous managers and employees who can be quickly summoned to deal with a fire, a possible outbreak of a food borne illness, a flood, or any other crippling crises. Although a catering crisis management team cannot *prevent* the crisis, the team can quickly *attack* the problem using a structured and pretested emergency plan.

The purpose of a crisis management team is to quickly respond to an unforeseen crisis. This team must be homogenous, meaning its members must be familiar with each other and able to work comfortably together. The team must be delegated immediate authority over all personnel in the organization during the crisis. They must have a blend of superior technical, human, and conceptual skills to deal effectively with the crisis and must have the immediate ability to make appropriate decisions to protect the interests of the clients and the organization.

A key factor of the crisis management team is the ability to respond immediately with action. Reconsidering the example of the caterer's fire and wedding event, a crisis management team might have previously devised a master plan with numerous, field-tested alternatives. The team might have already developed contingency plans with other caterers or nearby facilities to respond with help when a crisis occurs. The wedding reception could be immediately relocated to a nearby catering hall. They may have arranged contingency plans for renting, purchasing, or acquiring equipment. Flexible, detailed, and tested procedures must be established that prevent a *disorganized scramble* to replace lost or fire-damaged items. These procedures may be used to secure additional personnel, services, or anything else required to get the job done properly.

Even if the crisis management teams pulls off the event and the guests are happy, a bigger issue remains unsolved: What is the next step for the caterer? When the caterer begins the process of restoring the destroyed building, the local authorities may have passed new construction ordinances that will now pertain to the rebuilding of the catering facility and will likely increase the cost of construction.

Insurance

A catering crisis management team can help resolve the immediate needs of the situation. However, a well-designed **insurance program** will help protect the long-term interests of the caterer. When establishing the right insurance program for the organization, a caterer must:

1. identify and analyze the exposures or potential causes of loss.

2. know the options to address the exposures, and choose the best alternative for the organization.

3. monitor the insurance program and make incremental adjustments to the overall package.

A caterer will want an insurance policy that provides liability coverage and property coverage for the building and its contents. The package may include coverage for a caterer's loss of business income, extra expense, and ordinance.

Addressing Risk

Insurance coverage is not the only option for a caterer to address risk. A caterer may **avoid**, or **reduce**, or **transfer risk**. A caterer can implement a plan to avoid risk by eliminating all circumstances that cause it. One such method is the establishment of a catering *safety management team*.

The purpose of a catering **safety management team** is to continuously monitor the environment to identify and correct potential risks, ensuring the proper safety of the employees and the guests. The composition of a safety management team is up to the discretion of the caterer and is usually a combination of both management and hourly employees. Selection and the rotation of these members can be based on position, skill level, and length of service.

Figure 12-1
Safety procedures should be outlined to prevent unsafe operations, such as icing this cake while held in the air instead of supported on a flat surface.

A safety management team can be empowered to monitor safety procedures, help keep the work environment safe, make immediate recommendations, and implement a course of action to eliminate any identified hazards (Figure 12–1). The team should first create a plan to describe the format of an inspection. This plan must fit with the mission of the organization. The elements of the safety plan must be integrated into each individual event plan and dovetail with a caterer's HACCP plan. The team must structure a plan to include a detailed format of an inspection, the frequency of inspections, and who is responsible and accountable for its execution. Next, a checklist to inspect all areas in a catering operation is organized (Figure 12–2).

The philosophy of many successful caterers is to create an organization built with a commitment to safety. The challenge is for each employee to be an active participant in creating their own safe environment. An empowered safety management team that monitors the environment with the purpose of continuously improving safety is a key to success. Challenging each employee to use common sense and avoid taking shortcuts, especially on safety issues, is a simple but powerful policy (Figure 12–3). Employees can be rewarded for their active participation in safety.

Caterers can use the results of the safety survey to create a better work environment for the employees and guests (Figure 12–4). A caterer may integrate safety improvements in day-to-day operations. Weekly team meetings are often used to keep the management staff and employees aware of new developments.

ELEMENTS TO CONSIDER FOR A SAFETY CHECKLIST

❑ Operation of all equipment

❑ Flow of food through the operation, from loading dock to the customer, with emphasis on proper handling of all materials including lifting and carrying of supplies and equipment

❑ Storage areas, including dry, frozen, refrigerated, and nonfood supplies; cooler and freezer temperature storage alarms to alert the caterer to potential equipment malfunctions

❑ Work stations, including the use and care of knives

❑ Kitchen floors and aisles, with an emphasis on reducing slips and falls.

❑ Work procedures, including proper lifting techniques and prevention of slips and falls

❑ Outside areas, including keeping the perimeter of the building clean to prevent the infestation of insects and rodents

❑ All management personnel and employees trained in first-aid and CPR; access to first-aid kits for both on-premise and off-premise activities; local emergency telephone numbers, and standard procedures to respond to and report fires, including periodic fire drills

❑ Off-premise location(s)—buffet lines built on nonslip floors

❑ Defensive driving

❑ Housekeeping area

❑ Client services, including handicap accessibility and safety measures

❑ Maintenance of equipment and their records

❑ Implementation of security systems, such as video-surveillance systems; limited access to keys or electronic controls for valuable inventory storage areas; security procedures for the client and employee

❑ Warewashing area

❑ New employee orientation must include safety, fire emergencies, floods, storms, tornados, hurricanes, power failures, telephone failure, hazardous material spills, and automobile/truck accidents

Figure 12-2 *The catering safety management team should create a Safety Checklist for inspecting all areas of the operation.*

Figure 12-3 *This employee is not wearing protective mesh gloves — a safety procedure for preventing knife cutting injuries.*

BENEFITS OF A SAFETY SURVEY

A safety survey:

1. documents an active commitment to creating a positive safety record.

2. creates safety procedures that become standard operating procedures.

3. identifies training needs.

4. documents guest's comments and accidents related to safety issues.

5. provides for the continuous inspection and monitoring of the operation.

6. develops effective emergency procedures designed to protect the guest and the employee (Figure 12-5).

Figure 12-4 *Safety Surveys can be used as a development tool and to help create a better work environment.*

EMERGENCY PROCEDURES

1. In case of an emergency, keep calm.
2. Determine if emergency assistance is required. Do not attempt a rescue if it could result in an injury.
3. Determine if the area is safe for rescue personnel. Check for fire (heat), smoke, exposed electrical lines, and chemicals.
4. Dial 911. Stay on the phone with the 911 operator until told to do otherwise.
5. Know the location. Provide the name of facility, address, phone number, and your name. Speak slowly and wait for confirmation.

Figure 12-5 *Employee orientation should include review of the organization's emergency procedures.*

Reducing Risk

Risk can also be reduced. A caterer can have a sprinkler system or a central alarm system to reduce the risk of fire. A caterer can also transfer the risk of loss by renting a facility instead of owning the building. Some companies use a cross agreement with a competitor that basically states, "If you have an emergency, I will help you, and if I have an emergency, you will help me." Although this type of agreement is not commonly used, it can be effective. The point to remember is that insurance is only one option against risk. A complete, integrated plan can help avoid risk. A caterer can also reduce risk by the implementation of a safety program.

◆ INSURANCE SERVICES OFFICE (ISO)

Standard insurance policies are written on forms created by the **Insurance Services Office (ISO)**. Generally, insurance companies file their rates with the Insurance Commissioner's office in states where they desire to conduct business. They may also file a policy form that deviates from the standard ISO form to add coverage(s), making their product more appealing to their clients and prospective catering businesses. It is recommended that the caterer, to be an informed consumer of insurance, find out on what form the insurance company's proposals are written, and note any differences that may exist from the standard form.

◆ INFORMED CONSUMER

Becoming an **informed consumer** of insurance is very important to maintaining a healthy catering business. Caterers must be educated about the loss-control services offered by their insurers to take full advantage of the right mix for their organization.

Loss-control services offered by a caterer's insurer include basic coverages on property, liability, workers' compensation, and/or an umbrella coverage.

Property Insurance

A caterer has a few options regarding the coverage of **property insurance**. One choice is to have the building and contents covered on a replacement cost (RC) basis. An insurer will only pay the caterer the replacement cost when the property is actually replaced. Or, if the caterer does not intend to replace the property, an actual cash value (ACV) option can be used. A common formula used is:

$$ACV = RC \text{ less depreciation}$$

A caterer will also have options regarding the different levels of coverage with regard to causes of loss. These options are basic, broad, and special. The special cause of loss form is the broadest of the three and usually worth the extra cost. The special cause of loss covers all causes of loss except those specifically excluded. The insurer must prove a claim is specifically excluded under the policy language in order to deny payment to the caterer.

Liability Insurance

Premise/operations, or **liability insurance**, coverage, will protect the caterer against claims arising from the ownership, maintenance, or use of the premise and of the caterer's operations in progress. For example, say a potential client is meeting with the caterer on the premise to discuss future services. While touring the facility, the client slips and falls on a wet floor and becomes injured as a result of the accident. Liability insurance coverage provides protection against a claim made as a result of this type of injury.

Products and completed operations insurance covers the caterer for property damage and bodily injury to others as a result of a caterer's work when this damage or injury occurs off-premise. Say an employee, while serving hot gravy, spills it, severely burns a guest's leg, and damages her evening gown. Once it is confirmed that the caterer's employee was at fault, this policy would cover the medical bills, pain and suffering, and the replacement of the gown.

Personal and Advertising Injury Liability

Personal and advertising injury liability will protect the caterer against claims alleging false arrest, libel, slander, and false advertising if the caterer had no knowledge of the falsehood.

Fire Damage Liability

Fire damage liability provides coverage for the caterer's legal liability arising from fire damage to structures rented by the caterer.

Medical Expense Coverage

Medical expense coverage will reimburse all reasonable medical expenses incurred by anyone, except the caterer or the caterer's employees, as a result of an accident without regard for the caterer's liability. This gives the insurer some money to offer an injured party without concluding an investigation. This flexibility to respond quickly helps control the claim costs by settling claims early without delay.

Automobile Insurance

Laws regarding **automobile insurance** vary depending on the state in which the caterer is conducting business. It can be observed in the same light as property and liability coverages. Even if a caterer does not own a company vehicle, the caterer must have hired and nonowned liability coverage to be protected from liability imputed by the actions of an employee owning an automobile. A caterer can be named in a lawsuit resulting from an automobile accident involving an employee if the employee is found to be on a mission for the caterer, even if the caterer had not directed the employee's action as a result or purpose of the trip.

An employee stops on the way to work and purchases lettuce for the caterer. As the employee turns into the parking lot, he hits a pedestrian. Even though the caterer did not ask the employee to purchase lettuce, technically, and in the eyes of the law, the employee is on a mission for the caterer. This is reinforced if the caterer had ever, in the past, sent anyone anywhere for anything. Legally, this imputes liability to the caterer. This coverage also pays for the attorneys and their legal defense. Hired and nonowned liability coverage is very inexpensive, but very important.

Employment Practice Liability

This is a very hot topic in insurance, due to the high profile of some sexual harassment cases. **Employment practice liability** coverage has many options for deductibles and limits to help a caterer tailor a policy to fit the needs of the organization. It is recommended for a caterer to reference some of the excellent materials available to help prevent a claim of this nature. It is also important to obtain an estimate for this type of coverage to get as much information as possible before a decision to purchase or decline it is made.

◆ SELECTION OF INSURANCE

The most desirable program for a caterer is one that addresses all possible causes of loss with a combination of insurance, safety practices, and sensible transfers of risk at the least expense to the caterer.

Before a caterer can purchase the policy, he or she must design the best program to provide the maximum coverage for the business. To help make intelligent decisions regarding the purchase of an insurance policy, a caterer must answer the following questions. The answers will help build a strong foundation for an effective insurance program.

1. What is required by the law? Most states require a caterer to carry Workers' Compensation to cover the employees for medical expenses and wages if hurt in the course of employment.

2. What is required by a bank or lienholder for financed property or vehicles?

3. What must be covered to ensure survival in the event of a claim or loss?

An insurance grid will help a caterer to understand the process of designing the best program providing maximum coverage for the business (Figure 12–6).

A caterer must also be aware of **throw-ins**, which are added to policies by insurance companies to make their policies more competitive. Throw-ins are extra coverages at no extra cost to the caterer. Salespeople, called **producers**, will point out these throw-ins to a caterer to make their proposals more attractive than their competitor's policy.

Insurance Expense

A caterer trying to balance adequate coverage and the cost of insurance is considered to be making, at best, an educated guess. Therefore, here are some basic truths about insurance coverage. Higher deductibles, higher coinsurance clauses, low losses, if any, and competitive quotes will keep the cost of insurance down. The most important consideration is making sure a caterer has the right coverage to fit the needs of the business at a competitive rate. The caterer must learn about claims procedures by meeting with a representative and asking questions. The loss control services being provided should also be clearly understood. A good producer will be happy to promise the caterer that the policy about to be purchased will be kept, if needed.

The relationship between the caterer and the agent must be built on trust. When shopping for the best coverage, the caterer should look for an agent who would be trusted with a key to the business, because to some degree, this is what a caterer will be doing. The caterer should request credentials and expect honest and clear explanations. Agents should have a reputation of integrity, and the caterer should check references.

RISK	NON-INSURANCE	INSURANCE
INSURANCE CHART		
Building	Rent instead of own Install central alarm system Install sprinklers Use fire resistive material	Insure at replacement or actual cash value if no intention to rebuild Special cause of loss form
Contents	Separate flammables Safe storage Have alternate supplier	Insure at replacement cost Special cause of loss form
Loss of Income	Cross agreement	Business income coverage Include extra expense and consider ordinary payroll
Boiler and Machinery	Boiler inspections Back-up power supply Surge protection	Some packages include this to cover cooling equipment, electric equipment
Liability	Keep certificates of insurance on file for subcontractors and use hold-harmless agreements in contracts	Coverage to meet a caterer's organization's needs Protect company and personal assets
Automobile	Drug testing Check MVR and conduct safety meetings	Liability, physical damage, medical Hired and nonowned liability is a must, even if the organization does not own a vehicle
Workers' Compensation	Safety committee (some states require insurers to give a discount) Drug-free workplace	Required by law? A caterer may need employer's liability
Umbrella	Incorporate to protect personal assets	Sits over top of a caterer's liability Very broad coverage to protect against large awards

Figure 12–6 Caterers can use an Insurance Chart to design an insurance program that best meets their organization's needs.

◆ CONTRACTS

A caterer does not need to have an elaborate contract, but the contract does need to spell out some important details. Designing the right contract is but a matter of understanding the basics, using good judgement and following common sense. Figures 12–7, 12–8, and 12–9 illustrate various contractual arrangements.

To clarify the significance, it is important for a caterer to understand some basic business activities that involve a contract. A **contract** is a binding agreement between two or more parties. This may also be defined as an agreement creating an obligation.

The caterer is obligated to provide the food and service implied or detailed. The other party, referred to as the **engager** or client, is obligated to pay for food and specific services, if satisfactory. If either party fails to fulfill its side of the obligation, the other party may have the right to legal recourse. Every job a caterer agrees to execute, regardless of the party, requires a contract. One exception where no binding agreement is required, is when the caterer supplies catering services as a gift. This might include providing food and service for weddings, birthdays, and similar events for friends and family.

Execution of a contract enables a caterer to establish a firm business policy. Furthermore, putting agreements in writing ensures smooth and pleasant client relationships. A well-written contract will prohibit additional services demanded by the client to be provided by the caterer during the implementation stage of the function. It will also enable the client to better understand the services they are receiving.

TIPS FROM THE TRADE

It is an absolute must for a caterer to use a contract. Without contracts caterers would find themselves without a leg to stand on when attempting to collect payment for services and products rendered. We build almost everything into our contracts: when guarantees can be changed, cost of AV, minimum food and beverages per room night, cost of last minute changes, bar minimums, etc. Without a contract, the caterer would be subject to the honesty and memory of the client.

Jeremy Engle
Banquet Manager
Beaver Run Resort & Conference Center
Breckenridge, CO

Contracts are also valuable business assets for the caterer. They can be used as collateral to borrow money to meet short-term cash needs and are considered tangible assets in the sale of a catering business. Most contracts require customer signature and acceptance.

JARDINE'S CATERING
Monroe Road • Sarver, Pennsylvania
Phone number • Fax number • E-mail address

ORGANIZATION NAME: _____ (Client's Name)
ENGAGER: _____
ADDRESS: _____ STATE/ZIP_____
CITY: _____
PHONE: _____ FAX: _____
E-MAIL: _____
METHOD OF PAYMENT: _____ (cash, credit card)
WHO IS MAKING PAYMENT: _____ (e.g., wedding—bride/groom's family,
social event—Elizabeth 50% + Samantha 50%, celebration—Stephen 100%)
DAY: _____ DATE: _____ (function's day & date of execution)
FUNCTION: _____ (e.g., wedding, birthday, picnic, family reunion)
SPECIAL REQUEST: _____ (e.g., Tammie's birthday, Laurie & Tisha's graduation)
HOURS: _____ (exact starting and ending time)
LOCATION: _____ (exact location of function and directions)
APPROXIMATE NUMBER OF GUESTS: _____ (best estimate, based on historical data)
MINIMUM GUARANTEE: _____ (minimum guest count for this contract)
*FINAL GUARANTEE: _____ (guest provides in writing, attachment, guest will
guarantee to pay caterer for this number, regardless if fewer attend function)
*Final guarantee number will be charged unless adjusted prior to 1:00 P.M. on _____
(last day for guest to adjust final count without penalty)
MENU REQUIREMENTS: (All menu details as agreed upon with client)
Price Per Guest: $(_____) (If quote per person, amount specified in this contract)
All food and beverage subject to (____%) sales tax and (____%) service charge.
ENTREE AND SIDES: _____ (exact menu, portion size)
SERVICE STYLE: _____ (explicit description of service responsibilities)
BEVERAGE SERVICE: _____ (nonalcoholic/alcoholic beverages and service)
SET UP REQUIREMENTS: _____ (any special requests, floor plan and seating chart)
CHEFS: a flat $(_____) labor charge will be assessed for each chef required for buffet-line carving stations.
OTHER:
LINEN: Jardine's Catering will provide white linen from its inventory. Special requests for linen will incur an additional charge.
AUDIOVISUAL: Jardine's Catering recommended audiovisual company (_____) can handle any range of specialized audiovisual requirements.
FLORIST: Jardine's Catering recommended florist (_____) will arrange to meet your individual needs.
PHOTOGRAPHER: Jardine's Catering recommended photographer (_____) will arrange to meet your individual needs.
SPECIAL DECORATIONS AND SERVICES: Jardine's professional catering staff can enhance your event with ice sculptures, hand-carved centerpieces, individualized flower arrangements, and thematic decorations.
SECURITY: Jardine's Catering will not assume any responsibility for damages, loss, or stolen articles of clothing.
ITEMIZED INVOICE: Attachment, an itemized list of all function-related expenses incurred executing the function.
Engager: _____ Date: _____ Jardine's Catering: _____ Date: _____
Witness: _____ Date: _____ Witness: _____ Date: _____
Attorney's Signature: _____ Date: _____ (if reviewed)

Figure 12-7 *Jardine's Catering sample contract.*

TERMS AND CONDITIONS

All reservations and agreements are made upon, and are subject to, the rules and regulations of the Hotel and the following conditions:

In arranging for private functions, the attendance must be definitively specified and communicated to the Hotel by 12:00 noon, forty-eight (48) hours (2 working days) in advance. This number will be considered a guarantee, not subject to reduction, and charges will be made accordingly. The Hotel cannot be responsible for identical services to more than five percent (5%) over the guarantee for parties up to 500. For parties over 500, we will prepare for 25 additional guests. Guarantees for Saturday, Sunday, and Monday are due by 12:00 noon on the preceding Thursday. Guarantees for Tuesday are due by 12:00 noon on the preceding Friday. If a guarantee is not given to the Hotel by 12:00 noon on the date it is due, the lower number on the contract will automatically become the guarantee.

All federal, state, and municipal taxes which may be imposed or be applicable to this agreement and to the services rendered by the Hotel are in addition to the prices herein upon, and the patron agrees to pay them separately.

No food or beverages of any kind will be permitted to be brought into the Hotel by the patron or any of the patron's guests or invitees.

For private parties with groups of twenty (20) or less, the Hotel will charge a $60.00 labor charge.

Performance of this agreement is contingent upon the ability of the Hotel management to complete the same and is subject to labor troubles; disputes or strikes; accidents; government (federal, state, or municipal) requisitions; restrictions upon travel, transportation, food, beverages, or supplies; and other causes whether enumerated herein or not, beyond the control of management that may prevent or interfere with performance. In no event shall the Hyatt Orlando Hotel be liable for the loss of profit, or for other similar or dissimilar collateral or consequential damages, whether on breach of contract, warranty, or otherwise.

Payment shall be made in advance of the function unless credit has been established to the satisfaction of the Hotel, in which event a deposit shall be paid at the time of signing the agreement. The balance of the account is due and payable twenty-one (21) days after the date of the function. A deposit of twenty-five percent (25%) of the total balance of social functions is required at the time of booking; balance payable forty-eight (48) hours prior to the event.

Prices are subject to all applicable service charge and taxes; currently, 19% service charge and 7% sales tax.

The prices herein are subject to increase in the event costs of food, beverage, or other costs of operation increase at the time of the function. Patron grants the right to the Hotel to increase such prices or to make reasonable substitutions on the menu with prior written notice to the patron, providing, however, patron shall have the right to terminate the agreement within seven (7) days after such written notice from the Hotel.

The Hyatt Orlando does not accept any responsibility for the damage or loss of any merchandise or article left in the Hotel prior to, during, or following your function.

Patron agrees to be responsible and reimburse Hyatt Orlando for any damage done by patron or patron's guests of the Hotel.

The Hotel reserves the right to advance approval of all outside contractors hired for use by a convention group. The Hotel will, upon reasonable notice, cooperate with outside contractors. Hotel facilities are available to outside contractors to the extent that their function does not interfere with use of the facilities by other guests. Under such arrangements, the Hotel receives a ten percent (10%) commission from any outside contractors coming into the Hotel.

The Hotel has the following policy with respect to signs in the banquet and meeting areas:

The Hotel reserves the right to approve all signage. All signs must be professionally printed. No signs are allowed on the guestroom floors and main lobby areas of the Hotel or building exterior. Printed signs outside function rooms in the Convention Center only should be free standing or on an easel. The Hotel will assist in placing all signs and banners. Depending on labor and equipment involved, a charge for the services may apply.

Function rooms are assigned by the Hotel according to the guaranteed minimum number of people anticipated. Room rental fees are applicable if group attendance drops below the estimated attendance at the time of booking. The Hotel reserves the right to change groups to a more suitable room at the Hotel's discretion, and with notification, if attendance drops or increases.

The Hotel reserves the right to make the final decision regarding outdoor functions as follows:

a) The time to make the decision on whether the function will be outdoors or indoors;
b) b) Once the Hotel makes the decision, it is final.

_____   _____
Client Signature   Date

Figure 12-8 *Hyatt Orlando sample contract.*

BART'S CATERING COMPANY POLICY 2000

DEPOSITS

ONE-THIRD deposit of approximate cost of affair required to hold the date.

ONE-THIRD of fee required 30 days prior to the event. (Based on approximate cost of affair.)

BALANCE DUE: Day of event, prior to, or upon delivery of.

CORPORATE ACCOUNTS not received in 30 DAYS subject to 1.9% FINANCE CHARGE.

CORPORATE EVENTS have a minimum cost of $125.00 per event (unless prearranged).

CANCELLATIONS AND REFUNDS

All cancellations must be submitted in writing to Bart's Catering, 180 days prior to the event, to receive a full refund (less cost incurred).

All cancellations must be submitted in writing to Bart's Catering, 90 days prior to the event, to receive a 45% refund.

NO REFUNDS AFTER 90 DAYS

SERVING FEE*

18% includes Delivery and Equipment, 1-hour maximum setup, 1 hour maximum serving, and 1-hour maximum tear down.

* Setup of weddings or formal affairs an additional $100.00 fee.

Minimum serving fee $100.00 (Corporate minimum serving fee $50.00)

20% serving fee for extra services.

30% serving fee for china.

Minimum serving fee, china $250.00 (Corporate minimum serving fee, china $100.00)

SIT-DOWN FEE**

Additional Fee for:		
	50 guests or less	$200.00
	51 to 100 guests	$350.00
	101 to 150 guests	$500.00
	151 to 200 guests	$650.00

**Sit-down fee is over and above all other fees.

Delivery available for events not served (fee varies).

Delivery and set up with equipment rental available for events not served.

Disposable fee on all events not served.

ADDITIONAL SERVICES AVAILABLE UPON REQUEST

• Rental of china, crystal, and silverware – INSURANCE is required.

• Rental of chaffing dishes $20.00 each/plus deposit of $150.00 each.

• Rental of serving utensils $1.00 each/plus deposit of $50.00 total.

• Rental of hot boxes $20.00 each/plus deposit of $200.00 each.

• Rental of thermos coffee dispenser $15.00 each/plus deposit of $125.00 each.

Final guest count due 10 working days prior to the event.

24-hour notice for increased guest count.

(When guest count changes to next guest count level fee, price will automatically be adjusted.)

Sales tax on all orders (unless a tax-exempt number is presented).

Prices are subject to change. QUOTES VOID AFTER 30 DAYS

I have read and understand the above Company Policy.

_____   _____
Signature   Date

Figure 12-9a *Bart's Catering Company Policy 2000.*

BAR TENDERS & BAR SERVICE

PRESENTED BY

BART'S CATERING, INC.

(724) 727-2011

BARTENDER . . . .$100.00 FOR 6 HOURS MAXIMUM TIME
$12.50 EACH ADDITIONAL 1/2 HOUR
MAXIMUM NUMBER OF GUESTS 75
FOR 76-250 GUESTS (2) BARTENDERS
FOR 251-350 GUESTS (3) BARTENDERS

WALKING SERVERS . . . .$75.00 FOR 6 HOURS MAXIMUM TIME
$12.50 EACH ADDITIONAL 1/2 HOUR
MAXIMUM NUMBER OF GUESTS 75
FOR 76-250 GUESTS (2) SERVERS
FOR 251-350 GUESTS (3) SERVERS

BAR SERVICE . . . .$150.00 MAXIMUM GUESTS 200
$200.00 FOR OVER 200 GUESTS

INCLUDES . . . . PLASTIC CUPS
PLASTIC GLASSES
LEMONS, LIMES, & CHERRIES
PITCHERS
ICE
TABLE LINEN & SKIRTING
PAPER NAPKINS
MIXES **NOT** INCLUDED

OTHER SERVICES AVAILABLE:
- FANCY PLASTIC GLASSES ($50.00 PER 100 GUESTS)
- PLATIC CHAMPAGNE GLASSES ($1.00 PER GLASS)
- LINEN NAPKINS
- CRYSTAL
- MUGS
- WINE GLASSES

PLEASE SEE RENTAL GUIDE FOR ADDITIONAL DETAILS

BART'S CATERING AND FINE FOOD, INC. <u>WILL NOT</u> TAKE <u>LEGAL RESPONSIBILITY</u> FOR GUESTS OR PROVIDER OF AFFAIR!

I / WE DO NOT AND WILL NOT HOLD BART'S CATERING AND FINE FOOD, INC., IT'S OWNERS, OR EMPLOYEES LIABLE OR RESPONSIBLE FOR ANY PROBLEMS OR ACCIDENTS DUE TO ALCOHOL.

_____   _____
Signature   Date

Figure 12-9b *Bar tenders and bar service agreement*

TIPS FROM THE TRADE

Contracts are by far as important as the quality of food and service we are providing. If a contract is too strong you could lose business, it it is too soft you could end up with an event that is not profitable and could quite possibly take advantage of your business and its resources. **Please understand that this business is based on time. There is no way to ever return or exchange it; once it is consumed you will never get it back.** It is very important to include the following items in every contract: date and time of event, number of people, type of event, cancellation policy, and all pertinent hotel policies and procedures. I always include a minimum dollar amount, which must be met during the event. This minimum is determined by the type of event and its total estimated revenue. The hotel will be financially covered if the client's guarantees were to drop, or their budget were to decrease. Example: Let's plan a Christmas party for 500 people at an estimated charge of $40.00 per person. This party is on a Saturday in December. (Note: There are only three good Saturday nights in December for Holiday parties, so this is prime space.) I have a $1,000 deposit and the client is paying by credit card. What if ten days before the event, the group's guarantee drops to 300 people? If there is no minimum dollar amount in your contract you will be losing $8,000. That's $8,000 you will never be able to get back.

Dianne Herzog
Catering Manager
Hyatt Orlando
Kissimmee, FL

Basic Contract Stipulations

A contact must cover a standard set of basic contract stipulations or details (Figure 12–10). Before entering into a contract with the client, an attorney should be consulted to review its specific contents.

BASIC CONTRACT STIPULATIONS

1. **The exact number of people who will be served must be stipulated.**
   A stipulation requiring the final guarantee as to the number of guests attending this event to be given by 12:00 noon no later than (____) business days in advance of the function. Once given, this guarantee is not subject to any reduction. The caterer will permit a 15% increase if advised by 12:00 noon (____) days prior to the date of the function. The caterer will provide seating for an additional 5% beyond the guaranteed number at no extra charge. If, however, unexpected attendance exceeds 5%, then a $(____) per person surcharge will be applied.

   (continued)

Figure 12-10 *Every contract should include a standard set of contract stipulations and details.*

If no guarantee is received at the appropriate time, the caterer will attempt to contact the engager. If, after two documented attempts go unsuccessful, the caterer will assume that the original engager's expected count will be the guarantee, and all charges will be applied to this number.

2. **The exact menu to be served.**

In order for the caterer to assure the availability of the menu items selected, final confirmation of the menu selections must be submitted (____) weeks prior to the date of execution. However, unforeseen market conditions may require the caterer to make professional substitutions on menu items. Speciality and theme menus will be designed to meet individual needs and tastes.

3. **The type of service to be provided at the event by the caterer and staff.**

4. **The exact amount of time for each activity.**

Time limits are especially important. If the caterer runs into overtime, this must be carefully spelled out in advance on the contract. The caterer and client will agree to an exact beginning and ending time. Many caterers will include a clause granting the client permission to continue the celebration past the contracted ending time. If permission is granted, an overtime charge would be applied against the client.

5. **The exact price.**

The caterer may stipulate that all printed catering menu prices are subject to change without notice. In addition, all contracted prices would be honored. However, for contracted events at least six months in advance, the following stipulation would be included: This is an approximate price; the client grants the caterer the right to adjust the price based on unforeseen market conditions. The caterer will provide the final price (____) days before the function date.

6. **Payment Policy.**

A minimum deposit of 33 1/3% of the total bill is required when the contract is signed. Another 33 1/3 % of the total bill is required no later than (____) day(s) prior to the date of the event and the remainder of the final bill is due (____) day(s) prior to the event.

7. **Deposit and Refund Policy.**

All deposits are nonrefundable. Each event is different and if a function is canceled, it remains the judgement of the caterer to make this decision.

8. **Cancellation and Refund Policy.**

The caterer reserves the right to cancel this agreement without penalty and notice in the event of breach of contract by the client.

9. **Method for Counting Guests.**

An accounting method for tracking the number of guests must be determined. When the caterer is being compensated per guest, this is extremely important, especially if catering large events, such as a 1500-guest picnic. Techniques used may involve tickets, plates issued, bundled or rolled silverware with a napkin issued, an employee and guest assigned to each "count," and monitor attendance.

Figure 12–10 *Every contract should include a standard set of contract stipulations and details (continued).*

BANQUET EVENT ORDER

The **banquet event order (BEO)** is a multi-purpose catering management tool used internally to communicate the specific details for execution of a catering event to the appropriate personnel (Figure 12–11). It simultaneously functions

INDIANA HOLIDAY INN
1395 Wayne Avenue
Indiana, PA 15701
Telephone: (724) 463-3561 Toll-Free: (800) 477-3561
Fax: (724) 463-8006 E-Mail: IndianaSale1@CrownAm.com

BEO #:
Page 1 of 1
Date Created:

Banquet Event Order

Group Information	
Account:	**Event Date:** **Contact:**
Post As:	**Phone:** **Fax:**
Address:	**On-site Contact:** **Phone:** **Fax:**
Deposit:	**Booked By:** **Catering Manager:**

DATE	TIME	FUNCTION	SETUP	ROOM	EXP #	GTD	RENT

Menu Requirements	Beverage & Break Requirements
Meal Time:	Time:

Billing Requirements	Set Up Requirements

Miscellaneous Arrangements	Audio Visual Requirements

Figure 12–11a *Sample Banquet Event Order form (front).*

as an indirect control document because the BEO establishes accountability and assigns managerial responsibility by launching a concrete paper trail that is easily audited and confirmed. The BEO is often used by a hotel catering department to coordinate each catering event through communicating to the appropriate personnel or departments what participation is needed.

Additional Information

Guaranteed count of attendance is due by 11:00am three (3) business days in advance of the function or ____ ; *(list exact date)* if no count is received, the original count is considered the guarantee for billing purposes. Should your event cancel, deposit and payments are non-refundable.

All food and applicable beverage charges are subject to 16% Service Fee and 6% State Tax. All audio visual equipment is subject to 6% tax. Meeting room rental is subject to 6% tax.

Meeting room rental and set-up fees are subject to an additional charge should there be more than a 15% reduction in the contracted number of attendees.

Meeting/Banquet rooms are assigned by the number of people anticipated. We reserved the right to change groups to a room suitable for the attendance. We will make every effort to contact you in advance should this occur.

All food and beverage to be consumed in any public area must be purchased from the hotel and must be consumed on premise. The scheduled event time cannot be changed without prior approval by the hotel management.

In the event that the attendance exceeds the guaranteed minimum, the Hotel will make every reasonable effort to accommodate the extra number of guests with the same or comparable arrangements.

Any special dietary requests must be made 24 hours prior to the function.

All banquet checks must be signed by the person in charge or a designated representative at the completion of each function. Any discrepancies in counts or charges should be identified and resolved at that time.

Organization must obtain prior approval from Hotel for all activities which are planned for the event. The premises shall be used only for those approved activities. Organization agrees to assist Hotel in prohibiting any violation of this provision if Hotel deems it necessary.

The person executing this Agreement as Organization's representative expressly represents that he or she is over eighteen (18) years of age. Where the Organization is a corporation, an un-incorporated association, partnership or other legal entity, this Agreement shall be binding on such legal entity, its successors and assigns. The person executing this Agreement as the Organization's representative expressly represents that he or she is authorized to execute said Agreement on Behalf of the Organization.

_____
Organization Authorized Signature

Hotel Representative Signature
on behalf of the **Indiana Holiday Inn**

_____
Date

Date

Owned and Operated by Crown American Hotels

Figure 12-11b *Sample Banquet Event Order form (back).*

Summary

Catering management decisions regarding insurance and legal issues will help protect a successful catering business. *Ingredient for Success 41* reminds us *"The creation and maintenance of the right insurance and legal package, based on the mission of the organization, will protect the caterer against any unpredictable crisis."* A well-designed insurance program will help protect the long-term interests of the caterer. In addition to the appropriate insurance and legal package, a well organized catering business will anticipate a variety of potential crises that might occur. To be prepared for these unforeseen events, the creation of a crisis management team, comprised of a group of homogenous managers and employees, can quickly respond to any crippling crisis and attack the problem using a structured and pretested emergency plan. The caterer may also avoid, reduce, or transfer risk. The establishment of an internal safety team to continuously monitor the environment to identify and correct potential risks will ensure the proper safety of the employees and guests. Successful caterers create an organization built with a commitment towards safety, and empower each employee to become an active participant in creating their own safe environment.

Equally important as having the right insurance package, a caterer must always use a contract to spell out all of the important details for each and every event. Every contract must cover a standard set of basic contract stipulations or details. Remember, the contract will be very similar in descriptive detail to the caterer's written proposal that is accepted by the client based on exceeding their needs, wants, and demands. Before entering into a contract with the client, an attorney should be consulted to review its specific contents.

Review Questions

Brief Answers

1. Describe why insurance and legal concerns are important to the caterer.
2. Explain intrinsic and extrinsic rewards.
3. Describe why the caterer must develop and implement the right insurance and legal program.
4. Explain how a caterer can avoid, transfer, or reduce risk.
5. Explain the purpose of a crisis management team—why is this important to the caterer?
6. Explain the purpose of a safety management team.
7. Explain why a caterer needs to conduct frequent safety surveys.

8. Explain the basic insurance coverage for property, liability, and Workers' Compensation.

9. Explain personal and advertising coverage, fire damage liability, medical expense coverage, and automobile coverage.

10. Explain why a caterer must create a contract that covers the basics.

Multiple Choice

Select the single best answer for each question.

1. Rewards the caterer experiences as a result of executing the event are _____ .
   a. intrinsic rewards
   b. catering rewards
   c. customer rewards
   d. extrinsic rewards
   e. All of the above

2. A(n) _____ is a group of homogenous employees and a manager who are quickly summoned to deal with an emergency.
   a. safety team
   b. crisis management team
   c. risk management team
   d. sanitation team
   e. insurance team

3. When establishing the right insurance program, the caterer must:
   a. identify and analyze the exposures or potential causes of loss.
   b. know the options to address the exposures.
   c. choose the best alternative for the organization.
   d. monitor the insurance program and make adjustments to the overall package.
   e. All of the above.

True or False

Read each of the following statements and determine if it is true or false.

1. Caterers can use the results of the safety survey to create a better work environment.

2. Insurance policies are written on forms created by the Insurance Services Office (ISO).

3. A contract is a binding agreement between two or more parties.

Putting It All Together

Steven's Catering is a combination restaurant and bakery. The restaurant is managed by Paul while his sisters, Anne and Melissa, coordinate the catering operations and Richard manages the bakery. Each manager supervises 10 employees.

Upon closing, Carlos, a restaurant employee, forgets to clean and turn off the deep fat fryer. The fryer oil overheats and the grease catches fire. The entire production area begins to fill with smoke as the fire spreads. A bakery employee, Letitia, smells the smoke and is alerted to the fire raging in the kitchen. Letitia calls Emergency Control who alerts the local fire department.

Letitia, grabbing a fire-extinguisher, runs to the production kitchen to try stopping the flames from spreading. As she enters the production area, the fire prevention system discharges from the ceiling, causing her to slip on the wet floor, spraining her ankle.

The fire department arrives and extinguishes the fire, but extensive damage is done to the production area. Letitia is taken to the hospital to have her ankle x-rayed.

Who is liable? What insurance coverage is needed for the employee's injury, the fire, the equipment, and the supply loss? What safety procedures should have been in place to prevent this string of events from happening?

PART THREE

Total Quality Management Operations

335

Chapter Thirteen

Total Quality Management

Key Terms

system approach
subsystems
total quality management (TQM)
defects

Objectives

After studying this chapter, you should be able to:

◆ Discuss the importance of total quality management (TQM) for contemporary caterers.

◆ Identify how to adapt total quality management techniques into the catering operation.

◆ Explain the basic concepts of total quality management.

◆ Identify the early contributors to the total quality management movement.

◆ THE MANAGEMENT SYSTEM

Caterers use many different approaches to managing their business. The **system approach** to managing a catering operation helps the catering manager deal with the complexities of the organization and any unexpected contingencies that might arise from operations. Changing technological, economic, political, and sociological demands exert unforeseen pressure on the caterer. The system approach to management is one technique that enables a caterer to monitor and control these key activities and their interrelationships with the catering industry.

Common to all systems is the belief that they are composed of separate but interdependent parts working together to accomplish a common goal. A caterer's system is composed of the following interconnected **subsystems** or key activities: menu, purchasing, receiving, storage, issuing, preparation, production, hot and cold holding, service, exceeding customer expectations, and cleaning and sanitation.

Fundamentals of Quality

Total quality management (TQM) can be defined as the continuous process of incremental improvement in the key activities required by a caterer to produce quality goods and services through employee action (Figure 13–1). Quality is important because it defines the reputation of a caterer. A quality journey leads

Figure 13-1 *Employee actions and responses help a caterer produce quality goods and services.*

down the path to lower operational costs while increasing the value of the services to the customer. The pursuit of incremental improvement in these key activities will identify defects. **Defects** are breakdowns that occur in any of the key activities that cause the system to malfunction. Defects cause waste, increased costs, poor quality food and service, and unsatisfied customers. Innovation and creativity help generate creative solutions to fix the defects.

Quality Awards

In recognition of exceptional quality excellence, two awards have been established to recognize and honor the achievements made in the pursuit of quality.

◆ *The Deming Award.* This prestigious, international award was created by the Japanese to honor W. Edward Deming, an early pioneer of total quality management concepts.

◆ *The Malcolm Baldridge National Quality Award.* This award promotes an awareness of quality, achievements in the pursuit of quality, and a sharing of quality strategies so others can benefit. This award is presented to the organization that best exemplifies quality in manufacturing, the service sector, and the small business sector.

Theories on Achieving Quality

Each theorist tries to explain the best method and techniques for infusing quality into an organization, but many theories differ. The path to achievement of total quality management is dependent on the originator's philosophy. Each caterer must glean the philosophy from each theory and implement it into the organization to achieve quality improvement.

◆ *Philip Crosby* says an organization must be *injected* with 14 principles to achieve total quality. These 14 points relate to a system approach to management, communications, operations, integrity, and policies.

◆ *W. Edward Deming* says quality can only be achieved by continuous improvements in the process of production because the outcome is a better quality product.

◆ *Joseph Juran's* philosophy states that management may attain improvements in quality by studying symptoms of a commitment from the entire organization and a commitment from the mission of each individual department.

◆ *Shigeo Shigno's* philosophy states that quality can be accomplished by mistake-proof production systems. A catering system must be designed and continually adjusted to produce only quality products. For example, after the bread is baked is not the time to worry about quality.

◆ *Armand Feigenbaum* taught that any and all defects are detrimental to an organization. Therefore, every operation will become better over the long term if focus is on total quality management.

◆ THE RELATIONSHIP BETWEEN TQM AND SUCCESS

What is the mission of the organization? Where does a caterer begin? All the quality experts agree that active employee participation is a key to sustained success.

1. People can and will only manage themselves. Employees have to make decisions.

2. Employees will most likely know how to execute their tasks more effectively than the caterer. They will often be able to make better decisions. Therefore, the better an individual understands the mission of the organization, and how he or she can contribute to make it a success, the better off the organization will be.

3. To help an employee make a better decision, a caterer must share the organization's financial information with all employees. They should receive appropriate, timely, and pertinent information.

4. People have a need to feel pride in their work. Pride is derived from being associated with a winning team making a quality product. Key members of the management team teach the employee something new each day, build their confidence every day, and build pride and loyalty.

A caterer can implement quality management as related to continuous improvement by improving external customer satisfaction, developing supplier partnerships, ensuring communication between the front- and back-of-the-house, reducing waste, preventing variation in food preparation, improving production and service methods, providing for greater flexibility, and fostering creativity and innovation. One simple tool is the catering manager's daily Total Quality Management Report (Figure 13–2). This document may be formatted to meet the needs of any caterer.

CATERING MANAGER'S
TOTAL QUALITY MANAGEMENT REPORT

Manager _____ Day _____ Date _____

Operations:

1. Premanagement team meeting:
   - Outlines of objective(s)
   - Teaching tips for the day
2. Menus completely finished?
3. Recipes completed and distributed?
4. Food production sheets completely finished?
5. Raw materials on stock?
6. Schedules completed and posted?

Day of Function

1. Is it organized?
2. Has the team met with the caterer?
3. Does the team know what is expected of them?
4. Is the kitchen equipment turned on?
   - Fryers _____ Steamer _____ Food Warmer(s) _____
   - Ovens (convection set 25–50° lower than for a conventional oven?) _____
5. Baking area—breads, rolls, cakes, pies, and cookies started and on-time?
6. Employee review
7. Dispatch dish machine operator for any special activities
8. Food production on schedule?
9. Service staff understands menu items?
10. The end of day—follow up on all details

Catering Manager's Daily Walk

1. Record the following temperatures:
   Refrigerators: Walk-in _____ Pass-through _____ Loading dock _____ Production line _____
   Freezer: Walk-in _____ Production line _____
   Temperature of selected potentially hazardous food items:

Food	Temperature
_____	_____
_____	_____
_____	_____

Figure 13-2 *Total Quality Management Reports help catering managers evaluate their business's continuing improvements.*

Sanitation and Safety Report

1. Are critical control points being followed? Brief description.
   - Are potentially hazardous foods out of the danger temperature zone of 41°F to 140°F?
2. Dish tank area:
   - Wash cycle temperature?
   - Final rinse cycle temperature?
   - Soap in dish tank dispensing unit?
3. Three compartment sink
   - Wash in first sink and use clean water with detergent
   - Wash water is 110°F
   - Rinse in clean hot water at 120°F
   - Sanitize one minute in 220 ppm quaternary ammonium
   - Air dry and place in storage
4. Kitchen Report
5. Service Report
6. Identify Areas for Improvement
7. Customer Comments:
   - Service _____
   - Food _____
   - Recommendations _____
   - Equipment _____
   - Facility _____
   - Bathrooms _____
8. Safety and cleanliness of outside area?
9. Safety and cleanliness of inside area?

Figure 13-2 *Total Quality Management Reports help catering managers evaluate their business's continuing improvements (continued).*

Summary

Caterers use many different approaches to managing their business. The system approach to managing a catering operation helps the catering manager deal with the complexities of the organization and any unexpected contingencies that might arise from operations.

Tied directly to this approach of managing is the search for the continuous process of incremental improvement in the key activities required by a caterer to produce quality goods and services through employee action. This pursuit of continuous improvement in these key activities will identify defects which may cause waste, increased costs, poor quality food and service, and unsatisfied customers.

There are various theories on how a caterer can achieve quality in the organization. Each theorist tries to explain the best method and techniques for infusing quality into an organization. Each caterer must mine from these stories the ore to implement into the organization to achieve quality improvements.

Review Questions

Brief Answers

1. Discuss why the pursuit of total quality using management techniques is important to contemporary caterers.

2. Identify how a caterer may adapt total quality management techniques into the catering operation.

3. Explain the basic concepts of total quality management.

4. Identify the early contributors to the total quality management movement.

Multiple Choice

Select the single best answer for each question.

1. The management system most associated with total quality management is the:
   a. behavior system approach
   b. system approach
   c. contingency approach
   d. classical approach

2. A fundamental concept in TQM is for the caterer to identify _____ before improvement can be made in the operation.
   a. tasks
   b. clients
   c. employee skill level
   d. defects

3. The quality award established by the United States government in 1988 to recognize the achievements by an organization in total quality management is known as the _____ .
   a. Edward Deming National Quality Award
   b. Joseph Juran National Quality Award
   c. Phillip Crosby National Quality Award
   d. Malcolm Baldridge National Quality Award

True or False

Read each of the following statements and determine if it is true or false.

1. The Deming Award is the most prestigious international award given for recognition in achievements regarding total quality management.

2. The pursuit of total quality is not realistic, a management fad, and may never be achieved by a catering organization.

3. Total quality management is the continuous process of incremental improvement in the key activities required by a caterer to produce food and service.

Putting It All Together

Research the early pioneers of total quality management. Read about their different philosophies regarding how an organization can achieve total quality. How can a caterer apply the concept of total quality management to their own operation? What defects may occur in the production of food and service?

Chapter Fourteen

Emerging Benchmarks and Conclusion

Key Terms

benchmarking
best practices
value chain
backward integration

Objectives

After studying this chapter, you should be able to:

◆ Discuss the emerging business benchmarks being set by contemporary caterers.

◆ Identify how caterers are reinventing the catering profession.

◆ Explain how caterers are building technology into their organization's infrastructure.

◆ Explain how caterers are adapting communication technology into their profession.

◆ Explain how caterers focus on the global marketplace while remaining allegiant to their local community.

◆ REINVENTING THE PROFESSION

The catering profession still remains as one industry offering a motivated, dedicated, and goal-driven individual the opportunity to secure strong income, steady growth, and a challenging career. Many labor-intensive caterers across the country are benefitting from the big profits found in catering corporate luncheons, big events, and small gourmet parties. All over the world, both large and small caterers are following their forefathers' tradition of meticulously planning each minute detail to deliver exceptional, classical, European-style service. The presentation of professionally prepared cuisine in a splendid facility submerged in enchanting decor and applauded by a satisfied guest has remained unchanged since ancient times.

Traveling on the path worn by tradition, contemporary caterers are reinventing the profession, creating more value to the client and increasing the value of the organization with higher profit margins through exceptional operations. The emerging trend of today's catering business is establishing new benchmarks that are influencing and raising the standards in the management and art of catering.

The strategic management technique of **benchmarking** is the process of identifying innovative *best practices* by other caterers in the daily execution of their tasks. Then caterers can measure their own performance in a given area against the industry standard. **Best practices** introduce proven, successful techniques into the businesses of those astute enough to use them. Identification and adaptation of emerging best practices by outside competitors will excite the organization. If a caterer has identified new culinary techniques, the use of exotic foods, improved delivery of service, new applications of technology, employee training, and the solicitation of creative ideas as high standards being used by the competition, then that data can be used to improve their own processes.

A caterer uses benchmarking to compare their organization's internal key activities against a competitor's in the same market niche. An accurate assessment of a competitor's strengths, capabilities and weaknesses can be ascertained. This information is important to the caterer because it can provide clues to the strategic direction of this organization and will also identify activities that need improvement.

An important procedure used to establish benchmarks is analyzing a competitor's activities as food flows through the operation. The flow of food can also be called the *value chain* activities. A caterer's **value chain** is a detailed flow chart revealing the internal flow of activities and their costs involved in delivering the food and services to a guest. An accurate evaluation of the value chain must include the selling price and the profit margin of a catering event.

The value chain begins with the purchasing function and ends with a customer's perception of the goods and services they receive. Value chain analysis focuses on activities that include: formulation of the menu, purchasing, receiving, storage, issuing, preparation, production, hot and cold holding, service, and cleanup.

BEST PRACTICES FOR A CATERER

1. The negotiating ability to secure low margin pricing from a supplier
2. Better prices through volume purchasing
3. The ability to produce high quality food at lower production costs
4. Owning the distribution system in the delivery of goods
5. Quality training programs to develop management and staff skills regarding technical, human relations, and conceptual skills in all areas of the business, including technology, service, culinary arts, and production (this increases customer satisfaction and reduces employee turnover and related costs.)
6. Simpler management structure
7. Adaptation of technologically-advanced tools to increase employee productivity, streamline operations and reduce costs
8. Delivery of food and the execution of service

Figure 14-1 *Establishing a proven set of best practices helps caterers measure their own performance against the competition.*

The purpose of this analysis is for a caterer to compare their own internal cost-value relationships against the cost-value relationships of the competition. This analysis enables a caterer to strategically evaluate their business costs against a competitor's in the same marketplace and make necessary adjustments.

Benchmarking identifies the *best practices* in the execution of a *value chain* activity. A caterer may evaluate the best practices in relationship to the catering industry as a whole (Figure 14–1).

◆ TECHNOLOGICAL INFRASTRUCTURE

Primarily, today's trends utilize technology to coordinate the logistics of a catering business as never before seen in the history of the profession. At their fingertips, technology is the crystal ball that empowers them to expand control. They can monitor and control simultaneous functions located at diverse geographical locations, can grasp enhanced production equipment, acquire fresher foods, and touch the global marketplace whenever they want. At times, they can be engaged in each of these activities simultaneously.

Computer Applications

The immediate application of emerging advances in technology, by the innovative caterer, has always been a strength found within the profession. From ancient history to the new millennium, from the Egyptians to Fred Harvey and his *catering descendants*, caterers have always understood the need to adapt new technologies. They have sought out and applied these new technologies to create specialized tools whose purpose is to ease the logistics of executing a catering event.

Technology has delivered the personal computer, and the caterer has adapted this tool to provide great flexibility in the application of management techniques. Specific software allows the caterer to manage the overall operation of the catering business more efficiently. A computer can generate specific managerial reports that track inventories, conduct menu analysis, schedule events, monitor employee productivity, and control food costs by analyzing projected food usage against actual consumption. Today, food purveyors are finalizing development of proprietary software that will allow them to directly connect to the caterer. This umbilical cord permits a caterer instant access to a purveyor's warehouse to ascertain immediate product availability. One benefit is the instantaneous ability to verify costs of specific items that meet their specifications.

This type of software offers a number of different modules to assist the caterer in making better business decisions. Modules include menu construction and pricing that establish a selling price based on predetermined financial objectives. Using this technology, a caterer can place the purchase order online and receive the provisions without the interaction of a distributor sales representative.

CD-ROMs showing how to do just about anything will continue to be developed. These learning tools will become better integrated into a caterer's infrastructure and adapted on-site to guide employees in the preparation and service of food.

The computer can also be used to monitor the infrastructure of a caterer's facility. Systems are available that will automatically control utilities, such as the facility's internal temperature, by adjusting the heat or air conditioning, as well as its lighting system.

The personal computer has given caterers access to the World Wide Web. The Internet permits electronic access to information to support the efficient and effective execution of the tasks required in a catering function. Information is posted at Web sites and related links are often available to assist when researching themes, developing recipes, searching for equipment, and making business decisions.

Internet connection permits a caterer to keep an eye on the competition by monitoring their online Web page. An astute caterer can glean business information from a competitor's Web page that can help determine current and future strategic moves.

Using the Internet, a caterer can research clients, locate an off-premise location, or track food prices while following the volatile commodity markets. Caterers also create their own Web page to tell the world who they are and where they are located. The Web site is used to advertise, promote public relations, or to offer special announcements, coupons, and discounts.

The Internet has become a very important communication tool and it has emerged as an essential component of a caterer's marketing strategy.

◈ COMMUNICATION

A very basic but important managerial technique is the ability for a caterer to successfully communicate with all personnel. The purpose of communication is to share information with the catering team. The success of a catering event may often teeter on a fine line of demarcation; therefore, constant contact between a caterer and a team member is paramount, especially during the execution of the event itself. Reasons requiring a caterer to share information with the front- or back-of-the-house staff are almost infinite (Figure 14–2). Fulfilling a guest's special request, the prompt restocking of food or supplies on the buffet line, locating a guest's automobile in valet parking, or calling for an ambulance during an emergency situation are examples of why a caterer needs to have immediate communication capabilities.

Technology has given the caterer a variety of communication devices. Cell phones, walkie-talkies, and pagers provide efficient and effective management, and leadership, of the catering staff. Instantaneous communication is made possible by cell phone technology. Successful caterers have implemented cell phone technology to assist in their ability to deliver exceptional customer service. Whereas cell phones are used for on- and off-site locations, walkie-talkies are used primarily at on-site locations to direct the needs of both the front- and back-of-the-house staff. Communication between various members of the catering team ensures the smooth execution of the function.

The World Wide Web also permits the use of E-mail by the caterer to communicate with the staff, clients, purveyors, and other stakeholders.

Figure 14-2 *Smooth communication between front- and back-of-the-house staff enables this surprise champagne toast to come off without a hitch.*

◆ GLOBAL MARKETPLACE

The emerging ease of accessibility to worldwide locations in a matter of seconds has unlimited consequences for a caterer today. At the caterer's fingertips is the ability to access information quickly. E-commerce invites competitive purchasing of goods from either local business associates or directly from global-site sellers. Searching for products to meet the ever evolving needs of the sophisticated consumer is becoming much easier. The ability to negotiate without one-on-one, intimidating personal interaction, using Web-based services, is changing the rules of commerce.

The Internet provides the opportunity to directly link to the grower and bypass the traditional distribution network using large, established, local warehouses. The acquisition of fresher seafood, produce, and meats from aqua and other specialized farms will continue and genetically altered foods will become common. Faster response to new ingredients from indigenous peoples and areas around the globe will change taste preferences and lead to greater flexibility in menu design.

◆ COMMUNITY ALLEGIANCE

Access to global markets and the ability to purchase from sellers in distant places have not lessened a caterer's allegiance to their local communities. Today, more than ever, caterers have accepted the responsibility to share in the maintenance of the local community. Taking an active role, caterers donate to local charities, support fund-raising activities, and partner with local farmers.

Forming strategic partnerships with local farmers enables a backward integration into the distribution channel. **Backward integration** means gaining some control over the raw materials used in the production of the goods and services. When purchasing from farmers' markets, a caterer gains a primary local-supplier of produce, dairy, and meat. This may eliminate the worry as the price or availability of a product changes.

Forming strategic partnerships with local businesses creates a *differentiation-based* marketing and production strategy. Using a public relations and advertising campaign to promote the use of community business will greatly enhance the caterer's reputation. It is a win-win proposition for each team member. A caterer understands the success of their business is highly correlated to the success of the community.

◆ PROFESSIONAL DEVELOPMENT

The continued evolution of the catering profession demands trained professional caterers. Technological improvements in communication tools will necessitate learning new skills. The expansion of the Internet will require caterers to accept change more rapidly. The growing sophistication of the consumer will rapidly antiquate standard operating procedures and theme-based events. A continued demand for nutritionally healthy food, guaranteed free from bacteria contamination causing food borne illness, will challenge a caterer.

Professional development recognized by *certification* will continue to evolve. Continual training, education, membership in professional associations, studying magazines, and the Internet will provide useful information. Formal courses in strategic management, communications, marketing, sanitation, and business applications will contribute to sustained success.

Using the Internet from a stationary location will not become the *savior* for all applications. Gaining on-the-job experience at numerous global properties must still complement even the best academic preparation. Work experience will remain the best teacher; there is no substitute to prepare for the demands of the sophisticated consumer demanding global cuisine and customer service. Workshops, trade shows, and memberships will build networking opportunities.

◆ CONCLUSION

The catering industry may appear at the surface to be a subject that can be learned overnight. Unfortunately, it takes many caterers an entire lifetime to master an unfinished craft. *Introduction to Catering: Ingredients for Success* is intended to be a tool that can help future caterers master, succeed, and grow in the catering field.

This text is a useful summarization of forty years of untold successes and mistakes that can be utilized for many years to come. Although some areas were covered in relationship to their level of importance, there are still many areas of further research that may be conducted in the areas of catering. For this reason, we, as food service handlers, must understand that our jobs are never really completed. We must recognize that catering and food service establishments operate on a day-to-day basis and their success or failure is a direct correlation to each individual's enthusiasm, trust, and faith for an industry's continued development.

The authors hope you have learned from what was offered as a result of forty years of practical catering experience.

First, a caterer must be a leader. Leadership is about the character of the person. Building a relationship based on trust is a guiding principle for each one to follow. Establishing an honest reputation is the most important attribute a leader can create to run a successful business. A strong positive reputation is powerful.

Second, the caterer must articulate a vision that inspires the organization. Understanding where one wants the organization to be in the future, and maintaining the commitment to get it there, is inspiring. An articulated vision inspires and energizes the organization. A leader implies followers, and the followers must be loyal to the leader. The caterer sets the example, and others follow.

Third, effective communication is one of the oldest attributes of effective leaders. Every member must understand the organization's mission. The leader must communicate the organization's short- and long-term goals.

Fourth, the sign of a great leader is the ability to build a customer base. This is accomplished by attracting new customers and new resources to satisfy their evolving needs.

Finally, evolution, change, and adaptation are part of every successful organization. The successful caterer promotes success through their own adaptation to changes and their ability to lead.

Summary

The catering profession still remains as one industry offering a motivated, dedicated, and goal-driven individual the opportunity to secure strong income, steady growth, and a challenging career.

The emerging trend of today's catering business is to establish new benchmarks that influence and raise the standards in the management and art of catering. Caterers can measure their own performances against the industry standard and make necessary adjustments in their value chain. The value chain begins with the purchasing function and ends with a customer's perception of the goods and services they receive. A value chain analysis focuses on activities that include menu formulation, purchasing, receiving, storage, issuing, preparation, production, hot and cold holding, service, and cleanup. The purpose of this analysis is for caterers to compare their own internal cost-value relationships against the cost-value relationships of the competition.

Today's trends utilize technology to coordinate the logistics of a catering business as never before seen in the history of the profession. The emerging ease of accessibility to worldwide locations in a matter of seconds has unlimited consequences for a caterer today. At the caterer's fingertips is the ability to access information quickly. E-commerce invites competitive purchasing of goods from either local business associates or directly from global-site sellers.

The continued evolution of the catering profession will demand a trained professional caterer. A very basic, but important, managerial technique is the ability for a caterer to successfully communicate with all personnel. Technological improvements in communication tools will necessitate learning new skills and require caterers to accept change more rapidly to succeed in this ever changing marketplace.

Review Questions

Brief Answers

1. Explain the strategic process of *benchmarking*. Why is this process important for contemporary caterers?

2. Explain how a caterer can reinvent processes and tasks in the catering profession.

3. Explain how caterers are using technology to help execute catering functions.

4. Explain how caterers are adapting communication technology into their profession.

5. Explain how caterers have access to the global marketplace yet still remain allegiant to their own local community.

Multiple Choice

Select the single best answer for each question.

1. The strategic management technique of identifying innovative best practices in the catering industry is called:
   a. value chain activities
   b. benchmarking
   c. the World Wide Web
   d. the mission statement
   e. Total Quality Management

2. Benchmarking is a strategic management technique that examines the _____ to find innovative best practices by competitors.
   a. value chain activities
   b. negotiating skills
   c. production skills
   d. elimination of defects
   e. All of the above.

3. The purpose of the communication management skill is for a caterer to _____ .
   a. share information with the back-of-the-house
   b. provide information to the client
   c. share information with the front-of-the-house
   d. communicate processes
   e. All of the above.

True or False

Read each of the following statements and determine if it is true or false.

1. The catering profession still remains as one industry offering a goal-driven individual the opportunity to build a great career.

2. The value chain begins with the purchasing function and ends with a customer's perception of the food and services.

3. Backward integration is a term that describes how a caterer gains control over the raw materials used in the production of food and service.

Putting It All Together

Visit a caterer. Ask how the use of technology has been incorporated into their operation. What challenges were overcome when implementing this new technology? What is the vision as to the future direction of his or her business relative to advances in technology?

APPENDICES

355

Appendix A | Ingredients for Success

1 "Every customer served at the event is a possible referral."
2 "We cannot be all things to all people."
3 "Research every job."
4 "Build a relationship of trust."
5 "Everything must be 100%, 100% of the time."
6 "Never confuse being a nice person with being an astute business person."
7 "Always exceed your customer's expectations."
8 "Create a strategic growth plan."
9 "Build a positive reputation."
10 "Customer satisfaction grows your business."
11 "Understand why the customer has selected the caterer—what are the expectations? "
12 "To establish a long-term relationship with a customer and work, as frequently as possible, with each client one-on-one. "
13 "Presentations are important—create special, unusual, personable, and impressive competitive proposals."
14 "The closer the caterer gets to the event, the more difficult the event becomes."
15 "Every observable action exhibited by the caterer emulates from the public mission statement."
16 "Accurate forecasting of market trends and changes in food prices are keys to establishing correct pricing and meeting preestablished financial objectives."
17 "Cost control procedures are created for the acquisition of timely information to equip the caterer with the data to scrutinize controllable costs and make appropriate operational decisions."
18 "Strategies emerge as an outcome of planning."
19 "The longer the length of time between booking the event and its implementation date, the better opportunity a caterer has to create a detailed plan."
20 "To satisfy customer needs, the caterer must overproduce to exceed customer expectations."

356

21 "Outside suppliers are as important as a caterer's own key personnel."

22 "The main outcome of a recipe is to produce a food that will excite the consumer to become a repeat customer."

23 "A caterer must know the holding power of the food."

24 "When developing recipes to complement the menu mix, create them based on the preferred taste of the customer."

25 "The menu is a management tool from which the caterer can control operations."

26 "Structure is dependent on the mission of the organization."

27 "Every caterer should have at least two good suppliers, a principal supplier and a backup supplier."

28 "The supplier is only as dependable and responsible as the salesperson and the truck driver who delivers the food."

29 "Good receiving and planning provide the caterer with a major economical advantage. Good receiving principles provide control."

30 "The menu is the single most important tool used to determine precise equipment needs based on the type of food being prepared."

31 "Minimize utility costs through manageable conservation of natural resources by planning for the current and future selection of energy-efficient equipment."

32 "Needless steps and unnecessary movement cause worker fatigue, which leads to reduced productivity and increased labor costs, and contributes to preventable accidents that escalate workman's compensation claims."

33 "Insulated carriers will not only carry food but will also carry bacteria."

34 "Be sure that all hotel pans and small equipment units can be transported properly."

35 "The end result of the job relies on the entire staff working together— teamwork."

36 "Construct detailed diagrams of every buffet in advance."

37 "The more service given, and the better care taken of the customer through exceptional attention to detail, the happier the client will be and the more repeat business will be generated from that event."

38 "Consider every job a major production."

39 "A caterer's performance is a reflection of the business."

40 "A caterer's business success depends on enforceable controls. Creative acquisition, storage, preparation, and service of food and beverage will minimize labor requirements. Strong budgetary objectives derived from accounting systems will provide analysis of financial information."

41 "The creation and maintenance of the right insurance and legal package, based on the mission of the organization, will protect the caterer against any unpredictable crisis."

Appendix B | Weights, Measures, and Abbreviations

Basic Equivalents Used in Recipe Conversion

1 Tbsp	=	3 tsp, in liquids 1/2 fl oz
1/8 cup	=	2 Tbsp, in liquids 1 fl oz
1/4 cup	=	4 Tbsp, in liquids 2 fl oz
1/3 cup	=	5 Tbsp + 1 tsp
1/2 cup	=	8 Tbsp, in liquids 4 fl oz
2/3 cup	=	10 Tbsp + 2 tsp
3/4 cup	=	12 Tbsp, in liquids 6 fl oz
1 cup	=	16 Tbsp, in liquids 8 fl oz
1 pt	=	2 cups, in liquids 16 fl oz
1 qt	=	2 pt = 4 cups
1 gal	=	4 qt
1 lb	=	16 oz
1 pk	=	8 qt, approximately 12 1/2 lb
1 bu	=	4 pk, approximately 50 lb

Can Sizes Used in Food Service

Size of can	Approximate net weight or fluid measure	Approximate cups per can
No. 10	6 lb or 7 lb 5 oz	9–12
No. 5 - Squat	4 lb–4 1/2 lb	8
No. 3 Cylinder	46 fl oz or 51 fl oz	5 1/4
No. 2/12	26–30 oz	3 1/2
No. 303	16 oz	2
No. 300	14–16 oz	1 1/4
No. 1 - Picnic	10 1/2–12 oz	1 1/4
8 oz	8 oz	2

List of Abbreviations

Across	ACRS	Chop	CHP	Generous	GEN
Alternate	ALT	Clean	CLN	Glass	GL
Approximately	APRX	Cook	CK	Glaze	GLZ
Around	ARND	Copper	CPR	Gooseneck	GSNK
As purchased	A.P.	Core	CR	Grate	GRT
Assorted	ASSTD	Count	CT	Green	GRN
		Cover	CVR	Grill	GRL
Basket	BSKT	Creamer	CRMR	Ground	GRND
Beside	BSD	Cross	X		
Between	BTWN	Crosswise	X-WISE		
Blanch	BLNCH	Cup	CP	Half	HLF
Blend	BLND			Halves	HLVS
Blender	BLNDR			Handle	HNDL
Boat	BT	Dark	DK	Holder	HLDR
Bone in	B/I	Deep fry	DP FRY		
Boneless	B/L	Dice	DC		
Bottle	BTL	Diagonal	DIAG	Including	INCL
Bottom	BTM	Dining room	DNG RM	Individual	IND
Bowl	BWL	Doily	DLY	Inside	INSD
Bread	BRD	Drain	DRN		
Broil	BRL	Dressing	DRS	Julienne	JUL
Brown	BRN	Drops	DRP		
Brush	BRSH			Kettle	KTL
Bucket	BKT	Each	EA	Knife	KNF
Butter	BTR	Entree	ENT		
				Ladle	LDL
		Fill	FL	Large	LG
Can	CN	Flour	FLR	Leaf	LF
Center	CTR	Fork	FK	Lengthwise	LNTHWS
Change	CHNG	Fresh	FRS	Level	LVL
Cheesecloth	CHSCLTH	From	FRM	Lightly	LTLY
Chill	CHL	Frozen	FRZ	Line	LN

Marinate	MAR	Pre-heat	PRE-HT	Sprig	SPRG
Medium	MED	Purchase	PURCH	Sprinkle	SPRNK
Melt	NET			Stainless steel	S/S
Middle	MDL	Quarter	QRTR	Standard	STD
Miscellaneous	MISC			Standing	STNDG
Mix	MX	Request	REQ	Style	STYL
Mixture	MXTR	Roll	RL	Substitute	SUB
		Rosette	ROS	Supreme	SUPRM
Napee	NAP	Round	RND		
Napkin	NPKN			Tablespoon	TB
Neck	NCK	Salt & pepper	S&P	Teaspoon	TS
Number	NO.	Same	SME	Temperature	TEMP
		Sauce	SCE	Thin	THN
		Sauté	SAUT	Through	THRU
Open	OPN	Scatter	SCTR	Toast	TST
Optional	OPT	Scoop	SCP	Top	TP
Ounce	OZ	Score	SCR	To taste	TT
Outside	OUTSD	Section	SCT	Triangle	TRNGL
Oval	OVL	Server	SRVR	Trim	TRM
Over	O/	Served by	VIA		
Overlap	OVRLP	host/ess	SRVR	Under	U/
		Service	SV		
Package	PKG	Shell	SBL	Very	V
Paper	PAPR	Shred	SBRD	Volume	VOL
Partially	PART	Size	SZ		
Peel	PL	Skewer	SKWR	Warm	WRM
Pitcher	PTCHR	Skinless	S/L	Wedge	WDG
Planter	PLNTR	Slice	SLI	Weight	WT
Plastic	PLAS	Small	SML	White	WH
Plate	PLT	Spoon	SPN	Whole	WHL
Portion	PORT	Spread	SPRD	With	W/
Pound	LB			Without	W/O

Appendix C

Sample Business Plan

(Courtesy of Bruce Frankel and VirtualRestaurant.com)

Table of Contents

Company Description

Kundo, Inc., a Massachusetts-based company, will operate Abonda, a single unit, medium-size restaurant serving healthy, contemporary food. The restaurant will be located at 645 Deacon Street in Cambridge, MA.

Mission Statement

The company's goal is to gain a multi-faceted success. Our first responsibility is to the financial well being of the restaurant. We will meet this goal while trying to consider:

1. the effect of our products on the health and well being of our customers (and our staff)

2. the impact that our business practices and choices will have on the environment

3. the high quality of attitude, fairness, understanding, and generosity between management, staff, customers, and vendors.

Awareness of all these factors, and the responsible actions that result, will give our efforts a sense of purpose and meaning beyond our basic financial goals.

Development and Status

The company was incorporated in September of 1995 and elected sub-chapter S. The founders are Jack Morton and Wilma Mason. Jack is the President and Wilma the Vice President. There are a total of 10,000 shares of common stock issued. Wilma and Jack each own 3,000 and the remaining shares are retained by the company for future distribution. In addition, they have loaned the company $25,000 of their own money for research and start-up costs.

A suitable site for the first restaurant was found last month and lease negotiations are in the final stages. The location will be on Deacon Street, just outside Harvard Square, and close to a dense population of the target market. When the lease is signed there will be three months of free rent for construction, and in that time the balance of the start-up funds must be raised. With that phase completed, Abonda Restaurant can then open and the operations phase of the project can begin.

Future Plans

If the business is meeting its projections by month nine, we will start scouting for a second location and develop plans for the next unit. Our five-year goal is to have three restaurants in the greater Boston area with a combined annual profit of between $500,000 and $1,000,000.

Industry Analysis

Although the restaurant industry is very competitive, the lifestyle changes created by modern living continue to fuel its steady growth. More and more people have less time, resources, and ability to cook for themselves. Trends are very important and Abonda is well positioned for the current interest in lighter, healthier foods at moderate to low prices.

The Restaurant Industry Today

The food service business is the third largest industry in the country. It accounts for over $240 billion annually in sales. The independent restaurant accounts for 15% of that total. The average American spends 15% of his/her income on meals away from home. This number has been increasing for the past seven years. In the past five years the restaurant industry has out-performed the national GNP by 40%. The reasons given by the Folkney Report (November 1994) are lifestyle changes, economic climate, and increase of product variety. There are 600 new restaurants opening every month and over 200 more are needed to keep pace with increasing demand.

Future Trends and Strategic Opportunities

The projected growth for the food service sector is very positive in both short- and long-term projections. The National Restaurant Association released, in 2000, the *Restaurant Industry, 2010*, a comprehensive, futuristic report forecasting projections concerning the industry's evolution in the development and adaption of technology, the need for continued professional development, and the search for innovative solutions to satisfy customer needs by all sectors of the food service market. The National Restaurant Association suggested the food service industry will:

1. experience a positive growth, having a significant economic impact, with projected accumulated sales approaching 577 billion by 2010.
2. continue to be the largest employer, especially of women and minorities in the United States' public sector.
3. experience incremental growth in the annual household expenditure for food purchased away from the home.
4. continue the trend toward ethnic cuisine, with foods from Japan, China, Thailand, and the Caribbean region gaining in popularity.

Products and Related Services

Abonda Restaurant will be offering a menu of food and beverages with a distinctive image. There will be three ways to purchase these products: table service at the restaurant, take-out from the restaurant, and delivery to home or office.

The Menu

The Abonda menu (see appendices) is moderate sized, and moderate–low priced, offering a collection of ethnic and American items with a common theme—healthy (low-fat, low cholesterol, and natural ingredients), flavorful, and familiar. Our goal is to create the image of light, satisfying, and still nutritious food. There has been an increased awareness of nutritional and health concerns in recent years and a growing market of people who now eat this style of cooking regularly.

Production

Food production and assembly will take place in the kitchen of the restaurant. Fresh vegetables, meat, and dairy products will be used to create most of the dishes from scratch. The chef will exercise strict standards of sanitation, quality production, presentation, and packaging with the kitchen and service staff.

Service

There will be three ways a customer can purchase food. They can sit down at one of the 54 seats in the dining room and get full service from a waitperson. A separate take-out counter will service those who wish to pick up their food. Most take-out food will be prepared to order with orders coming from either the telephone or fax. Delivery (an indirect form of take-out) will be available at certain times and to a limited area.

Future Opportunities

There is a market segment that prefers to eat this type of cooking at home although they do not have the time to cook. There are already caterers and mail order companies that provide individuals and families with up to a month's supply of pre-prepared meals. This opportunity will be researched and developed on a trial basis. If successful, it could become a major new source of income without creating the need for additional staff or production space.

The Target Market

The market for Abonda's products covers a large area of diverse and densely populated groups. Although it will be located in a downtown urban setting, it is an area where people travel to eat out and one that is also frequented by tourists. It is an area known for catering to the demographic group we are targeting.

Market Location and Customers

The Harvard Square area is one of the most desirable retail locations in New England. The Massachusetts Chamber of Commerce rates it as the third best retail market in the state. There are more than 400 businesses in a one-quarter square mile area with average sales of $330 per square foot.

The customer base will come from four major segments.

1. Local population—The city of Cambridge, with a year-round population of 145,000, is centrally located in the Boston area and is within a fifteen minute drive of eight major suburbs.
2. Colleges and universities—Harvard alone has six different schools within walking distance of Deacon Street and a seasonal population of 22,000. In addition five other colleges near the square have large student bodies.

3. Tourism—Between hotels, motels, bed and breakfast rooms, and inns, there are over 8,500 rooms available. Last year they were at 92% occupancy.
4. Local businesses—The Cambridge Chamber of Commerce lists over 900 businesses with an average of twelve employees in the Harvard square area.

The food concept and product image of Abonda will attract three different customer profiles.

1. The student—More and more young people have developed healthy eating habits. Some also go through a health food phase while in college.
2. The health-conscious person of any age or sex—This includes anyone on a restricted or prescribed diet, or those who have committed to a healthy diet.
3. The curious and open-minded—"If you try it, you will like it." Through marketing, publicity, and word-of-mouth, people will seek out a new experience and learn that nutritious food can be tasty, fun, convenient, and inexpensive.

Market Trends and The Future

The population and demographics of Harvard Square have remained steady for the last fourteen years. Tourism has increased 24% over the last three years and is predicted to keep growing. Local businesses are increasing at a rate of 18% yearly.

The idea of a health consciousness through nutritional awareness and dietary change has been slowly building for the last seven years. The extensive government studies and new Food Guide Pyramid have given everyone a new definition of a balanced, healthy diet. This is not a fad but a true dietary trend backed by the scientific and medical community, the media, the government, and endorsed by the big food manufacturers. As the *Foodservice 2000* report stated, this trend would be even more important by the turn of the century. As people want to stay home more and cook less our strategy of delivering prepared meals on a weekly or monthly arrangement may be a widespread, accepted new way of eating.

The Competition

There are over two dozen restaurants in the Harvard Square area that sell food at similar prices. Although this presents an obvious challenge in terms of market share, it also indicates the presence of a large, strong potential. The newest competitors have made their successful entry based on an innovative concept or novelty. Abonda will offer an innovative product in a familiar style at a competitive price. Our aggressive plans of take-out and delivery will also give us an advantage to create a good market share before the competition can adjust or similar concepts appear.

Competitor's Profile

Competing with Abonda for the target market are the following categories of food providers:

- independent table service restaurants of similar menu and price structure
- chain restaurants
- commercial foodservice companies serving students directly

Independent operators include Grendel's Den, Iako, Bombay Club, Iruna, and The Border Cafe. Most are ethnic based and will carry at least two similar menu items.

Grendel's and Iruna are long-standing businesses, while the others are fairly new. They all are doing very well.

The major chain restaurants are House of Blues, Chili's, and Bertucci's. All are relatively new but well established and profitable. They have big resources of marketing and/or a specialty product or attraction (House of Blues is also a live music club). Ogden Foods and Cysco both service 24,000 Harvard students but their product is not appealing enough to prevent students from eating out five to seven meals a week. In addition, there are two local catering companies that deliver prepared meals daily to offices.

Competitive Strategy

There are three major ways we will create an advantage over our competitors.

1. product identity, quality, and novelty
2. high employee motivation and good sales attitude
3. innovative and aggressive service options

Abonda will be the only restaurant among the competition that focuses the entire menu on healthy, low-fat cooking. Each of the competitors offers at least one healthy selection on their menu. Grendel's Den has an entire section called *On the Lighter Side*, but in all cases they are always seen as alternatives to the main style being offered. The target market will perceive Abonda as the destination location for healthy, low-fat cooking. Once they have tried the restaurant, their experience will be reinforced by friendly, efficient, knowledgeable service. Return and repeat business will be facilitated by accessible take-out and delivery options. Most of the competitors offer take-out.

Marketing Plan and Sales Strategy

Market Penetration

Entry into the market should not be a problem. The store has high visibility with heavy foot traffic all day long. The local residents and students always support new restaurants and the tourists do not have fixed preferences. In addition, $10,000 has been budgeted for a pre-opening advertising and public relations campaign.

Marketing Strategy

Focusing on the unique aspect of the product theme (healthy, tasty foods), a mix of marketing vehicles will be created to convey our presence, our image, and our message.

- print media—local newspapers, magazines, and student publications
- broadcast media—local programming and special interest shows
- hotel guides, concierge relations, Chamber of Commerce brochures
- direct mail—subscriber lists, offices for delivery
- miscellaneous—yellow pages, charity events

A public relations firm has been retained to create special events and solicit print and broadcast coverage, especially at the start-up. The marketing effort will be split into three phases.

1. opening—an advanced notice (press packet) sent out by the PR firm to all media and printed announcement ads in key places; budget: $10,000

2. ongoing—a flexible campaign (using the above media), assessed regularly for effectiveness; budget: $10,000

3. point of sale—a well-trained staff to increase the average check as well as enhance the customer's overall experience; word-of-mouth referral is very important in building a customer base.

Future Plans and Strategic Opportunities

Catering to offices (even outside of our local area) may become a large part of gross sales. At that point a sales agent would be hired to directly market our products for daily delivery or catered functions.

Operations

Facilities and Offices

The restaurant at 645 Deacon Street is a 2,400-square-foot space. It was formerly a restaurant and needs only minor structural modifications. The licenses and codes issued are all in order. New equipment and dining room furnishings will be purchased and installed by the general contractor. Offices of the corporation are presently at Jack Morton's home but will be moved to the restaurant after opening.

Hours of Operation

The restaurant will be open for breakfast, lunch, and dinner seven days a week. Service will begin at 7:00 A.M. and end at 10:00 P.M. The restaurant will be closed Christmas, Thanksgiving, and Fourth of July.

Employee Training and Education

Employees will be trained not only in their specific operational duties, but also in the philosophy and applications of our concept. They will receive extensive information from the chef and be kept up-to-date on the latest developments in healthy eating.

Systems and Controls

A big emphasis is being placed on extensive research into the quality and integrity of our products. They will constantly be tested for our own high standards of freshness and purity. Food costs and inventory control will be handled by our computer system and checked daily by management.

Food Production

Most food will be prepared on the premises. The kitchen will be designed for high standards of sanitary efficiency and cleaned daily. Food will be made mostly to order and stored in large coolers in the basement.

Delivery and Catering

Food for delivery may be similar to take-out (prepared to order) or it may be prepared earlier and stocked. Catering will be treated as deliveries.

Management and Organization

Key Employees and Principals

Jack Morton is President and is also the owner and manager of Grains & Beans, a local natural food wholesaler and retail store. Since 1977 his company has created a high-profile mainstream image for natural foods. In 1992 Grains & Beans opened a small café within the retail store that became so popular and profitable that he decided to expand the concept into a full-service restaurant.

Jack brings with him a track record of success in the natural foods industry. His management style is innovative and in keeping with the corporate style outlined in the mission statement.

Compensation and Incentives

Abonda will offer competitive wages and salaries to all employees with benefit packages available to key personnel only.

Board of Directors

An impressive board of directors has been assembled that represents some top professionals from the area. They will be a great asset to the development of the company.

Consultants and Professional Support Resources

At present, no outside consults have been retained, except for the design department at Best Equipment.

Management to be Added

We are presently searching for a general manager and executive chef. These key employees will be well chosen and given incentives for performance and growth.

Management Structure and Style

Jack Morton will be the President and Chief Operating Officer. The general manager and chef will report to him. The assistant manager and sous chef will report to their respective managers, and all other employees will be subordinate to them.

Ownership

Jack Morton and the stockholders will retain ownership with the possibility of offering stock to key employees if deemed appropriate.

Long-Term Development and Exit Plan

Goals

Abonda is an innovative concept that targets a new, growing market. We assume that the market will respond, and grow quickly in the next five years. Our goals are to create a reputation of quality, consistency, and security (safety of food) that will make us the leader of a new style of dining.

Strategies

Our marketing efforts will be concentrated on take-out and delivery, the areas of most promising growth. As the market changes, new products may be added to maintain sales.

Milestones

After the restaurant opens, we will keep a close eye on sales and profit. If we are on target at the end of year one, we will look to expand to a second unit.

Risk Evaluation

With any new venture, there is risk involved. The success of our project hinges on the strength and acceptance of a fairly new market. After year one, we expect some copycat competition in the form of other independent units. Chain competition will come much later.

Exit Plan

Ideally, Abonda will expand to five units in the next ten years. At that time, we will entertain the possibility of a buy-out by a larger restaurant concern or actively seek to sell to a new owner.

Company Information

Company name	Kundo, Inc.
Business form	Corporation
Business name	Abonda
Address	128 Dew St. Montrose, MA
Contact person	Mr. Morton
Telephone	413-477-3345
Hours of operation	
Breakfast	7–10 A.M.
Lunch	11–3 P.M.
Dinner	5–10 P.M.
Days open	7 days
Closed for holidays?	52 weeks
Opening date	3/1/01
Length of lease	10 years
Type of restaurant	Limited menu

Sources of Capital and Debt Service
Kundo, Inc.
3/7/01

Total start-up capital	$300,000
Loans and notes	50,000
Stock sales	0
Partnerships	250,000

Loans and notes

	Amount	Rate	Term	Source
#1	50,000	10%	5.00	Friends
#2	0	0%		
#3	0	0%		
#4	0	0%		
#5	0	0%		
Total	$50.000			

Stock

Total shares	0.00
Outstanding shares	0.00

Shareholders

	Amount Paid In	Shares	%
#1	0	0	0%
#2	0	0	0%
#3	0	0	0%
#4	0	0	0%
#5	0	0	0%
#6	0	0	0%
#7	0	0	0%
#8	0	0	0%
#9	0	0	0%
#10	0	0	0%
Total	$0	0	0%

Dividend schedule _____

Partnership information

Number of limited partners	5
Amount paid in by each partner	50,000
Total capital	250,000
Percentage of profits for general partner	50%
Percentage of profits for limited partners (group)	50%
Interest on principal amounts	10%
Cumulative?	N

Total yearly interest   **$25,000**

Use of Funding and Start-Up Costs Summary
Kundo, Inc.
3/9/01

Total start-up capital $300,000

	Amount	Expense	Depreciation	Amortization	Amort. Lshld.	Balance
Security Deposit	10,000					
Construction Rent	10,000			10,000		
Construction Utilities	2,000			2,000		
Liquor License	2,000					
Yearly License Fees	3,000			3,000		
Utility Deposits	2,300					
Insurance-Prepaid	2,500					
Advertising & Promotion	5,000			5,000		
Graphics & Printing	5,000			5,000		
Architects/Decorators	10,000			10,000		
Bank Note Payment	0					
Other Note	0					
Legal & Accounting	3,000			3,000		
Inventory	10,000					
Uniforms	2,000			2,000		
Contractor Fees	0			0		
Cash Reserves	**80,700**					
Furniture, Fixtures, Equipment	60,000		60,000			
Leasehold Improvements	60,000				60,000	
Payroll, Training	5,000			5,000		
Consultants	15,000			15,000		
Research & Development	2,500			2,500		
Landscaping	0			0		
Debt Consolidation	0					
Employment Agency Fees	0			0		
Other	10,000			10,000		
Other	0			0		
TOTALS	300,000	0	60,000	72,500	60,000	
	Amount	Expense	Depreciation	Amortization	Amort. Lshld.	Balance
	$300,000					

Gross Sales Calculation
Kundo, Inc.
3/9/01

Breakfast	Covers	Food	Wine	Liquor	Total
Average check		$2.57	$0.00	$0.00	$2.57
Monday	100	$256.75	$0.00	$0.00	$256.75
Tuesday	100	$256.75	$0.00	$0.00	$256.75
Wednesday	100	$256.75	$0.00	$0.00	$256.75
Thursday	100	$256.75	$0.00	$0.00	$256.75
Friday	100	$256.75	$0.00	$0.00	$256.75
Saturday	100	$256.75	$0.00	$0.00	$256.75
Sunday	100	$256.75	$0.00	$0.00	$256.75
Weekly Totals	700	$1,797.25	$0.00	$0.00	$1,797.25
Monthly Totals	3033	$7,788.08	$0.00	$0.00	$7,788.08
Yearly Totals	36400	$93,457.00	$0.00	$0.00	$93,457.00

Lunch	Covers	Food	Wine	Liquor	Total
Average check		$6.04	$0.62	$0.45	$7.10
Monday	250	$1,509.38	$154.38	$111.25	$1,775.00
Tuesday	250	$1,509.38	$154.38	$111.25	$1,775.00
Wednesday	250	$1,509.38	$154.38	$111.25	$1,775.00
Thursday	250	$1,509.38	$154.38	$111.25	$1,775.00
Friday	250	$1,509.38	$154.38	$111.25	$1,775.00
Saturday	250	$1,509.38	$154.38	$111.25	$1,775.00
Sunday	250	$1,509.38	$154.38	$111.25	$1,775.00
Weekly Totals	1750	$10,565.63	$1,080.63	$778.75	$12,425.00
Monthly Totals	7583	$45,784.38	$4,682.71	$3,374.58	$53,841.67
Yearly Totals	91000	$549,412.50	$56,192.50	$40,495.00	$646,100.00

Dinner	Covers	Food	Wine	Liquor	Total
Average check		$7.64	$1.24	$0.43	$9.301
Monday	150	$1,145.63	$185.63	$63.75	$1,395.00
Tuesday	150	$1,145.63	$185.63	$63.75	$1,395.00
Wednesday	150	$1,145.63	$185.63	$63.75	$1,395.00
Thursday	150	$1,145.63	$185.63	$63.75	$1,395.00
Friday	150	$1,145.63	$185.63	$63.75	$1,395.00
Saturday	150	$1,146.63	$185.63	$63.75	$1,395.00
Sunday	150	$1,145.63	$185.63	$63.75	$1,395.00
Weekly Totals	1050	$8,019.38	$1,299.38	$446.25	$9,765.00
Monthly Totals	4550	$34,750.63	$5,630.63	$1,933.75	$42,315.00
Yearly Totals	54600	$417,007.50	$67,567.50	$23,205.00	$507,780.00

(continued)

Combined Totals	Covers	Food	Wine	Liquor	Total
Weekly	3500	$20,382.25	$2,380.00	$1,225.00	$23,987.25
Monthly	15167	$88,323.08	$10,313.33	$5,308.33	$103,944.75
Yearly Gross Sales	18,2000	$1,059,877.00	$123,760.00	$63,700.00	$1,247,337.00
Covers/day	500	84.97%	9.92%	5.11%	100.00%
			AVERAGE FOOD CHECK		$7.64

Beer and Wine		Avg. Price	% Buying	Total
Beer		2.75	5%	0.14
Wine Glass		4.00	10%	0.40
Wine Bottle		14.00	5%	0.70
	AVERAGE BEER AND WINE CHECK			$1.24

Liquor		Avg. Price	% Buying	Total
Drinks		3.50	5%	0.18
Drinks		5.00	5%	0.25
Drinks		0.00	30%	0.00
	AVERAGE LIQUOR CHECK			$0.43

Dinner	
AVERAGE FOOD CHECK	$7.64
AVERAGE BEER AND WINE CHECK	$1.24
AVERAGE LIQUOR CHECK	$0.43
TOTAL AVERAGE CHECK	**$9.30**

Appendix D

Suggested Web Site Addresses for Interested Caterers

Alaska Seafood Marketing Institute - www.state.ak.us/local/akpages/COMMERCE/asmihp.html

Almond Board of California - www.almondsarein.com

American Association of Meat Processors - www.aamp.com

American Bakers Association - www.americanbakers.org

American Center for Wine, Food and the Arts - www.theamericancenter.org

American Cheese Society - www.cheesesociety.org

American Correctional Foodservice Association - www.corrections.com/acfsa

American Council on Science and Health - www.acsh.org

American Culinary Federation - www.acfchefs.org

American Dairy Products Institute - www.americandairyproducts.com

American Dietetic Association - www.eatright.org

American Dry Bean Board - www.americanbean.org

American Egg Board - www.aeb.org

American Emu Association - www.aea-emu.org

American Frozen Food Institute - www.affi.com

American Hotel and Motel Association - www.ahma.com

American Institute of Baking - www.aibonline.org

American Institute of Wine and Food - www.aiwf.org

American Lamb Council - www.lambchef.com

American Meat Institute - www.meatami.org

American Meat Science Association - www.meatscience.org

American Mushroom Institute - www.americanmushroominst.org

American Ostrich Association - www.ostriches.org

American Public Health Association - www.apha.org

American Poultry Association - www.ampltya.com

American School Food Service Association - www.asfsa.org

American Sheep Industry Association - www.sheepusa.org

American Society for Healthcare Food Service Administrators - www.ashfsa.org

American Society of Baking - www.asbe.org

American Soybean Association - www.oilseeds.org/asa

American Spice Trade Association - www.astaspice.org
American Sugar Alliance - www.sugaralliance.org
American Wine Society - www.vicon.net/~aws
Aseptic Packaging Council - www.aseptic.org
Association for Dressings & Sauces - www.dressings-sauces.org/index.html
Association of Food Industries - www.a-fi.org
Bakery Equipment Manufactures Association - www.bema.org
Biscuit & Cracker Manufacturers Association - www.thebcma.org
Blue Diamond Growers - www.bluediamondgrowers.com
Bunn-O-Matic Corporation - www.bunnomatic.com
The Bread Bakers Guild of America - www.bbga.org
California Artichoke Advisory Board - www.artichokes.org
California Asparagus - www.calasparagus.com
California Aquaculture Association - aqua.ucdavis.edu
California Avocado Commission - www.avocado.org
California Date Commission - www.californiadates.org
California Egg Commission - www.eggcom.com
California Fig Advisory Board - www.californiafigs.com
California Kiwifruit Commission - www.kiwifruit.org
California Olive Committee - www.calolive.org
California Poultry Industry Federation - www.cpif.org
California Pear Advisory Board - www.calpear.com
California Pistachio Commission - www.pistachios.org
California Prune Board - www.prunes.org
California Raisin Marketing Board - www.calraisins.org
California Salmon Council - www.calkingsalmon.org
California Seafood Council - www.ca-seafod.org
California Strawberry Commission - www.calstrawberry.com
California Table Grape Commission - www.tablegrape.com
California Tree Fruit Agreement - www.caltreefruit.com
Cambro Manufacturing Company - www.cambro.com
The Catfish Institute - www.catfishinstitute.com
Center for Disease Control and Prevention - www.cdc.gov
Cherry Marketing Institute Inc. - www.cherrymkt.org
Chilean Fresh Fruit Association - www.cffa.org
Chocolate Manufactures Association of the U.S.A. - www.candyusa.org
The Club Foundation - www.clubfoundation.org
Club Managers Association of America - www.cmaa.org
Concord Grape Association - www.concordgrape.org
Confrerie de la Chaine des Rotisseurs - www.chaineus.org
Council for Responsible Nutrition - www.crnusa.org
Council of Hotel and Restaurant Trainers - www.chart.org
Council of Independent Restaurants of America - www.indrest.org

Council on Hotel, Restaurant, and Institutional Education - www.chrie.org

Cranberry Institute - www.cranberries.org

Culinary Archives & Museum Johnson & Wales University - www.culinary.org

Dairy Management Inc. - www.doitwithdairy.com or www.dairyinfo.com or www.ilovecheese.com

Diamond Walnut Growers - www.diamondwalnut.com

The Duckling Council - www.duckling.org

Dudson China - www.dudson.co.uk

Ecolab - www.ecolab.com

Education Institute of the American Hotel and Motel Association - www.ei-ahma.org

Family Features Editorial Syndicate - www.culinary.net

Farmer's Rice Cooperative - www.farmersrice.com

FDA Model Food Code (1999) - http://vm.cfsan.fda.gov/~dms/

FDA Plan Review Guide - http://vm.cfsan.fda.gov/~dms/prev-toc.html

FDA Seafood and Information Resources - http://vm.cfsan.fda.gov/seafood1.html

Flexible Packaging Association - www.flexpack.org

Florida Dept. of Agriculture and Consumer Services - www.fl-seafood.com

Florida Dept. of Citrus - www.floridajuice.com or www.fred.ifas.ufl.edu/citrus/

Florida Fresh Fruit & Vegetable Association - www.ffva.com

Florida Tomato Committee - www.floridatomatoes.org

The Food and Beverage Institute - www.ciachef.edu/fbi/ciavid.html

Food and Drug Administration (FDA) - www.fda.gov

The Food & Drug Law Institute - www.fdli.org

Food and Nutrition Information Center - www.nal.usda.gov/fnic

Foodborne Illness Education Information Center - www.nal.usda.gov/fnic/foodborne/statemen.html

Foodchain- The National Food-Rescue Network - www.foodchain.org

Food Distributors International - www.fdi.org

Food Institute - www.foodinstitute.com

Food Marketing Institute - www.fmi.org

FoodNet - www.foodnet.com

Food Processing Machinery & Supplies Association - www.fpmsa.org

Food Processors Institute - www.fpi-food.org

Foodservice Consultants Society International - www.fcsi.org

Foodservice and Packaging Institute - www.fpi.org

Foodservice Educators Network International - www.feni.org

Foodservice Equipment Reports - www.fermag.com

Food Service Industry Links - www.gernsbachers.com/indlinks.htm

Georgia Peach Commission - www.agr.state.ga.us

Georgia Pecan Commission - www.georgiapecans.org

Glass Packaging Institute - www.gpi.org

Grocery Manufacturers of America - www.gmabrands.com

Hazelnut Council - www.hazelnutcouncil.org

Hazelnut Marketing Board - www.oregonhazelnuts.org

Hobart - www.hobartcorp.com

Horseradish Information Council - www.horseradish.org

IACP Culinary Collection Directory International Association of Culinary
Professionals - www.iacp-online.org

Idaho Bean Commission - www2.state.id.us/bean

Idaho Potato Commission - www.idahopotatoes.com

Insurance Services Office (ISO) - http://www.iso.com

Independent Bakers Association - www.mindspring.com/independent-baker

Institute of Food Technologists - www.ift.org

Institute of Shortening & Eddible Oils Inc. - www.iseo.org

International Association of Culinary Professionals - www.iacp-online.org

International Association of Food Industry Suppliers - www.iafis.org

International Association of Milk, Food & Environmental Sanitarians Inc. -
www.iamfes.org

International Bottled Water Association - www.bottledwater.org

International Commission on Microbiological Specifications for Food -
www.dfst.csiro.au/icmsf.html

International Dairy-Deli-Bakery Association - www.iddba.org

International Dairy Foods Association - www.idfa.org

International Food Information Council - www.ificinfo.health.org

International Food Service Executives Association - www.ifsea.org

International Foodservice Manufacturers Association - www.ifmaworld.com

International Herb Association - www.iherb.org

International Jelly & Preserve Association - www.jelly.org

International Society of Beverage Technologists - www.bevtech.org

International Union of Bakers & Baker-Confectioners - www.bakeruib.org

The James Beard Foundation - www.jamesbeard.org

Just-food.com - www.just-food.com

Kansas Wheat Commission - www.kswheat.com

KitchenAid - www.kitchenaid.com

Leafy Greens Council - www.leafy-greens.org

Learn2 Set a Table - www.learn2.com/06/0608/0608.asp

Les Dames d'Escoffier International - www.ldei.org

Libby Glassware - www.libbey.com

Maine Lobster - www.mainelobsterpromo.com

McClancy Seasoning Company - www.mcclancy.com

Meat & Poultry Hotline U. S. Dept. of Agriculture Food Safety & Inspection
Service - www.fsis.usda.gov

Meat Industry Suppliers Association - www.meatpoultry.com/misa

Michigan Apple Committee - www.michiganapples.com

Michigan Asparagus Advisory Board - www.asparagus.com
Micros Systems - www.micros.com
Midwest Food Processors Association - www.mwfpa.org
Milliken Table Linen - table setting & napkin folding -
     www.visatablecloth.com/main.html
The Mushroom Council - www.mushroomcouncil.com
Napa Valley Vintners Association - www.napavintners.com
National Association of Catering Executives - www.nace.net
National Association of Fruits, Flavors & Syrups - www.naffs.org
National Association of Margarine Manufacturers - www.margarine.org
National Association of Catering Executives - www.nace.net
National Assn. For the Specialty Food Trade - www.fancyfoodshows.com
National Caterers Association - www.nacater.org
National Cattlemen's Beef Association - www.beef.org
National Cherry Foundation - www.nationalcherries.com
National Chicken Council - www.eatchicken.com
National Coffee Association - www.coffeescience.org
National Confectioners Association - www.candyusa.org
National Corn Growers Association - www.ncga.com
National Country Ham Association - www.countryham.org
National Fisheries Institute - www.nfi.org
National Food Distributors Association - www.specialtyfoods.org
National Food Processors Association - www.nfpa-food.org
National Food Safety Database - www.foodsafety.org
National Frozen Food Association - www.nffa.org
National Honey Board - www.nhb.org
National Hot Pepper Association - www.peppergal.com
National Ice Carving Association - www.nica.org
National Juice Products Association - www.njpa.com
National Meat Association - www.nmaonline.org
National Nutritional Food Association - www.nnfa.org
National Onion Association - www.onions-usa.org
National Pasta Association - www.ilovepasta.org
National Pest Control Association - www.pestworld.com
National Pork Producers Council - www.nppc.org
National Potato Council - www.npcspud.com
National Potato Promotion Board - www.potatohelp.com or www.uspotatoes.com
National Research Council - www.nas.edu/nrc
National Restaurant Association - www.restaurant.org
National Restaurant Association Educational Foundation - www.edfound.org
National Specialty Coffee Assn. of America - www.scaa.org
National Soft Drink Association - www.nsda.org
National Sunflower Association - www.sunflowernsa.com

National Turkey Federation - www.turkeyfed.org

National Watermelon Promotional Board - www.watermelon.org

Network of Executive Women in Hospitality - www.newh.org

New York Apple Association - www.nyapplecountry.com

New York Wine & Grape Foundation - www.nywine.com

North American Association of Food Equipment Manufacturers - www.nafem.org

North American Blueberry Council - www.blueberry.org

North American Meat Processors Association - www.namp.com

North American Olive Oil Association - www.naooa.org

Northarvest Bean Growers Association - www.northarvestbean.org

North Carolina Sweet Potato Commission, Inc. - www.ncsweetpotatoes.com

Northwest Cherry Growers - www.nwcherries.com

NSF International (National Sanitation Foundation) - www.nsf.org

Oldways Preservation & Exchange Trust Chefs Collaborative 2000 - www.oldwayspt.org

Occupational Safety and Health Administration - www.osha.gov

Oneida Foodservice - www.oneida.com

Oregon Raspberry and Blackberry Commission - www.blueberries.com

Organic Alliance - www.organic.org

Organic Trade Association - www.ota.com

Pacific Northwest Canned Pear Service - www.pnw-cannedpears.com

Peanut Advisory Board - www.peanutbutterlovers.com

The Peanut Institute - www.peanut-institute.org

Pear Bureau Northwest - www.usapears.com

Pomegranate Council - www.pomegranates.org

The Popcorn Institute - www.popcorn.org

Professional Association of Innkeepers International - www.paii.org

Processed Apples Institute - www.appleproducts.org

Produce Marketing Association - www.pma.com

Rare Fruit Home Page - www.gate.net/~tfnews/tfnhome2.htm

Research Chefs Association - www.researchchef.com

Retailer's Bakery Association - www.rbanet.com

Roundtable for Women in Foodservice - www.rwf.com

Salt Institute - www.saltinstitute.org

Second Harvest Network - www.secondharvest.org

Share Our Strength - www.strength.org

Snack Food Association - www.sfa.org

Society for the Advancement of Food Service Research - www.safsr.org

Society for Foodservice Management - www.sfm-online.org

Southern Bakers Association - www.sba.org

Squab Producers of California - www.squab.com

The Sugar Association - www.sugar.org

Tea and Coffee Trade Journal - www.teacofmag.com

Tea Assn. of the USA, Inc - www.teausa.com

Thomas Food Industry Register - www.tfir.com

Tortilla Industry Association - www.tortilla-info.com

Tyson - www.tyson.com

Uncle Ben's - www.masterfoodservices.com

United Soybean Board - www.unitedsoybean.org

U. S. Apple Association - www.usapple.org

United States Department of Agriculture - www.usda.gov

USA Dry Pea & Lentil Council - www.pea-lentil.com

United Fresh Fruit & Vegetable Association - www.uffva.org

USDA Food and Nutrition Information Center at the National Agricultural
Library - www.nal.usda.gov/fnic

United States Department of Agriculture Food Safety and Inspection Service -
www.fsis.usda.gov

U. S. Pastry Alliance - www.uspastry.org

U. S. Personal Chef Association - www.uspca.com

U. S. Poultry & Egg Association - www.poultryegg.org

USA Rice Federation - www.usarice.cpm

Veal Committee of the National Cattlemen's Beef Association - www.beef.org

Vermont Cheese Council - www.vtcheese.com

The Vinegar Institute - www.versatilevinegar.org

Virginia Marine Products Board - www.virginiaseafood.org

Walnut Marketing Board - www.walnut.org

Washington Red Raspberry Commission - www.red-raspberry.com

Washington Wine Commission - www.washingtonwine.org

Washington State Apple Commission - www.bestapples.com

Washington State Fruit Commission - www.nwcherries.com

Wheat Foods Council - www.wheatfoods.org

Wild Blueberry Association of North America - www.wildblueberries.com

Wisconsin Milk Marketing Board - www.wislink.org

Women Chefs Resource Center (WCRC) - www.chefnet.com/womenchefs

Women's Foodservice Forum - www.womensfoodserviceforum.com

World Association of Cooks Societies (WACS) - www.wacs.co.za

World Mustard Association - www.mustardweb.com

The authors and Delmar guarantee that the Web site URLs referenced here were accurate at the time of printing. However, due to the fluid nature of the Internet, we cannot guarantee their accuracy for the life of the edition.

Glossary

American service — Food is preplated and brought out to the guests. Sit-down dinners are considered American service where portion control is maintained keeping food costs low.

amusement park catering — This is a dimension of corporate catering. The management of an amusement park may cater their own functions internally or may outsource the responsibility of providing the food and related service for all on-premise catering events to an independent caterer.

appropriate personnel — The human resource standard as defined by the caterer to describe the required individual needed to accomplish the specific task.

automobile insurance — Insurance to protect the caterer from liability imputed to him by the actions of an employee. Laws regarding insurance for vehicles vary depending upon the state in which a caterer is conducting business.

avoid risk — The catering management processes meant to eliminate all circumstances that may cause a risk to materialize. One example is the creation of a safety team whose purpose is to monitor the environment to identify and correct potential risks to ensure the safety of the employee and guest.

back-of-the-house (operations) — Physical, mechanical, and financial activities performed by a caterer that the customer generally does not get to witness.

backward integration — To gain control over the raw materials used in the production of food and services by a caterer.

balance sheet — The statement of financial position that shows the accounting equation: total assets = liabilities + owner's equity.

banquet event order (BEO) — This form is a multi-purpose catering management tool used internally to communicate the details for execution of an event to the appropriate personnel.

barriers — These include obstacles that inhibit or challenge the caterer. The two main types of barriers include *operational barriers* and *human resource* (or *communication*) *barriers.*

base recipe — A standardized recipe changed by adding additional ingredients to create another menu item to complement the menu mix.

benchmarking — A strategic management technique. The process of identifying innovative best practices by other caterers. A measure against a caterer's own performance that can be measured against an industry standard.

benchmarks — Predetermined standards. A caterer establishes these standards to compare against the actual operational performance.

best practices — These include proven, successful techniques from the catering industry that one adapts to improve their own organization's service delivery.

blueprint — A detailed outline of a plan used to guide organizational behavior.

branded menu items — Food items produced by a principal, backed by its name to guarantee a consistent level of quality.

broadline distributor — A market intermediary who bundles a number of specialized product lines, such as food, nonfood, equipment, chemical, and cleaning supplies together.

budget — A financial, tactical, single-use plan used to set the parameters for each event.

buffet service — A common style of service used to serve food. The distinguishing characteristic of buffet service is that the customer actively participates in supplying part of the service by serving themselves from an organized table offering a variety of food.

bundle of tasks — The catering management procedure to identify and group all similar employee tasks together based on the event's tactile plan. It is used to assign or delegate tasks to the appropriate employee for their execution.

business growth plan — A strategic plan based on the answers to key questions used to identify a caterer's market niche that provides for controllable growth in the appropriate direction as established by the caterer.

capital resources — Includes the facility, equipment, land, and inventories of raw materials managed by the caterer to exceed customer expectations.

cash flow — The uninterrupted series of cash installments by the client to the caterer for executing the catering function.

caterer's market — The group of all actual and potential customers in a caterer's geographic service area who have an unmet need, want, or demand requiring the service of a caterer

catering management — Tasks of planning, organizing, influencing, and controlling each activity involved in the preparation and delivery of food, beverage, and related services at a competitive, profitable price that meets and exceeds the customer's perception of value.

client-based pricing method — This pricing method bases the cost of a function on the client's perceived value rather than the direct food and labor costs to produce the event.

code of ethics — A formal statement used to describe the caterer's philosophy regarding an employee's professional conduct and behavior.

commercial segment — Traditionally considered the "for-profit" catering segment, it includes the independent caterer, the restaurateur and caterer, and the home-based caterer whose financial goals include a profit gained from revenue minus expenses.

communication barrier(s) — A type of barrier (also called a human resource barrier) caused by the staff that disrupts the elements of a catering event. These may include human error, lack of communication, and deviation from standard operating procedures.

competitive-based pricing method — This pricing method bases the cost charged to a client for a function on the relative cost charged by competitors in the market, rather than on direct food and labor costs or demands.

contract — The legal agreement between the client and caterer outlining details of the event. It does not have to be elaborate, but should cover the basics including time, date, menu items, number of guests, the price and payment policy, and provisions for extenuating circumstances beyond the caterer's control.

controlling — One of the most important catering management functions. Ensures the effective and efficient utilization of the caterer's resources in the process of producing food and beverage to accomplish organizational goals.

control point — Any point in a specific food system at which loss of control does not lead to an unacceptable health risk.

convenience foods — Manufactured or processed by a principal and delivered to the caterer in a ready-to-eat or ready-to-cook form.

convention catering — One of the most profitable types of catering events. Distinguishing feature is the ability to simultaneously prepare and serve food and beverages to support professional, business, and social activities of a large group of people. These events are held in a closed environment, at a hotel or convention facility, using multiple meeting rooms and/or a large banquet or ballroom.

corporate catering — The professional caterer's target market is a clientele of corporate and business accounts such as meetings, ceremonies, anniversaries, recognition dinners, training sessions, seminars, conventions, and other related events.

cost-based pricing method — Adding a standard markup to the direct labor and food cost to determine the client's final cost for a function.

cover — The complete place setting for one guest at the start of the meal including the service plate, flatware, napkin, and water glass.

creativity — Combination of imagination, ability, and understanding customer needs to create excitement, wonder, and anticipation for the client attending a catering event.

crisis management team — Group of homogenous management and hourly employees who can quickly respond to an unforeseen crisis with the purpose of protecting the interests of the guest and the organization.

critical control point (CCP) — As defined in the Food Code, means a point at which loss of control may result in an unacceptable health risk.

critical limit(s) — As defined in the Food Code, means the maximum or minimum value to which a physical, biological, or a chemical parameter must be controlled at a critical control point to minimize the risk that the identified food safety hazard may occur.

customer appeal — Professional expertise, such as proper food preparation techniques, sanitation procedures, attractive thematic presentations, and related amenities offered by the professional caterer.

customer base — A solid foundation consisting of current and potential clients upon which a caterer continuously builds to support the catering business now and in the future.

customer-satisfaction objectives — These objectives are developed by the caterer specific to the client's needs and wants for each individual event. Exceeding these objectives should be the goal.

defects — These are breakdowns that occur in any of the key activities of the caterer, that cause the system to malfunction.

delegate — The assignment of responsibility and authority to an appropriate employee to execute a "bundle of tasks" or a job in the catering operation.

demands — Derived from the client's needs and wants, demands also include the client's ability to purchase them.

deviation — The failure during the implementation of the HACCP plan to satisfy a required critical limit for a critical control point.

distinct competence — This is achieved when a caterer defines their target market exclusively and hones their skills to enable them to do something uniquely better than the competition. It also provides a competitive advantage that is difficult to copy or penetrate.

distributor (or purveyor) — These individuals purchase items directly from the principal (manufacturer or farmer). They set up huge warehouses to handle large volumes of food and supplies for a specific geographic region. (see specialty distributor; broadline distributor)

distributor sales representative (DSR), supplier sales representative, territory sales manager, merchandising associate — Terms used interchangeably to refer to a purveyor's sales representative—the contact between the caterer and the distributor.

dual restaurant-catering — When a restaurant operator evolves into catering services to strategically increase the efficiencies of the base operation.

employee work schedule — The catering management task of assigning tasks to be completed by the employees predicated on the production schedule and event plan.

employment practice liability — Coverage of day-to-day activities in the workplace.

engager — This is the client or person who is contracting the services of the caterer.

equipment — Caterers determine equipment needs based on the menu, service requirements, type and location of the event, and any special needs of the client.

exclusive caterer — A caterer owns the sole rights to all catering functions held at a specific facility.

execution of tasks — The physical action by an employee to accomplish predetermined goals defined as tasks.

extrinsic rewards — The tangible rewards gained from executing a successful catering event, such as earning a competitive salary.

family-style service — In this self-service type of catering, food is delivered to the table on platters or large serving dishes with enough for everyone seated. The guests pass the platters and help themselves.

field testing — Procedure of serving food, prepared from a new recipe, to an unbiased sampler to ascertain its fit in the caterer's menu mix.

financial catering activities — Back-of-the-house catering activities. Procedures that help to accomplish predetermined profit objectives by controlling operational resources in the daily execution of catering tasks.

financial objectives — These are based on the needs of the client and developed from the event budget. They're crucial to the initial planning process and will vary with every event.

financial resources — The management process of procurement, allotment, investment, and control of monetary resources by the caterer to provide a desired financial return with its appropriate investment.

fire damage liability — Insurance coverage for a caterer's legal liability arising from fire damage to structures rented to the caterer.

flow of food — This concept refers to the order in which food will travel through a catering operation, from receiving, to storage, to preparation, to production, and finally to service.

food broker — A market intermediary whose fundamental task is to bring the caterer and the principal together in the marketplace to facilitate a sale. Brokers identify trends, conduct training programs, educate caterers to new ideas, products, and culinary techniques, and build recipes by bundling product lines together.

formal payment policy — The explanation and guidelines created by the caterer to describe for the client how payment is made. Creates a positive cash flow into the organization.

formal structure — Created by the caterer, its purpose is to help allocate and control organizational resources while supporting its evolving strategy as determined by the mission statement and outlined in the catering plan.

formulating (a plan) — To design a specific plan of action to meet the client's needs based on the proposal and contract.

French service — An elaborate style of service where food is prepared at table-side using a *gueridon* (a small table with wheels) and a *rechaud* (a pan set over a heating element).

front-of-the-house (operations) — Extremely visible, customer-driven service activities designed primarily to please the guest in the dining area, where customer expectations and a caterer's performance intersect.

fund-raising events — Usually catering services are required to support various fund-raising events sponsored by the corporate community. These provide excellent business opportunities for a caterer.

HACCP (Hazardous Analysis and Critical Control Point plan) — A HACCP plan, as defined in the Food Code, means a written document that delineates the formal procedures for following the HACCP principles developed by The National Advisory Committee on Microbiological Criteria for Foods.

hazard — As defined in the Food Code, it means a biological, chemical, or physical property that may cause an unacceptable consumer health risk.

Hazardous Analysis and Critical Control Point plan (HACCP) — A HACCP plan, as defined in the Food Code, means a written document that delineates the formal procedures for following the HACCP principles developed by The National Advisory Committee on Microbiological Criteria for Foods.

hidden costs — Any unknown (to the client) costs levied against the caterer for providing food and related services in a third-party owned catering hall.

high school/elementary school catering — An on-premise catering service offered by the food service director exclusively for the school's own population.

home-based caterer — A caterer who operates from their home facility.

hospital catering — Primarily on-premise catering operation that occurs within a hospital's environment servicing internal associations and/or a department's special needs.

human resources — Skill levels, knowledge-base, experience level, and maturity (length of service) of the caterer's employees.

human resource barrier(s) — A type of barrier caused by the staff that disrupts the elements of a catering event. These may include human error, lack of communication, and deviation from standard operating procedures. Also called a *communication barrier*.

implementing (the plan) — The catering management processes of using effective communication skills to launch a plan into action.

income statement — The statement of revenues, expenses, gains, and losses for the accounting period.

informal structure — The interpersonal relationships that emerge as a result of employees working together to accomplish a common goal.

informed consumer — A caterer educated about the loss-control services offered by an insurance carrier. The mix of loss-control services includes basic coverages on property, liability, and workers' compensation.

insurance program — The complete package written by a professional carrier to protect the caterer against the potential of loss.

Insurance Services Office (ISO) — The property/casualty insurance industry's leading supplier of statistical, actuarial, underwriting, and claims information.

intrinsic rewards — The internal satisfaction or feelings of achievement a caterer experiences as a result of executing a successful catering event.

key activities (subsystems) — Part derived from the whole catering management system. Common subsystems of the catering operation include purchasing, receiving, storage, production, transportation, service, and cleanup.

legal concerns — All activities and specific obligations the caterer must meet, including adhering to the legality of a contract, charging appropriate sales tax, understanding differences between an employee and independent contractor, and identifying and pursuing legal recourse against a client who fails to pay.

liability insurance — Premise/operations coverage to protect a caterer against claims arising from the ownership, maintenance, or use of the premise and of the caterer's operations in-progress.

life cycle of customer events — The cycle of lifetime celebrations: bridal shower, wedding reception, anniversary, birthday, baby shower, baptism, prom, sporting banquet, college graduation, marriage, and death that requires the services of a caterer. The cycle repeats itself.

manufacturer's agent — A market intermediary who is employed by the principal and has direct responsibility for accomplishing sales goals for each product in an assigned geographical sales area. Does not take title to the goods, issue invoices, or set prices.

market-penetration pricing strategy — This pricing strategy sets a low initial price to penetrate a new segment or to gain an overall market share.

market-skimming pricing strategy — This pricing strategy sets a rather high initial price to skim profit from the market.

master menu — Standard lists offering a variety of both entrees and side dishes based on the caterer's skill level from which a client selects to create their own menu based on their individual needs and budgetary requirements.

mechanical catering activities — A back-of-the-house catering activity that focuses on the effective and efficient use and maintenance of the equipment.

medical expense coverage — This insurance will provide reimbursement for all reasonable medical expenses incurred by anyone, except the caterer or caterer's employees, as a result of an accident, without regard for the caterer's liability.

menu — This is the most important factor in the catering plan and is built around client needs and wants, availability of products, and the caterer's financial objectives and capabilities.

menu development — The process of defining the function of a menu; forecasting, pricing strategies, and item popularity and mix.

merchandising associate, supplier sales representative, distributor sales representative (DSR), territory sales manager — Terms used interchangeably to refer to a purveyor's sales representative—the contact between the caterer and the distributor.

military segment — The catering segment that encompasses all catering activities involved in association with the armed forces and/or diplomatic events. Traditionally operates on a break-even basis whereas revenue equals expenses.

mission statement — A written statement to define why a caterer is currently in business and communicate this purpose to stakeholders in the marketplace. Is a caterer's guiding light.

mobile catering — A caterer who employs one or a fleet of trucks specially equipped to support an assortment of food and beverages for customers located at diverse locations, such as construction sites.

monitoring step — The planned sequence of observations, or measurements of critical limits, designed to produce an accurate record and intended to ensure that the critical limit maintains product safety. Continuous monitoring means an uninterrupted record of data.

multitasking equipment — Food production equipment that offers the ability to be used for multiple procedures or processes in the preparation of food. For example, a tilting braising pan can perform multiple cooking duties such as braising, frying, roasting, thawing, and hot or cold holding.

napperon (overlay) — A small table cloth placed over the larger one to help protect it and accent it with additional color.

needs — The complex set of human needs that include the need for food, beverage, and related services.

noncommercial segment — Traditionally considered a "not-for-profit" catering segment that operates on a break-even basis where revenue equals expenses.

Catering and services are provided as an adjunct service to complement the catering required by a business and industry account, college and university account, health care facility account, recreational food service account, school account, social organization account, or transportation food service account.

nonprofit (or private) caterers — These caterers provide the hall, food, beverage, and servers for an occasion. Usually, the events are held on-site since many nonprofit caterers lack the expertise and equipment to handle off-site events. Catering is used as a supplement to their internal financial budgets.

objectives — Framed by the mission statement, they are established to serve as benchmarks against which actual performance can be measured against a predetermined target.

off-premise catering — The caterer transports all of the food, equipment, and personnel to an external location to execute the event.

one-stop shop catering — A full-service catering operation that supplies the client with a choice of a variety of services designed to satisfy their needs, wants, and demands.

on-premise catering — When all of the tasks, functions, and related services that the caterer executes in the preparation and implementation of food and service for the client, are done exclusively within the caterer's own facility.

operational barrier(s) — A barrier that disrupts the physical elements of a catering event and may include human error, accidents, time constraints and *Act of God* disturbances.

operational task(s) — A singular, identified activity that must be executed in order to accomplish an objective.

operations — A term used by a caterer to describe the task of implementing and executing the daily elements of a catering plan.

ordering — The catering management process of communicating the exact needs to a purveyor.

organizing (function) — The catering management function of formally creating a structure to support the efficient and effective execution of each delegated task in the accomplishment of stated objectives.

overhead — The cost of operating the catering business regardless of the type or number of functions executed. It describes indirect labor, utilities, indirect material costs, insurance, taxes, depreciation, and the repair and maintenance of equipment.

overlay (napperon) — A small table cloth placed over the larger one to help protect it and accent it with additional color.

personal and advertising injury liability — Insurance coverage to protect against claims alleging false arrest, libel, slander, and false advertising if the caterer had no knowledge of the falsehood.

personality conflicts — An unexplainable dislike of the client based on the intuitive feeling of the caterer, formed by the initial interview, that causes the caterer to refuse the function.

physical catering activities — The back-of-the-house interrelated management activities of purchasing, receiving, storage, preparation, and transportation.

planning — The process of detailing and outlining all tasks required to accomplish an objective. Planning is the first of seven catering management functions.

plate presentation — The arrangement of good tasting food and its colorful and attractive display on the serving plate.

preventive measure — An action to exclude, destroy, eliminate, or reduce a hazard and prevent recontamination through effective means.

primary caterer — Handles approximately 75% of a client's total catering need.

prime cost(s) — The sum of the direct food cost plus the direct labor cost to produce a menu item for a client.

principal — A common term used in the hospitality trade to denote a source who manufactures or processes food.

private (or nonprofit) caterers — These caterers provide the hall, food, beverage, and servers for an occasion. Usually, the events are held on-site since many private caterers lack the expertise and equipment to handle off-site events. Catering is used as a supplement to their internal financial budgets.

private-party catering — Many restaurants have separate rooms that can accommodate small groups for private parties such as bridal showers or retirement and award dinners. Off-premise caterers can service private parties at an individual's home.

producers — A term used in the insurance industry to describe the individuals who sell insurance.

professional sales staff — Based on need and budgetary requirements, this team's purpose is to represent the caterer in the target market by communicating to potential clients a caterer's skills and capabilities to satisfy customer needs, wants, and demands.

property insurance — This insurance provides protection against the loss of property.

proposal — A communication tool used to effectively inform and educate the prospective client about everything the caterer can do for them during the particular event.

prospecting strategies — Methodologies used by a caterer to introduce them to a prospective client with the purpose of building a sustainable customer base.

psychographic segmentation — The process of segmenting a catering market by variables such as lifestyle, social class, or personality characteristics to identify a target group of customers based on these characteristics.

purveyor (or distributor) — These individuals purchase items directly from the principal (manufacturer or farmer). They set up huge warehouses to handle large volumes of food and supplies for a specific geographic region. (see specialty distributor; broadline distributor)

receiving — The catering management task of the following specific procedures to inspect, verify, and confirm the delivered item meets the caterer's needs by checking it against a set of written specifications. It includes receiving, storage, and the internal distribution of raw materials to meet production needs.

recipe — Specific plan or formula used to describe the preparation of a certain food.

recipe development — Process of creating new recipes in response to changing consumer trends and tastes. Function of a caterer's love of food, experience, and the application of the basic knowledge of food preparation.

recipe research — Begins the process of recipe development by seeking to understand the relationship between a client's needs and a caterer's skill level.

reduce risk — A process, procedure, or tangible element specifically designed to reduce the element of risk. One example is the installation of a sprinkler system to reduce the risk of a fire.

referral(s) — When a satisfied customer recommends a caterer to others.

relationship — The bond that connects the caterer with a client based on mutual respect for each other.

reputation — The character of the caterer, whether favorable or not, that is held by a customer. A customer's expectations predicated on the past performance of a caterer. One of the most important considerations a client uses to select a caterer.

retail grocery store — Caterers who shop for their goods and services here should be careful to purchase the specific quantity needed. It would also be wise to negotiate a fixed markup or pricing formula rather than pay consumer prices.

rethermalization (retherm) — The process of taking a prepared product, either prepared from scratch or purchased in a prepared state, that was either chilled or frozen, and applying heat to bring it to a desired serving temperature. Depending on the item, final rethermalization temperature is based on HACCP-recommended procedures for reheating prepared foods. For example, a temperature of 165°F is required to retherm a poultry product before serving it.

risk — An estimate of the likely occurrence of a hazard or the change of loss, damage, or injury.

risk management — A complete analysis of the potential causes of loss inherent in a caterer's business and the appropriate defense to provide protection or to avoid, reduce, or transfer the risk.

Russian service — This formal and elegant style of service distinguishes the use of silver serving platters, the skillful handling of the serving utensils, and the arrangement and presentation of the food.

safety management team — A group of employees who continually monitor the environment to identify and correct potential risks, ensuring the proper safety of the employees and guests.

scheduling — The catering management task to balance a precise number of employees against a given volume of work.

scratch foods — Menu items prepared on-premise by the caterer's staff using standardized recipes.

seasonal niche — Special events that may occur during a specific time or season of the year. One example is a county fair.

secondary caterer — This caterer manages approximately 25% of a client's catering needs. Often maintained to back up the primary caterer.

segment — The part or submarket derived from the total of all potential catering customers. Members of these various submarkets have similar, identifiable needs, wants, and demands.

sensitive ingredient(s) — Any ingredient historically associated with a known microbiological hazard that causes or contributes to production of a potentially hazardous food as defined in the Food Code.

service — Caterers define service as it applies to their mission statement. Their reputation is built on delivery of service so developing hiring and recruiting strategies should complement a caterer's service objectives.

service standards — Predetermined levels based on the organization's mission established to gauge an employee's performance.

severity — The degree of seriousness of the consequences of a hazard if it were to become an actuality.

signature menu item — Special or unique food giving the caterer a distinct recognition as the sole supplier of this specialized item.

signature recipe(s) — A recipe that has been tweaked or adjusted to be unique to a specific caterer. (e.g., adding a unique seasoning or marinade, adding an additional preparation step that alters the recipe in some unique way.)

silencer/silence cloth (under cloth) — A cloth placed beneath the table cloth to prevent it from sliding. It also protects the table surface, provides cushioning for the table cloth, reduces the noise of placing or moving china and glassware, and brings out patterns on the table cloth.

sit-down dinner — A very elegant event where the caterer must be well organized and have a good plan. Typically, the food costs are lower than with a buffet dinner because the caterer prepares a set portion per guest with a slight (2–3%) overage.

small wares — The additional service items placed on the table including sugar holders, salt and pepper shakers, ashtrays, pitchers, creamers, ice buckets, and compote dishes.

social catering — A distinct field of catering which provides food and service to clients engaged in social events such as weddings, birthdays, and similar events. A distinguishing facet is that the event is usually held in someone's home.

speciality distributor — Basic type of market intermediary who specializes in the distribution of one product category, such as produce, cleaning supplies, or chemicals.

speciality wholesaler — A specialized market intermediary. This wholesaler furnishes the food service industry with a specialized line of products, such as produce or chemicals.

specifications — Concise statements communicated internally and externally, of the exact products needed by a caterer in the operation to maintain standards and exceed a client's needs, wants, and demands.

speed scratch cooking — Foods that are made from scratch and finished off in the caterer's kitchen with little preparation.

staffing — The catering management task of identifying the correct number of employees needed to execute an event.

stakeholders — Anyone who has a direct relationship with the catering business including employees, suppliers, clients, guests, community, neighbors, competitors, or government agencies.

standardized menu — Exact listing of the type of food, beverage and related service offered by the caterer without a client's option to modify, change, or make substitution.

standardized recipe — A specific plan. A standard operating procedure that communicates how to use the exact ingredients in the preparation of a specific food. It delivers a consistent quality, exact yield, and portion size each time it is produced. The achievement of financial objectives is supported by ensuring consistency, controlling costs, and preventing food borne illness.

storage — The correct placement of all items on-premise in the storeroom, refrigerators, and freezers. Providing protections from spoilage, pilferage, and theft are some key tasks of the storage function.

strategic plan — Plan established to guide the entire catering organization over the long term, three to ten years into the future.

strategic vision — A long-term outlook that focuses on where the business is headed over the next ten years. All possible demands that may exert pressure on the business during this time are also identified.

subplan — Plan developed for each individual catering function derived from the parameters of the caterer's master or strategic plan and the specific needs of the client.

subsystems (key activities) — Part derived from the whole catering management system. Common subsystems of the catering operation include purchasing, receiving, storage, production, transportation, service, and cleanup.

supermarket catering — A traditional supermarket prepares food in their deli department. The customer will purchase this food and carry it themselves to the event location.

supplier sales representative, distributor sales representative (DSR), territory sales manager, merchandising associate — Terms used interchangeably to refer to a purveyor's sales representative—the contact between the caterer and the distributor.

SWOT analysis — A strategic management tool used by a caterer to match their business strengths to market opportunities. An acronym that stands for identifying internal strengths and weaknesses, and the external opportunities and threats.

system approach — A management technique that enables a caterer to break the management of their operation down into subsytems or smaller, more manageable pieces.

tabletop — This includes any items placed on the table that are needed by guests for their dining experience.

tactical plan — Specifically created to provide the caterer precise short-term guidance as required for each catering event. This requires precise detail and precision execution.

teamwork — A collective staff working together to implement the catering plan. A necessity to executing any event successfully.

territory sales manager, supplier sales representative, distributor sales representative (DSR), merchandising associate — Terms used interchangeably to refer to a purveyor's sales representative—the contact between the caterer and the distributor.

throw-ins — A term used in the insurance industry to describe when extra coverage is given at no additional charge to make the policy more competitive in the marketplace.

total quality management (TQM) — The continuous process of incremental improvement in the key activities required by the caterer to produce quality goods and services through employee action.

transfer risk — The caterer may assign the ownership of the risk to another party. One example is for a caterer to rent a facility rather than owning it.

under cloth (silencer or silence cloth) — A cloth placed beneath the table cloth to prevent it from sliding. It also protects the table surface, provides cushioning for the table cloth, reduces the noise of placing or moving china and glassware, and brings out patterns on the table cloth.

university/college caterer — On-premise catering service primarily responsible for providing food and related services to the students, faculty, administrators, and guests.

upgrading the event — To enhance the delivery and showmanship of the food and/or service by tweaking elements of the event package to exceed a client's basic needs. These professional suggestions may be based on the caterer's expertise.

value chain — A detailed flow chart revealing the internal flow of activities and their relative costs to deliver the food and services to a catered guest

verification step — The methods, procedures, and tests used to determine if the HACCP system in use is in compliance with the HACCP plan.

wants — A client's basic needs as communicated to the caterer.

"what if" scenarios — The caterer's plan should include provisions for unanticipated or unexpected problems. (e.g., "What if" the equipment fails? "What if" the weather conditions don't complement an outside event?) By determining these problems in advance, the caterer will have a backup plan in place should they occur.

wholesale clubs — A large warehouse stocked with a variety of bulk foods, equipment, clothes, and other items. A membership fee is required for the privilege to purchase at the warehouse location. Caterers may find it advantageous to become a member and purchase food at these clubs.

word-of-mouth advertising — A type of referral when a satisfied customer recommends the caterer to others.

work production schedule — A communication tool used to guide the appropriate behavior of the caterer's staff in the execution of tasks.

workstation — Areas in the production kitchen influenced in design by three basic dimensions: method of preparation, type of cooking method utilized, and volume of food produced. Common workstations include preparation, hot food, cold food, final preparation, warewashing, and transportation.

Index